PICK YOUR THRILL

＊◆＊◆＊◆＊◆＊

Whether they're coupling the fabulous old-fashioned way... or loving on the edge. Whether they're watching... or being watched. Whether they're reveling in the intimacy of one man and one woman... or losing themselves in the deliriously multiple madness of three or more. Whatever their pleasure, their greatest joy is telling readers of *Penthouse* all about it, leaving out no delectable detail. Because they know you'll be listening...

OTHER BOOKS IN THE SERIES:

LETTERS TO
PENTHOUSE
IX

SHARE
THE
SECRETS
OF THE
SEXIEST
PEOPLE
ON
EARTH

THE EDITORS OF
PENTHOUSE MAGAZINE

GRAND CENTRAL
PUBLISHING

NEW YORK   BOSTON

Copyright © 1999 by General Media Communications, Inc.
All rights reserved. Except as permitted under the U.S. Copyright Act of 1976, no part of this publication may be reproduced, distributed, or transmitted in any form or by any means, or stored in a database or retrieval system, without the prior written permission of the publisher.

Cover design by Tony Russo

Grand Central Publishing
Hachette Book Group
237 Park Avenue
New York, NY 10017
Visit our website at www.HachetteBookGroup.com

Grand Central Publishing is a division of Hachette Book Group, Inc. The Grand Central Publishing name and logo is a trademark of Hachette Book Group, Inc.

Printed in the United States of America

First Printing: November 1999

16 15 14 13 12 11 10 9 8

This book is dedicated to my mentor, the editor and publisher of *Penthouse Letters,* Don Myrus. He has walked me through the wonderful world of pornography and will always be affectionately known as *"The Potentate of Porn."*

—*Kathy Cavanaugh 1999*

Table of Contents

The joys of sex are too many to number but so much fun to explore. Everyone has different tastes, positions, needs and expectations and we all deserve to be satisfied. Beyond these pages lies a world to call your own.

Let this book be your guide to freeing yourself of all the pressures daily life has to offer and indulge yourself with stories of the erotic lifestyles of people just like you who want to share their sexcapades. What are you waiting for?

Kathy Cavanaugh
Managing Editor
Penthouse Special Publications

Someone's Watching

WAIT A MINUTE, ISN'T THAT YOUR WIFE WITH THAT GUY'S DICK IN HER CUNT?

My wife Lori and I have been married for almost seventeen years, and at thirty-seven she's still a hot-looking lady. At five feet seven inches tall and a hundred and eighteen, she's still in good shape. Do the numbers 35-27-36 mean anything to you?

Recently, to make a little extra cash, she took a job in a titty bar. Last night was her first night.

We left the house and got to the club when they were opening the doors for business. Lori was nervous but wildly excited. I sat at the bar as the other girls showed my wife the dressing room and told her the rules. She could keep as much of her clothes on or get as naked as she wanted. She could do whatever she wanted for the guys, but she couldn't allow them to touch her.

I sat and talked to the barmaid and had a drink as Lori went to get ready. My cock was already hard, and there wasn't another soul in the place yet.

After several guys came in, the music started playing. The first dancer was a pretty girl who did an excellent job dancing. I was watching her when I noticed my wife come out of the dressing room. She was dressed in a skimpy little outfit that showed a lot of skin. It had a thong bikini that let her ass-cheeks show. She walked up to the bar and played like she didn't know me, ordering herself a drink. We'd decided to act this way all night, to add to the fun.

A couple of guys started talking to her, and I was excited with this arrangement, because I could watch as if I weren't her husband.

When it was her turn to dance, she went up on the stage. She danced to about six guys sitting in the front row. She was smiling, and one could tell she was having fun. On the second song, her top came off. I was hard! My wife was topless in front of half a dozen guys, onstage, stripping for the first time in her life. She was bending over in front of strangers who were giving her dollar bills. Her hands rubbed her tits and pinched her nipples. The second song wasn't even over before she was removing her bottoms, throwing them to the side and dancing completely naked (except for her heels) in front of guys with money in front of them. She was having so much fun, she'd have danced to them even if they hadn't been giving her money.

She came over to the end of the stage and smiled at me, giving me a very sultry look. Her pussy was completely shaved. I almost came.

She turned and went back to the guys in the front row, lay down on the stage and spread her legs. She struck many poses while rolling on the floor, most all of them showing her pussy. She looked especially good when she got on all fours, facing the guys on the other side of the stage. Her ass pointed toward those behind her, and her pussy was spread open for all to see.

The guys only a couple of feet from her cunt were leaning forward to get the best look they could. All too soon, her set of songs ended and she was off to the dressing room.

After she changed and came back out, she came to the bar. I started talking to her like we'd just met. It was fun role-playing. She was very excited about what she was doing. Her new outfit was just as sexy as the last.

When it was her turn to dance again, I went to the stage and put my dollars up. She was one hot number! I was so proud of her! She danced for me like she had for everyone else, squatting and spreading her legs. Her big clit poked out of her sexy lips. I stayed there as she went to the next guys, four of them celebrating a birthday. They mentioned this to her, and she did a special dance for the birthday boy.

Facing him and squatting with her knees on both sides of his head, she positioned her pussy just inches from his face. The guys sitting by his side were leaning to look at her cunt. She took the guy's hands and pointed both his index fingers up, then guided them down her tits to her nipples. One of the bouncers came over and motioned no to her, but she didn't care and continued for a few more seconds.

After she was done dancing this set and went to change, I went back to the bar and sat. She appeared later in another outfit and came to the bar to get a drink. Acting as if she was making small talk, she suggested I come downstairs and watch her. The birthday boy's buddies had bought him a lap dance.

I went downstairs and sat at the bar as she went to get him. I ordered a drink and waited. She showed up with him and I watched. She got topless as he sat on the couch. She danced and rubbed her tits over his body. According to the rules, his hands were on the couch back and he wasn't touching her. I would have enjoyed watching him feel her up.

I spent the rest of the evening watching her dance buck naked on the stage and give private dances on the downstairs couches.

One particular guy seemed to get her attention. He bought her a couple of drinks and she danced for him for three songs. I could tell she liked him. I went and sat at the stage to watch and listen.

They were making small talk and he was giving her a lot of dollar bills. He was telling her how much he liked her shaved pussy and her big clit. She just smiled and spread her legs, even going so far as to rub her clit with her fingers and spreading her pussy lips for him to see. I could tell she was getting off on what she was doing. It was highly erotic sitting two seats away, listening to a stranger telling my wife how hot she was and seeing her get sexually charged.

After changing again and coming out of the dressing room, she had on one of my favorite outfits: a one-piece, patent leather, crotchless teddy that's cut out around her tits, leaving them exposed. After more dancing, mainly to this one guy, her set was over.

She got dressed and went downstairs with this guy to give him a lap dance. I followed them about ten minutes later. Except for me at the bar and the bartender, they were the only ones downstairs. The couch they were in was at an angle, facing away from the bar. The guy was sitting with his arms on the couch back, Lori's knees straddling his legs.

She would take each tit in her hands and place a nipple on his nose before sliding it down into his mouth. He would eagerly suck it. I was surprised she was doing this. She whispered into his ear and he looked around the room and said something back. I could make out Lori saying, "He's okay," as she looked my way.

My wife's hands were in front of her as they continued to talk. As she motioned with her head for me to come over, her hands grabbed her tits again and she resumed sliding her nipples over the guy's face and in his mouth. As I walked up to them, Lori asked me to put some quarters into the jukebox. I walked around in front of the couch to the jukebox and, as I put coins in, I turned and looked at them. My heart leaped into my throat! I had a perfect view of a huge cock splitting my wife's crotchless outfit wide open, stretching her cunt lips as she had impaled herself on him. As she would raise herself to put her tit in the guy's mouth, his cock would slide partway out before she plunged back down onto it.

Her movements were so sporadic that you couldn't tell they were fucking. I sat down on a couch next to the jukebox so I could watch. When a song ended, they'd just sit still so some of the others who had come downstairs wouldn't know what they were doing. One of the other dancers entered the room just as Lori was coming, and hollered toward her that it was her turn to dance on stage. Lori bit her lip and nodded her head okay.

Then the guy tensed, and I watched as his dick slid out of my wife's stretched-wide cunt lips as she got up, his come shooting onto the floor. Lori gave him a quick kiss and ran upstairs.—
Name and address withheld ⊙┠▪

A DILDO WRAPPED IN A PUSSY INSIDE AN ENIGMA

The area was finally given a break from the scorching summer heat, perfect for lying outside and getting a tan. My house is surrounded by woods; the nearest neighbor is two hundred feet away, barely visible through the trees, allowing me to lose any inhibitions about sunbathing in the nude.

After covering my body with oil, I lay upon the blanket, enjoying the soft breeze, and started massaging my thighs and breasts, rolling my fingers over my nipples, which were quite taut by that time. Suddenly, I felt that hot surge coming up from my loins, and I knew right away that I was going to be a naughty girl.

I found myself rubbing my pussy and in quite a horny state of mind. In the distance I could hear the construction of a new highrise apartment building, and I noticed that the voices of the workmen were a little clearer than usual as they echoed off the trees around me. Upon looking in the direction of the site, I saw that the building had now reached above the tops of the trees that surround my pleasure dome.

I could see the workers at the top of the structure, setting up the beams for the next story. Maybe that would be the penthouse floor, from where you could see for miles around all the homes below with their manicured lawns and glamorous swimming pools. One could even see my house, for instance. I grimaced at the thought of losing my privacy. On the other hand, this could lead to a new sexual intrigue. The idea of masturbating with my toys on my lawn, knowing that someone from afar could actually see me, was pretty exciting! So I went in to get my playthings to start practicing.

I returned to my playground, but before I resettled onto the blanket, I dove into my pool to completely refresh myself. The cool water felt so good as it reduced my horny fever and cleansed me of the body oil and sweat. I walked out feeling my long hair cling to my back as it dripped water down the crack of my ass. My nipples were so erect they ached at my touch. I left my skin glistening with the water as I nestled onto my blanket, placing my vibrators beside me. I glanced up to check that the workers were still in sight, and I thought to myself, Boys, I'm going to tease the fuck out of you!

I reached for my vibrator with the tingling fingers and held it against my pussy. I thought of the time I screwed my husband's boss right here beside this very pool. I acted like he was coming on all suave as hell, and I gave him the indication that I had no idea he was seducing me. But I knew it, and I didn't mind, because I'd wanted to screw him ever since we were transferred here.

I opened my eyes to see if my construction friends were keeping an eye on me, and I was pleased to see that half of them actually had binoculars. They must have been waiting for this day for a long time.

Back in my memory, I remember that while Dick's boss was talking to me about stock options and surreptitiously (he thought) staring at my tits, I just reached forward and cupped his nuts through his pants. He acted surprised, but he wasn't so surprised that he couldn't follow my lead and get undressed as fast as I did. While I remembered this, I stuck my vibrator halfway into my pussy, hearing muffled whoops and hollers from my distant audience.

Laying me back on a poolside chair, my husband's boss mashed my knees into my tits and slipped his huge cock into my tight hole. I must admit, it hurt a little at first (kinda like this dildo was doing now), but that only made the payoff that much more special. Once I got good and wet, his rod was slamming so deeply into me that I thought I was going to catch on fire from the friction.

I pushed my vibrator all the way into my hole, letting the little fingers explore every space there was inside me. Remembering my husband's face when he discovered me boning his boss brought me to a very loud climax. It turns out he'd been watching too.—*Name and address withheld* O—▬

YOU CAN HAVE THIS WONDERFUL PRIZE PACKAGE IF . . . THE PRICE IS RIGHT

My wife and I have been married for seventeen years. Although we are still very much in love, I must admit that our sex life is not what it used to be. Jackie is as attractive today as she was the day I married her. She is five two and weighs just over a hundred pounds. She has a gorgeous set of legs, her ass and bush are perfect and her tits are firm.

Needless to say, she still turns me on very much, but she has pretty much lost interest in fucking me. We tried doing different things in the bedroom, and these experiments served to rekindle her interest a bit, but soon her fire would fade again.

This has obviously left me very frustrated. The new things we tried turned me on so much that being denied them just added to my frustrations. I masturbated more often, relying on my fantasies for arousal. One of the things we did to add spice to our sex life was to take pictures and videos of ourselves. When I would be taking pictures of her posing in provocative ways, I would be thinking about her posing like this for other men and even screwing other people. The thought of Jackie fucking some good-looking guy while I watch became a very big turn-on for me. It was the main thing I fantasized about when I beat off. Before long, it was the only thing I thought of, and I started to think of ways to make it actually happen.

One night, while we were lying in bed, I decided to tell Jackie what was on my mind. I told her I'd had a dream about her fucking a friend of ours named Mark while I watched, and I let her know how much just thinking of it turned me on. At first she said I was sick, but as I told her the details of the dream, how big his cock was and how wild she became while riding it and sucking it, she became hotter and hotter.

I started massaging her pussy as we talked about it. Her snatch was so wet and hot it soaked her panties. She started asking me questions about the dream, and when I filled her in on the details, she moaned and got even hornier. I reached for a ten-inch vibrator, and as I held it up, I said, "This is how big Mark's cock is."

She pulled her panties off and in a sexy voice loaded with desire she said, "Fuck me with that big cock of yours, Mark. Let Phil see how much I love your big, hard dick."

I slowly pushed the vibrator into her, and she went wild and started thrusting her hips, screaming, "Give me all of it, Mark, I want to feel your hard cock all the way up my cunt. I want Phil to see you fill me with your come."

I fucked her hard with the vibrator. She squirmed with pleasure as she neared orgasm. "Oh, yes, come for me Mark. Oh, Stubbly (Jackie's nickname for me), he's coming inside of me. I'm going to come too."

As she came, she reached down and pushed my hand to get the vibrator in as far as it would go. It all but disappeared into her hot box. Watching my wife come as she yelled another man's name drove me nuts, and my cock was ready to explode. I moved around so my dick would be near her mouth. She grabbed it and pulled it into her waiting lips, sucking me off like she had never done before. I was still working the dildo in and out of her, and I asked her what she was thinking about as she sucked my cock. She stopped long enough to say she was thinking about sucking off Mark while I watched.

Before wrapping her lips back around my cock, she asked me what I was thinking about. I told her the same thing, only with another well-hung guy who was fucking her as she sucked.

She moved her ass so it was above my face. We were now in a 69 position, with her on top. As I removed the vibrator, she lowered herself so I could lick her clit. In no time she was coming again, and as she did I exploded with the most intense orgasm I ever had. Jackie sucked my cock and swallowed every last drop of my come—something she had never done before.

After we regained our composure, I turned around and held her as we talked about what had just happened. She agreed that that was the best sex we had in a while. She said that the thought of her fucking someone else, not only with my approval but with me there watching drove her wild. She admitted that she often fantasized about men with extremely large cocks. (My own dick is barely five inches hard.) We discussed doing this for real, about how we would set it up, etc. As we talked about it, my dick began to rise again. Seeing this, Jackie mounted it and started to slowly fuck me while we talked. We both came again and fell asleep in each other's arms.

The next day at work all I could think about was what had happened the night before. I couldn't wait to get home and start making plans for our adventure. To my disappointment, when I got home Jackie did not want to talk about it. She said that what we'd done was okay as a fantasy, but she could never do it for real.

"But you were more turned on last night than I've ever seen you before," I said.

"I don't want to talk about it anymore," she said.

When we went to bed, I pulled out the vibrator again and started to rub it against her cunt. She told me to stop.

I rolled over and spent the rest of the night confused. Why was it that every time we found something we both enjoyed when it came to sex, she would refuse to do it anymore? I couldn't figure it out.

For the next three or four months, I kept trying to figure it out. Was the fact that she liked big cocks and that mine was not very large the reason our sex life was dying? I convinced myself that I just could not satisfy her. Maybe she had a lover. Although I wanted to see her fuck another man, the thought of her doing it behind my back made me mad. I became obsessed with the thought of watching her fuck some guy with a big cock. I wanted to see how she would really act. I wanted my wife to be sexually satisfied, and if I couldn't do it with my small dick, then I wanted her to have the big cock that she craved.

Still, I could only be happy if it was something we did together, not something she looked for on her own. I tried to be honest with her and tell her how I felt, but when I did she would say forget about it and quickly change the subject. This only helped to damage our sex life more. The few times we did attempt to make love, I started to have performance problems. This just compounded the frustrations.

Then there was a breakthrough. One night when we went to bed, she snuggled up close to me and asked, "If I were to tell you that I wanted to fuck someone while you watched, who would you want it to be?" My dick sprang alive and I didn't ask any questions. I just started to name a few of our friends that I thought she would like to screw. Although she agreed with some of the names I rattled off, she said she didn't think she could go through with it with someone she knew. I then suggested that we go out to a bar, pick someone up and bring him home and fuck him. She liked this idea but was worried that if she chickened out at the last minute it wouldn't be fair to the guy she brought home.

"I would feel bad getting some guy all turned on and then leaving him hanging," she said.

"Well," I said, "I guess you could always use your hand or your mouth to finish him off. Do you think you could do that?" I asked.

She thought a minute and said, "I guess."

We were getting horny now and I said, "We can always hire someone."

"Hire someone, eh." The thought of paying someone to fuck her seemed to make her even hotter. "That's right," I quickly added, "we wouldn't have to worry about how he felt with having me be there or anything."

"Where does one hire such a person?" she asked. I had no idea, but I told her, "There are several male escort services around. I heard that that is what they are for. We'll have to call a few."

"Not we. You," she replied. "Wouldn't you want to pick out the guy?" I inquired. She was now stroking my cock with her hand as she moved her mouth down to it.

"If this is going to happen," she said, "you will have to make all the arrangements. You know what I want. I'm not going to mention it again. You just tell me when," and then she slurped my rock-hard dick into her mouth. We made fantastic love all night.

For the next couple of days I racked my brain on how to set this up. I had no idea where to find a male prostitute, and I was too embarrassed to ask anyone.

One Wednesday evening, as I was getting out of the shower at the health club I go to, another guy that I'd seen but never met was just going in. He was about thirty-two years old, five eleven with a muscular build and a cock that hung about six inches — soft! I estimated that it had to be at least eight or nine inches erect. I remembered having thought on many occasions how much Jackie would love that cock. I'd been thinking so hard about finding a male prostitute, and the solution was right here in front of me. Jackie would love this guy. Now all I had to do was get him to like the idea.

I hung around the club awhile until Alex came out. I said hello to him as I approached, and he said hello back. He asked me what I was doing and I explained I was waiting for some people, but that I didn't think they were going to show. He said he was going to a bar he usually goes to after his workouts and asked if I wanted to join him. I said yes.

Once we were in the bar we started to talking, and eventually the conversation turned to sex. I asked him if he had a girlfriend, and he said, "I've been out of circulation for so long that I don't know how to meet women anymore. Besides, I don't need a relationship, just some wild sex."

Bingo!

I took advantage of the opportunity and started telling him of my wife and our plan. He sat there in shock as this practically total stranger told him of how he was supposed to hire a man to bring home and fuck his wife.

"Since you're looking for wild sex and I'm looking for someone to satisfy my wife, maybe we could help each other out," I told him. "Interested?"

Not knowing what to say, he said, "It depends. What does she look like?"

I pulled out a picture of her taken at the beach and showed it to him. When he saw the picture of my wife, he exclaimed, "Wow, what a fox. You're serious, aren't you?"

I assured him I was and that if it wasn't him, it would be someone else. He eagerly agreed and we set it up for the following Saturday. He would come to our house and pretend he was a hired gun, so to speak.

I didn't say anything to Jackie until Saturday afternoon. When she got back from her weekly errands, I helped her with the bags and then kissed her. "Tonight's the night," I said, out of the blue.

At first she was unsure of my drift, but then a look of panic came over her face. "Tonight? Oh, my gosh. When? Where? I don't know if I'm ready," she blurted out.

I kissed her again and smiled reassuringly. "You have until eight o'clock to get ready. He's coming here."

I went out to buy some booze, and when I returned she was in the bathtub getting ready. I went into the bathroom and she was trimming her pussy. "Why are you doing that?" I asked.

"I want everything to be perfect. But I have to keep stopping because when I put my fingers near my snatch I start to come," she explained.

"Well, I'll let you get ready," I said, and I left the room. When she came out, she started asking me all sorts of questions about the guy. I just assured her she wouldn't be disappointed. We picked out what she was going to wear. Sheer black G-string panties that barely covered her pussy lips, thigh-high stockings and black high heels. Over this she wore a white polka-dot sundress that was very short and low-cut in front and clung to her perfect hourglass figure. She was gorgeous.

"I'm nervous. What am I supposed to do?" she asked. I lit a joint and said, "That's easy. Relax, fuck him any way you want and have the time of your life."

It was seven o'clock. An hour to go and I couldn't wait.

The bell rang at eight on the head. I answered it and Jackie went to the living room and waited. She had smoked a couple of joints and downed a few drinks to loosen up, and she was glowing. I walked Alex into the living room and introduced them. It was obvious from the look on her face that she liked what she saw. They sat down on the couch making small talk.

I excused myself to go and make drinks. I went into the kitchen and made them, then lit a joint and smoked it. I wanted to give them some time alone to relax. When I brought the drinks back they were sitting right next to each other. Jackie was asking him about his line of work. I was worried that Alex might blow it and give away that he wasn't a pro, but he handled it well and played right along.

"When I have the opportunity to be with a woman as beautiful as you, I don't consider it work," he told her. "Believe me, the pleasure is all mine."

"Let's hope not," she teased as she moved towards him and they locked lips in a deep French kiss.

It was started and there was no turning back. As their tongues worked, their hands were exploring each other's body. Alex pulled my wife's dress aside and cupped her breasts. He kissed his way down her neck and took her hard nipples into his mouth. His hand found her thigh, and he slid under her dress and found her wet bush. Jackie was totally into it now, and she let out soft moans as Alex fingered her through her panties and sucked her tits.

Her hand was on his swollen dick, massaging it through his pants. She started fighting with the zipper, trying to get at it. Alex got up and started to undress. Jackie did the same as she let her dress fall down her body. When Alex saw her standing there in her G-string, stockings and heels, he grabbed her and pulled her to him, kissing her as his hands went to her ass and fondled it.

She pushed away and sat down, helping him finish undressing. When he pulled his shorts down, his erect cock sprang out. It was easily ten inches. Jackie was awed at its size. She wrapped her hand around it and started stroking it as she exclaimed how beautiful it was. She started licking it up and down the entire length, then she slowly took it into her mouth. She began sucking it in more and more. My cock was ready to burst through my pants as I quickly got undressed.

I stroked my pecker slowly as I watched my wife suck Alex faster and faster. Alex warned her he was about to come, but she was loving his dick fucking her mouth so much that she couldn't stop and he exploded into her mouth. She swallowed as fast as she could, but there was so much that some ran out of her mouth and down her chin. She was fingering her soaking wet snatch with her left hand as she milked every last drop of come from his dick with her right. She eagerly licked his cock clean, then wiped the come from her chin and swallowed that up, too.

Alex's cock remained hard as he sat down and started to pull Jackie's panties off. His hand went to her cunt and he buried his middle finger in it as their mouths met. Jackie spread her legs wide as her hand expertly stroked Alex's cock back to a full erection. Alex got on his knees and buried his face into my wife's burning pussy. She screamed with delight as he fucked her with his tongue. Never in my life have I seen Jackie so wild with lust. She came with a screaming fury, and she grabbed Alex's head and pressed it hard into her crotch.

As she came, so did I, stroking my cock furiously. I swear, my come shot three feet into the air.

Alex stood back up as my wife's legs wrapped around him. Her pussy was rubbing against his stomach as they kissed and tried to catch their breath. "Let's go into the bedroom. I want you to fuck me with that gorgeous cock of yours. I want you to fill me with your come," she said. As they walked into the bedroom, my wife took hold of this man's cock and led the way. She looked back at me and asked, "You coming, Stubbly?"

"I'll be right there," I replied.

They went ahead and I got our camcorder. I guess they couldn't wait, because by the time I got in there they were already in a 69 position, with Jackie on top devouring his cock and Alex on the bottom with Jackie's pussy hovering above his mouth. I started the camera and zoomed in on Jackie as she slowly deep-throated Alex's tool. She would let the head pop out of her mouth and lick his shaft up and down, then she would suck the entire length back in. I had no idea how she got that thing all the way down her throat without gagging, but she did. Alex was alternately tonguing and fingering my wife's love box. They were totally oblivious to anything else going on.

Alex's cock swelled even more and he was about to come again. Jackie pulled his rod out of her mouth and said, "Not like this. I want you inside of me."

She moved around and positioned her waiting cunt lips above Alex's dick. She lowered herself onto it, guiding the swollen head into her. She let out a gasp as she took about half of his length in. She worked herself up and down on his cock, each time taking more of it in until she had all ten inches of him inside her. She rotated her hips for a few seconds, then leaned forward and started to kiss him.

She would slide up and he would suck her tits, then she would slide back down on his cock and their tongues would meet.

Each time she slid up, about six inches of his dick would be exposed. When she slid down, he would bury himself in her. They fucked real slow like this for quite a while before Jackie sat up and started to quicken the pace. She rode up his pole until just the head was in her and then she rode it back down.

As they moved faster, she suddenly jumped off and turned around on her hands and knees. Alex did not have to be told what to do. He quickly got up and entered Jackie from behind, thrusting his entire ten inches into her all at once. She let out a gasp as she put her shoulders onto the bed, arching her back to push hard against Alex, making sure she had every inch of his cock inside her. Alex started to fuck her hard, pulling out and thrusting in. He was hitting home so hard his balls were slapping against her stomach. With each thrust Jackie would push her ass to meet it. I had a good angle with the camera and got a good view of that monster cock going in and out of my wife's snatch. Stroking my cock with my free hand, I was ready to come again.

Jackie was now completely out of control. As she met Alex's every thrust, she came so hard that she made Alex's dick start pumping come deep into her tunnel. As Alex continued to hammer her, his come started to run out of her cunt and drip down her legs. His big cock was wet with her juices and his own jism. Jackie was biting the bed to keep from screaming. As they both reached the end of their orgasms, they collapsed onto the bed, exhausted. Alex wound up spending the night, fucking my wife several more times.

My wife and I have since had several experiences where I was able to watch her get totally satisfied. Hiring a "pro" to get started helped Jackie over any inhibitions she had. She goes out now and picks guys up and brings them home to fuck while I watch. She has seduced several of my friends and has fucked three guys at once while I videotaped them. —*P.M., Truth or Consequences, New Mexico* ⚬—▪

PARTY ANIMAL UNLEASHES INNER BEASTS

Since my husband and I moved to our new neighborhood, I've really been wondering about myself and my sexuality. I was once rather active and have had quite a few guys, but since we got married seven years ago, it's just been Bill and I. After the bizarre events that took place last week, though, I've been reevaluating my priorities.

We were invited to a party. I only knew a few people there, and those only slightly. They all seemed to be an average group of professionals, similar to ourselves.

One of the first people I met was Cynthia. She was young, friendly and likable. She had a pleasant smile and very pretty eyes, dark and deep. You could see her trim, athletic body very clearly through the thin summer dress she wore. She was good-looking but didn't really make an issue of it or anything. I had a little chat with her just as we got there, about how Bill and I were getting on in our new home and his new job and all. I didn't think much of it at the time, just the pleasant chitchat that people exchange.

A little later I caught sight of her among the other guests, chatting with some guy. I didn't know him. I later found out that his name was Mike. The way she smiled at him and stood close to him, and the way she fiddled with the belt on her dress, made me think there was something going on between them. As it turned out, they'd never met before that night.

A little while later, on the way to the kitchen to get another glass of wine, I caught sight of her sitting on the couch, grinning across the room at Mike. He was smiling back at her, obviously enjoying her attention. It kind of amused me.

On my way back I caught sight of Cynthia and Mike in the hallway by themselves. They were pressed against one another, talking very intimately, while his hands ran up and down her body. She seemed to quiver at his touch. I watched this teasing and bantering, feeling a little ashamed of myself. No one else was paying any attention—or maybe everyone else just had the good taste to ignore them.

But I was fascinated and kept out of sight, watching their flirting advance to outright lust. His hands began to clutch her ass more firmly. Her ass-cheeks were so round beneath the filmy dress. Cynthia, who was obviously getting off on his attention, squirmed and grinned up at him. Her eyes darted to his lips, as if enticing him to kiss her. He basked in this for a moment (as did I, observing unseen) and then leaned slowly down to kiss her, her expression encouraging him.

Just then the music suddenly changed from a slow song to loud, pulsing, dance music. Cynthia yanked herself away from Mike, then pulled him behind her into the living room. I discreetly followed, lingering at the edge of the crowd. Some people were dancing in the middle of the room, and that's where Cynthia and Mike started to move to the throbbing rhythm.

She moved like a dancer, her whole torso gyrating in a slow, slinky grind against him. Her dark eyes flashed up at him, a sultry smile on her face. I was obviously not the only one watching them because, before long, they were the only ones dancing. Everyone else had stepped aside to make a circle around them.

Her dancing was a blatant seduction. She might as well have been wearing a neon sign that flashed "SEX" as she slithered about, undulating her hips seductively and rubbing her ass up against him. Mike seemed momentarily taken aback, as if too embarrassed to keep this up.

She squatted low before him, keeping in perfect rhythm with
the music, and gave him a look that said, "Are you man enough
to go for it?" as she shimmied up against him. She made sure the
whole length of her body made contact with the very evident
bulge in his pants. From that point on, Mike accepted her challenge. There was no turning back for either of them.

She lifted her leg and wrapped it around her waist. His hands
clutched at her ass, holding her up as she ground her pelvis into
his. Their eyes locked. It was clear to everyone by now that she
had nothing on beneath her dress.

The people around me were all amazed—some fascinated,
others amused, still others embarrassed. I, too, wondered how
anyone could make such a spectacle of themselves, but I could
not look away. Then I noticed that Bill was on the opposite side
of the room from me, and his eyes were also fixed on Mike and
Cynthia. Then Bill looked across the room and our eyes met. An
electric shock seemed to pass through me as I looked at Bill. I
shuddered with excitement while Cynthia and Mike pushed their
erotic romp even further.

As she twisted herself around and back and over, gyrating to
the pulsing music, her dress loosened and her right breast tumbled out, her nipple erect and dark. Some of the audience snickered, some clapped and cheered and some, perhaps unsure if she
was aware she was exposing herself, felt a little uncomfortable.

But she leaned back against Mike, arching her back and thrusting herself forward as he reached around and clasped her naked
breast. As she grinned at the crowd, making sure that we were all
watching, her eyes connected with mine and she winked at me.
That's when I knew the naked tit wasn't an accident.

As she stared at me, Mike's other hand worked its way down
her body, easing her dress up her thighs, revealing the little
clump of hair beneath. I couldn't keep from looking down to see
her pussy. The thin line of her labia was clearly damp. I must
have gasped or looked stunned, for when I looked back into her
eyes, she seemed to laugh with delight at my shock.

She then twisted around, her dress above her waist, and jutted
her naked ass out. She started to gyrate her round, white ass-
cheeks. I was fascinated by the sight of her cheeks squeezing
tight, then releasing and spreading before clenching again. She
didn't protest in any way when Mike pulled her flimsy dress up
over her head, leaving her entirely naked.

I looked across the room at Bill. From the look on his face, I could tell that Cynthia was giving him the eye. But not for long, because it was soon obvious from her lewd and passionate kisses that Mike again had her full attention.

The people around were either getting into it or were growing even more disturbed. One woman was so outraged she dragged her reluctant husband out in a big huff. It was kind of funny—I knew how the woman must have felt, but there was no way I was going to miss any of Cynthia's extraordinary performance.

I watched her coil and curve her sinewy body around Mike. I watched her tongue lap hungrily at his. I watched her thrust her pussy against him, welcoming his fingers as they prodded and parted her lips. She spread her legs to make sure everyone could see all the action. I was stirred—repulsed yet fascinated. I had never seen anything like this. Cynthia was exuding pure, raw lust. She didn't care what anyone thought—I think she was beyond caring. She was into some amazing zone of sensation where her body and mind fed not just on Mike, but on all the eyes trained on her—on her saucy little tits rubbing against his body, on her ass swinging about in proud display, and her pink cunt, all spread open and moist. The harder Mike thrust his finger in, the more she splayed herself for all to see.

Next she began tearing at his shirt, and then she yanked open his trousers and jerked them down and off. I held my breath and sensed everyone around me do the same. We all wondered how far she would take this.

Mike's prick was fully extended and already leaking precome. He, too, appeared to be in a trance as Cynthia kneaded his balls and stroked his long shaft. She then dropped to her knees before his cock, as if praying to it. She kept massaging it and caressing her face with it. Her cheeks were getting sticky with its fluids. All the while she grinned up at Mike, her eyes dancing with delight.

Then she looked around the room at all of us, making eye contact with as many of us as possible, including me. I shuddered as she looked right at me and crammed his prick into her mouth. She let out a moan, savoring the taste and texture with unabashed enjoyment.

I began to feel almost faint as my own body quivered beyond my control. Across the room I saw Bill in a similar state, his crotch not just bulging, but with a damp patch starting to show.

Beside me, some guy was standing very close, his breath coming fast and excited, warm on my neck. A clearly sexual energy emanated from him, and most definitely from me too. Around the room people were smiling, their bodies moving, their own appetites stirred. Sucking and slurping sounds could be heard over the music as Cynthia filled her mouth, then moved around and up and down that sleek, wet staff. She was in a frenzy, attacking Mike's dick with total abandon, as if she had lost all control of herself.

But she was actually very much in control. She pulled Mike to the floor and laid him down. His organ, pointing up ramrod straight, gleamed with saliva. I had a clear view as she squatted over his face. Her pussy hovered over his mouth. He reached up and delicately spread her open with his fingers. She smiled lasciviously at his touch, her eyes darting about the room, making direct contact with her rapt audience. Then she lowered herself as his tongue darted out, lapping at her wet lips and hair. She gasped, like a laugh and sigh combined. Her eyeballs rolled back and forth and she continued to pant and whimper.

She seemed so completely outside of herself, or so far into herself, that she was no longer present. She seemed lost in a welter of extraordinary sensations beyond description. But then her eyes would come back to us, checking up on us: were we still here? Still watching and enjoying her total exposure? As if that fed her, she'd disappear back into herself, to feed that tongue lapping at her clit.

Cynthia shifted away from Mike's face and, like an agile cat, turned her back to me and poised herself over his magnificent cock. Again she looked around the room, then glanced over her shoulder at me, before smiling down at Mike and sliding down onto his prick, letting it slip deep into her.

I gazed, enthralled, at her pussy, all red and wet as it swallowed up his cock. She rode up and down on his shaft, slowly at first, then quicker. Her round white ass was spread wide and her little asshole winked at us as she plunged up and down with unrelenting force. Mike thrust up into her in perfect rhythm.

It was an awesome spectacle that left me limp and damp. Cynthia was taking us all with her, to the very threshold of total sexual release.

She rode Mike's prick with total abandon. Her head rolled and jerked, her legs pulsed, her buttocks quivered. Little shrieks and moans burst out of her. Her eyes, now glazed, roamed the room to seek us out, her conspirators in wanton carnality. The whole room throbbed to the rhythm of their fucking, and I thought it was actually possible I myself would come just standing there watching this exhibition.

And then, at the last possible moment, she lifted herself off him as that cock popped, and a fountain of white jism gushed up and out. Mike filled the room with his roars at each spurt. It splashed onto his belly, gushed onto her arm, her tits. She leaned down to catch some in her mouth.

The whole room seemed to convulse as Mike roared and erupted. I nearly passed out. Thank God for the guy beside me or I would have hit the floor.

Giggling, Cynthia licked the come off his prick and slurped it up off her lips. She made it look so delicious, I could almost taste it myself. Then everyone started to applaud and cheer. The man beside me let go of my hand to clap, and I had to steady myself before I could join in the ovation. The tension in the room had been released. We all breathed easier.

The party broke up soon after. What can you do after that? Some hurried upstairs to the bedrooms to indulge their urges in more private quarters, others, including us, hurried home to their own bedrooms.

That night I sucked and fucked Bill like I never had before. Together we connected with something we'd never touched. We followed Cynthia's ground-breaking trail and unleashed the rawest, most primal parts of ourselves. I could never do what she did, but I have to admit I envy her. I'm also grateful to her for showing us the way. —*J.G., Cincinnati, Ohio* ⚷

ANNIVERSARY COUPLE CELEBRATES
BY GIVING A FAIR SHARE FOR CAB FARE

My first experience with two partners happened on the very date of my third anniversary of marriage to Ian. Ian is tall, very muscular and extremely well-endowed, both physically and sexually. I am always very satisfied with him, but the turn of events on this particular night led me to want even more.

We went out to dinner at a romantic Italian restaurant, where we shared two bottles of wine. After dinner we strolled along the river and smoked a joint. It was a beautiful night. I was more than a little buzzed as well as somewhat turned on. As we turned away from the water and walked back toward a busy street, we embraced in a long, heated kiss. We then hailed a taxi to take us to our next stop, a local club for some dancing.

In the back of the taxi, Ian began to stroke my bare legs, tracing little circles, getting closer and closer to my moist heat. I was wet already. He leaned into me and kissed me deeply, sliding a finger into my unclad pussy. I glanced up and caught the driver watching us in the rearview mirror.

Ian leaned down a little farther and pulled the strap of my dress off my right shoulder. As he hungrily brought his mouth to my right breast, the driver's eyes bored into us. I realized I didn't care in the least—in fact, it turned me on.

Ian kept up his attention to my pussy with his finger until I begged for more. He clumsily unzipped his trousers and let his rock-hard dick come out. He pulled me over on top of him and my wetness took him in with the greatest of ease. After just a few strokes, I was jerked to attention when the cab rolled to a stop.

The driver was staring intently into the rearview mirror. We sat still and acted, unconvincingly, as if nothing was happening. The driver said, "You guys are killing me."

Red-faced, I answered, "We're sorry. We didn't mean to get carried away." Cabbie, as I'll call him, was apologetic for interrupting and explained that this was a first for him. He admitted it was making him so horny he could just burst.

To my total surprise, Ian, after making sure I didn't mind, asked the cab driver if he wanted to join us. Strangely enough I realized I wanted them both, and said so.

Ian asked the driver to guess what I love the best. When he said he didn't know, Ian responded, "You know what she likes? She really loves a tongue in her. You want to taste her?"

Cabbie jumped at the chance. He got out of the cab and came around to open my door. He gently turned me sideways in the seat, then spread my legs and shoved his face between them. He licked and sucked and tickled my clit. I thoroughly enjoyed it. He continued this as I lay back and began to suck my husband hungrily. Then, all of a sudden, I felt a huge rod thrust inside me. I knew it must be larger than Ian's, because it seemed to tickle all the way to my stomach. For a minute I completely forgot about my mouth. Ian quickly reminded me by guiding my head back up and down. All this was most thrilling, and exhausting too!

We skipped the dancing and went straight home, with a free

cab ride, of course. Ian and I showered together and made beautiful love under the cascading water. Soon thereafter we snuggled into bed together.

I felt a little guilty for a few minutes, but Ian held me tighter, placed a gentle kiss on my forehead and whispered, "Happy anniversary, my love." I felt completely at peace and we slept a deep sleep together. — *T.L., New York, New York*   O⊢▪

HOLIDAYS AREN'T BORING WITH A WIFE LIKE HIS

Well, anybody who says that holidays are boring is wrong. It all started on the Fourth of July. My wife Lanie and I decided to attend the picnic at the local park. We both like to go every year because we get to talk to a lot of old friends whom we don't see very often, while downing a few cold ones.

This year Lanie really dolled herself up for the occasion, and was looking extremely edible. She's twenty-nine years old, five foot ten and has a great figure. She was wearing tight, faded jeans and a tasteful blouse left unbuttoned enough to reveal some sexy, tanned cleavage. To top it all off she was having a great hair day. To sum it up, Lanie and her sexy ass could stun the average male in seconds.

When we arrived at the picnic, it was a typical mob scene, but the crowd in the beer tent was kind of thin.

Lanie and I got a couple of beers from the bar and somehow got into a conversation about fantasies we used to have. Things started to heat up a bit from all the sex talk and Lanie's slinky body. She was getting me hot without even trying. I suggested to Lanie that we play a little game. I would pick out a guy who I thought would be a good sex partner for her and she would select a woman for me. With a little giggle and a smile, Lanie said okay.

I scoped out the tent and saw a guy who looked just right for Lanie standing by the entrance. I pointed him out to her. "Check out the dark-haired guy with the green shirt and light-colored jeans." Lanie smiled and said that he looked interesting. I have to admit that I cheated a bit. I'd seen Lanie checking out this guy when we'd walked in. "Now it's your turn," I told her.

Lanie's task was going to be much harder than mine. She was

having trouble finding a woman she thought would appeal to me. She finally picked someone she thought was right for me: a short blonde with a bad attitude whose clothes didn't really fit well. "Nice try," I said, "but she's not for me." There just weren't any sexy women there that night.

As Lanie and I got up and started to walk around, we bumped into an old friend of hers. I figured I'd let them catch up a little and excused myself to fetch a round of beers. As I walked up to the bar to order, the guy I'd selected for Lanie was there, watching the football game on TV. I asked him who was winning, and we soon got into a conversation about sports. We introduced ourselves. His name was Andy.

My beers finally came and I figured I'd better return. The last thing a man wants to do is leave a horny female by herself. When I got back I found her standing there alone. As I handed Lanie her beer, I told her whom I'd run into at the bar, and her face lit up with excitement. I asked her if she wanted to meet Andy. I told her he seemed like a really nice guy.

We walked over and I introduced them. Right off the bat I could tell they hit it off. We all started talking, and I could tell that Andy was attracted to Lanie. It was pretty obvious to me that she was wet for him. After several beers and many laughs, I asked Andy if he wanted to come to our house and watch the rest of the football game. He seemed kind of unsure, but I convinced him with the promise of better booze and good food at the house. Andy said he'd follow us in his car.

I could tell Lanie was happy with the invitation. By this time hormones were pouring out of us, and if anything sexual was going to happen, it was going to happen soon. On our way home I asked Lanie what she thought of Andy. She smiled and said, "Todd, you know what happens to me when I drink. I get very horny. If his cock is like the rest of him, he'll be perfect." I'm proud that Lanie can tell me anything because our marriage is so secure.

When we arrived at our house, I turned on the game and broke out the Jack Daniel's. We were all soon laughing it up. By now Andy and Lanie were checking each other out, but trying not to be too obvious. Lanie and I looked at each other and I could tell she was thinking of making a move, but to be honest I didn't think she had the nerve.

Lanie excused herself and went into the bedroom. Andy and I talked and watched the game. At this point, we were flying high from the drinks and I asked Andy what he thought of Lanie. "Todd, you're a lucky man to have such a sexy woman," he replied, but I think he knew what I really meant.

A few minutes later Lanie came out wearing nothing but a skintight, white see-through teddy, with white stockings and white pumps. Our jaws dropped. With her bronze skin contrasting with that white teddy, her golden nipples erect and her shaved mound dripping wet, Lanie looked incredible. Andy and I were speechless as Lanie twirled around, modeling for us.

"So what do you think boys? Do I look good enough to eat?" she asked coyly. I couldn't believe my eyes. She walked over to where Andy was and sat down next to him, spreading her legs and languidly stroking her wet mound. Andy and I were still in shock. Neither of us could say a word. "Todd," Lanie said, "you are going to sit there and watch me and this stranger fuck and suck."

That's when it finally hit me. Earlier, Lanie and I had been talking about our old fantasies, things that we'd never had the nerve to make happen. Lanie had always wanted to get it on with a stranger and never see him again. Just pure lust with a stranger, nothing more. My fantasy was to watch some guy, either a friend or a stranger, balling my wife. Well, it looked like both of our fantasies were finally going to come true.

Andy looked at me, confusion on his face. I just said, "Go for it. Just don't hurt her and don't make a baby!" Andy smiled. I could tell he couldn't wait to explore her mound.

As Lanie rubbed her wet throbbing pussy with one hand, she started stroking Andy's bulge with the other. They both started to groan, and Lanie's box actually started dripping. Andy reached over and replaced her hand with his as he leaned over and started kissing and sucking her neck. Deep groans came from Lanie. I could tell she was loving it. I was going crazy. My pole was like cement. This was incredible. I couldn't believe it.

Lanie pushed Andy down onto his back and said, "I'm going to fuck your brains out. I'm going to fuck you like you've never been fucked before." She bent over and pulled out his rather large cock. She groaned as she slid her tongue around him. Andy started moaning and held the back of her head to steady her while Lanie worked her magic. The stranger was finding out how good Lanie was at giving head. After lapping him for a minute, she lay back and told him, "Eat me."

Andy leaned over and started rolling his tongue over her wet clit. Andy was a pro and it didn't take long for Lanie to explode. "Now ride me hard and don't stop," Lanie instructed. Andy slipped it in and started riding her. I don't think they noticed, but I had my cock out and was going to town as I sat there watching all this. After some wild riding, Lanie made me get the K-Y jelly from the bedroom. They kept going while I got it. When I returned, Lanie was on all fours waiting for me.

"Give him the K-Y," she told me. I did, and Lanie told Andy to put some on his cock and her asshole. I was shocked. Lanie never wanted to have anal sex before, but she was going for it all. Andy slowly slid his cock into her well-greased rectum. Lanie started to scream with passion. "Faster, faster," she yelled. "Pump my rump." Andy went faster and was almost there. "Before you get there, pull it out and squirt it all over my cheeks," Lanie told him. Andy pumped harder and harder. "Keep going," Lanie encouraged. Finally Andy pulled his cock out and spurted all over Lanie's butt. Wow! What a trip this was!

After Lanie and Andy cleaned up in the shower, Andy left knowing we would never see him again. Lanie gave me a great blowjob, and told me, "I hope you enjoyed it as much as I did."

It was the best sex I'd ever seen. Who says holidays are boring?—*R.G., Harrisburg, Pennsylvania*   O┼▄

BLAME IT ON THE BELLBOY
WHEN A SHY WIFE GOES WILD

What follows is a true experience my wife and I would like to share with your readers. We are an average couple in our early forties, and what happened brought us closer together than we had ever been before.

I had been married to Beth for fifteen years. Like many marriages of that length, ours was in sort of a down period as far as sexual excitement went. It was not that Beth is unattractive. She is a pretty five-foot-six-inch woman with shoulder-length brown hair, a trim figure, lovely long legs and beautiful 36C breasts. I guess you could say she's easy to look at. It was just that, after fifteen years I was bored with the same old thing. To add to that, Beth was never very inventive. Though she was really hot when the right buttons were pushed, she never tried to vary the routine. She always dressed conservatively, even though she had a great body. She was a virgin when we married and I was the only man she'd ever had.

A couple of years ago, I read an article in a magazine about men who liked to watch their wives with other men. At first the idea seemed strange to me. I figured if I ever saw my wife with someone else I would flip out. But, to my surprise, the more I thought about it the more turned on I became.

I began to imagine Beth trying to attract other men. I thought about her showing herself off to other men or being made love to by someone else. At first these thoughts proved to be very confusing for me. However, the more I thought about it or read about it the more real and exciting it became. When I had these thoughts while we made love it seemed to heighten my pleasure. I began to be consumed by the idea of my wife teasing or making love with another man.

When we went out on our boat I would talk her into removing her suit or taking off her top to sunbathe. All the while I assured her nobody could see her, but all the time I was hoping somebody would.

This went on for over a year. Every letter I read in men's magazines about women making love to men while their husbands watched turned me on more. I would read the letter and imagine the woman was Beth. Needless to say, I got myself off time and time again with this fantasy.

I began to buy Beth sexy underwear and nightgowns, low-cut blouses and short skirts. Every purchase was made with one thing in mind: to show her off to other men. My goal was to make my average wife so desirable that she would be hounded by other men. Sometimes she wore the clothes I bought her and sometimes she didn't. I didn't have the courage to tell her what my motive was.

To celebrate our fourteenth wedding anniversary, we went to Toronto for the weekend. It would turn out to be a truly momentous weekend. After years of trying I finally talked Beth into going without underwear on Friday night, our first night in town. We were going out to dinner and the theater. She reluctantly agreed because it was our anniversary and she wanted to please me. It was a real turn-on to know that under her very modest button-front dress she was nude except for her thigh-high nylons.

As we walked down the hall to the elevator I noticed how her breasts swayed and undulated under the thin material of her dress. Her nipples became erect from rubbing against her dress and their outline was very evident as they pushed against the material.

In the cab on our way to the restaurant, I ran my hand up her leg until it made contact with her uncovered cunt. This was a first for us both. Her pubic hair felt like silk, and she was so very warm. As we sat in the dark backseat of the taxi I gently stroked her. She leaned over to kiss me, moaning ever so softly into my mouth. All the while I was hoping the driver would see what we were doing.

After a great meal with a couple of bottles of wine followed by a wonderful play during which we teased each other, we headed back to our hotel. We decided to walk since the weather was nice. We walked arm in arm, kissing and laughing, feeling very much in love. Twice along the way I pulled Beth into the shadows of a building to kiss her and feel her up. I managed to open several buttons on her dress during our passionate embraces. I was thrilled when I realized that she was not aware they were open.

As we walked along, a little tipsy and both of us quite horny, I glanced over and saw that her dress, shifting with her movements, occasionally exposed a side view of her lovely breast right down to the nipple. I had a raging hard-on as we walked through the hotel lobby and she unknowingly exposed herself to some lucky onlookers.

Once in our room we had several more drinks. I was sitting in a chair by the window, looking at downtown Toronto. Beth stood at the foot of the bed. She walked toward me with a seductive smile as she reached down to unbutton her dress. When she discovered the open buttons on her dress, she gasped in shock.

"Oh, no. I must have exposed myself to half of Toronto tonight. I'm so sorry. I shouldn't have had so much to drink. Please don't be mad. I just wanted to celebrate with you."

I got up and held her. I knew the time had come. It was now or never. I said, "I'm actually very turned on by the thought of some other guy seeing you like that. I know it sounds crazy but you're a beautiful woman and I enjoy the way men look at you." Beth looked a little stunned.

"But you're so jealous. Are you just saying that or do you really mean it?"

"I'm very serious," I said. "Sometimes I imagine other men watching you, or being with you. Tonight, walking around the city knowing that you weren't wearing anything under your dress, with other men so close, had me excited from the moment we left the room. Beth, I love you more than anything in the whole world. I hope you don't think I'm disgusting."

She said she loved me and that anything we did together to please each other wasn't disgusting or wrong. She said she loved me so much that she would do anything for me.

"Even flash other guys?" She kissed me and said, "I'll do whatever I can to please you."

We fell onto the bed and made passionate love. We didn't close the curtains or turn out the lights. Afterward, Beth got up and walked over to the window and looked out at the city. She looked beautiful standing there, her breasts firm, her nipples large and hard, her legs long and inviting, her ass so very pert and smooth.

Seeing her at the window gave me another hard-on. She walked over to the bed and took my cock in her mouth.

The next morning we ordered breakfast from room service, and I was in the shower when it arrived. When I came out of the bathroom, it was obvious that Beth had answered the door in her robe. Through the thin white cotton, I could see the slight dark shadows of her pussy and her nipples. The sway of her breasts made it clear she was naked underneath. In the past, she would have gotten dressed before letting anyone in, but today she was evidently feeling a little looser.

I told her she looked great and that room service must have enjoyed their stop at our room. Blushing, she admitted that the bellhop who had delivered breakfast had checked her out, even though she was probably old enough to be his mother. She said it was kind of fun knowing that he was looking at her with obvious lust. She also admitted that teasing him had been kind of exciting.

I leaned back in my chair and opened my robe to show Beth the huge hard-on she had just given me. I said, "Just imagine what that guy would have done had you been wearing some sheer negligee."

"I didn't bring one with me, so I guess we'll never know," she sighed wistfully.

I told her it was still fun to think about and, with that, I drew her down on the bed and made love to her. Just before I came I whispered how turned on she had made me by turning on the bellhop. We both had powerful orgasms. The only thing Beth could utter was that it was the very best she had ever had.

Later that day we passed a lingerie display in a large department store. I pointed out some of the sexy negligees to Beth. I told her I wanted to buy her one, adding that she might have a chance to use it before we left. She reluctantly agreed. I felt like she might be humoring me.

I was looking for just the right one when I heard Beth say, "Boy, this one's beautiful." She was holding a long black nightgown, sheer except for black satin stripes. It came with a matching robe that tied at the neck and hung partially open. Then she added, "But this is more revealing than anything I have. I don't know if I could wear this. It's just too much. I wouldn't be very comfortable. Let's look for something else."

"If I was the only one to see it and I like the way it looks on you, why not get it to make me happy. Nobody else will ever see you in this." That seemed to reassure her, and I bought the gown. The rest of the day, I told her how much she turned me on.

In bed that night, I began to kiss and suck her nipples, while my fingers stroked her cunt. She became very hot and excited.

I whispered in her ear how much she turned me on and how wonderful she was for letting the bellboy see her. She grew more highly aroused, moaning with each stroke of my finger.

I told her the bellboy must have gotten a huge hard-on just looking at her. "Right now, he's probably making love to his girlfriend, thinking of you," I said. "It turns me on to know that other men want you, but you're all mine."

As I continued to arouse her with my fingers, I asked if she liked teasing the bellboy. She moaned a little. I asked if it made her feel good to know she could turn a man on like that. She moaned again.

When Beth was about to orgasm, I asked if she would do it again. She moaned, "Yes, oh yes! Anything for you!" and, with that, I took her over the edge to a shuddering orgasm. Without hesitation, I crawled on top of her and sunk my throbbing cock into her hot, moist pussy. We fucked well into the night.

The next morning, while Beth was showering, I laid out her new finery. When she saw the negligee on the bed she said, "I don't know about this. If the bellboy sees me in this he might get the wrong message. He might think I really want to, you know, do it with him."

I told her that would be my ultimate fantasy. She asked softly. "Do you really want to see me make love with another man?"

When I told her it was my deepest desire, she kissed me and said, "I would do anything for you."

Beth took her time dressing. She applied her makeup carefully, and even darkened her nipples with lipstick. Her hair was brushed and hung down around her shoulders like silk. When she had finished her nails, she stood there looking at me and I told her she was the sexiest woman in all of Toronto.

In her new gown, her nipples and breasts were clearly visible, as was the dark triangle between her legs. She said, "I'm really nervous. I hope I can go through with this." I poured her a drink to help her relax and ordered breakfast from room service.

Then I laid her down on the bed and told her I was going to help her relax while we were waiting. I knelt between her legs, and raised her gown. Before me was her beautiful pussy. I inhaled her aroma and began to run my tongue up and down her slit. I tongued her clit and made it stand proud. I inserted my tongue and then my finger into her hole. She began to moan. When I moved up to suck her nipples through the gown, they were larger than I had ever seen them before. Her thighs and buttocks grew moist with her juices. For twenty minutes, I kept her on the brink of pleasure.

When we heard the knock on the door, I gave her cunt one last lick, and then we stood up. She adjusted her robe, and stood there, her cheeks flushed, her eyes glazed. She wore an expression of pure lust, and her nipples were obviously erect through the sheer material of her gown. Best of all she smelled of sex. Her thighs and cunt glistened, and gave off an aroma of womanhood. She was ready.

She kissed me and went to the door, while I stepped into the bathroom and turned on the shower as we had planned.

Beth opened the door and let in the bellboy. He was about twenty-two years old and very good-looking. His eyes lit up when he saw my wife. She slowly turned and walked into the room, directing him to bring the tray in. She took her time getting her money, giving him a good look at her luscious body.

From my vantage point behind the partly opened door, I could see them in a mirror on the wall. He had a noticeable bulge in his slacks. He couldn't take his eyes off her and the longer he looked the harder his cock got.

Beth handed him some money and told him to wait. She looked at me from across the room, then smiled and said, "I don't seem to have any more money for a tip. Maybe there's something else? From that bulge in your pants I bet you could think of something."

I saw the bellboy move to Beth's side. He kissed her neck as his hand came up to caress her breast. As he lowered his hand to her dripping cunt and felt it through her gown, he asked, "What about the guy in the shower?"

"Don't worry. He likes it when I fuck other guys," Beth said. With that, she turned and kissed him full on the lips, then guided him to the bed. I stepped out of the bathroom, still staying out of sight, my cock throbbing. I was about to live out my ultimate fantasy.

I watched as Beth disrobed him. When she pulled his slacks and underwear down, his nine-inch cock sprang to attention. It was much longer than my six inches and a little larger in girth.

Beth dropped to her knees and began to blow the stranger. It was a delight to see my wife of fifteen years sucking this young man's cock. She moaned with every thrust as he slid it in and out of her mouth. She acted as if she couldn't get enough.

After five minutes or so he stood her up and peeled her gown and robe off. He gasped when he saw her body, and laid her back on the bed.

I moved in to get a better view. As he kneeled and buried his head in her crotch, she looked at me and said, "Come here, honey. Be with me."

Aware of me now, he started to pull away from Beth's juicy snatch but she put her hand behind his head and guided him back between her thighs.

I walked to the bed and she took my hand and guided me down so I was next to her on the bed. She leaned over and kissed me, and then started to talk to me in a soft whisper while he ate her cunt.

"Honey, he's licking my pussy. He just put his tongue in my hole. Nobody else except you has ever done that to me. It feels so good. Just think, someone I never met before is eating me. I'm letting him do it to me for you. I'm so hot I can't wait until I can feel his cock in me. It tasted so good and it felt so big and smooth. I loved it in my mouth. Do you want him to fuck me now? My cunt is on fire. I already had two orgasms but I really need to feel him pounding into me. Tell me if you want me to let him fuck me, honey. Tell me if you want this man's cock buried deep in your wife's pussy. I want it bad, honey. Tell me it's okay."

"Fuck him, Beth. Fuck him good. Let him pump you full of his hot come. Do it for me, baby." I kissed Beth again and she moaned into my mouth as she had yet another orgasm.

Beth guided the bellboy up and began to lick her juices from his face. "Fuck me for all you're worth," she said. "I want your big cock in my pussy."

When the stranger lifted her hips, about to penetrate her, Beth stopped him and told me to watch his cock enter her pussy. I slid down until my head was about a foot from her moist cunt. She reached down and guided the head of his cock to her opening. Ever so slowly he began to sink his big prick into my wife. I watched until it was buried to the balls. When he slowly withdrew, his cock was covered with Beth's juices. Her pussy grasped his dick as if trying to prevent it from ever leaving her. He soon established a steady fucking rhythm, and Beth moaned with each stroke. They fucked furiously.

After a few minutes, he rolled onto his back and Beth rode his cock. As she bounced up and down I stood by watching. She took my hand and pulled me to her, and kissed me as she fucked him. He rolled Beth onto her back again and began to pound her. I could tell he was about to come. Beth had me lie down next to her, and she was kissing me when the stranger stiffened and moaned. As I lay there kissing my wife, another man was pumping her cunt full of jism. Then Beth moaned and stiffened as she climaxed. Her legs were wrapped around the bellboy, holding him deep in her cunt.

I watched him pull out, and his large, softening cock was covered with their fluids. As he stood up and began to dress, I sat between Beth's spread thighs, gazing at her freshly fucked cunt. Her pussy hair was soaked with their sweat and juices. Her lips were swollen and her slit was oozing another man's come. It flowed from her cunt down between her ass-cheeks and pooled on the bed beneath her. She looked more beautiful and desirable than I had ever seen her.

As I heard the bellboy close the door behind him, Beth gently stroked the back of my head, and slowly pulled me forward, directing my face to her dripping pussy.

To my surprise I ate her out. I then moved up and kissed her. Just as I was sinking my cock into my wife's well-used pussy, she licked my face clean and tried to suck my mouth dry. We fucked until one that afternoon. It was the best sex we ever had. Beth is now a changed woman and every day is as exciting as the first. — *Name and address withheld*

COUPLE'S NEW MOTTO: IF THE SHOE FITS, BARE IT!

I'm a forty-seven-year-old man blessed with a wife twenty-one years my junior. I met her four years ago at a local college where I was taking a refresher course in real estate. We dated for about one year before getting married. We had both been raised to believe in a strict moral code; so—although we did plenty of petting and necking—we didn't have intercourse until our wedding night.

It wasn't until a year and a half later, however, that we opened up to each other enough to discuss our sexual fantasies.

We were reading the "Someone's Watching" section of *Penthouse Letters* when my wife suddenly confessed that she was a closet exhibitionist. Nothing, it seemed, turned her on as much as the idea of cockteasing men by exposing herself to them in public places. Fortunately, this was one fantasy my wife could easily accomplish. She is an extremely attractive woman who has little trouble arousing men even when fully clothed.

That very night my wife and I agreed that we would try to fulfill her fantasies. After working out certain guidelines to minimize risk, we embarked upon our new sexual adventure. I'm writing this letter in order to share some of the great experiences we've had.

At first we started off simply. One day we got on a bus together and pretended not to know each other. My wife sat across from a nerdy, pimple-faced eighteen-year-old who had "virgin" written all over him. I sat nearby. She was wearing a short skirt over a pair of sheer, white panties. Slowly but surely she hiked up her skirt and parted her shapely thighs. I don't know which popped out further, the kid's eyes or the bulge in his pants.

Several times we've gone to adult bookstores together, knowing they're excellent places to hunt for horny men. Upon entering a store, my wife would browse the shelves of steamy X-rated materials. She assumed a variety of provocative poses beneath walls covered with photos of flesh.

But soon, reaching for the top shelf and letting a guy glimpse her firm, panty-clad ass wasn't enough of a thrill for her. She began making eye contact with her victims, especially the young, well-built ones. She'd wink and leer at them and slowly circle her lips with her hot pink tongue. Sometimes, when she thought it was safe, she'd lock eyes with a guy, reach her hand underneath her skirt and finger herself to a powerful orgasm. I began to think she wouldn't be happy until she had guys dropping their pants in public and beating off. Several times, we had to leave the stores in a hurry, fearing for her safety.

As her nerve increased, we tried wilder and wilder things. Once, she arranged to have a masseur come to our home. I hid in the closet while he gave her the massage. To tell you the truth, I almost pitied the poor guy as I watched my young, sexy wife tease the hell out of him. She let him touch and rub oil over every part of her nude body. But (because of an agreement we had made earlier) she wouldn't touch him back; nor would she allow him to relieve himself in any way. After he limped out the door, I came out of the closet and we had great sex.

The last incident I'll share took place in a shoe store of all places. We entered the store about ten minutes before closing time, when the store and the mall surrounding it were nearly deserted. I told the clerk that my daughter needed a pair of blue shoes to match her blue panties. My wife then lifted her skirt, took her panties off and handed them to the startled young clerk. She then sat down demurely and waited for service. The clerk was back out with a pair of shoes before I could even blink. A second clerk also materialized, ready and willing to provide my wife with any service she might require.

My wife allowed each clerk to fit one shoe. Even though there were two men on the job, it took a lot longer than usual. It's quite possible they were distracted by the view.

Suddenly, with both clerks still kneeling before her, my wife spoke up. "Do you like feet?" she asked them coyly.

The clerks nodded dumbly.

"I just figured that since you work in a shoe store, you must really like feet," she continued. "Would either of you like to kiss my feet?" she asked, wiggling her manicured toes in front of their eyes.

The clerks said nothing but the next thing I knew, I was witnessing the wildest thing I had ever seen: two young guys we had never met before were kissing my wife's feet and rapturously sucking on her toes as if they were small, hard cocks.

I could tell that my wife was really hot for these guys, so I let things go a little further than I normally would have. I handed her a dildo and said, "Show the guys what you do at parties." She immediately grabbed the dildo and crammed it into her tight, wet twat. She was on fire now, and the two clerks were devouring her with their eyes. I handed her a second dildo and, after lubricating it with her juices, she forced it up her ass.

At this point, I suggested to the guys that they give her a hand. (I think they would have done so whether I wanted them to or not.) They brought my wife to an unbelievable orgasm. She then brought out the guys' cocks and masturbated each of them to orgasm. Later she told me that it had been only the second time she had done that to a man besides me.

I love showing my wife off and she enjoys it too. Our sex life is now very satisfying because we dared to let our fantasies come true. —*K.L., Muncie, Indiana* ○┼▬

MORE SHOE STORE HIGH-JINX! WILLING WIFE SHAKES HER BOOT-Y

Heather is the most wonderfully sexual woman I have ever met, and it has been my great pleasure to be married to her for the past sixteen years. She is more than willing to accommodate my perversions and more than able to think up many of her own.

Heather is also a real beauty. She stands five feet, nine inches tall and has light brown hair that cascades over her shoulders and around her angelic face. Her body is perfectly proportioned. Her breasts are gorgeous and are adorned with large dark-brown areolae and nipples that stick out a full half inch when aroused.

To top it all off, Heather has remained in tremendous physical shape. She walks five miles every day, which keeps her body as hard and shapely as a granite sculpture. Her long, firm legs are strong enough to squeeze the come right out of you when she wraps them around you to fuck.

Needless to say, when Heather walks by men, they (and their cocks) sit up and take notice. This brings me to one of my favorite pastimes: I love to watch men looking at my lovely wife. The more she shows, the better. I love it, and you better believe she likes showing off as well.

One day, about two weeks ago, Heather and I took a day off from work and decided to go shopping at a new mall located about ninety miles from our home. We rose at six in the morning to make the one-and-a-half-hour drive. When Heather came into the kitchen that morning my dick immediately sprang to attention. She had on a tight semitransparent top through which I could clearly make out the outlines of her large nipples. She also wore a black, pleated mini-skirt. Her long, slender well-tanned legs were bare. Her outfit was topped off by a pair of three-inch high heels.

The moment I saw her, I wanted to lay her on the table and bury my face in her sweet pussy; but the day was young, and her outfit (as well as the mischievous twinkle in her eyes) told me to wait and see what the day would bring.

We arrived at the mall just as it was opening for business. After about half an hour of window shopping, we bought some coffee and seated ourselves on a bench near the top of a spiral staircase. I soon noticed that Heather had not chosen our bench at random: anyone coming up the stairs had only to glance slightly upward to see her lovely legs. Soon a well-built man with a mustache started to ascend the stairs. When Heather spotted him she slowly uncrossed and re-crossed her legs. This caught the man's eyes instantly.

Pretending she was looking over her shoulder at a store window, Heather seductively spread her legs once more, giving the young stranger an unobstructed view up her skirt at (I assumed) her customary lace panties. At this point our young voyeur tripped and nearly fell down the stairs. Watching his reaction made me hard as stone.

After teasing a few more passers-by, we got up and continued our stroll through the mall. As we walked hand in hand, Heather turned to me and asked if I had enjoyed the show so far. I gave her a kiss on the cheek and briefly placed her hand on the raging hard-on hidden in my jeans. "Judge for yourself," I said.

Our next stop was a shoe store. Stopping in front of the store, Heather pointed out a good-looking young man helping an older gentleman try on shoes. With a twinkle in her eye, she announced that I too needed a new pair of shoes. I entered the store alone while Heather went to the bathroom to freshen up.

The young salesman, whose name was Ross, was quite helpful. I had been trying on shoes for about ten minutes when Heather waltzed in looking incredibly sexy. She sat in a chair directly across from me. Spotting her, Ross dropped me like a hot potato and instantly turned to help her. Looking at Heather, I couldn't really blame him.

She told him she would like to try on a pair of red heels. Ross looked at me and I told him to go ahead and wait on the young lady since I was really in no hurry. Ross turned back to Heather, gently raised her foot up onto his stool and removed her shoe. As he did so, Heather let her thighs fall slightly apart. It was only then that I discovered that Heather had not worn her usual panties. She was wearing a pair of hot-pink crotchless panties with black, lace trim. Ross froze as he caught sight of my wife's beautiful pussy. Then, without a word, he rose to retrieve a new pair of heels. When he returned, he again placed her foot on his stool.

Leaning back in her chair, her nipples taut against her tight top, Heather once more spread her legs for all to see. Her pussy—which she keeps shaved clean from the top of her pussy-lips all the way to her asshole—was cherry red from excitement. The lips were full and succulent, and her love juice glistened as it flowed down to her asshole. It was the most unbelievably sexy thing I have ever witnessed, period.

I was more turned on than I ever imagined possible, and I imagine the same was true for Ross. He looked over at me and I just shrugged my shoulders. Since we were the only three people in the store and I had made no sign of objecting, Ross decided to go for it. He turned back to Heather and ran his hand lightly up the inside of her thigh. Heather closed her eyes and spread her legs even further.

Encouraged, Ross tossed caution to the wind.

Slowly sliding forward on his stool, he inched his hand higher and made contact with Heather's hot, wet box. Heather emitted a low guttural moan. He then started to gently caress my wife's lovely pussy. He inserted two fingers into her cunt and began to massage her clit with his thumb. Heather was hot as fire. She began to rock back and forth on his fingers, riding them as if they were a hard, throbbing cock. The juices flowed over his fingers and dripped onto the faux-leather chair. Within minutes Heather was in the throes of an intense orgasm. She threw her head back and grunted loudly. Her cries of passion were so loud, I was afraid a crowd might gather in front of the store.

After Heather had settled down she stood, straightened her clothes, thanked Ross and walked away. I soon followed.

I met Heather down the hall from the store. Without saying a word, we hurried to the parking garage and climbed into our minivan. I lay her down on the back seat, dropped my pants and draped her long legs over my shoulders. With one swift thrust I buried my diamond-hard cock in her wonderfully hot canal. Neither of us lasted more than three minutes before we simultaneously came.—*J.F., Minneapolis, Minnesota* O╼▬

IT TOOK BEAUTIFUL STRIPPERS
TO EXPOSE HER PASSION FOR HIM

I have been an occasional reader of your magazine for many years. Like many of your letter writers, I didn't think I'd ever have the opportunity to write a letter of my own. As a married thirty-five-year-old with children, I thought my glory days were over; but on one September day, I was proven wonderfully wrong.

I work at a franchised national chain in a middle management position. One September day I had to go to a meeting in a large city with another manager from our firm. The other manager is a beautiful lady in her early thirties. In spite of her beauty, I had never considered trying anything with her because I knew she was happily married with a nice house, a sweet dog, a two-car garage and all the other accouterments of a dull but happy life.

Sioban and I had a good relationship at work but other than an occasional collision in the hallway, we had never had any physical contact. I must admit, however, that I treasured those encounters and had often dreamt about how things might develop from these encounters.

Anyway, on the day of our trip, I went to pick Sioban up at her house at six in the morning. The city was about three hours away so we had to get an early start. As I pulled into Sioban's driveway, she walked out of her front door, looking as beautiful as ever. She was wearing a light blue dress that fit rather snugly around her ample bust and waist line, but was loose and flowing below her waist.

She got into my car with a big bright smile and a grand good morning. We headed for our destination chatting about our work, our mates, vacations and various other safe subjects. All of a sudden, though, Sioban asked me if I intended to visit the strip joint that all of the other men in our office frequented whenever they got the chance to visit the city. I was actually kind of shocked by this comment and I just laughed it off by saying, "Yeah, right!"

Shortly thereafter, we arrived at the hotel where our meeting was to take place. As we walked in through the huge front entrance, I kept picturing how nice it would be to have a private meeting with Sioban in one of the hotel rooms.

The meeting was pretty much a standard affair. It ended with a buffet lunch, but Sioban and I blew it off and decided to eat somewhere a little more interesting. We proceeded downtown to an old building that had recently been converted into a series of shops and eateries.

The restaurant we chose had an old-world ambiance and great food, but it was the conversation I enjoyed the most. It was very intimate, kind of like a first date when you get as much from looking deeply into your date's eyes as you do from the conversation. We spent a lot of time discussing past relationships. The conversation was at times intense, but always very pleasant.

Once in the car, Sioban asked me if I regretted missing out on the strip joint. I thought to myself: This is the second time this woman has brought this subject up. Could she actually be interested in going there? So I turned to her and said: "Do you?"

Sioban blushed and averted her eyes. I asked her if she wanted to go there with me. After what seemed to be an eternity she responded, "If I said I did, would you tell anyone back at the office?"

I assured her that I would not, because I didn't think it would be a good idea for my wife to find out. As we discussed what we were about to do, I noticed that she was no longer her usual calm cool self. She was nervous, but it was much more of an excited nervousness than an apprehensive one. It was obvious that she could hardly wait to get there. I didn't tell Sioban, but she wasn't the only one.

I paid her cover charge and we entered the smoke-filled front door. It was midafternoon and the place was far from packed. Only one of the three stages was being used, so I guided Sioban towards an empty table about ten yards away from it.

The dancer teased for a while before finally removing her g-string. She teased and rubbed her twat in several guys' faces and collected as many tips as she could before the song was over. I had to explain to Sioban how the whole thing worked. It was arousing just telling her about the process.

After a couple of different dancers had performed, Sioban

asked if I was going to sit up near the stage. I didn't want to act like a chicken, so I assured her that I would and asked if she would join me. She declined and said that she would keep an eye on me from the table.

I got to the stage just as a very well-endowed, dark-haired dancer stepped into the spotlight. At this point, there were only two of us up near the stage: myself and an older man who must have weighed a good three hundred pounds. The dancer (her stage name was "Ginger") gave me more than my share of attention. Towards the end of her third song, she reached down my pants, gave me a quick squeeze and nodded at the audience as a sign of approval. After getting an appreciative chuckle from the crowd, she asked if I would like a private dance later. I tucked a buck into her garter and said, "You betcha!"

When I sat back down at our table, I noticed a big smile on Sioban's face. I smiled back and asked her what was so funny? She said she thought that the way I tucked the dollars into the dancer's garter was really cute. I asked again if she wanted to move closer to the stage but once more she declined.

A few minutes later, Ginger came to our table, grabbed my hand and said, "It's your turn, honey!" She pulled me out of my seat and led me to the back corner of the club. This part of the club was designed for only one thing: private dances.

Ginger was good and she knew it! She worked me over in every possible way short of giving me a blowjob. About halfway through the song, I noticed that Sioban had moved to a different table, one which allowed her to keep a closer eye on my activities.

When the dance was over and I had caught my breath, I asked Ginger if she could arrange to have one of the dancers put on a special show for Sioban. She agreed that this could be arranged and took my money.

I returned to my seat. Sioban and I talked and watched a few more dancers until a dancer named Tammy showed up to show us her stuff. She began to strip in front of us, shaking her tits in both of our faces. Then, gradually, she began to pay more attention to Sioban. I could tell Sioban was excited and so could Tammy. Soon, Tammy was dancing solely for Sioban's benefit. Her bra came off and her large firm breasts bounced free. Then she leaned over and swayed her breasts just inches from Sioban's upturned face.

As Tammy worked on Sioban, she occasionally paused to give

my swollen cock a rub and me a big wink. When the show was over, Sioban smiled but didn't say much. After watching a few more dancers perform we decided it was time to head home.

As we headed for the car, neither one of us said anything. Once in the car we didn't say much either. Instead, Sioban turned to me without a word, put her arms around me and began to kiss me— a French kiss at that!

The only sounds in the car were moans of passion. Sioban rolled towards me so that her chest was rubbing against my arm. I slowly put my right arm around her and began to rub her back. She responded by going straight to my swollen groin. The heavy kissing went on for a few more minutes before I pulled away from her to gaze into her eyes for a moment. Then I told her how beautiful I thought she was and softly kissed her.

Without speaking, she grabbed my hard cock and began her intense kissing again. I slowly moved my hand to her tits. I massaged her breasts through her dress. Her nipples were erect and her breasts were very firm. In fact, the only thing in the car firmer than Sioban's chest was my aching cock wrapped in her right hand.

Next, I popped the top two buttons on her dress open, revealing a bright red lacy bra. After enjoying the feel of her breasts through the silky material of her bra for a while, I found the front release clasp on her sexy bra and used it. Since her large globes were now exposed for all to see, I suggested we move the car to a more secluded spot. She agreed and temporarily released her stranglehold on my swollen member.

As we drove to the rear of the parking lot (neither of us wanted to take the time to drive any further), she told me how she had long admired me and how watching the dancers grabbing my crotch had looked like so much fun that she just couldn't keep her hands off of me when we got in the car. I didn't argue. I just parked the car and grabbed her again, picking up where we'd left off.

Sioban picked up where she'd left off too—at my belt buckle. It didn't take long for her to release my manhood and suck it deep into her mouth. Back at the strip club, I had pictured Ginger doing this to me, but I had never dared hope that Sioban's lips would be wrapped around my penis that very evening!

While Sioban was working away, my hands roamed over as much of her body as I could reach. It didn't take long for me to unload in her mouth. She moaned with pleasure as I filled her up.

She kissed her way up to my mouth and I could taste my own juices as I probed her mouth with my passionate tongue.

Our kissing continued as I resumed massaging her tits. Finally, she undid the last few buttons of her dress. The final button revealed red panties matching her red bra. (I almost came a second time just at the sight of them.) Traces of her bush were poking through the lace on either side of her tiny panties. I worked my mouth and tongue down from her face, stopping briefly when I reached her tits and belly button. When I reached her aromatic crotch, I paused and kissed her mound. Then I worked at her inner thigh with my tongue, kissing and licking along the edge of her panties. The aroma of her wet twat was driving me wild.

My first foray beneath her silky panties was limited to just one finger. The warm slickness of her pussy lips tempted me to slip my finger inside her, but I waited. Her panties were now stained by the abundant moisture running from her slit. I continued to kiss my way around her groin before finally pulling her panties to one side and revealing an absolutely beautiful pussy. Her curly black hair was neatly trimmed, leaving just a narrow swath of carpet at the top. The sides of her dripping slit were perfectly clean-shaven.

I dove in head first, working her clit over and occasionally letting my tongue stray to her opening. As I happily tongued away at her, she moaned as if she hadn't received this kind of service in years. Before long she was trembling with pleasure as a powerful climax overcame her. Her screams of pleasure quickly quieted to heavy breathing as she returned to reality.

I kissed my way back up her body to her mouth. I kissed her, letting her taste her own juices. This was wonderful, but the job wasn't done yet—my rigidity had returned. I slowly slid my prick up and down the length of her slit, stopping briefly when Sioban moaned, letting me know I had made contact with her clit. After a few moments of this, she grabbed my ass and pulled me in as deep as I could go. We both started going as if there was no tomorrow. I looked and watched my dick pumping in and out of her beautiful, black-haired pussy and glistening with its shiny coat of vagina saliva. The sight of this brought me to the brink once again. I got kind of worried about coming inside her, so I asked her permission.

"Please do," she answered. Her words released the floodgates. With a loud cry I exploded within her. With my cock still erect and inside of her, we kissed and caressed for a few minutes before getting dressed. As I looked out of the car, I noticed that the parking lot was much more crowded than when we'd first entered the car. Some cars were only ten or twelve yards away. How could they have not noticed us?

Anyway, we both got dressed and commented about how much fun it had been, and how we had never expected something like this to happen, even though we had both wanted it to happen for years.

We had an enjoyable conversation on the way home. Sioban had to use a Kleenex to mop up her panties because my semen was running out of her. After the sun had gone down and we were nearly home, Sioban leaned over, gave me a big smooch and said that she had really enjoyed our trip and that she couldn't wait to go again. She also wanted to make sure that I kept our little secret.

With a big smile on my face, I assured her that I would. I drove the rest of the way home with the windows down, hoping to air out the car. It had the unmistakable odor of passion, and my wife would no doubt recognize it.

The next day at the office, it was business as usual. We both acted as if nothing had happened. Now every time that I see her walk down the hall my mind wanders back to that special day in September. I just hope that I don't have to wait till next September to go again. —*F.G., Boston, Massachusetts* ᴏ╼▪

SHRINKING VIOLET BLOSSOMS BENEATH THE STROBE LIGHTS

My wife Nancy had a part in a play that ended in two weeks. To celebrate, I took her out for an expensive dinner, and then dancing at a new club. My plan was to see how she would behave in a club if I wasn't around. While we were dancing at the nightclub, I got a prearranged message on my pager. I pretended to use the phone and then went back to Nancy to tell her I'd have to be gone for at least an hour. If I had to be gone longer, I added, I would leave a message on our home answering machine. Nancy offered to leave with me, but I told her to stay and have a couple of drinks because I would probably be back. I then pretended to leave the club. My friend Steve, who works at the club, led me to a small room where I could watch Nancy through a two-way mirror. She was sitting at a table near the main dance floor. It took less than a minute for a guy to sit across from her and buy her a drink.

At that point, I noticed a group of three well-dressed black men in their mid-thirties checking her out. They were seated in a semi-circular booth—one of those old-style ones with a curtain that could be drawn for privacy. By their table, a magnum of champagne was being chilled. The nicest looking of the three men got up and approached Nancy. He was probably six-five, and he was wearing an expensive Italian suit. Steve had rejoined me earlier, and he now informed me that the black guy's name was Jim, and that his two friends were Tim and Doug. "Jim's a real operator," he added as he left the room.

After a while Jim asked Nancy to dance. She seemed a little tipsy walking toward the dance floor. Jim folded Nancy in his big arms. Soon he started rubbing her back. Eventually his hand was squeezing her ass. Nancy reached around and pushed his hand away, but it soon drifted down there again. After pushing him away a couple of more times, she gave up and nestled closer to him.

I guess this was the encouragement Jim needed. With his hand between her legs, Jim said something to her and she nodded. The guys pushed the table out a little bit and drew the curtain. From my vantage I could see everything, while from down in the club, you'd have to go out of your way to get a peek.

Nancy climbed onto the table and turned to face Jim. She reclined on her back, resting on her elbows, her pussy right in Jim's face. She lifted her ass up off the table and he removed her thong, balling it up and putting it into his coat pocket. He then pushed her dress up and spread her legs. Slowly he ran his tongue up and down the seam of her little red bush. Tim and Doug just smiled and sipped their champagne, watching the proceedings with relish. It wasn't long before Nancy was moaning and pulling Jim's head into her crotch. Finally, she began trembling as a huge orgasm coursed through her.

When she had caught her breath, Nancy sat up on the table and pulled the dress over her head. The guys' eyes nearly popped out of their sockets when they saw how big and firm her tits were. All Nancy had on now was a pair of black stockings and high heels. She reached over, undid Jim's buckle, unzipped his pants and pulled down his slacks and underwear. Out sprang a huge black cock nearly twice as big as mine. Nancy grinned devilishly, wrapped a hand around it and gave it a few pumps. Then she leaned back on the table and let her legs dangle over the edge.

Jim stood before her, and with his hand he guided his cock up and down along her wet slit, coating it with her copious juices. Then he slowly started to penetrate her, inching his way deeper with each stroke.

Nancy's box is really tight, so I wasn't sure he'd be able to fit it all in; but after about twenty strokes he was buried to the hilt and his big balls were draped over her asshole. There was a look of sublime satisfaction on Nancy's face when she realized she'd taken his whole cock inside her.

Jim proceeded to give her a nice slow fuck. With each stroke, he pulled his cock nearly all the way out and then slowly slid it back in till it disappeared inside her. Doug and Tim, not wanting to be left out, leaned in from either side to suck on a tit. Nancy's nipples are really sensitive, so I knew this would get her super hot. Jim then started fucking her harder. Nancy met his every thrust, trying to get every inch of his dick inside her. Soon she was squirming about so much, Doug and Tim had a hard time keeping their mouths on her nipples.

This scene was better than I'd even imagined. Nancy's milky white skin contrasted amazingly with Jim's deep umber. The sight of that huge, black, glistening hose stretching out her little pink slit was making my heart pound and my dick ache. I knew he was reaching places inside of her I'd never been.

Nancy was so transported by the fucking Jim was giving her she didn't even notice when Doug took his mouth off her tit and opened up the booth's curtain. The dance floor was treated to the sight of a lovely young redhead, totally naked, her legs spread wide to accommodate the immense black cock ramming into her. Jim lifted her legs onto his powerful shoulders and really started giving it to her. Nancy panted and writhed, yelling at him to fuck her even harder. Finally she began convulsing and tossing her head from side to side as a massive orgasm swept through her.

I guess the sight of her come sent Jim over the edge. He growled and his thrusts became short jabs as he blasted his cream into my wife's spasming pussy. He shot the first few spurts deep, then he pulled out and sprayed thick jets of gooey cream all over her pubic hair.

Just then, a song ended and people started clapping. I thought Nancy would turn fifty shades of red when she realized she'd had an audience. But, to my utter dismay, she smiled, stood up and took a bow. She was shiny with sweat, her nipples were stiff and aroused and her pubic hair was visibly matted with come. While everyone watched, my wife got on her knees in front of Jim, sucked the come off his dick and zipped him up.

By now it was getting late, and (perhaps due to Nancy's fine example) the club really started to hop. I saw women dancing topless and a guy getting a blowjob from a cute blonde.

After they finished their champagne, Jim took Nancy by the hand and led her, like his personal slut, up the stairs and into the VIP rooms. Doug and Tim went along. I had to go down a corridor and look through several different two-way mirrors before I found where they went. My efforts weren't wasted.

They were in an empty room that had an upholstered table in the middle of it. Jim told Nancy to lay back and spread her legs. She willingly obeyed. Tim and Doug then undid their pants. Their cocks were as big as Jim's. Doug's was even a little thicker. When he slipped that thing into Nancy's slick cunt, she just about went crazy, but her moaning was soon silenced when Tim pushed his tool into her mouth. When passers-by saw that a hot young redhead was being doublefucked by two big black men, they came in to watch.

Soon a good-sized crowd had gathered. A nice-looking brunette in a mini-dress leaned over, braced herself against the table with her arms and started wiggling her ass provocatively at the guy behind her. The guy lifted her dress, freed his cock and penetrated her. She formed an "O" with her lips and began grinding her hips, all the while staring in rapt arousal at Nancy.

Nancy was well worth staring at. She was on her back, her legs spread wide and Doug's dark meat sliding back and forth in her wet pussy. Her sweet lips were wrapped around a second, big black cock, and she was massaging her own breasts and tweaking her nipples with her hands. She seemed to be coming every two minutes.

It was so incredible. I had to remind myself time and again that this was my wife down there, enjoying the thrill of carnal pleasures in a room of strangers.

The two guys picked up the pace as they approached their climaxes. Nancy thrust her pelvis to meet each of Doug's strokes even as she gently stroked Tim's big balls, trying to coax the cream out of them.

"Here it comes baby," Tim bellowed. His cock started pulsing and a torrent of come erupted into Nancy's mouth. She tried to swallow it, but she was panting so hard that much of it spilled over her lips and chin. Suddenly she started shaking wildly. Tim's cock slipped out of her mouth and she gasped, "I'm coming! I'm coming! Fuck me, yeah, fuck me!"

Doug bore deep into her, groaned and filled her box with come as her hips shook wildly.

A minute later, the brunette and her guy went into their own orgasms. Then, without taking her eyes off Nancy, the brunette removed the cock inside her and took off her dress. As Doug and Tim backed away from the table zipping up their deflated dicks, the brunette climbed up and started sucking Nancy's nipples. Seconds later they were kissing passionately, mixing saliva and jism with their tongues.

A few moments later, the girl shimmied up Nancy's torso and put her knees on either side of Nancy's head. Her come-soaked pussy was just inches above Nancy's face.

My cock got even harder when my wife reached up and pulled the girl's hips down so that her chestnut snatch landed on her open mouth. I could see Nancy's tongue probing vigorously, causing the girl to let out a long, low moan.

She rode Nancy's face for a while, then turned around and went down on her. Now they were locked in a furious 69. It seemed like they were competing to see who could make the other one more excited.

I thought Nancy had won when she slicked her index finger with saliva and worked it into the girl's asshole, but then the girl did the same to Nancy. Finally, they exploded together, hips shaking and tongues writhing against spasming pussies. It was quite a scene.

The girl climbed off Nancy and they both stood up. Their faces were shiny and slick with juices and perspiration. Jim handed Nancy her dress and she put it back on. Then Jim, Tim and Doug escorted her out of the club. It was three-thirty in the morning.

I left the club by a back door and raced home to wait for Nancy. I was so worked up by what I'd seen, that I couldn't wait to fuck her silly. Once I got back home, however, it quickly became clear she wouldn't be back anytime soon. I paced, looked out the window and drank beer as the hours passed. There was no way I could sleep—not with all the images of Nancy's night out playing in my mind.

At dawn a shiny black Jaguar pulled into the driveway and deposited my disheveled wife at the doorstep. She was tired, a bit hungover and her pussy was stretched and sore—I could tell by the way she was walking.

She said she'd been to an all-night party. All in all, she said, she'd had a great time and she'd tell me about it after she'd had some sleep. As soon as she woke up that afternoon, I got the whole story, never letting on that I knew most, if not all of the details already. The only thing I didn't know was where she'd spent the time between leaving the club and getting home. She said, "When I get good and horny sometime, I'll tell you all about it."—*R.R., Marietta, Georgia* ⚬—▪

SHE'S SPENT A LIFETIME MOONING, AND SHE'S HAPPY TO SHOW YOU HOW

My wife Janie and I are both thirty-three and have been happily married for nine years. Janie is a very sexy and passionate woman. Her shapely long legs make heads turn wherever we go. Janie's auburn hair matches her lovely bush but what's most impressive about Janie is her luscious ass, which she just loves to have licked and fingered.

Janie has always been very sexually active. After we were married, Janie would tell me about some of the more memorable fucks she'd had while I played with her wet pink slit.

She'd ask her dates to stick their tongues and fingers into her pussy and asshole, which was especially sensitive, and she told me how when she was fucking, she enjoyed feeling the hot come squirt in and fill her cunt. But what really surprised me was when Janie revealed to me the thrill she got from mooning.

My wife, though sexy, also has a very sweet and proper appearance and I was astounded. At parties Janie would hike up her skirt and pull her panties all the way down her legs when she was dared to moon. She said the guys would nearly fall over themselves and I couldn't blame them.

One particularly memorable night, I invited two of my most muscular friends over to help me move our new furniture into the living room. After they finished moving, Janie brought out some beer for us all. I could see Janie was excited by Mark and Jerry by the way she kept looking at their broad-muscled chests and arms.

When Mark kidded Jerry that he had done most of the heavy lifting, Janie stated that she could have lifted the couch herself. Then Janie said that she used to moon and any girl that can moon can do anything. The guys kidded her and said that girls didn't have the guts to moon. At that Janie stood and turned her back to the guys.

She hiked her skirt up to her waist to reveal her pink satin panties, then she hooked her thumbs in the waistband and slowly lowered them to her ankles, completely exposing her creamy-white ass. Mark and Jerry were speechless as she spread her legs wide and bent over.

Janie looked back at us between her long legs and said, "No guts to moon, huh?" All eyes were glued to her spread cheeks revealing her puckered asshole surrounded by curly hair with her full cunt lips protruding.

Janie remained in this pose for a few seconds before she straightened up and pulled up her panties. I was rock-hard after having witnessed this scene, which I had only fantasized about before. I knew Janie was hot, too, by the way her pussy glistened.

I wanted Janie to show the guys more and I wanted to be there to see it. I retreated into the adjoining room and waited for Janie to break away. She soon excused herself and sauntered up to me. I told her it had excited the hell out of me when she showed the guys her ass. I asked Janie if she would like to have sex with them and she said yes.

I reached into her panties and slipped a finger into her dripping hole. She was hotter and more excited than ever before. I told her my plan and then said, "Go for it."

I told Jerry and Mark that I would be going to the store for some more beer. I went out and made my way behind the bushes which covered the living room window. I had an unobstructed view of the entire room and the open screen allowed me to hear everything.

Jerry brought Janie the last beer and they continued to chat. Mark really started to tease Janie. "When guys moon, they do it for a full minute," he said. Then Jerry said that she still looked too prim and proper to moon.

To these comments Janie replied, "Mark, kiss my ass!" Mark jokingly got down on his knees at Janie's feet, but she was serious. She turned her back on him and knelt on the couch. Once more she pulled down her cute lacy panties just enough to expose her full butt.

Mark knew an opportunity when he saw one. With my wife's ass only inches from his face, he started to plant kisses on her soft cheeks. Then Mark tugged her panties all the way down her long legs and left them at her ankles. Jerry started to squeeze an asscheek as a huge boner filled his pants. Watching my buddies feel and examine my wife's beautiful ass got me yanking at my own hard-on.

"Make sure you hit the bulls-eye," Janie whispered as she reached back with both hands and spread her cheeks apart to reveal her asshole. Mark sank his stiff tongue all the way into her butt. Janie moaned in ecstasy, which caused Jerry to remove his trousers and start jerking at his meat. He too watched as Mark alternately licked Janie's butthole and pussy.

Janie groaned hoarsely and Jerry knelt by my wife's face. She hungrily gobbled up his hot cock and began slowly sucking it as Mark flicked his tongue deep into her cleft. Then Mark stood up and unzipped his pants to reveal his ten-inch member.

He placed it at the entrance to my wife's vagina and slowly started to push its entire length in. Janie growled deeply and continued to deep-throat Jerry's cock. Mark wet his finger and pushed it all the way into her asshole as he continued to ball her vigorously.

I watched with mounting excitement while Janie was getting it from both ends. Mark then pulled his boner out of my wife and lay down on his back. Janie straddled his lap and reached back, sinking his swollen cocktip into her wet hole. I watched in fascination as her large hairy cunt lips enveloped the head.

I could hear the liquid sound of her wet snatch as it slowly swallowed the entire shaft right up to his balls. Janie started to ride him while moaning in ecstasy. It was so freaking hot watching Mark's huge dick appear and then disappear into my wife's pussy. Then Jerry, his cock still wet from my wife's saliva, stepped behind them and placed his cockhead against Janie's butthole.

He inched his meat into her hungry rectum as he moaned in pleasure. They got into a slow, deep rhythm and the sounds of lovemaking filled the room. They fucked like this for fifteen or so minutes before Janie bucked into a deep orgasmic moan, whereupon both Mark and Jerry let go, filing her butt and cunt with a double load of come.

As my buddies removed their shrinking cocks from Janie, I saw their sperm dripping from her snatch and asshole. Janie then kissed Jerry and Mark and told them good night.

When I entered the house I knew Janie was still hot and horny, and one look at my hard-on told her I had witnessed the whole scene and enjoyed it. Janie quickly undressed me and straddled my face as she lowered her buttered pussy onto my mouth. We slipped into a 69. She took my throbbing member into her throat. I could taste my buddies' salty come mingled in with hers as I dug my tongue deep into her well-lubed pussy and then her asshole.

It became too overwhelming and I shot my load far into Janie's sucking mouth. I tongued her clit into another shattering orgasm. We slept like logs and woke up the next afternoon, fully rested.

Over a late breakfast Janie started to tell me more mooning stories, but this time I believed her one hundred percent. I'd seen the evidence with my own eyes, and I couldn't wait to see more. My wife's hot ass looks so much hotter knowing that other guys have seen it. —*Name and address withheld* O┼■

Swinging & Swapping

RENO ROMP RAISES STAKES FOR MARRIED COUPLE

My wife wanted me to write this letter and describe what happened on our trip to Reno last week.

Beth is a very beautiful forty-two-year-old woman. This is the second marriage for both of us. We have been married for twelve years, and have talked many times about past relationships, so I know Beth had quite a sex life even before me. When we were dating, she openly confessed that she'd once been fucked by three guys at one time. Each of the men, she said, had exceptionally large penises, which they had used to fill each of her available orifices. As she told me about this story, which she went into in great detail, Beth got incredibly turned on, and we ended up having one of our best sexual experiences ever.

In Reno, we found ourselves at the blackjack table with this guy named Larry. He sat next to Beth. We started talking and soon we were all getting behind in the cards so we decided to play the slot machines. I asked Larry what he did, and he answered he occasionally acted in adult movies. A look crossed Beth's face I will never forget.

After Beth and I went back to our room to get ready for dinner, she was curious and couldn't stop talking about Larry and how sexually charged everything was in Nevada. "Sex is in the air out here," she said. "It makes it hard to think of anything else. I wonder if Larry has a big dick, he's a good-looking guy," she said.

I told her guys in that business did not necessarily have to be well-endowed but it helped if they were short on looks, sexual stamina or acting skills. I could tell she was thinking about it and getting turned on, so I told her if we saw Larry later that evening we would ask him up to our room for a drink. With that, she went wild. We went to bed and had one hell of a fuck as we talked about what he would do to her with that big dick.

When we did get around to dinner, she asked me if it would be alright if we went through with our fantasy. "Oh, baby, this is for you, whatever you desire," I said, agreeing to go along with her fantasy. After dinner we went back to play blackjack, but we didn't see Larry. After an hour I told Beth I was going to the restroom. Instead I went looking for Larry, who I found playing the slot machines. I walked over and asked him how he was doing. "Pretty badly," he replied. I told him we were not doing so hot at blackjack either.

"Why don't you come to our room for a drink?" I asked. There was an implication in the tone of my voice, and an understanding passed between us with nothing said.

You should have seen Beth's face when we walked up. When we got to the room, Larry said he would go and get the ice. When he left the room, Beth gave me a big kiss. "What should I do?" she asked nervously. I ran my hand over her pussy.

"Don't worry," I told her. "I will take care of everything." At twenty-six Larry was considerably younger than us so I knew we were in for some hot and heavy action. After three drinks, which I made doubly strong for Beth, I asked Larry about some of the pornographic movies he'd made. He told us about one that was very good because the female co-star really got into it. She was a good fuck so it was more than a job for him. I told him we had seen a few movies, and most of the men had large cocks. I asked him if his was big, and he said, "a little bigger than average."

Beth had not said a word. "I bet Beth would like to see it, wouldn't you, honey?" She just nodded her head. Larry looked at me. I told him to take his pants off and walk over and show his cock to Beth. He stood up and pulled his pants down. Out fell his dick, which although it wasn't erect, was so long and fat that my wife said, "Oh my God! It's as big around as my wrist."

He walked over to Beth. She reached out, took hold of his dick and played with it lovingly. Once, when she pulled her hand up to the head, there was a drop of clear come on the tip. She took it off with her finger, then licked it off, giggling like a school girl. Larry helped her to stand and we both undressed her. He gave her a deep kiss while he moved his dick into position between her legs. I could tell he was on her love-button because she started to moan and shake. Larry picked her up then put her on the bed. Beth looked up and said, "Fuck me, Larry. Please fuck me."

Larry got between her legs while Beth raised her knees to make room for him. She closed her eyes as he put the big head of his cock to her pussy. As the head went in, she looked at me and said, "Oh my God, it's so big it's beautiful." Larry started to slowly fuck her, putting more and more into her with each stroke. He moved faster so she raised her ass off the bed to meet him. Then she started to scream, "Fuck me, fuck me with that big cock!"

Beth put her arms around his neck and her legs around his ass. She screamed out, "I'm coming, oh baby, I'm coming, fuck me, yeah!" All the time he was giving her long hard strokes. Beth was trying to get it all as she raised her ass off the bed, to milk him dry, something she does to me all the time. He fell on top of her as he moved it in and out. Larry rolled off on his side as Beth screamed "No, no don't take it away from me."

Larry told her what a great fuck she was. He was not done, however. She put her hand on his dick, which was still hard. She put as much of his cock into her mouth as she could, holding onto the base with her hand. Then she said, "I have to have more, I can't stop."

She got on top, put a leg on either side as she guided his cock back into her pussy. Then she rode him like a wild woman, screaming, "It's so deep. He is fucking the hell out of me." Beth moaned from deep inside her body.

"Baby I'm going to come with you," Larry yelled.

Beth screamed, "I can feel you coming. I'm coming too! My whole body is coming." She fell on top of him as she went limp. He pushed her over on the bed as he got up but she didn't move. Her pussy was open and the bed was wet.

"You're a great fuck," Larry said.

Here was a professional, calling my wife a great piece. It made me proud to think someone in the sex business would find my forty-two-year-old wife so desirable. I was beaming like I'd won first prize at the high school science fair.

Beth was mopping up the spunk between her legs, smiling at both of us. "You are not bad either. Either one of you." —*T.H., Denver, Colorado* ⚷

WIFE BECOMES A PARTY FAVOR

I wrote you a letter a few weeks back about my wife's first multiple-partners experience, which occurred this past winter. We have subsequently joined a swingers' network and enjoyed some good and bad multiple-partner relationships. One in particular helped us discover that my wife prefers having sex with multiple black partners.

A few weeks after we had joined the swingers' club we received a member number and password that allowed us access into the online network, which you can browse by area code or by zip code. Upon returning home from work one day, I came across a message on the answering machine. It was from another member, who said he had received my wife's message and was returning the call. He also left a number and address where he could be reached. When Brenda arrived home I asked her about the message. She said that she had contacted a few different members the past several days, and that this must have been one who was calling back.

Later that evening Brenda returned the man's call. As she was sitting down at the table she asked me for a pen and paper. After introducing herself she started talking and writing down some vital information on the piece of paper. She wrote, "six-foot-three, two-hundred-twenty-five pounds, black, well-hung, good shape." She spoke for a half hour or so. Finally, she told him that everything sounded pretty good and that she would get back with him to possibly set up a time to meet.

After she hung up, Brenda asked me my feelings. I wanted to know if he had a partner, and if it was just going to be him and her, or if others were going to be involved. Brenda said that he discussed just the two of them. If I was interested in doing more than just watching, she said, this was fine by him. He said that if we were interested he could definitely arrange for additional people. I told her to give me a few days to think about it.

A few days had passed when she brought the subject up. I told her to give him a call and make the arrangements. Later that night they agreed on a date and place. We were to meet him at his apartment that coming Saturday around seven. He was having a small party and we were invited. We were going to play it by ear. We live in Cincinnati and his apartment was located in Dayton, Ohio, which is about a forty-five minute drive. We left a little early to make sure we had no problem finding it. We also wanted to get there a little before the party started so we could talk with him and see what he was like.

We arrived at his place around seven, found his apartment number and knocked on the door. A tall, well-dressed black man answered the door and introduced himself as Tim. He asked if we had any problem finding our way. We introduced ourselves and he invited us in.

Tim told us that he had been a member of the swingers' network for a few years and that he was pretty happy with most of the people he had met. We were there for about forty-five minutes when there was a knock on the door. As Tim got up to answer it, Brenda looked at me and said that she was feeling pretty comfortable. I turned to see who was at the door. I noticed three other black men walking in. They introduced themselves as Brad, Anthony and Mike. Each one was checking out Brenda as she stood to shake their hands. Tim then told us that maybe a few more people were going to show up, but that was going to be it.

Tim put some music on the stereo, and Brad asked if anyone would like something to drink. We sat around talking for a little while and drinking a few beers. Mike took out a small bag from his jacket and asked if anyone wanted to really get the party going. He rolled one up, and as we passed the joint around things started to loosen up for everyone. After a few more beers and a couple more joints, Tim went over and turned the music down low. Then he hit the VCR and put a videotape on. The porno flick starred two black studs and one white chick. He then turned to Brenda and said, "I thought things were starting to get a little boring. This might loosen things up."

Brad, who was sitting next to Brenda on the couch, put his arm around her and said, "I got something that will loosen you up." He then began to take his hand and run it across her chest, stopping on each tit to give it a little squeeze. I got off of the couch and moved over to a chair in the corner of the room, where I could see Brenda and the couch clearly. When I got up Tim took my place. He reached down and spread Brenda's legs apart. Brenda suggested that they find a more comfortable place, one with a little more room. Anthony then came over and took her by the hand and said, "Sounds like the bedroom to me."

Once we arrived in the bedroom, Anthony told Brenda to remove her clothes and lay down on the waterbed. Tim looked over at me and asked if I was okay and comfortable with what was going on. I told him to go ahead. As I stood there watching Brenda undress, Tim went over to a closet and removed a shoe box, placing it on a table next to the bed. By this time Brenda was down to her panties and bra. She removed her bra, revealing a soft, firm set of breasts. As she took off her panties, exposing a shaved pussy, everybody let out a collective sigh of admiration.

Tim told her to take the shoe box and lay down on the bed. He told her to open it and take out whatever appealed to her most. Brenda opened the box and dumped the contents onto the bed—three sex toys in different shapes and sizes. She chose a battery-operated dildo that stroked up and down with multiple speeds. Mike told her to put it into her mouth and suck it.

She began to lick and kiss the head of the toy, then turned it on to let it stroke and hum inside her mouth. After just a few minutes of this she took it out and inserted it between her pussy lips, turning it up to full speed. Her nipples were like bullets and her toes were curling as the buzzing toy moved against the pleasure center at her clitoris. She looked over at us, fucking herself, and said that the real thing would feel a whole lot better.

"We got plenty of the real thing, baby," Tim said.

The group proceeded to remove their clothes. Brad was the first to approach her. His cock was huge. I then looked around at the other three, who were also positioning themselves around the waterbed. Their cocks were nothing to be ashamed of either. All four were hung, especially Mike. His was not only long but very round. As Brenda laid there still stroking herself with the dildo, Brad knelt next to her face and started to stroke his cock. When he rubbed it on her erect nipples, Brenda reached over and guided it toward her lips. She licked the cockhead and, little by little, inserted the bulbous knob into her mouth.

Tim was removing the dildo from her pussy and positioning himself between her legs. He placed her knees forward, exposing her wet, hot pussy. He thrust his swollen black cock into Brenda's pussy with one fast stroke. Brenda let out a few groans and moans, while Mike and Anthony were getting into position. Mike moved to one side of her face, while Anthony got behind her at the top of her head. They each placed their cocks next to her face.

Tim was pounding her pretty good, while she was taking turns on the three cocks in her face. Tim finished fucking her and buried his face in her pussy. Someone eating Brenda's pussy was all it took for her to come.

She was moaning and writhing around, having one long, multiple orgasm. Anthony told Brenda to get on her hands and knees. As she knelt on the bed Anthony positioned himself next to her rear, and began banging away with fast, hard thrusts. Brad had gotten underneath her and was licking her pussy while she gave head to both Tim and Mike.

Tim then got out of bed and went into the bathroom. He was

only gone for a few minutes when he returned with a jar of Vaseline. Anthony opened the jar while still fucking away. He inserted a few globs on his fingers and began to rub them inside Brenda's asshole. As soon as he touched it, she jerked her head back and said that was one thing she did not do. Tim said that with four guys and only two holes they needed a little more out of her.

I know that I had tried several times over the years to have anal sex with Brenda, but I never could accomplish it. Anthony took his fingers and slowly began to probe her rectum. Once it was inside and he began to slide his finger in and out, Brenda willingly put her face down on the bed and stuck her ass invitingly into the air. It still took her several minutes to let him penetrate her. Every time he would try she would lift up off the bed and say, "I do not think I want to do this."

Finally, after some convincing, he took his cock and started to enter her juiced-up asshole. The tip of his head went in gradually. Once in, the rest of his head fell into the tiny crack, which gaped widely to accept the stem of his manhood. Anthony stroked with steady thrusts.

Mike was getting a blowjob while Brad positioned himself underneath Brenda, who was forcing her pussy down onto his cock. Finally, he got her into a position so he could enter her cunt. I sat there in front of the bed and could not believe that my wife was taking on all three men at the same time. Each of her holes was plugged and she was loving it. I couldn't let a good thing pass. I had to try it one time, easing my rod deep inside the tight clasp of her anus.

When I was finished getting her in the rear we dressed and left the room so Brenda could get cleaned up. When she entered the living room I asked her if she was all right. She said that she was fine and that what had happened was the best sex she had ever had. Tim asked that we stay, and we took him up on his offer. I do have to admit that since that night anal sex with my wife has just been great. —*T.L., Cincinnati, Ohio*

MARRIAGE MADE IN GANG-BANG HEAVEN

I recently began buying your fine publication. My wife and I enjoy it immensely. Reading the letters from husbands who enjoy watching their wives with other men has led us to believe that our relationship is not as unusual as we had once thought.

Cheryl and I had been living together for over four years, and we enjoyed what most people consider an open relationship. We had agreed that we could date others; however, I never felt the urge to do so. I was a virgin when we met and had always been quite shy around women. Cheryl had been quite promiscuous throughout her high school and college days and she saw no reason to alter her behavior just because we were living together. Cheryl is five feet tall and has long red hair, perky tits and a vivacious personality.

About a year ago I started to get the feeling that Cheryl was less than excited whenever we made love. In contrast to our lovemaking when we had first met, Cheryl rarely climaxed. In fact, while Cheryl continued to see other men on a regular basis, whenever she and I made love she acted rather indifferent to my efforts to bring her to orgasm. It was on one such night, after vainly trying to bring Cheryl to orgasm, that I confronted her with the problem. "Honey, I'm so sorry. I love you so much, but I'm afraid I'm going to lose you if I can't make you come," I said. Cheryl seemed touched by my concern but she didn't spare my feelings.

"I'm sorry Mike," she said. "Don't take this the wrong way, but I just can't get turned-on with you like I used to. I still love you, but I guess I just like to make love to bigger guys."

I was heartbroken but gradually got over my hurt with the assurance of her love and support. Since that night Cheryl and I became even closer. She began to freely discuss her sexual needs with me, treating me as she would a close girlfriend and confiding all her secret desires and longings. During this time, I began to work on my skills at licking and sucking Cheryl's juicy pussy. It was something I had always enjoyed but never felt like I had completely mastered. I concentrated on it like it was a real task, and I became a cunnilingus expert as a result. I got to the point where I was able to bring her to orgasm most every time we made love. My tongue was one little talented teaser.

For my own sexual release, I began to masturbate more and more, not only when Cheryl was out with one of her lovers, but also while hearing the juicy details upon her return. Although Cheryl never actually refused me sex, it was clear that upon returning home after a passionate lovemaking session, she preferred me to lick her pussy clean while bringing myself off.

Over time I began to have the urge to actually watch Cheryl

make love to one of her lovers. Just imagining one of her big studs move up between her legs and insert his thick shaft deep inside her eager pussy gave me an immediate erection. When I brought this up she said she would ask Bob, one of the men she was currently seeing, if he minded if I tagged along on one of their dates.

Bob was a guy she had met at her health club and they had been carrying on an affair for over three months. Cheryl had told me about several of their previous dates and it seemed that Bob really encourages Cheryl's exhibitionism, going as far as having her do a sexy striptease in front of two of his envious friends.

As a condition for letting me accompany them, Bob had requested that Cheryl abstain from sex for two weeks before their date. Cheryl told me that Bob wanted her to be extra horny, and as for me, well let's just say that it took quite an effort not to masturbate while anticipating the upcoming event. At her suggestion, Cheryl and I spent the entire day before her date shopping for a sexy new outfit.

I took a special interest in helping her choose extremely provocative clothes, including a tight black miniskirt and a sheer white blouse. Cheryl also selected white fishnet stockings along with a lacy white garter belt and G-string panties. To top off the look we got a sexy pair of black platform shoes with five-inch heels.

Throughout the day Cheryl continually teased me, saying things such as, "I'm in the mood to be really fucked hard tonight. Wait till you see Bob's cock, it's huge."

It was all I could do to keep from coming as I sat on the edge of the bed, massaging my rigid member and watching Cheryl dress. It's become something of a ritual for me to help Cheryl prepare for her dates. Earlier that evening I had carefully shaved her pussy until it was smooth as silk. As she dressed for a date, Cheryl performed what I like to think of as a reverse striptease, and I often ended up jacking off. Tonight was no different.

I watched her bend over to fasten a delicate gold chain around her ankle. I was quite close to orgasm when Cheryl noticed me in the mirror.

"Oh Mike you are a naughty little boy, aren't you? Don't come yet, though. Wait until later, okay?" giggled Cheryl as she straightened the seams in her stockings. I reluctantly took her advice and tucked my erect cock back into my pants while she continued to primp.

Cheryl had just put the finishing touches on her makeup when the doorbell rang. I quickly excused myself to answer the door. Cheryl said she would be about twenty minutes more and so I offered Bob a drink while waiting. I felt a sharp pang of jealousy as I saw that he was extremely handsome, well over six feet tall with a strong, muscular physique. At the same time my cock stiffened as I imagined Cheryl making love to this Adonis.

Bob wasn't paying much attention to me as he surveyed the living room from his seat on the couch. It was clear from the way he looked at me that he considered me a nuisance, so I resolved to be as inconspicuous as possible throughout the evening. Nevertheless, I tried to start up a conversation by remarking, "You know, Cheryl says that you and her have had a lot of fun over the past three months."

"Yeah, man, you could say that. Your woman sure does like to fuck. That's for sure," he said with an arrogant flourish. I was about to respond when I was interrupted by Cheryl bouncing down the stairs to meet Bob. She greeted him with a lingering French kiss.

On the way to the restaurant, I drove Bob's Lincoln Continental while Cheryl and Bob made out in the backseat of the car. After a quiet dinner, Bob and Cheryl spent an hour dancing at a local nightclub. As she and Bob danced, I could see her grinding her pussy against his crotch. Watching Cheryl's blatant seduction, I developed a raging erection. After a particularly sexy dance, Bob and Cheryl returned to our table and said, "C'mon boy, let's go. It's late and your girlfriend says she needs my big pole."

Cheryl ran off to the ladies room as we exited the bar. While walking to the car, Bob told me how he planned on fucking Cheryl on the way to his house, but that he didn't want me hanging around after that. Although I was quite disappointed that I wouldn't be able to watch their entire session, just the thought that my beautiful girlfriend would soon be spreading her legs for this stud had my cock straining in my pants. When we reached the car, Bob climbed in the backseat while I got behind the wheel.

It was only a couple of minutes before Cheryl joined Bob in the backseat and we were soon on our way. As soon as I had driven out of the parking lot, Bob unzipped his pants to unleash his hard cock. "Suck it baby," he growled. Cheryl immediately leaned over and began to mouth his swollen rod. I glanced into the back and saw a sight I'll never forget. Cheryl was kissing the head of an absolutely enormous cock. It must have been at least ten or eleven inches long and three times as thick as my slender rod. My cock had formed a tent in my pants as I frantically tried to find a secluded spot to observe Cheryl and Bob. It took about five minutes, but I soon found a deserted street and quickly pulled the car over to the side. By this time Bob was lying somewhat uncomfortably across the backseat and Cheryl was on top of him, straddling his huge cock. Her blouse was unbuttoned to expose her firm tits and her skirt was bunched up around her waist. I immediately pulled out my cock and began to stroke it.

It so happens that earlier that day I had purchased a diamond engagement ring and I had hoped to ask Cheryl to marry me the following week while on our annual vacation. However, the beautiful sight of Cheryl impaled on Bob's massive pole inspired me to ask Cheryl to marry me then and there. When Cheryl heard my proposal, she just giggled, "Of course I'll marry you, Mike. I love you." Hearing these words, I was ecstatic and immediately pulled out the diamond engagement ring I had recently purchased. Cheryl didn't even miss a beat as she continued to rock back and forth on Bob's dick while allowing me to place the diamond ring on her finger. "It's beautiful, sweetheart. I love you," declared Cheryl, leaning over to give me a kiss.

When Cheryl leaned forward to kiss me, Bob's cock slipped out of her pussy. Bob pulled Cheryl back towards him while furiously roaring, "What the fuck is going on? I thought I told you I don't want this wimpy guy anywhere near you tonight!" Cheryl immediately turned her attention back to Bob as she cooed, "Oh, Bob, I'm so sorry. He won't get in the way anymore, I promise. Come on, you get on top. I want you to fuck me hard." She then lay back on the seat while Bob positioned himself between her luscious thighs.

All the while I continued to stroke my dick. I noticed Cheryl's diamond engagement ring sparkling in the moonlight as she reached between her legs to insert Bob's swollen rod. The lust and pride I felt when I saw her ring made me truly appreciate the fact that we were to be married. It was a truly incredible sight as I watched my fiancée with a muscular stud between her legs, her platform shoes draped over his broad shoulders with his glistening manhood pounding in and out of her soaked pussy. The car was rocking back and forth with Bob's thrusts, and Cheryl's moans and whimpers of orgasm created a real soundtrack of lust.

As I watched I felt an incredible craving to feel, taste and even smell my wife-to-be's delicious body. Remembering the angry tone of Bob's earlier remarks, I realized that for tonight at least Cheryl was to be Bob's alone. Grasping about for some method of enjoying all the beautiful sensations of my fiancée, I finally reached over the seat and grabbed Cheryl's discarded G-string. Clutching it in my hand, I immediately brought it up to my nose and savored the delicate smell of her perfume mingled with the musky scent of her pussy. As I watched Bob thrust in and out of Cheryl's cunt, I slipped the silky panties over my hard cock and began to masturbate in time to their lovemaking. It was only a matter of minutes before Cheryl's cries of pleasure triggered my orgasm. I squirted my pent-up sperm all over the tiny white triangle of her panties.

"Oooh, yes, yes. Fuck me harder!" moaned Cheryl as Bob brought her to yet another climax with his driving penis. Meanwhile, even a stud like Bob had his limit as Cheryl's skillful caresses coupled with her luscious pussy pushed Bob to the limit.

He threw his head back and growled, "I'm coming, baby!" while unloading his seed into the depths of her pussy. After Cheryl and Bob had straightened up, I drove them over to Bob's house.

"Would it be alright if I came in for awhile?" I asked, as I carefully parked Bob's car out front.

"No way! I promised Cheryl I'd let you watch us once, but I'm not going to have you hanging around my house. You can get the bus down at the corner," responded Bob. Cheryl noticed that I was very disappointed.

"Just a minute, Bob," she said. "I've got an idea. Mike, why don't you take out your dick and play with yourself for me." I wasn't sure what to do, but one look at Cheryl leaning forward with a mischievous grin and I immediately unzipped my pants to free my soft prick. "C'mon Mike, stroke it. Make it hard," urged my fiancée. I began to slowly stroke my cock with my right hand while fondling my balls with my left. "You liked watching me fuck Bob, didn't you Mike?" teased Cheryl as her eyes never left mine. "Did you see how many times I came? His cock is so big I just can't get enough of it. It feels so good when he's inside me I just want to fuck forever," cooed Cheryl.

Giving Bob a sexy smile she reached over to run her hand over his crotch. I was quite close to coming for the second time that evening when Cheryl reached down between her legs and scooped up some of the copious semen leaking out from her pussy. She then brought her fingers to my lips so that I could smell and taste the remnants of their coupling. "That's it Mike, lick it up," whispered Cheryl while I licked and sucked her fingers clean, savoring the delicious taste of Cheryl's juices coupled with Bob's tangy semen. Bob, meanwhile, was chuckling softly, as he found the whole situation quite amusing. I ignored him completely, however, as I continued to stroke my manhood. Cheryl's sexy teasing soon brought me to another tremendous orgasm as I spurted semen all over my hand.

As soon as I had finished spilling my load, Bob ordered me out of the car. I stood there, come dripping off my hand as Cheryl and Bob walked up the steps to the door. I longed for another opportunity to observe their passionate lovemaking, but it was not to be. As I learned later, Bob and Cheryl spent the remainder of the evening together engaged in a fabulous sex session. I took almost an hour to get home where I ended up masturbating to one more tremendous orgasm while just imagining Bob and Cheryl engaging in all manner of erotic escapades.

Cheryl and I were married last September in a beautiful small chapel in the mountains. We had planned on spending our honeymoon at a nearby resort, so after saying our goodbyes to the guests at the reception, we drove off to the resort. What I didn't know was that Cheryl had planned a surprise for me when we finally reached our hotel. It was almost ten when we arrived. Following the custom, I lifted Cheryl up and carried her through the threshold into our suite.

As soon as I had closed the door, out came three enormous men from the bedroom. All three of the guys were well over six feet tall and played for a local semipro basketball team. "Congratulations Mike, my name is Larry and that's Bill and Jim. Let me be the first to kiss the bride," laughed one of the guys as he took Cheryl from my arms and gave her a wet kiss.

I guess I must have looked pretty shocked as Cheryl giggled, "Surprise, honey. I thought you might want our wedding night to be extra special, so I invited some friends. Why don't you pour us some champagne to celebrate while we get comfortable in the bedroom."

In Larry's arms Cheryl looked like a tiny doll. As he walked into the bedroom my cock stiffened at the thought of these massive men making love to my bride. I poured five glasses of champagne while shedding my clothes. As I entered the bedroom, I noticed that even in her five-inch heels, Cheryl was over a foot shorter than any of the guys. Two of the guys had sandwiched

Cheryl between them. While Larry was kissing my wife, Bill was intent on unzipping her dress. It wasn't long before Bill had unzipped my wife's wedding dress, tugging it down over her hips and tossing it unceremoniously into a corner of the room. Cheryl's bra and panties didn't last long either, leaving my lovely bride wearing a white lace garter belt, sheer white stockings and white satin heels.

My cock was near bursting as I watched Cheryl slowly unbutton Larry's shirt to expose his muscular torso. She covered his chest in kisses, slowly working her way down towards his crotch. Cheryl then undid Larry's belt and unzipped his slacks, pulling them down around his ankles. Cheryl repeated her actions with Bill and Jim until all three men were standing in their underwear. With a naughty little smile over at me, Cheryl knelt down in front of them and slowly tugged down first Bill's then Larry's and then Jim's underwear to reveal their semihard cocks.

"Oh, wow, I love your big cocks," moaned Cheryl as she began licking and sucking Larry's large rod. It grew to at least ten inches! Next, Cheryl turned her attention to Bill. Within a couple of minutes his prick was also fully erect. Bill and Larry had by far the largest cocks I had ever seen, but when Cheryl had finished with Jim, I was shocked to see that his manhood was almost as big as my forearm!

As I learned later, Cheryl had contacted them through a local swingers' magazine and she had carefully culled the ads looking for a group of well-endowed men. My pretty bride was absolutely fascinated with their cocks as she alternated between each of them, kissing and licking up and down the entire length of their shafts.

After enjoying my wife's oral worship of his cock, Bill lifted Cheryl up and placed her on the bed. He immediately moved up between her outstretched legs and began to rub his giant cockhead between Cheryl's juicy pussy lips. Just the touch of his prick on her clit excited my wife.

"You're going to like this, baby," Bill said.

"Hey, ditto, my man," Cheryl retorted. "You are going to like this, too."

I saw Cheryl shudder as the monster cock penetrated her inner walls. It wasn't the first shudder nor would it be the last. I wasn't sure if it would fit in my wife's tight pussy, but with her copious juices easing the way, Bill's meaty cock was soon buried balls deep.

I couldn't have imagined a more incredible wedding night as I softly rubbed my throbbing penis. Larry was standing near me sipping his champagne as he chuckled, "Man, I couldn't believe it when your wife said she wanted us to fuck her on her wedding night. But hell, it sure looks like you are enjoying yourself."

"Yeah, she's the greatest," I responded. "This is kind of a twist on the old bachelor party routine, isn't it?"

I couldn't help but bless the luck that had brought us together. From my vantage point all I could see of my wife was her clean shaven pussy, the soft creamy globes of her ass cheeks resting on the bed, and her high heels kicking wildly in the air. Jim was seated on the bed next to my wife and he was running his hands all over Cheryl's firm tits, pulling and teasing her erect nipples. I was stroking my cock when Jim reached back with one hand and began to toy with Cheryl's pink asshole. This in itself was enough to give me a tremendous climax as I spurted semen all over my wife's moist panties.

Bill continued to fuck my bride for almost thirty minutes as Cheryl experienced numerous orgasms. Larry and Jim were becoming somewhat impatient as they awaited their turns, so they stood at the edge of the bed while Cheryl eagerly alternated on sucking their glistening rods.

Since I had previously brought myself off, I was able to hold back, timing myself so that at the same instant Bill threw back his head and grunted, "I'm coming," I came too, shooting my cream for the second time all over Cheryl's panties.

When Bill pulled out of my wife, he got up off the bed and invited Larry to take his place. Larry immediately mounted my wife, using his large cock to fill and engulf her completely. As soon as he started thrusting she began to climax once again.

"Baby, you've got one hot little pussy. I'm going to make sure you don't ever forget this night, that's for sure," Larry said as he banged her box.

Hearing this, Cheryl glanced over at me and sighed, "I love you, Mike. So far this has been the best day of my life."

Cheryl's attention was soon diverted by the pleasurable sensations emanating from her busy love-canal. Larry fucked my wife for at least thirty minutes, pounding her with a steady, pulsating beat until he came in a rush of orgasmic bliss.

Larry was quickly replaced by Jim, who eased his enormous rod into Cheryl so that she sighed in pleasure. I didn't know she could take so much loving in one setting. They fucked for almost twenty minutes, both of them heaving and writhing as Jim's cock slammed against Cheryl's heated twat. I masturbated to another incredible orgasm watching them climax together.

When Jim finally pulled his cock from my wife, I immediately leapt onto the bed and began to kiss and caress my sexy wife. She was numb with pleasure, I thought, but still able to accept my attention.

I had a decision to make. I knew there was no way my cock could compare with the three massive members that had recently entered my pretty bride. Rather than fucking my sweet bride, I decided to lap up the juices oozing from her opening. It turned me on to think I could ingest the fruits of all this lust. Cheryl's pussy was so loose from Bill, Jim and Larry's huge cocks that my tongue immediately slipped deep inside her.

The taste and the smell was pungent. Gobs of tasty semen, mixed with the copious outpouring of Cheryl's vagina, flooded into my mouth. I noticed her snatch was warm to the touch, a result of all the incredible friction and the huge demands placed on her sex by the three hunks.

"Oh, Mike, that's it. Suck the come from my pussy," moaned Cheryl as she rolled over on top of me, grinding her creamy snatch into my face.

The next day Cheryl would be sore, but for now she egged on my cunnilingus technique with total enthusiasm. For the next ten minutes I licked and sucked every drop of juice from Cheryl's pussy, taking extra care to dart inside the walls of her cunt and titillate the knob of her clit as I did. The three guys were taking a smoke break as we performed our little marital ritual for them. Cheryl was squeezing her nipples as I rimmed her asshole and cunt with my moistly elongated tongue. We finally maneuvered into a 69 and she sucked my throbbing erection until I pumped what little sperm remained in my balls into her silky mouth.

Even after I had come, I remained so engrossed with licking and sucking Cheryl's pussy that I didn't even notice her sucking Bill's cock. Before long I felt Cheryl's hands on my head as she pushed me away so that Bill could move up between her legs. The two of them began to fuck hard and fast. Bill's hips looked like a rivet machine, blasting my wife's tender hole with feverish intensity. Soon they were joined on the bed by Larry and Jim. By this time I decided to give the four of them a little privacy so I quietly left the bedroom. I promptly fell asleep on the small couch in the other room.

It was almost three in the morning when I awoke to find

Cheryl's lips on mine. "Oh, sweetheart, I love you," she whispered while taking my hand and leading me into the bedroom. The guys had just recently left and the room still had the musky aroma of semen mixed with Cheryl's pussy juices. Cheryl was exhausted from her sexual marathon so we both instantly fell asleep in each other's arms.

Since our wedding, Cheryl and I couldn't be happier. She has a small group of lovers to choose from. About once a month she will invite one or more of them over to our house for a wild session of fucking and sucking. On these occasions, I'll sit quietly nearby, masturbating to one orgasm after another. I can't imagine a more perfect marriage.—*M.R., Phoenix, Arizona* ⊙━▪

HAPPY COUPLE GETS AWAY TO PLAY,
WITH ONE BEST FRIEND AND TWO STRANGERS

I have read in *Penthouse Letters* about husbands watching their wives make love to other men, but never figured I would be involved in it myself. I was never sure how I'd feel about it, either.

My wife is thirty-seven and I'm thirty-three. Gina is five feet five inches tall, has beautiful, platinum blonde hair and 34B boobs tipped with sensitive, lickable nipples. Her best feature is her butt. She weighs under a hundred pounds, so you can imagine she's got a tight little "microbutt." It is incredibly shapely even at this age.

We both keep in tip-top physical shape by exercising, playing baseball and tennis, biking and so forth.

During a troubled time in our relationship, she used to sneak off with a coworker to "talk" at a park near where they both worked. They only kissed; it never went any further than that. I had a sixth sense something was going on and asked her during the heat of lovemaking if she had ever kissed her coworker, Bobby. She whispered no, but then immediately changed it to yes as she quickly decided to get it off her chest, since it had been bothering her. While I was certainly turned on, I was also upset, and asked her to cease the physical part of the relationship with Bobby. She did that in one more trip to the park the next day.

Fast forward to Christmas of last year. We drove across the

state to her hometown to celebrate Christmas with her parents. While we were there we saw her old best friend, Tracy, who had just gotten divorced. Tracy is thin and striking, though very small-breasted. Such a pretty face, with brilliant green eyes looking out through long, kinked blonde hair. She has an all over tan that she gets at the exercise club she practically lives at.

I asked Tracy if she had the cash to go with us to Jamaica to celebrate our tenth wedding anniversary and Gina's birthday. She said yes, and the trip was on.

The whole thing was a surprise, so Tracy stayed at another friend's house the night before we were to leave. When Gina woke up I presented her with two of the three tickets. She packed her suitcase excitedly as I shuffled the kids like playing cards to a variety of friends and relatives.

When I returned, Tracy had arrived. We walked in to let Gina know that Tracy was coming with us.

Gina was thrilled, and traveling was a breeze. We arrived in the afternoon, got our act together at the hotel and went in search of some serious eating and drinking. As we danced through the night, Tracy, Gina and I all became a lot closer. We giggled, drank and became physically festive. Both girls were wearing minidresses that clung to their bodies.

I took some liberties with Tracy on the dance floor, with double entendres and tight dancing during the slow songs. Of course I made sure Gina got equal treatment. While I never got a full hard-on while dancing with Tracy, I knew she felt me at half mast, because I was holding her so tightly and she whispered that what I was doing felt so good.

We all stumbled back to the hotel in a drunken stagger. No one bothered to turn a light on as the moon shone in, giving us just the right amount of ambient romantic illumination. I quickly got cleaned up in the bathroom, and came out in just my underwear and cutoffs with the top button undone. Gina and Tracy lay on the two beds giggling and toasting themselves with tequila shots.

Their dresses had ridden high on their thighs, exposing their panties. Gina wore thigh-high black stockings under her black dress, with oh-so-French-cut black thong panties. Tracy had red panties on under her red dress and no stockings, since her tan legs were something you never wanted to cover.

I attacked Gina. Tracy ripped off her dress, revealing her red bra-and-panty set, but just as quickly got in under the covers. She rustled around under the sheets removing her undergarments, which she threw on our bed as I disrobed Gina. We're not exhibitionists, so we threw the covers over us as I got my two stitches of clothing off as well.

Tracy was obviously beginning to masturbate under her blankets, holding one hand behind her head, lying on her side, and the other buried in her pussy. I played happily with Gina's nipples and pussy, and we both started to moan quietly.

I teased Gina's pussy lips with my penis, then finally plunged in with one long stroke. From then on I didn't stop until we both came about five minutes later, sweat on our brows. I lay next to Gina, listening to Tracy frigging herself, and rubbed Gina's clit. I stared over at Tracy. We locked eyes as she brought herself off in a very obvious way. She came violently, then licked her fingers clean. Gina came shortly after that from my finger ministrations.

I had another boner from watching Tracy and Gina, but Gina'd had enough, and Tracy wasn't ready at that point to schtup her best friend's husband, even with her best friend there.

I asked Tracy to turn on the lamp in the corner of the room for some ambient light. Then I arranged Gina and Tracy on either side of me, both very naked, and both talking very dirty, while I showed them how I masturbate. It took about ten minutes of teasing, with both of them blowing lightly into my ears, before I erupted my second geyser of the night past my left ear as I lay on my back.

The next day we rode bikes and hung out on the beach. Little was said of the night before. What were they plotting, I wondered, but then I decided my imagination was a little overactive.

Night number two was more subtle, as we didn't dance but went to a very laid-back bar, where everyone was chatting quietly and drinking conservatively while being friendly. We went back to the hotel room, none of us certain what was to transpire. The amount of alcohol we'd consumed certainly helped us figure things out. Gina and Tracy lay in their respective beds. I washed up, and when I came out of the bathroom I switched off the TV, turned the stereo on and proceeded to do a mock strip. I can't dance worth a lick, but was down to my silk Speedos in ten minutes. The girls played along, pointing out that I sported a "semi."

Tracy had on frayed faded cutoffs and a white vest, with a white teddy underneath. She sat upright on the bed and opened her legs. I sat back into her. Gina joined us as well, lying atop my chest. We took in each other's smells and lightly caressed each other. Tracy had started wetly kissing my neck, unbeknownst to

Gina, which made it more erotic. I turned my head to kiss Tracy directly, and Gina got up to move back to our bed again, simultaneously whipping off her jeans and T-shirt.

Gina watched as I made mad, passionate love to Tracy, all the while masturbating up a storm herself. Seeing Tracy in her white teddy was too much for my tender mind. I quickly unsnapped the garment's crotch and plunged my tongue deep inside her warm, waiting vagina, at the same time reaching up to fondle her nipples underneath her teddy. As she neared orgasm I got up and mounted her quickly. Excited beyond belief, both of us came within thirty seconds. Fortunately, to save face, I was able to stay hard after coming, and I continued to plug away. About ten minutes later we both fell in a heap, after a second intense mutual orgasm, and fell asleep together.

On day three we went to a nude beach to enjoy the sun. Unfortunately, there was more cock than cunt, but I didn't feel the need to have a perpetual boner all day, so that was fine by me. Tracy and Gina seemed to be enjoying all the attention they received, as they went topless part of the day and nude for about an hour at the end. When they did I had to plunge into the ocean to hide my erection.

We went dancing again that night, because it was our last night. We ran into several of the guys they had seen at the beach earlier that day. They both admitted to me that they were very horny, because they already knew which men had the big penises.

Gina started hinting that she wanted it to be a night for her to get some fresh man-meat. I told her to go for it. After all, I had just schtupped her best friend, so who was I to argue. Gina was making her desires quite obvious with her dirty dancing, and periodically told me some of the men were pressing their legs and penises into her crotch, which was making her crazy.

Gina and Tracy picked two guys, and we went back to our hotel suite. Both girls were wearing one-piece lycra outfits that consisted of shirts and shorts rolled into one. They were so tight they could have been painted on, and they wore only thongs underneath. Tracy and Gina are not models, but they have their curves in all the right places.

More drinks flowed, and one of the guys had some pot, so everybody enjoyed that, and got nice and relaxed. We all lay around together in an assortment of poses, and our clothes came off, slowly but surely.

When we got hot and heavy, I was with Tracy. My wife Gina was flat on her back with an eight-inch penis in her pussy and a six-inch penis in her mouth. She was moaning uncontrollably, something I had never seen her do before. I was lying on my back as well, and Tracy kept asking me if I liked watching that other guy's dick slide into Gina. I told her I did.

Tracy used her mouth on me, sucking me slowly and gently while I watched Gina. When my excitement got to be too much Tracy jerked me off lovingly into her waiting mouth. All the time I was spraying my sperm my eyes feasted on Gina being jammed in two orifices.

Gina told me to come over to the chair next to the bed so I wouldn't miss any details of what was about to happen. Gina announced that she had never had anal sex, and that she wanted to try it with the guy who had the six-inch penis, since she thought it would be the easiest to accommodate. I was desperately jealous, since I had always wanted to do her butt, but had only gotten my head in before she decided my penis was just too wide for comfort.

Gina lay on her belly, spread-eagle, all four limbs flung wide, no clothes and no blankets hiding her beauty. Ronnie, the guy with the six-inch penis, was working his dick along her thighs while the other guy rubbed some oil into her butthole, slowly inserting his finger to get her loose and slick.

I was rock-hard as Gina moaned with each thrust and Tracy licked my penis and caressed my balls again and again. Gina looked me right in the eyes and groaned as loudly as I'd ever heard her before as Ronnie slowly inserted his cockhead. Five minutes and about a quart of oil later he was all the way in.

They put pillows under her to raise her butt, which made her look all the more sexy. The other guy quickly got underneath Gina and entered her vagina with his penis. Gina said later that she had the longest, most intense orgasm of her life at that point, as they developed a very slow rhythm. She moaned, "Oh, honey, I feel him all the way up my ass, and it feels so good."

She felt so free that she came again when Ronnie started to fuck her ass more quickly. He stayed all the way inside her as he came violently. Gina yelled, "Ah, sweet Jesus, he's coming all the way up my ass. Oh, it feels so good." Tracy sat on my dick, her back toward me, and rode me for all I was worth. I came quickly, and had to send her over to the other guy to be fucked so she could come as well.

So, not only did I get to see my wife make love to another man, I got to see her do it with two men and watch while one took her anal cherry. That was quite a vacation.—*P.S., Trenton, New Jersey* ⊙┼▄

THEY MET THE COUPLE OF THEIR DREAMS AT A SMALL SWING CLUB IN THE BIG CITY

I've read so much in *Penthouse Letters* about swinging. Even though the subject never fails to give me a diamond-tipped erection, I was not sure about trying it. I finally did, though, and oh boy, did it ever change my life for the better.

This took place several years ago now, but I remember it better than I do what happened to me yesterday.

My husband and I had been married for about ten years, and our sex life needed a good airing-out. We had once gone to a club in Houston that had turned out to be a swingers club. We went with it. That was the first time I had sex with a man other than my husband. Jack and I did a lot of talking after that first swing, and we both decided we wanted to try it again.

One Saturday afternoon Jack suggested we drive into Houston and go to the club for a little fun. I was thrilled. I thought and thought about what to wear. I wanted to dress sexy, like most of the other women at the club. I wanted Jack to be proud to be seen with me. I chose a wrap blouse, with no bra, and a skirt to match. I wore white lace panties and no hose, just sandals. I'm five-three, with long brown hair and nice-sized tits with large nipples. I love my husband, and was looking forward to learning some new sexual techniques to try on him.

On our trip into Houston, Jack and I did a lot of laughing and talking. My pussy was getting wet just thinking about what might happen. The club wasn't very big. It was like a neighborhood bar. Most of the people there seemed to know each other. It had a comfortable, homey kind of feeling.

There were several people dancing when we entered. I had butterflies in my stomach from anticipation. We ordered drinks and sat listening to the music. It was a little early and we had a table to ourselves for a while.

Soon two other couples sat at our table. They seemed nice, but the guys didn't really spark my interest, and I don't think the women interested Jack either, although he did dance with one of them.

A couple of guys from other tables asked me to dance. I enjoyed the attention, and didn't mind that they copped a feel or two. I liked it, as a matter of fact, but we just didn't click. One guy asked if we'd like to come meet his wife, but she had already picked some other guy to swing with.

I wanted to find a couple that my husband and I could both enjoy swinging with. Then Rand came to our table, introduced himself and asked Jack if he minded if I danced with him. Jack said it was fine. I'd been enjoying watching the other dancers fool around. A couple of women were dancing in their sexy undies. Then they took their bras off, and the other dancers closed in around them so the host couldn't see what was going on and put a stop to it.

Rand was not tall, but I really enjoyed dancing and talking with him. Something clicked inside me, and I knew that I would enjoy exploring him and seeing how his dick felt inside me. The more we danced the bolder Rand got. He started feeling me up. He had one hand on my ass, and the other was playing with my tit. His dick was rubbing against my cunt. My pussy was getting wetter and wetter.

We started kissing, and I got even hotter. I wondered if my husband was watching, or if he was doing the same thing to some other woman. The thought of him watching really turned me on.

Rand said that he would sure like to fuck me. He said that he would bring his wife over to meet my husband. He was hoping they would hit it off and we could all go to their house for a party. When Rand took me back to our table I told Jack that we'd been invited to Rand's house if he was agreeable. Rand went and got his wife and introduced her to us.

Her name was Sue, and she seemed really nice. Jack asked her to dance, and Rand and I had one more dance too. This time we both did a little more exploring. I was happy, when I looked over, to see that Sue was pressing her big breasts into Jack's chest. He had a big smile on his face. When we all got back to the table we were all in favor of going to Rand and Sue's place.

Rand asked me to ride with him, and Sue rode with Jack, in case we got separated. The minute I got into Rand's Honda Civic he gave me a long kiss, tongue and all. My pussy was drenched, and needed attention. It did not take Rand long to have my tits bared to the world. He felt them, then kissed me again. My nipples were both standing at attention. We hadn't gone far when his hand was on my knee, squeezing it. He moved his hand ever so slowly up to my panties. He was exploring my cunt through my thin, white, lacy panties.

I put my hand on Rand's crotch, and began playing with his peter through his pants. It wasn't long till it was hard as a rock. We continued playing around all the way to his house, with me damn near nude most of the way. My breasts were bared and my skirt was up around my waist as we sped through Houston.

Somewhere along the way we lost sight of Jack and Sue. We waited in the driveway till they pulled up next to us. Of course we were a little busy necking while we waited. I'd never been so bold before. While necking, I hauled out his beautiful dick and began to stroke it. He was fingering me, with my skirt pushed out of the way and his finger snaking up the leg of my panties. I had my first major orgasm the minute he touched my boiling cunt.

I think he would have fucked me in the car if they hadn't finally driven up. We headed into the house, and straight to the master bedroom. It was a big room, with a king-size bed. There was a bathroom off this room, and in a corner was a wooden box about the size of a desk. I asked Rand what that was for, and he told me it was a darkroom, where he developed pictures. He said he'd take my picture later if I didn't mind.

Then he walked over to me and began kissing my neck and lips. Slowly he took off my top, and gave my nipples a quick, sucking kiss. Very nice. As we kissed, he put his hands on my hips and slowly pushed my skirt to the floor, along with my slip. All I had on was my panties. Rand stepped back and took a look. He said I was beautiful, but he wanted me naked, so he took off my white lacy panties. I watched as he stripped his clothes off, then he led me to the bed.

He spread my legs wide open, getting a good look at my hairy pussy, before he jumped in and began licking my cunt. My juices were so thick, he said, he just had to fuck me, right then and there. He slowly moved up and put his hard dick into my hot cunt. He started slowly, but before long he was flying along, and all the time his dick was rubbing my hard clit.

I can't tell you how many orgasms I had, but it damn sure felt good. Pretty soon Rand filled my cunt with his hot love-juice. We were out of breath, so we just lay in each other's arms for a while.

When we had recovered, Rand sat up and asked if I would mind if he took my picture. I didn't mind, so he went to get his camera.

He told me I could pose any way I wanted. I sat up in the middle of the bed, with my back to the headboard. I raised one leg up and crossed the other one over, and Rand took my picture. Having my picture taken in the nude turned out to be a real turn-on for me.

Rand joined me back on the bed. He said it would be a while before he could get it up again, but he sure wanted to fuck me again. While we were waiting I rubbed his back. He rolled over on his stomach, and I straddled him and began rubbing softly.

I don't know how long I rubbed for, but I could tell he was ready for me to rub something else. He turned over, and I rubbed his chest, his arms, his legs, but I ignored his dick. I could tell it was getting to him, but he didn't say a word. Finally I took his semi-erect dick in my mouth and began to rub my tongue around the head. Rand moaned, enjoying my tongue-lashing.

He asked me to stop and let him fuck me again, so I did. He thrust into me and started hammering my pussy fast and furious. I was wondering if Jack could hear the sucking noises. The more I thought about it, the more noise I made. It didn't take long before Rand shot his load in me again.

When our breathing slowed down, I could hear moans coming from out front. I was so happy. Rand suggested that I clean up a bit, and then we would go see what Sue and my husband were up to in the other room.

When I came back from showering Rand had on a robe. I didn't feel like wearing anything so I followed him into the living room nude. There sat Sue and Jack. She had on a housecoat too, but my husband was nude. I smiled at Jack, and he gave me a loving smile back.

Rand and I sat across the room from them. We had a nice talk.

It was getting late, and Rand said he wanted to take me back to the bedroom for another quick fuck. I followed him. He sat down on the edge of the bed and pulled me to him. He sucked one nipple, then the other, while his hands explored my body.

I was getting turned on all over again. Rand noticed this, and guided me back to the bed. He didn't lie on top of me. Instead he slid his butt and dick up between my legs while his legs moved past my butt. We were in kind of a sitting position. Rand slid his dick back into me and began rocking back and forth. It felt wild; a new part of my cunt was being massaged. Rand kissed me and played with my breasts as he moved. My cunt contracted around his dick and that was all there was to it. He came again.

We slid down in the bed and held each other for a while. Rand said he'd sure enjoyed our lovemaking.

I dressed, while Rand sat on the bed and watched me. We walked back to the living room. Jack and Sue were just coming out of the other bedroom. Jack was still getting dressed. We said our goodbyes to Rand and Sue and headed for our truck.

I was a little tired, but exhilarated too. I slid over close to Jack as we drove off, and put my hand on his leg. We started talking about the evening's fun. I could tell that he was getting horny. So was I. He opened my wrap blouse and let my breasts out. He was tweaking my nipples with his free hand. I was having little spasms each time he did it.

We had not gone more than a mile before he pulled off the road. He had his hands in my panties, pulling them off. He asked me to move over and lean up against the door so he could eat me. I moved over and spread my legs wide apart. Jack dove for my pussy. Each time he batted my clit with his tongue, I came. I suddenly realized that I still had Rand's come inside me. Jack was bound to be tasting it. I don't know how many times I came before Jack slid up and stuck his dick into me. I exploded again in another orgasm. He pumped away for a while, then he filled me with his come.

Jack pulled up his pants, but didn't fasten them. I slid back over close to him. I had no idea where my panties were, but I didn't need them. We played with each other all the way home.

When we got there we drifted off to sleep. I'm not sure what time we woke up, but we were still horny, and made love again.

Our little swing kept our love-life heated up for several months. I learned to be more adventurous sexually and more vocal about what I wanted and needed. We met Rand and Sue again at Lake Travis, and it was as much fun as the first time. Camping out and skinny-dipping can really turn a person on— not to mention the pictures we took of each other.

We lost track of them finally, but we think of them often. They will always be special people to us. Just writing this made me as horny as on that memorable night. I sure would love to meet up with them again.—*N.K., Galveston, Texas*

A HAPPY CUCKOLD MANAGES TO PUT HIMSELF IN THE PICTURE AT LAST

When I married Adele I introduced her to *Penthouse Letters,* and since then she has also been reading it regularly. Adele often gets inspiration for various adventures from what we read.

I often read letters from horny guys getting their jollies watching other men fuck their wives, and I always get so turned on that I wind up beating off. To be truthful, I would also get very envious. Ever since we got married I've fantasized about seeing some well-hung stud fuck my lovely wife. Adele knows how much I've wanted to see her with another man, but she always steadfastly refused to grant my wish.

Her reluctance wasn't based on any great disdain for taking another man to bed. Adele was twenty-two when I married her, and she willingly admitted she had been with numerous men before me. We slept together on our very first date, which she said was common practice for her. When I proposed to her, she was hesitant, saying I fit her ideal in every way except one: I wasn't as well-endowed as other guys she'd been with. She said I just didn't satisfy her in bed.

Adele finally agreed to marry me, but it was understood she would share her bed with other men. In our four years of marriage Adele has had numerous lovers, maintaining at least one full-blown extramarital affair at all times. She doesn't neglect me, either emotionally or sexually, regularly giving me fantastic blowjobs. She also lets me fuck her now and then, usually serving me sloppy seconds. She loves for me to go down on her when she's been with another man, and I've learned to at least tolerate the taste as I lick my wife's swampy, sperm-saturated snatch.

In spite of all this, though, Adele refused to let me watch her have sex with another man. To her, making love was intimate and personal, not something to be done in front of an audience. She loved to read about other women doing just that, but refused to do it herself.

Yesterday that all changed. It all began with Adele going to work out. She loves the gym because it's such a good place to meet prospective lovers. With her good looks and fantastic body she always has several guys hitting on her when she goes there.

I stayed home, as usual. When she got home she had a real surprise for me. She told me she'd been talking to a guy at the club and he was coming over in half an hour. Now, Adele has brought guys to our house on a couple of occasions during our marriage, but it's very rare. But Richard was married, so she couldn't meet him at his house.

Adele asked if I would straighten things up a bit while she went upstairs to get ready. Adele keeps the house very neat, so it took me just a few minutes to pick up the newspapers I'd strewn around and pick up the toys our oldest son had left on the floor when he went to bed. Twenty minutes later, the doorbell rang.

When she returned she was wearing only a very short, transparent nightgown. It was black, barely covered her crotch and hid nothing. Adele's fluffy blonde pubic fuzz was clearly visible, and her smallish breasts were in plain view. Her nipples were standing out, firm and erect.

Richard's eyes opened wide at the way she greeted him, and a broad grin appeared on his face. My eyes opened wide also. Standing there in our doorway was a handsome, very well-built, extremely dark-skinned black man. I had not expected that. This was to be her first experience with an African-American.

No sooner was the door closed than Adele was in Richard's arms making out with him. She didn't even bother to introduce me.

Their mouths met in a tongue-probing kiss, and Adele's abdomen ground against the bulge in Richard's slacks. His hands went under her short nightie, gripping her bare ass-cheeks as he pulled her hard against him. His mouth moved to her neck and ears, and Adele got hotter and more passionate than I'd ever seen her in my life.

Her hands clumsily fumbled with the zipper of his trousers, trying to free his manhood. He kept mouthing her neck, and I heard her gasp. "Uh, uh, oh, oh yes. Keep doing that. Yes! Don't stop, keep doing that."

Richard's powerful hand was up under her nightie between her legs. Adele's lower torso was frantically twitching as he fingerfucked her. His entire hand was already wet with her juices, and I could see she was about to come. Adele closed her eyes, shuddered, moaned loudly and a flood of juice came out of her, further coating his hand and running down her inner thighs.

"Where's the bedroom?" I heard Richard gasp.

"No," I heard her respond. "Just fuck me. Here, now. I want you in me now, Richard. Fuck me now."

Richard pulled his hand from between my wife's legs. As he

helped her work his trousers and his boxer shorts down his legs I heard Adele say to him, "Just remember what I said earlier. I can't take a chance on getting pregnant, so don't come in me. Okay?" Richard nodded as he gave a few tugs on his huge cock to bring it to full hardness.

I saw Adele look down between them and smile when she saw his rigid cock sticking out. She looked back up at him, smiled and then feverishly began kissing him. Adele was hotter than I'd ever seen her. She literally climbed up his body.

Richard's hands grabbed my wife's butt and helped support her as she grabbed his shoulders, hoisted herself up and put her legs around his waist. Adele's hot gash lined up with the head of Richard's prick and she sank her crotch down on it. I was undoing my own trousers by then. I took out my dick, stroking it as I watched my wife impale herself on Richard's cock.

They were only a couple of feet from the closed front door. Richard took two choppy steps and leaned her against it. The door banged and rattled as Richard began thrusting at her. I could tell they weren't going to last long, and I knew I wouldn't either. As Richard lunged at her, Adele worked her wet, slick tunnel up and down his thick shaft.

I heart Richard grunt, then saw him stiffen and I heard him moan. "Gotta come, Adele. Oh God, I gotta come. I'm gonna come in you. Yes! Yes! Coming, oh shit, coming." When he did that, I heard my wife give out a deep, guttural sound. I also saw her thrust at him, hold and shudder as her orgasm hit her. Richard pushed in to the hilt and really pinned Adele to the door as he shot his wad. She was crying out, shaking, appended to Richard's body, as they climaxed. Seeing them in the throes of an intense mutual orgasm, I shot my wad on our living room carpet.

Adele went limp and Richard's knees buckled as they finished spending. For a second I thought he was actually going to fall.

Richard regained his balance, though, and helped lift Adele off his body. She just hung onto his shoulders and leaned against him.

Richard spoke first. "I'm sorry, I couldn't pull out. I got too worked up. I'm sorry."

Adele looked up at him, grinned and replied, "I'm not." She then kissed him, passionately, for a long time.

When she ended the kiss she looked at him and said lovingly, "Now we can go to the bedroom. If you can get that hard again, you can do me some more. Interested?"

When they were gone, I looked at our front door and saw a wet, sticky spot, the mixture of Richard's come and my wife's juices.

Richard wound up staying in our bedroom with Adele a full two hours. I beat off again as I listened through our bedroom door. I could hear Adele's moans of pleasure and the headboard of our bed thumping against the wall as Richard repeatedly fucked her. It was past eleven when he finally came out. A smug smile my way and a nod was his only acknowledgment of me. He left without our having even been introduced.

I guess I'll be seeing a lot of Richard around here from now on. — *V.S., Akron, Ohio*   ⊶▪

<u>Serendipity</u>

THE GREAT OUTDOORS HAS NEVER BEEN GREATER FOR THESE LOVERS

My lover Rosie and I decided to watch an X-rated movie one night recently. We sat close beside each other on the sofa, started the tape and were soon getting hot from kissing and watching the writhing bodies on the screen. Rosie's hard nipples stood up under her shirt, and I couldn't resist gently pinching them.

It wasn't long before she slid off the sofa onto the floor in front of me, unzipped my pants and freed my cock. She ran her tongue slowly up and down its full length before taking the tip into her mouth. I was transfixed by the sight of her full lips sliding down the shaft, and it was the visual as much as the physical sensation that made my cock so hard.

Once she had me good and wet, Rosie stroked me with her hand and fondled my balls until a drop of clear, sticky come oozed from the tip. Rosie licked it up and told me she loved the taste.

I asked her to turn the TV off so we could concentrate on our own pleasure. Rosie stripped off her jeans and panties. Running a hand over her partially shaved mound, then slipping a finger inside to spread the gathering moisture over her labia, she straddled my lap. She slowly lowered her hot, wet pussy down over my cock. We both watched as her beautiful sex swallowed me deep inside her. I groaned with pleasure as she slid all the way down to my balls. Rosie began fucking me while I kneaded her large breasts. The feeling was incredible, perfect.

I suddenly got the urge to make love standing up, so I reached under her legs and grabbed hold of her bottom. She was surprised when I stood up, still holding her, and continued pumping into her. Recovering quickly, and delighted with our new position, she held onto my shoulders, and wrapped her legs around my waist, bouncing up and down on my cock. Rosie got very excited and asked me to fuck her from behind, definitely our favorite position.

We went into the dining room and Rosie leaned over the table. She reached back to spread her lips, and I rubbed the head of my cock along her pussy. The pink folds glistened with her juices. I held her by the hips and slowly drove my full length deep into her. She moaned with pleasure and so did I. I started to fuck her faster, and she responded with cries of "Oh God, it feels so good!" and "Fuck me harder!" Rosie came twice. Each time she stopped pushing back against my hips and just stood with her mouth open, unable to make a noise, her legs rigid and her body trembling from top to bottom.

By the time she came the second time I was getting close to coming myself. I told her she felt so good that I had to slow down to make it last. I asked if she would suck my cock some more. Rosie loves to suck me until I come in her mouth, and she eagerly agreed. I suggested we try something a little different: going out onto the back porch. Rosie just grinned her sex-hungry grin at me and out we went. It was a warm summer night on the New Hampshire coast, clear and still. She sat in a lounge chair and began to drive me wild again with her mouth while I stood in front of her. Her sucking soon made my knees weak, so I asked if she wanted to try something really daring—would she like to fuck out in the backyard, down in the grass. She was hesitant at first, but some passionate kisses and stroking of her pussy persuaded her to try it.

I took her by the hand and led her out the screen door and down the steps into the moist night air, enjoying the heavy, expectant feeling in my balls that I get when I've been putting off a good orgasm. Rosie got down on her hands and knees in the dew-covered grass. I then gripped her firmly by the hips and kneeled behind her.

Neither of us could believe we were really about to fuck outdoors, where we might be seen by neighbors out for a walk or drivers passing by. But we were so hot to fuck each other by this time that we couldn't have stopped even if we had wanted to try. I slid my cock teasingly between Rosie's thighs, and she reached back to guide me into her. We wasted no time and started pounding into each other. Rosie and I both came quickly in a hot, sweaty, mutual orgasm, shuddering with pleasure, certain someone would hear our moans in the dark.

It seemed like a long time before we were able to regain our senses and move again. Finally we helped each other up off the grass and ran back into the house, laughing at the craziness of it all. Rosie is a wonderful lover and that was one midsummer night that I'm glad wasn't a dream!—*S.T., Portsmouth, New Hampshire* O┼▪

COLLEGE STUDENT GETS AN EDUCATION FROM GIRLFRIEND'S MOM

My girlfriend Gwen and I are seniors at a small college. Gwen is a cute girl, with small breasts and a nice little ass. Her idea of sex, though, is to give me an occasional hand-job, or maybe a suck on her little A-cup titties. Gwen refuses to let me fuck her, as she intends to remain a virgin till she's married. I've never even laid eyes on her pussy. I've often thought of breaking up with her, just to satisfy my need for a good fuck, but I decided to stick it out.

A couple of weekends ago, Gwen went away on a ski trip to Colorado. I was just getting out of the shower when there was a knock at the door. I pulled a towel around me and answered it. I was greeted by a hot-looking blonde babe who introduced herself as Rachel. "I'm Gwen's mom," were the first words out of her mouth, followed by, "The way you look in a towel, it's no wonder she likes you." A little embarrassed, I invited Rachel in, though I told her that Gwen was gone for the weekend.

"It doesn't surprise me," Rachel said. "Gwen invited me up to spend the weekend and now she isn't here. She was never terribly considerate." Rachel was the total opposite of her daughter physically, with a pair of nice big boobs and a fine-looking ass. I could already tell they had different views about sex. Rachel asked me if Gwen had given me blue balls. I confessed she had. Smiling, Rachel said that, in that case, maybe she hadn't wasted a trip after all.

Next thing I knew, my towel was on the floor and Rachel was rubbing my cock and French-kissing me. Sinking to her knees, Rachel touched her tongue to my cockhead, slowly circling that sensitive organ with the warm, pink tip of her tongue. My cock disappeared into her mouth and she proceeded to give me a wild blowjob.

Rachel didn't have to work long before I let loose into her hard-working mouth. She swallowed my entire load, then kept my dick in her mouth, sucking very gently, until it went limp.

"That's just a sample of what we can do," Rachel said, smiling as she undressed and lay back on the floor. "Now it's your turn to do me." I sucked hungrily on her hard, hot nipples while feverishly fingering her clitty. "Come on, baby, give it to me hard. I love feeling like a slut," she cried. She was creaming in no time. "Please. Get your fucking cock inside me," she begged. "Fuck me hard." I buried my bone deep in her sloppy pussy and fucked her fast and wild for another several minutes, thoroughly enjoying her eager cooperation before coming at last inside her.

Rachel and I showered together and went out for some beer. On the way back home Rachel sucked me off in the car and asked me if I had ever fucked a woman in the ass. When I confessed I hadn't, Rachel purred that it was time I had a lesson. "I've been itching for a good butt-fucking," she told me, "and your young, hard dick is perfect for the purpose."

We went into the bedroom. Rachel took a jar of Vaseline and coated my cock. She got on all fours on the edge of the bed. I stood behind her and aimed my erection, which was harder than hell at the prospect of what we were about to do, at her tight brown hole. I plunged my dick into her butt.

"Come on, butt-fuck me," she howled. "Plunder my ass. Do me like you'd like to do Gwen." I banged her hot butt for a good ten minutes, then filled her asshole with come.

We fucked each other silly for the rest of the weekend. As Rachel was leaving she told me her pussy and ass were sore, and I started to apologize. "Are you nuts?" she asked. "It's the best feeling on earth. It's going to keep me reminded for the next couple of days of everything we did. Every time I think about it I'll have to beat off."

Gwen came back on Monday, and everything has gone back to the way it was, but I keep thinking about the weekend and shaking my head. I can't wait to see what the future brings. —*M.O., Des Moines, Iowa* ⊙┼▪

YOU DON'T HAVE TO TEACH THIS OLD BABE
ANY TRICKS

My mother suffered a stroke that impaired her speech and weakened her right side to the point where she cannot care for herself.

Business commitments kept me from traveling to North Carolina to be with her immediately. By the time I could arrange the trip, Mom had been returned to a nursing unit at her retirement community.

I arrived at the nursing unit in the middle of a violent thunderstorm. I was only able to visit with Mom for a few minutes before the unit closed to visitors for the evening. My mother's friend Erica escorted me from my mother's room. On the way out I asked Erica to suggest a nearby motel.

Erica suggested that I stay in her apartment. I gratefully accepted.

Erica and I hurried through the pouring rain, but we were both drenched by the time we reached the front door of her apartment. She instructed me to get out of my wet clothing, and then disappeared. She returned shortly, wearing a short terry cloth robe tied at the waist. I stood before her, naked except for my wet cotton briefs. Erica smiled, commenting that if she was fifteen years younger I would not be safe parading in front of her dressed as I was.

Later, as we sat drinking coffee, I took a good look at the lady who had come to my rescue. Erica was much younger than my mother, probably in her early sixties. Her black hair was highlighted with gray. Large glasses were perched on a small pointed nose, and lines were carved deep into her stately, handsome face. Plenty of skin was exposed from her neck to the point where her robe overlapped, but there was no hint that any portion of her breast was about to be exposed. Erica's hips were wide, her butt more than ample, but her legs were still shapely and toned.

Erica finished her coffee. She placed a pillow and a single blanket on the couch and quietly retired to her room. I realized my underwear was still damp, so I removed it and drifted off to sleep

Before my sleep-filled eyes could focus I was greeted by her cheerful voice. "Good morning. You must have had one hell of a dream." Erica sat on a chair next to the couch on which I reclined. It was several seconds before I realized that I had kicked off the blanket during the night. My entire body was exposed, and I was painfully aware that my erect cock hovered above my stomach.

I sat up, aghast. Very matter-of-factly, Erica asked me to keep myself hard. Before I could respond, there was a knock at the door. Erica tossed me the blanket, which she had folded and placed by her chair.

As I spread the blanket over me, Erica let a totally gray, stocky lady into the apartment. Brendenna took a chair, while Erica forced her way onto the end of the couch. Erica apologized for my lack of formality, explaining that I wore nothing other than the blanket, placing her hand firmly on my thigh.

"Yeah, right," Brendenna said, her voice filled with disbelief.

"See for yourself," Erica replied, tossing the blanket over the back of the couch.

"Oh, my God. Look at that boner," Brendenna squealed. "You sly old slut."

Erica gently grabbed hold of my erect cock. Brendenna watched momentarily, but quickly excused herself. Erica told her not to let the door hit her in the ass on the way out. Erica continued to gently jerk me off.

Brendenna and Erica, it turned out, regularly swapped stories about their sexual encounters. Erica confessed that her stories were pure bullshit, and she suspected that Brendenna's were too, but she was never quite sure. This was Erica's chance to give her stories some credibility. I didn't care what her motivation was, I just wanted to get my rocks off. Suddenly the senior tease stopped stroking my cock, saying she shouldn't be doing this.

I grabbed her around the waist, pulling her on top of me. I kissed her passionately. My tongue explored her mouth as I slid my hands inside her robe and lifted it off her shoulders. I sucked on her little tits for all I was worth.

Turning my attention to my dick, I tried to guide it to her cunt. She stopped me, explaining that she would need some Vaseline. I decided I could get her juices flowing. I buried my face in her crotch, licking and sucking every crevice of her cunt. I massaged her buttocks as the horny old lady rode my face. She bucked and thrust her hips into my face harder and faster with every stroke. Her cunt now moist, I tried to lick my way up her body so I could bury my prick deep inside her. Erica was no longer interested in cock. She pushed my head back down between her legs.

Somewhat disappointed, I licked and sucked on her clit. Erica pulled my head against her crotch. I licked faster and faster until she exploded.

We lay caressing each other while Erica calmed down. The doorbell rang.

Without bothering to cover herself, Erica answered the door.

Again Brendenna entered. Brendenna apologized profusely for the intrusion, explaining that she had left her purse by the chair. "Oh, stop, Brendenna. I knew it was you. I knew you'd need another glimpse of my young man," Erica insisted.

Erica took a wide stance in front of me, pulling my face to her cunt. As Brendenna watched, I buried my tongue in Erica's pussy. She fucked my tongue in a nice, slow rhythm. With Brendenna still looking on, Erica pushed me onto my back, grabbing hold of my cock on the way down. Then she straddled me, aiming my erection at her pussy.

"Eat your heart out," Erica cried, smiling at Brendenna as she impaled herself on my dick. Erica bounced on my cock, telling Brendenna how good it felt. Brendenna left before I came. My cock wilted too soon for Erica to get off again. Erica was not going to be denied, though. She planted her pussy over my mouth, insisting that I suck her to another orgasm.

My sister cannot believe I am already planning to visit Mom again. But since Brendenna has invited me to stay with her this time, I think I will hurry back.—*N.T., Toronto, Ontario* ⚷

AN OLD LOVER COMES OVER
TO SHOW OFF HER NEW TALENT

A few years ago I was in a situation where I'd been dating the same girl on and off for years, but just wasn't getting what I needed from her. One night, when I was working at my computer, an old ex-girlfriend called me, and we started to chat. Eventually the conversation got around to sex. We started to get into a deep conversation about how we would like to get together and do it. Well, my girlfriend was going home early the next day, so we set it up that Regina would come over after she left, and we would fuck.

Regina came over, and was sitting on the edge of my loft bed, undressing. She was down to her bra and panties, and all I had on were my boxers when I got a phone call and had to climb down. I was the sports editor of the school yearbook, and the call was from the managing editor. Regina followed me down and was rubbing my cock while I talked. It was soon hard as a rock. It

was, like, impossible to get this guy off the phone, but I finally
managed it, then crawled back up to the loft and begged Regina
to suck my cock, which she proceeded to do in great fashion.

She was licking and sucking my shaft and playing with my
balls, then using her hand to jack me off while using her mouth
on my balls. She even stuck her finger in my ass, because she
knows I love that. I was grabbing her hair and moaning when she
deep-throated my rod. I can't take much of that, and I blew a
huge load, which she noisily gobbled.

After I blew my load, Regina just kept right on sucking my
dick, which never went soft. She was running her tongue up and
down, sucking my balls into her mouth from time to time, and
even licking my asshole. After a while I blew another load into
her mouth. It was so cute when she looked up and asked me to
fuck her silly, a drop of my come dripping out of her talented
mouth.

We rolled over. Regina mounted me and began to ride my hard
cock for all she was worth. She was sliding up and down my
shaft at blinding speed. Her tits were softly calling my name, so
I began to squeeze and suck her nipples. That sent her over the
edge, and she began heaving her hips around in sharp, spastic little movements. She held my shoulders hard and suddenly went
still. All I could feel was her pussy pulsing around my cock, trying to milk me of what little semen I had left. She'd had a little
orgasm, but Regina wanted more, and began rubbing her clit
against my pubes in short, hard thrusts. Soon she was screaming
and grabbing at my chest.

Without a pause, we rolled over and I mounted her. I began to
slam my cock into her as hard as I could, and she was loving it.
She kept looking into my eyes and saying, "Come on, come on.
Come in me." I fucked her for what seemed like an eternity.

She wanted me to fuck her from behind, knowing that it is my
favorite position. I slid my cock into her cunt from the rear and
began to fuck her in good, long, steady strokes. She was playing
with my balls and fingering her clit as her juices poured out of
her and down both of our legs.

All at once Regina turned and looked me in the eye, then asked
me to fuck her ass. I had never done that to her, but she had told
me that she had let her last boyfriend, who has about a nine-inch
cock, do it to her. I was ecstatic! I have always wanted to fuck
her luscious ass.

I reached into a nearby drawer, got a tube of lube out and

coated my cock with it. I stuck a finger in her ass to loosen her up, then placed the head of my cock at the entrance to her anus and began to push.

She was so tight that it was really hard the first few tries. Her ass finally gave way, and I was in with one huge stroke. Her passage was so tight and hot. I slammed my cock all the way in on every stroke.

Finally she said she was getting a little sore, so I pulled out, not expecting to get any more that morning. Regina surprised me by taking my cock right back into her mouth. She was giving me the blowjob of a lifetime. I was getting close to blowing another load in her mouth when she slipped two fingers into my ass. That proved to be my final undoing, and I shot my third load of the morning down her throat.

At that point we were totally spent, and just lay back and talked about past lovers. We haven't fucked since then, but I am hoping one day we'll get together again. Maybe next time she'll even fuck my ass.—*H.G., Billings, Montana* ⊶▮

THE OLD TOOL SHED,
WHERE FANTASIES ARE BORN AND SATISFIED

About ten years ago I was home from college, preparing for my senior year. Both of my parents were working so I used my time at home doing yard work and minor house repairs. But I had another motive as well: the girl next door. She had also just finished her junior year, but at another college. Boy, did I have the hots for her.

I used every possible excuse I could to go into the yard wearing almost nothing, with the hope of catching her eye. My favorite shorts were an old pair of cutoffs with a large rip across the back. Of course I wore no underwear, and several times I caught Gillian looking my way when I was bent over to start the lawn mower.

One particular day she was sunning herself in an unbelievable bikini. I had just mowed the front yard of my parents' place and was sweating up a storm. We lived in a small town and the property was large, although our houses were not far apart. Gillian watched me closely as I mowed the backyard. As I neared her I could see her erect nipples pressing against her bikini top. I immediately had a hard-on. At first I thought I should turn around and conceal it, but I changed my mind and mowed near enough to her that she could plainly see my dick's outline in my tight jeans. Then she winked, and that was all it took.

I turned off the mower and went her way, noting that she was as hot and sweaty as I was. After all, the sun was bright. "I see a young man who needs a bigger pair of shorts," she said. I asked her if she thought they should come off, and she gladly offered to help. "Not here, though," she said. "My parents could catch us." We ran to an area near the back of the yard, next to a tool shed. No one could see us there unless they were looking from one of the large upstairs windows. But we would hear her parents when they returned, and we could split from behind the house before they got inside and up the stairs.

It seemed as if the gates of heaven had opened when she began stroking my crotch. The top of my cock stuck out of my jeans as she rubbed. Our tongues met. I removed the top of her bikini. She unzipped my cutoffs and squeezed my rod, causing a small stream of pre-come to run out and onto her hand. She licked it up as I bent down to kiss her again. We tumbled together to the ground where I pulled off her bikini bottom and dove into her wet pussy. Our bodies slithered easily against each other as the sweat lubricated us, and I tasted salty perspiration mixed with her love juices. I entered her from on top and pushed so hard that I could hear her ass tearing the grass. I was about to come like never before, but she told me not to.

Instead, she instructed me to sit up and lean back against the shed. "Scoot closer to me," she demanded. As I did so, she swallowed my throbbing member into her mouth so far I thought she would choke. She reached under my balls and began rubbing the sweat around and toward my asshole. Then, with a sudden push, her sweaty finger slid into my ass. She developed an unbelievable rhythm, sucking my cock and pushing her finger slowly in and out of my butt. I was delirious.

As I pushed my dick into her face, I wanted more of her finger in my ass. But when I pushed my ass down further onto her finger, my cock slid away from her mouth! The exquisite joy and tension were driving me crazy! My own pumping got faster, until Gillian knew the moment was near. Watching her suck me, with one hand on my pole and the other on her clit, sent me into ecstasy. I told her I was going to come, and she pulled my cock out of her mouth to watch. I erupted with a thousand pounds of pressure per square millimeter.

Come went everywhere! There is nothing remarkable about my prick, but when I shoot it seems like it will never end. That had been true since I first masturbated, and still is today. After a few jets, Gillian tried to swallow the rest of my cream, but it just kept going, and when she pulled my penis out again, still spasming and dribbling, she grinned and giggled like a little kid.

After resting her cheek on my spent rod, she reached up to offer me a gentle kiss. I had tasted my own come once before, but this time it was much more salty because of the sweat. Gillian and I lay together awhile before noticing that we were covered with grass stains and come. Then we heard a car in the driveway in front of her house. Gillian kissed me and ran into the house naked. As I quickly put my shorts back on, I looked up to see her wave from her upstairs bathroom window before jumping into the shower.

Then I noticed something else. On the opposite end of the upstairs level was a full-length window in a separate bedroom. Gillian's nineteen-year-old brother was standing there with his pants down to his knees pulling on his pecker. Evidently he had been watching us the whole time, and was now so involved in his own fantasy that he hadn't noticed that we were finished. I watched as he exploded come on the window, then I snuck away.

Gillian and I had other adventures, which I'll relate in later letters. — *H.P., Sarasota, Florida* ⊶▪

ONE-WOMAN LEAGUE OF NATIONS OFFERS MORE THAN HANDS ACROSS THE WATER

My wife Allison and I are avid readers of *Penthouse Letters*. We've recently developed a hobby which may be of interest to your readers. In brief, this hobby consists of her seeing, from amongst her lovers, how many countries she can collect.

Allison is a gorgeous blonde who sticks out in back and front in an enticing way. We have been very happily married for eight years. Our sex life at first was outstanding, but over time it gradually deteriorated. For some time, we had discussions as to what to do about this. Finally, Allison suggested that what she needed was more variety in her sex life. I agreed that it would be good to try this out, even though she wouldn't agree to my following the same course of action.

My wife works in an office where there are many visitors from other countries. It seemed the ideal setup for our new hobby. The male visitors are all capable, sophisticated gentlemen, generally without any accompanying spouse, who have an appreciation for good-looking girls and a desire for blonde Americans and their sexual favors. In addition, they stay at elegant hotels, which are quite suitable for extramarital sex events. The fact that these eligible studs are here for only short periods of time eliminates the problem of possible long-term emotional attachment.

So, we began the "foreign assistance project," and it has turned out to be a huge success. A little flirtation from Allison almost always brought forth an invitation for dinner and a few drinks afterward. This would be followed inevitably by an invitation to the stud's bedroom, with invariably interesting results.

In the first year of the game, Allison chalked up the following countries for her collection: Canada, Costa Rica, Ecuador, France, Honduras, India, Ireland, Japan, Liberia, Nigeria, Russia and Saudi Arabia. She had many exciting experiences, and even learned some new tricks, which happily she shared with me in both words and action. For example, there were some interesting variations of cunt-eating from the French entry, some new twists in the cocksucking field from a Saudi prince, and a new position for fucking from the Honduran.

Allison's goal is to be sucked and fucked by macho guys from at least half the countries in the United Nations. In any event, our sex life has been greatly enhanced—my wife's by the additional and greatly varied activity, and mine by the terrific improvement in our joint lovemaking, as well as the thrill of hearing about her sexual exploits with so many different men. The only problem is that I can't get her to permit me to undertake a similar project. However, I'm trying hard to convince her, and very much hope that I'll soon be successful.—*L.L., New York, New York* O⊢▪

THE BIGGER THE BETTER,
SAYS ONE WOMAN WHO HAS BEEN THERE

I've seen in many sex surveys the question of whether women prefer large penises to smaller ones. For my part, there's no question. I prefer the big ones.

Several years ago I met Georgie at a going-away party for one of my coworkers. He was slightly younger than I am, tall and slender, with a dazzling smile.

Georgie and I hit it off immediately, and by the end of our second date I knew that I would be sleeping with him. To skip the preliminaries, we ended up at his place. After some kissing, he removed my top and began to gently suck on my nipples. He then moved further and started to caress my moist pussy. I was getting hotter by the minute. When he finally moved between my legs and started licking me out, I came within seconds. Georgie was patient, though, and ate me to two more fantastic orgasms before coming up for air.

I felt that I should do something to return the favor so I began to remove his pants, which of course he had no objection to. When I finally grasped his cock in the dim light, I thought to myself, this can't be real. I couldn't see exactly how big it was, but I could definitely tell it was bigger than any cock I had held before. I couldn't even get my hand around it. I did my best to give him a good sucking, but it consisted mainly of licking the shaft and the underside of his balls. After several minutes of my eager if unsuccessful attempts, Georgie suggested that I lie down.

I was a little apprehensive at first, but when I felt the bulbous cockhead touch my pussy lips I knew that I wanted it all inside me. Georgie rubbed his monster at the entrance of my cooze for a minute, then started to make his entry. As his cock slowly nudged forward I could feel my pussy stretch to let him inside. He wasn't even fully inside when I felt a climax building. I came once very powerfully, and then began a succession of what I can only describe as miniorgasms. After about every fifth miniorgasm I would have another huge one. And he wasn't even all the way in yet! Finally Georgie got all the way inside me, and truly gave me one of the best fucks I've ever had. He pumped in and out with a steady rhythm that rolled me from one orgasm to another.

When he finally came he was so deep inside that I could feel his boner twitching and spurting his load. We lay still for several minutes, and even after he had stopped coming I had another climax.

The next morning in full light I was able to really take a look at that monster, and was truly amazed to discover that it was even bigger than I had thought. I once measured it at just under eleven inches long and five inches around. One time I climaxed a total of twenty-three times with the help of Georgie and his fabulous tool.

We continued to see each other for several months, until Georgie was transferred across the country. I've heard that he is married now, and I can't help but be a little jealous of his wife and the great sex she's having with him. I have been with a few other men since Georgie, but none has ever been able to drive me the way he could.

To sum up my feelings about big cocks: Ladies, if you've never had a monster dick churning inside of your pussy, you are truly missing out on one of the most pleasurable experiences a woman can ever have. Of course, if Georgie hadn't been so patient about getting me good and wet and ready for his monster, I might have been less enthusiastic, but the combination of a big dick and good technique is unbeatable.—*R.G., Boston, Massachusetts* O⊢▪

NOW THAT YOU'RE GROWN UP, YOU CAN SCREW RIGHT HERE IN THE FRONT SEAT

My wife and I were returning from a vacation up north when I asked her to play a game to kill time on the road. We started asking each other questions that we had to be completely truthful about and both answer.

One question she asked me was, "What would you do if you could be a member of the opposite sex for a day?" Part of my answer was that I wanted to have sex with two men and a woman at the same time. Roxanne asked me how I would feel if she did that. I said that I didn't know, but that I would be as supportive as possible.

One question I asked was, "What was the most erotic thing you've ever done in a car?" Roxanne said that hers was giving me a blowjob while a friend of ours was in the backseat. That was mine as well, actually, but she asked me to tell her about something else I'd done. I told her about a girlfriend who had stripped while we drove down the interstate so that I could masturbate her. After she came, she knelt on the seat with her ass against the window, so that truckers could see her pussy, and she gave me a blowjob.

Roxanne asked me if I wanted her to do that. I felt selfish, but said, "Sure!"

Roxanne pulled off her sweater, dress and panties and placed her back against the passenger door. She spread her legs, one foot on the dash and one on my seat back, so that I could easily get at her pussy with my free hand. I could smell the sweet, pungent aroma of her sex and it made me dizzy with lust. When I stroked her pouting labia with my fingers she was soaking wet. I plunged into her with my forefinger, and she softly and sexily moaned and moved her pussy against my hand for more penetration. As her moaning became louder and her bucking became more urgent, I put two fingers into her and began to rub her straining clit with my thumb. She looked so beautiful, caught up in herself, with her hair in her face and her exquisite skin pale in the cloudy moonlight.

Soon her breathing quickened and she began to shudder as she frantically impaled herself on my fingers. The orgasm that rocked her seemed to start deep in her stomach, and rolled out to her sexy toes and fingertips.

Once Roxanne caught her breath, she decided it was my turn to come. She unzipped my jeans and delicately began licking and sucking my cock. As she went down on me, she made little moaning sounds and began to sway her beautiful ass. I began to rub her bottom with my right hand and slid a finger into her soaking pussy from behind. The more I masturbated her, the more enthusiastically she worked her mouth and tongue on my dick.

I started to gently finger Roxanne's asshole between rubbing her ass and fingering her cunt. She stopped sucking me long enough to push her long red curls aside and say, "That's it. Shove it in there, Christopher! I want to feel you in my ass!" I was already loving the feeling of Roxanne working on my cock as I attempted to drive down the coast, but I was elated by her request.

I began to finger her harder and with a more deliberate rhythm. She responded by sucking me more vigorously and moaning around my cock with each stroke. Roxanne's mouth and moans were slowly but surely driving me to the edge, and I was more than ready to come.

I said, "Suck my cock like you mean it, girl!" With that encouragement, she began bobbing her head and sucking me like never before. I kept saying "That's it! Suck it like you mean it!" I continued to shove a finger into her butt, and soon felt myself going over the edge. I exploded into her warm, waiting mouth with an orgasm that left me quivering and breathless.

Roxanne kept sucking me until I was hard again. Then she sat back against the passenger door. With her legs spread wide, she plunged two fingers into her cunt. After a few seconds, she pulled them out so that I could taste her wonderful juices. She was so wet and tasty that I was quickly ready for more driving fun.

Roxanne was ready for some driving fun too, but the driving she wanted was my cock in her glistening pussy. She leaned forward slightly and said with authority, "I want you to stop the car and fuck me. Now!" Then she began sucking me again while I looked for a place to pull off the road.

We parked in a turnout in front of a farm. Roxanne reclined her seat as far as possible while I stripped. She turned around and lay down on the seat with her bottom slightly raised so that I could fuck her from behind. As enticing as fucking her was at that moment, I couldn't help stopping and sampling her sweet pussy. After a few licks she looked over her shoulder and said, "Fuck me, damn it!" I raised myself level with her ass and slowly pushed my throbbing cock into her. She was so hot! It felt like the muscles of her vagina were pulling me into her.

After a few minutes like this, we switched our positions so that she was facing me with her knees up high. I started with long, slow strokes again as Roxanne quietly exhorted me to fuck her. I started talking to her about the earlier fantasy of being with two men and a woman at the same time. I asked her if she would like someone to fuck her from behind while someone else worked his cock into her little mouth and down her throat. Would that turn her on? Would she cry out with pleasure?

Needless to say, all this fantasizing and her hot body had made me pick up my pace. I was tearing in and out of her pussy like I was one of the men I had been describing. It was incredible! We were making so much noise I'm surprised that the farmer didn't come outside to see what was going on. Roxanne began to come again, with another tremendous rolling orgasm. I love looking into her eyes while I can feel her coming.

We quietly put our clothes back on and started down the coast again toward home with a twinkle in our eyes and the smell of sex filling the car.—*C.L., Palo Alto, California* ⊶▪

TALK ABOUT GETTING IT ON BEHIND YOUR PARENTS' BACKS!

There's a thrill to screwing in secret, right under the nose of someone who has no idea of what's going on. My wife and I were near the end of a long trip, vacationing with both sets of our parents. My wife Lisette's parents were driving the minivan, my parents were in the middle seat and we were in the back. The interstate stretched for miles ahead of us, and we sat silently in the dark, for after a week together there was little small talk left. Lisette had fallen asleep with her head on my lap, and I was in that mesmerized state you get in when waiting for the highway to end.

I felt her stirring as she woke up, and reached down to stroke her head. In response she lifted my T-shirt and kissed my belly. I absentmindedly reached out and stroked her tits and felt a shudder go through her body. To my amazement, I felt her hands on my zipper. She was soon digging into my open fly to expose my cock, which lay flaccid beneath my jockey shorts. I wondered just how far she was planning to go, right there in the car with both sets of parents. I didn't have to ask. She let me know that she had decided to suck my cock.

In complete silence, she surrounded my drooping dong with her lips and began to suck gently. Her mouth covered my prick completely, the warmth of it like a blast furnace in the air-conditioned minivan. Her attentions soon caused my cock to grow and fill her mouth. Her lips slid up my pole as it expanded. Soon only the glans was covered, and her wonderful tongue ran swirls of delight around the tip of my cock. She sucked gently, and very lightly, never hard enough to make a telltale slurping sound and draw attention to us. With exquisite slowness I felt her lips slide down my cock, a band of liquid heat surrounding my manhood, until I was fully sunk between her lovely lips, then another achingly slow withdrawal as she pulled back.

I worked hard to keep my breathing steady, even as my body

was sent racing by Lisette's attentions. Once again she clamped my glans between her lips and began to suck, drawing my juices from the depth of my balls. I felt the excitement begin to rise, felt my balls tighten and my prick get even stiffer. It was all I could do to maintain my silence when I began to pump my come into her mouth. Lisette maintained her steady sucking, draining me silently in the backseat of the van. At last the rush was over, and to my amazement neither set of parents had noticed a thing.

Lisette let my prick drop out of her mouth and rolled over. I quickly slid the strap of her halter top down one arm and pulled back the cup to expose one tit. With trembling hands I began to play with her nipple, gently pinching it and rolling it between thumb and forefinger. I could feel it hardening as I played, and soon the rhythmic motion of her head in my lap told me she was enjoying the attention. I reached my hand farther down, sliding it under the band of her shorts. The angle was wrong to be able to penetrate her warm bush, so I contented myself with sliding my fingers over her slippery cunt hair and cupped my hand over her clit. Using short strokes, I massaged her and felt her hips begin to move.

Keeping time with her motion I rubbed her clit, feeling her tension build. I felt her hand grip my arm as she grew more excited, her lips firmly sealed to keep from making a sound. I kept rubbing and nearly lost my arm as she tightened her grip on it. At last I felt her hips rise in the seat, and she drew in one sharp breath as she went over the edge. I struggled to keep rubbing her clit as she came, slowing as she rolled over the peak. At last she lay still on my lap, and we continued down the highway. With no one but ourselves having any idea what had just happened.—
K.T., Saint Paul, Minnesota O╾▪

SHOWERING AT A TRUCK STOP
LEADS TO A HIGHWAY FUCK STOP

Sally and I were going away for the weekend, and we had to hurry and get on the road. We hit the freeway wearing shorts and shirts, nothing fancy. We had a four-hour drive, and only five hours to arrive, get cleaned up and be ready to attend a play with my parents.

While we were driving we came upon a truck stop that advertised showers, so we decided to get cleaned up there. We separated to our respective locker rooms and agreed to meet at the grill. Forty-five minutes later she came out, looking absolutely stunning. Sally is five feet seven inches tall, and has a very nice figure. She was wearing a loose white blouse that buttoned up the front, a black skintight miniskirt and white heels. I got a hard-on just looking at her. Sally walked up and said, "Do you like? I bought this outfit to wear for you tonight." I was so stunned I couldn't answer.

We jumped in the car and hit the road again so we wouldn't be late. I couldn't keep my eyes off her. The bulge I was sporting grabbed her attention as well. That was all the signal she needed.

Sally turned in her seat so that her back was against the passenger door, put one foot on the back of the seat and the other on the dash. She pulled up her skirt. To my surprise, she wasn't wearing any panties. She slowly started rubbing her pussy and asked, "So you didn't answer my question. What do you think?"

I growled, "I want to eat you."

"Not yet, my hasty friend," she responded. "I have a lot more planned for you."

She started rubbing harder and faster. I could smell her excitement, and my cock felt like it was going to burst through my pants. I started fidgeting in my seat, trying to get more comfortable, but it didn't help. Sally leaned over and took my cock out of its cloth prison. She leaned back and rubbed my throbbing muscle with her foot. Reaching up, she undid her blouse. I started stroking myself. When Sally saw this she removed her hand from her cunt and stuck her fingers in my mouth. "Find somewhere to pull over," she moaned. "I want to fuck you."

She returned her hand to her cunt, at the same time leaning over to suck my aching dick. I found an isolated road and pulled off. Once we were parked, Sally pulled my pants down around my ankles, then lay back on the seat.

I slid down and started eating her pussy. Her flowing juices were sweet as honey. Her moans became louder and louder until she screamed out, "Fuck me!" I didn't need to be told twice. I propped her up on all fours and fucked her doggie-style. The way she controls her muscles is fabulous. She gripped my tool tightly. I pushed and pushed, working my prick in and out of her clenched cunt, and we both came with a roar. I pulled out, leaned

down and cleaned her of both our juices with my tongue, then
shared the cream with her in a passionate tongue kiss.

We pulled ourselves together and hit the road again. We arrived with ten minutes to spare. When we approached my folks
they commented, "You two sure look happy this evening!" We
looked at each other and just smiled. It was the most wonderful
experience I've ever had.—*P.D., Taos, New Mexico* ○┼▪

LOOKING FOR SOMETHING DIFFERENT, SHE DECIDES TO TURN OVER LEIF

I was at my boyfriend's apartment one evening while he was still
at work. Ray's roommate Leif was there too, and looking good,
as always.

I was wearing tight sweatpants. When I bent over to pick
something up, I felt a hand on my butt. I let Leif have his way for
a moment before I spun around and asked him what he was
doing. "Sorry, I just couldn't resist," he said.

I told him he'd better watch it. "I have been watching it," he
stated with a sly smile that drove me crazy. "I watched it twitch
around here in those short shorts you wore all summer, and now
I've watched it twitch around here in those tight sweats all fall,
and I couldn't resist touching it." I was already worked up,
knowing he had been eyeing me as much as I had been eyeing
him.

"I don't think so," he responded sarcastically, when I told him
he might get slapped. Leif and I have gotten along well since we
first met, about nine months ago. His muscular build and his
"country coolness" to my flirting have had me hot for him ever
since.

I asked him what it was he liked about my short shorts. He
said, "Come here," and led me to his room, where he handed me
a beat-up old tank top. "This would go good with those shorts,"
he said. Making him turn his head, I slipped out of my sweatshirt
and into the flimsy top. My 36D boobs weren't too well covered
up by the little bit of material, and the fact is my nipples were
about as hard as they could get. "It doesn't go so well with those
sweats, though," he mused. "Go put on something that looks

good with that top and you'll look the way you do when I fantasize about you."

I couldn't resist playing with my boobs as I stood in front of a mirror getting ready to change into a pair of pink G-string panties.

I was soon standing in front of him. His eyes ran slowly up and down my body. "You mustn't like the change, since you're not fondling me like you did in the kitchen a while ago," I complained.

"I might get slapped," he responded.

"I don't think so," I laughed, and moved toward him. Leif's hands played over my boobs, then crept behind me to outline my tiny panties. He picked me up and carried me into the living room. Once there, we kissed for the first time, our hands exploring each other's body. I love to talk a little dirty while having sex. Ray hates it, but I was hoping Leif would feel differently. I knelt before him, undid his pants and said, "I can't wait to suck your dick." That sly smile came over his face again, and I nearly ripped his pants in my hurry.

Soon I was sucking the most beautiful cock I'd ever seen. I positioned myself so that Leif could play with my butt while my head went up and down his shaft. "I want you to come in my mouth, but not until after you fuck me," I told him in between slurps, gazing into his eyes, with his cock resting on my lips.

We switched positions, with me on my knees on the edge of the couch and him directly behind me. He gave me the best tonguing I had ever received. I squealed as his tongue ran up my crack and stopped long enough to tease my asshole. (I love to play with my asshole, but Ray doesn't like that either.)

Soon Leif was sliding his big cock in and out of me. "I want you to fuck me in the ass," I said. I got on all fours, with my butt up in the air, and he slowly worked his big cock into my ass. It felt so good I could hardly stand it, and I knew right then that Leif and I were going to be making love a lot more in the future.

We switched positions several more times, and he was on top of me, driving away, when I realized that Leif was ready to come. "Come in my mouth," I begged.

He sat on the couch and I lowered my head, waiting for my prize. It wasn't ten seconds before he gushed his come into my hungry mouth. I slurped and played with his load, then climbed onto his lap to share it with him in a lingering kiss.

I love Ray, but I really love fucking Leif. I later told Ray that

I had given Leif a blowjob that evening. He looked at me funny, but said he knew I wouldn't be able to resist Leif for very long. He even said he didn't mind, because Leif is a good buddy and had recently gone through a rough breakup with a girl he had dated for several years. Now Leif and I fuck each other a lot, sometimes even when Ray is home. I don't know how long he'll stay cool about it, but for the moment I have a perfect world.
—*S.B., Pontiac, Michigan*

ONE LARGE HOUSEGUEST

When my husband called from his office Monday afternoon to inform me that his old college roommate was in town on business and would be spending the rest of the week with us, I was not very happy. I had been complaining for several months about Joe's lack of attentiveness to my sexual needs and viewed this as just another excuse for him and a boon companion to hit every singles bar in town and run up a world-class drinks bill while I sat at home with a bad case of the hornies. But much to my delight our houseguest turned out to be exactly the right medicine for my problem.

The next morning I had to run some errands after Joe left for work, and didn't get back home until about ten o'clock. As I walked down the hall past the guest bathroom I saw that the door was slightly ajar and heard the sound of the shower. Glancing through the cracked door from where I was standing in the hallway, I could see Danny's reflection in the mirror. He was in the clear-glass shower enclosure, and the water streamed down over his naked body as he lathered himself with soap. I shivered with excitement and anticipation. But I couldn't get a full-frontal view of him in his present position. "C'mon, baby," I whispered, "turn just a little bit more." When he did, I gaped in astonishment at the marvelous sight that presented itself.

Danny's cock hung down nearly halfway to his knees. Even in its flaccid state it had to be eight or nine inches in length, and it was twice as thick as my husband's larger-than-average tool. Without even thinking about it, I slipped my hand under my dress to touch myself and found my panties were already damp from excitement. I somehow knew that if I didn't go for that prize prong now I probably would never get up the courage again. Within seconds my clothes were on the hallway floor and I was stepping into the shower with Danny.

His eyes nearly bugged out of his head when my twin 38Ds pressed against his hairy chest and my hand grasped and started stroking his hambone.

"Lucille," he mumbled, "are you sure you want to . . . ?"

"Yes," I told him, "I've been sure what I wanted since I first saw you last night." Danny's lollapalooza was now half erect and so big that I could barely get my hands around it. He needed no further encouragement. Now his hands were all over my wet body. He fondled and massaged my tits, caressed my ass, explored my hot and welcoming pussy.

When I felt his dick as he rubbed the head up and down in my crack, I nearly lost it there and then. "If you keep that up for very long I'm going to come," I told him.

"That's what it's all about, isn't it?" He had a big grin on his face as he concentrated on my throbbing clit. I couldn't hold back any longer and exploded in a quick but intense climax that caused my body to shake uncontrollably.

"Wow," Danny said when I had calmed down a bit. "You are one very hot lady, aren't you?" And he continued, "Now that you've had the appetizer are you ready for the main course?" I nodded. My body was still on fire with lust. Danny grasped the cheeks of my ass and easily picked me up. He lowered me slowly onto his cock. I moaned as he slowly eased me down that massive rod until it slipped into my cunt, buried to the hilt. The sensation of being that full of cock was unbelievable. Without either of us even moving I started coming again in one long, shattering orgasm that seemed to last for five minutes.

When I realized Danny had not come yet and that his massive prong, still hard as a rock, was still buried in my pussy, I knew what I wanted next.

"Let me down, lover," I told him, "I want to suck you off." I immediately dropped to my knees in front of him and sucked that large muscle into my mouth. Pumping his thick shaft with one hand and fondling his huge balls with the other I blew him in a near frenzy. Now I felt another climax building inside me. I was so hot I knew that when he started to climax I would go over the edge for the third time.

I heard Danny start to moan and felt his stretcher twitch in my mouth and throat. Seconds later, he erupted, filling my mouth with so much come I couldn't swallow fast enough. I had to release that cock and he shot several streams of jism onto the glass shower door and onto my avid face. As expected, this set me off again. I shuddered as another orgasm rolled through my body until I thought I would pass out.

We had been at it for so long the water had gone completely cold. We were so hot for each other we didn't notice the change in temperature. Danny laughed and shut the water off before helping me stand up. Then he kissed me hungrily. "Goddam, Lucille, that was fantastic!" he said, "but what the hell do we do for an encore?"

I gave his cock a gentle squeeze before answering. "Well, baby, it's only Tuesday, so we've got the rest of the week to think of something."

And believe me, we did. But that will take another letter.
—*O.P., Kansas City, Kansas* ⚯

CLEANING UP AT THE DRIVE-IN

I am a regular reader of your journal and enjoy very much the spectacular pictorials and stimulating articles. I would like to share one of my recent experiences with your readers.

Not long ago, I acquired a used van. I quickly seized the opportunity and invited my girlfriend Barbara out to a flick at the local drive-in. I was uncommonly lucky this night and we were into each other's pants in minutes. I loved it when she ran those luscious lips over my throbbing johnson as I thrust my face into her cavernous gorge. Then I licked her labia and let those pussy juices slowly trickle across my countenance while at the opposite pole her throat anxiously awaited delivery of a hot load of semen.

Suddenly we were interrupted. A gentleman rapped on the window and politely asked for a light. It was obvious from the bulge in his pants that he had had a good look at what was going on in the van. We did the only gracious thing and invited him to join us. He seemed hesitant at first. My girlfriend went into a frenzy when he unveiled a twenty-centimeter cock. She begged him to shove his rotor-rooter into her plumbing. He was not prone to argue, and he immediately complied. Actually, at this point I must admit that I was getting pretty excited at the sight of his enormous shaft as it penetrated the depths of Barbara's dripping cunt.

He was extremely polite, and after depositing his load of jism he invited me to clean up. I eagerly jumped in and ate his hot come out of her inflamed pussy. As he got dressed and left for his own car, we thanked each other and agreed to meet again. —*M.P., Louisville, Kentucky* O—■

SAMPLING A VINTAGE WINE

This all happened when I visited my older brother Jim in Carson City. He said he had promised two girls that he would help them move the next morning and that I could just stay in bed until he got back. But I was up before he was, so I drove him over to the girls' place in my pickup truck and dropped him off. I went on to an X-rated movie house, which can't be found where I live. But after four films in one hour I decided to go and help with the move.

That's when I met Jane, a twenty-five-year-old redhead who obviously had her eye on Jim, and Vanessa, a beautiful twenty-eight-year-old woman who I will surely remember for a long time. We finished the move in about three hours and after one case of beer. Then Jim and I went home to clean up and allow the girls time to straighten up their new place. Jim told me the girls had invited us to come over that evening and play some cards, and he also said we might not be going home that night. I thought he might not come home, but I was pretty sure I would. I didn't think Vanessa would be interested in someone six years younger. But I'm glad to say I was wrong.

After a tour of the house we all sat down at the dining room table to play spades. The conversation soon turned to sex, and the more we drank and smoked the more open we all became. When the talk got around to birth control, and both girls assured us that everyone was safe, I began to feel maybe Jim was right about not going home. Vanessa and I were partners, and after we lost in the card game we suggested that we all go in the living room and listen to music. But no sooner were we all comfortable than Vanessa said she had to run out to the liquor store, since it would be closed the next day, Sunday. Vanessa and I went together, and since we had had no dinner, we also bought the groceries for a meal for all of us. By the time we got back, Jim and Jane were in the bedroom, which was fine. It gave me a chance to be alone with Vanessa. When Jane and Jim came out of the bedroom the steaks and French fries were cold. Neither of them complained.

We talked until it was late, and we all agreed it was best for Jim and me to spend the night. It seemed a dream come true to me. Vanessa and I went in her bedroom and simply held each other close for a long time. Then we fell onto her king-size waterbed. I had never even slept on a waterbed, and I certainly had no experience in what was to follow. I tried to be subtle in getting off Vanessa's clothes and my own on the waterbed, but I was woefully clumsy. It was then I began truly to appreciate who I was with and to treasure the experience. Things were awkward and getting worse when Vanessa gently suggested, "Why don't we get off the bed to take off our clothes?" That doesn't sound like much, but it opened a line of communication that stayed open for the rest of the night. We undressed, and I marveled at Vanessa's pendulous breasts, her full ass, and her mature figure.

We wasted no time in getting back in bed and it was continuous ecstasy from then on. We started by kissing and fondling each other but the pace quickened when Vanessa kissed and licked her way down to my blood-engorged prick. Cocksucking is too crude a phrase for what she did for me that night. I've had other girls give me head, but she was practicing an art. I had never experienced the feeling that went through me then. She slowly ran her tongue up and down my shaft, then sucked it as contentedly as a newborn baby at its mother's breast. As much as I was loving it I didn't want to come in her mouth, so I turned her around so that her pussy was over my mouth and returned the favor. I have always loved the joys of cunnilingus. Although I don't feel I am an expert, I certainly practice whenever I can. As I kissed, nibbled and gently sucked the lips of her vagina she reached down and guided me to exactly where and how she was excited the most. I'm a fast learner. I redirected my attention to her now stiff clitoris and flicked my tongue over it as I massaged her breasts with light circular strokes. Before long she moaned, "I'm coming." As I quickened my strokes both on her breast and on her clit she reached a quiet screaming orgasm.

I couldn't believe how naturally everything had happened. We took a break, joking around and caressing each other, but not for long. As soon as we caught our breaths we took up where we had left off. This time, after a little more foreplay, I had the privilege of sinking my roscoe deep into her warm moist pussy. Now I know what paradise is like—and for once I knew I had all night and day if I needed them. I was in no hurry. Both of us savored every sensation with easy, full, rhythmic strokes. When I reached the point of no return I slowed my pace to make it last. Vanessa started nibbling my neck. She said she was about to come again and wanted us to come together. We did, matching one another's strokes and intensity precisely, thrusting in perfect unison at high speed. I was amazed to find that after I came powerfully and thoroughly I had no need to stop and rest. It was like defying gravity.

Our night together was over after about three hours and three climaxes. Vanessa had to leave town, but she came back the next day and brought with her a film projector. Jim was working that night, so I went over to the girls' house alone. Jim would join us later. I had told the girls of Jim's aversion to X-rated films, so the three of us watched several together. These were the first girls I had ever known to show any interest in them. As we watched the fuck-flicks, Vanessa said that she was getting excited and had already creamed her jeans. We decided it would do Jim some good if he saw a few X-rated films. As soon as he arrived, I rolled one. Vanessa was sitting at my feet, which gave me the opportunity to reach down and remind myself just how perfectly round and firm her breasts were. Jim raised no objections. From the sound of things, he and Jane seemed to be exploring their possibilities. Before long we all went to bed. I don't know about Jim but my night was, like the whole weekend, unforgettable. I know that a time like that may never come again but I live in hope.—*G.D., Fargo, South Dakota* ⚷▪

WORKS HARD, KEEPS CLEAN

I've read your magazine for years and never believed even half of the encounters I've read until recently. I was earning some extra money to pay for a blind date my friends had set up by cleaning out the basement parking lot and trash room where I live. I was hot and horny and the job was dirty and smelly.

I was almost through cleaning the trash room dumpster, reaching over it to pick up a stray newspaper, when a paper bag of garbage slid down the chute. It burst and showered garbage on my head and back.

"Great!" I complained as I picked eggshells and coffee grounds out my hair. "I can't wait to get my hands on the dope who did this." I went up to my apartment hoping to avoid running into anybody when to my dismay the elevator stopped at the floor just below mine.

Standing there was the most gorgeous brunette in three counties. She snickered at first at my garbage-bedecked appearance. But then a look of comprehension came over her face.

"Oh my God," she gasped. "I'm sorry. That was my trash that hit you." To make amends she offered me the use of her shower and laundry room to clean up. I had nothing to lose, so I accepted. The brunette, who introduced herself as Colleen, led me to her apartment. She said to leave my dirty clothes on the floor when I climbed into her shower. Colleen took the clothes to her laundry room while I scrubbed myself clean. I wondered as I soaped myself if my hostess looked as hot without clothes as she did in them.

As if in answer to a prayer, things took a turn for the better. I'd barely finished washing my hair when I suddenly heard a husky feminine voice.

"I need this too," said Colleen. "Mind if I join you?"

"No indeed," I said, over my delight and confusion. "No problem." Then my eyes popped at the sight of her grapefruit-sized breasts. As I backed away in the shower stall to give her room as she stepped under the water, my gaze immediately zeroed in on her firm and generous ass. She looked over her shoulder and saw me soaping up my chest.

"Would you wash my back?" she asked.

"Sure," I said, with sincere enthusiasm. I lathered up my hand and worked my way slowly from her freckled shoulders down her splendid tapered torso. She leaned slightly forward and tensed when my hands briefly cupped her full breasts.

I knelt behind her then, and gently soaped her ass. I spread the cheeks as she spread her legs and leaned forward. The sight of Colleen's hairless snatch was as arousing as her moan of approval when I gently touched her labia. I gently washed both her legs, then stood back and suggested it was my turn.

Colleen faced me and her eyes focused on my semi-rigid prick. "You missed a spot," she said. "I think I can fix that." She took the soap from me and knelt down. Then she slowly lathered first my pubic hair, then kneaded my balls. Now there was nothing semi- about my erection. She gripped my cock to pull me under the stream and rinse me off. Still kneeling, she took my newly washed John Thomas between those luscious lips. She started at the base and licked and kissed her way up to the tip. Then she sucked in my stiff shaft as if she hungered for it.

I was already horny, so I soon shot a load of come into her mouth. She swallowed every drop. We washed again and dried one another off. I sat on the couch in the living room wearing a towel.

"It'll be about an hour before your clothes are dry," Colleen said when she returned. "Would like something to eat?" She took off her T-shirt and lay down on the couch with her legs apart and her pussy open to me. I dived into her honey-pot like an Olympics competitor. I think I proved I could give as well as take. I licked circles around her mound of Venus, then worked my way to her sweet-tasting twat. I watched her pinch her nipples as she clutched my head and pulled my tongue deeper into her honey-pot. I puckered my lips and sucked her pussy hard. Now I had another roaring erection, and I pulled my face away from her grotto so that I could slide my cock into this eager pussy. I prolonged our pleasure with long hard strokes. Then we switched positions. She straddled my prick and her beautiful tits bounced wildly as she bounced happily on it. I lost track of time, but I know we came together, with me shooting what seemed like buckets of jism and Colleen's pussy lips happily squeezing out every bit. She fell down on me exhausted and I held her close.

Needless to say, I now make this place the cleanest building in town.—*P.C., Calgary, Canada* ○╾▪

THE TRUTH, SO HELP HER

I know you don't receive many letters from women and I suspect few of the stories are true, anyway. But here is a true story from a woman that your readers may like.

My name is Georgia. I am a twenty-five-year-old homemaker. I am petite and sport strawberry blonde hair almost down to my waist. I have green eyes and measure 35C-23-35. I'm probably attractive—I get a lot of longing looks—and I am definitely a nymphomaniac.

I love my husband dearly but he does not satisfy me. This, coupled with his absences on sales trips, often leads me to seek extramarital pleasures. Yesterday's adventure was fairly typical.

The telephone rang and woke me at nine a.m. It was my friend Callie inviting me for coffee. Usually, with Callie, that means a session with her in bed as well. She is thirty years old, five-foot-six, 36C-24-36, black and beautiful. Callie is addicted to the way I lick her pussy. Yesterday, we had our morning coffee, jumped in bed, and did a lot of petting. Then I ate her pussy.

Once Callie came, it was my turn. I tend to flow like a river when I reach a climax, and Callie drinks it all up greedily.

By eleven, our fingers and tongues having done all they could, I was out cruising the local roads looking for likely sites to stage a breakdown and break out the air mattress I keep handy in the back of the van.

As usual, I was rewarded. There were a couple of good-looking guys among the good Samaritans who stopped and, also as usual, both gentlemen elected to drop their pants upon invitation. I always wear a garter belt and stockings under a loose short skirt when I'm cruising. Leaving my underpants at home helps, too. The men are understandably in a hurry.

Home, showered and changed by four is a must since I'm screwing the paperboy. I enjoy Herbert mostly because he was a virgin until I broke him in, and I can still safely dispense with condoms. Like any eighteen-year-old, that lad can get it up again in a hurry. A few sucks help sometimes, in an emergency. I try to meet and seduce a college student at least twice a month. Needless to say, the males are easy, once you overcome their fright. You have to spend a great deal of effort becoming a young woman's friend and confidante before you can bed her.

Whenever my husband is away I spend part of an evening at a second girlfriend's home. Bernice is a call girl. She is quite pretty and consequently very busy. Because I am not interested in the fee part, she never minds letting me take on a couple of interesting, well-hung Johns.

I typed this letter with a vibrator in my pussy, so please overlook any errors. And guys, if you see a blue van and a lady in distress one afternoon on a side road on the west coast, stop and say hello!—*B.M., Pacifica, California* O┼▪

SHOWTIME FOR SUZETTE

I have been an avid reader of your magazine for years, I can't believe I finally have a story to write about. I have a passion for exotic dancers. I love to watch them dance and strip. Lap dancers are my favorite. My girlfriend knows about this and dances for me at home. She is quite attractive, with a fine body: small and firm breasts, flat stomach, nice hips. Her tight, bouncy butt is probably her best feature.

Until recently I was her only audience, although her home dance routines are excellent. She seems to take naturally to the art of stripping. When we took a trip to Baltimore where there are a lot of bars that feature exotic dancers, I talked her into going into one of the bars with me. She was reluctant at first, but I told her she could just watch the other dancers and maybe pick up a few pointers.

When we got ready to go to the bar, she wore one of her stripping outfits from home. It included black lace thong panties, thigh-high stockings, a white lace bra under a lace top that is quite transparent and a black spandex miniskirt. She looked great. You could see her dark nipples through the lace top and when she sat down her skirt rode up to show a lot of thigh. If she spread her legs a little you caught a glimpse of her panty-covered pussy. I told her sincerely I was sure she would probably look better than most of the dancers, but she didn't believe me. In fact, she got a little apprehensive, not really sure if she could go out in public dressed in such a revealing outfit. Little did she know that before the night was over I was hoping that she would be showing off all of her body.

I suggested we have a couple of drinks and a joint for courage, and we did. She always gets real horny after smoking so I knew everything would work out fine.

Walking through the hotel was an experience for her. She really turned a few heads, which helped build her self confidence. When she got into the cab her legs opened up and the cab driver got quite a view. We were on our way to a very enjoyable evening.

The bar we chose was a little more upscale than most, and it was crowded. It had a large stage in the center and there were smaller ones in dark corners for the lap dancers. When we entered the bar the featured dancer was just finishing her routine.

As she removed her G-string she rubbed her middle finger along her pussy lips and into her slit, then licked her fingers. The crowd really loved that and so did I. Turning to my girlfriend I said, "Now there's a new trick for you, Suzette." Suzette nodded, enthusiastically, and watched the dancer closely. She was really getting excited by the dance. And even with all the professional dancers around, a lot of guys were checking her out. That got her even more excited.

We found a seat at the bar and when she sat she gave everyone a good view of her crotch. I asked her how she felt about showing her pussy off. She said she wasn't sure. "What do you think about everyone seeing my pussy?" she asked me. I told her I not only didn't mind but was hoping she'd go a little further, let everybody see all she had.

Suzette loves to fuck and suck cock but she was not sure she could strip in front of all those horny men. She protested that she was not attractive enough, I told her I would prove her wrong. I found the manager and told him I had a girl who wanted an audition, that she was a little nervous but wanted to try out. We walked over to her and I introduced him.

"Call me Jim," he said. "If you're nervous, come to my office and dance for me there." Suzette said she would only do that if I accompanied her. The manager said, "No problem." Then he asked if she knew what the men might want her to do.

Suzette said she had a pretty good idea, and that she understood there were rules about touching and stuff.

Jim said men would pay more if she let them touch her. "Some might want you to suck their cocks while you dance," he added.

Suzette said she wouldn't suck anyone's cock but mine. The manager said that was up to her. All this was quite an advance for Suzette—from not being sure about dancing in the nude to talking about sucking some strange guy's cock.

In his office, Jim put on some dance music. He and I sat in chairs in the middle of the room. It was show-time. Suzette danced around the room, slowly at first, and let her skirt ride up. As she danced over to Jim she pulled off her top. When she reached him, he stroked each of her breasts.

She pulled away from Jim and slipped off her skirt, leaning over to give us a full view of her ass. Now dancing only in her bra, panties and stockings she really got into it. I didn't know how far she would go but I soon found out. She danced over to the manager and asked, "Do you want the works, sweetie?" It was obvious to me Suzette had overcome a lot of her shyness.

"Give it your best shot," he panted. She unhooked the bra and it fell away. Then she placed his hands on her tits. He fondled each nipple. She bent closer so he could kiss her nipples. Then she pulled away and danced over to me. I ran my hand up her inner thighs and fondled her pussy. It was soaked. I asked her if she wanted to stop now.

"I'm doing fine," she said. "I'm not going to stop now!"

"Do whatever you want," I encouraged her. Suzette danced back to Jim and stood between his legs. She put her hand on his crotch and grabbed his prick through his jeans. Jim opened his belt and gave her better access to his cock. She sat in his lap and rubbed his prick all over her legs and pussy. Then she removed her panties. When she slipped them over her legs you could see just how wet her pussy was.

"Let us see how wet your pussy is," I asked her. She put Jim's hand right on her honey-pot. When she removed it she licked her cream off her fingers.

What a turn-on! She was really putting on a good show. Now Jim told her she could dance later in the evening, but first invited her to suck his cock. He wanted her to suck his cock!

Jim had said the right thing. He then got the blowjob of his life. Suzette knelt in front him and slurped his cock into her mouth. She licked and sucked it, then took it all down her throat. It did not take long for him to come, and she swallowed it all. As she dressed, he told her she could dance for him anytime.

We returned to our seats to await her turn, but that will be another letter.—*G.C., Kenosha, Wisconsin*

GETTING TO KNOW A NEW NEIGHBOR

In our six-year relationship my former girlfriend Louise and I have spoken of many fantasies. Some we fulfilled. Others will always remain just fantasies. Either way, we love sharing them.

One very hot fantasy was our all-time favorite, and it included another man—a threesome. The idea of watching Louise wrap her soft wet lips around a thick, long hard cock made us both extremely horny as well as creative. One night we had smoked a good joint and got pretty drunk. I lay down in our bedroom. Louise stayed in the living room to watch one of our favorite porn movies. (You guessed it, a threesome.) Later Louise came into the bedroom. I was stroking my hard cock. She liked to watch me jack off. She climbed in next to me and asked what I was thinking of. Well, I first told her of how horny I got just watching her get excited as we talked about our threesome fantasy, in which she fucked a man with a thick hard cock as I watched. Then I would lick all the juices from her well-fucked, ruby-lipped pussy. "His come too?" she asked. "Yes, everything from the lips to the deepest point of your sweet cunt," I answered. She kissed me gently, gave my hard tool a peck, ran her tongue over the crack of my ass and told me not to come until she got back. She wanted to finish the movie. She was wearing a sexy black G-string and a teddy I had bought for her. She loved to show it off. Moments later I heard her open the patio door, as we often do to cool off the apartment when there's a breeze. Then I heard a rustling of clothes. I assumed Louise was getting comfortable on the couch. But then I heard slurping noises and very soft moans of passion. Louise loves to play with a monster-size dildo as we watch our movies, so I thought nothing of it. The sound of the TV got louder, as did the moans. It all sounded like good hot sex. A half-hour later Louise turned off the TV and came to bed. She was naked and I felt a light film of sweat on her body. I was nearly asleep and my cock was soft now.

"I'm going to get your cock fat and hard," she said, "and then you're going to fuck me to an earth-shattering orgasm." She kissed me deeply, groaning passionately, and ground her honey-pot against my John Thomas. I realized then that she reeked of sex. Her lips were all swollen, as if she had just finished giving a well-hung stud a dedicated blowjob.

My cock stiffened. "Please eat my pussy," she begged. I spread her legs and dove into a very wet and puffy-lipped pussy surrounded by matted pubic hair. Her cunt was filled with come. I smelled and tasted another man's jism and his musky sweat.

So Louise had just finished fucking another man. But who? How? I loved it.

"Eat me," she cried again. I can't remember being that excited. Like a mad pussy hound I explored every crack and fold of her sweet cunny. "Oh yes," she shouted, "eat my pussy good." I swallowed every drop of fuck-juice in her quim. "Do you like my pussy? Do you love the taste?" she cried.

I growled deeply, grabbed her ass, rubbed the honey-pot all over my face. "I've never tasted your pussy like this. The taste and smell makes me hornier than I can ever remember. I love the taste of your pussy!" She came immediately. Her body shook as never before. Her screams of orgasm pierced the night. "Yes, oh yes. I'm coming," she cried. I played with her clit as my tongue made deep passes through her beautiful pussy.

Finally, she pushed me away. She could take no more. I rolled her over on her stomach and with one stroke easily thrust into her asshole the entire length of my very hard nine-inch cock. She arched her back and made the penetration even deeper. I fucked her with long leisurely strokes. "Your cock feels bigger than ever," she said. "Fuck me." She looked up at me over her shoulder as I lunged within her. "Why are you so horny?" she asked.

"The smell and taste of your sweet pussy does that to me," I told her, my voice husky with passion.

I didn't want to let her know I knew her secret. She reached back, grabbed her ass-cheeks and spread them even wider. I exploded with an orgasm surpassing all others I had ever had. I kissed her face and neck, telling her how much I loved her. We soon fell asleep.

The next morning while drinking my coffee on the balcony, I saw our newly moved-in next-door neighbor, also outside and reading his newspaper. His robe opened slightly to reveal a robust chest and a flat stomach. I introducing myself and he uncrossed his legs to shake my hand. That revealed his monster cock. I kept glancing at it as we spoke. It was at least ten inches long and thick as a Coke can. This, I realized, was the man and the prick that had deposited the load of jism that I had eaten out of Louise's pussy. The new neighbor made no attempt to hide his prick as we continued to make small talk. He leaned his head back to soak up the morning sunshine and his legs widened to show off a large pair of balls. He knew my eyes were fixed on his cock. He also knew I would be less embarrassed if he looked away. He was enjoying my curiosity.

My cock began to thicken as I pictured Louise's hot mouth trying to swallow his prong whole. I could almost see her lips and tongue massaging this mammoth cock. I fantasized her straddling his cock, and this made my prick peek out of my robe. I couldn't help but picture him fucking Louise doggie-style, thrusting deep inside her. My hand had now begun to stroke my own hardened tool. He looked up and asked, "What's on your mind, neighbor?"

I realized what I was doing and was embarrassed. I answered, "Women must love your cock, eh?"

"Yes, they do," he said. "They like it any way, from sucking it to my fucking them doggie-style."

I immediately came on myself.

"Damn," he said. "What can you be thinking of?"

"Well," I said, "I love the fact that you are fucking my girl-friend. We always fantasize about her and another man—hoping his cock looks like yours."

"Then you know?" he asked.

"Yes, I do," I said, "and when she came back to bed, I cleaned out her come-soaked pussy and swallowed every drop."

He looked surprised.

"Relax," I said. "I would like to keep this our secret."

"Fine, anything special you want me to do?"

"Yes," I said. "Fuck her good and deep and have her suck every inch of your cock. Fuck her in every position, and come in her doggie-style."

"You got it," he said.

"When the time comes," I said, "I would like to have a three-some with you and Louise."

"Sure," he said. "We would have a great time."

"So, tonight, same time?" I asked.

Just then I heard the shower going, and went to join Louise. I knew the evening would be fantastic because, knowing I'd be watching, he had promised to fuck her well.

That evening I tried to replay the night before. This time I crept to the living room and watched my new partner in fantasy. I loved the whole thing. I came all over the curtains, watching them fuck in every position. His handsome cock was like a giant piston as he thrust deep in Louise's cunt. I have never enjoyed sex or fantasy so much. I rushed back to bed just as they both or-gasmed. Again she ran to me, spread her ass-cheeks and sat on my face.

"Eat me. Lick my hot pussy," she cried. Again I swallowed her come and his. It was fantastic. My orgasms were so powerful I almost fainted. He certainly filled her up with his seed.

Louise and her not-so-secret lover have repeated this hot and nasty sex session about fifteen times now. I know she wants to tell me, but deep down she realizes I know. For now, things are too good to blow her cover.

Sometimes I watch through the cracks. Other times I lie in bed and listen to their cries of passion, always waiting for my turn in the fantasy. Soon I will share with you our threesomes. — *A.B., Fort Lauderdale, Florida* ⚬┼▪

Boy Meets Boy

CHICAGO COPPERS DISPLAY IRON-HARD RODS IN STEELTOWN, USA

I'm writing this letter to let you know about an amazing event that I experienced, and which I am finding impossible to forget.

Alex and I have been partners for about seven years. Not sexual partners, squad partners—we're cops. We both work the juvenile section of our police department.

Last month Alex and I went to a convention in Pittsburgh for five days. We spent the first night there checking out the town and doing some drinking. The next day we had to sit in seminars all day long, and by the time evening came we were ready to let loose again. We went to our room and cleaned up, and then we went out to dinner. After that, not wanting to spend a lot of money, we picked up a couple of fuck magazines and went back to the room. First thing I did was take a shit, and while I was in the bathroom I decided to wash my face, using one of the hotel washcloths. When I came out of the bathroom, Alex was lying naked on his bed reading one of the magazines we had picked up.

We've been to these conventions before, and we've learned a lot about each other. After being partners for as long as we have, you know so much about the other guy you don't even think about it. I probably know as much about Alex's personal habits as his wife—that's how long we've been together.

I grabbed one of the other magazines and lay on my bed, going through and looking at the great-looking cunts which were plastered on every page. After a while, I looked over at Alex. His prick was starting to grow out of the dark pubic hair which covered his balls and cock. Alex saw I was looking and said, "Man, I'm horny."

"Me, too," I said. "But don't forget, we promised our wives we would not fool around with any women on this trip."

Alex said that still did not stop him from being horny. As we lay on the two beds, I noticed that every once in a while Alex would pull on his cock, making it grow even larger than it was before.

Now, reading the magazines and watching Alex pull on his prick was about all it took for my own prick to start getting hard. Alex kept reading and pulling his cock when all of a sudden he said to me, "Hey, read this letter," and he passed the magazine to me. The letter was about two gay men and how they liked to suck each other off. After I read the letter, Alex asked if I had ever done anything with a guy. I told him that once, when I was in the army, this guy and I fooled around and jacked each other off. Alex then said that once, when he was in college, he and another guy on the football team sucked each other off.

"Get the fuck out of here," I said. "You, king dick of the Ninth Precinct, have sucked cock?"

"What did I tell you, man. Yes, I sucked a dick."

"What was it like? I mean, what did it taste like?"

"I don't even remember, brotherman. It was a long time ago. I barely even remember doing it. It's more like I remember remembering doing it. You know what I mean?"

"No."

"Well . . . ah hell, forget it. What do you remember about jacking another man off?"

I told him that it was a lot of fun at the time. Alex and I kept talking, and soon the conversation turned to the things we did with our wives. The longer we talked, the harder our cocks grew. Alex's prick had a drop of pre-come hanging off the tip which looked like a pearl in the light. I told Alex how one night, when my wife and I were having sex, she was in a silly mood and after she sucked my cock she came up and kissed me, squirting the last few drops of my own come into my mouth. Alex, at hearing this, reached over and took hold of my prick and started rubbing it back and forth.

"Alex," I said, "we have been through so many things together, if you're interested, we can try something together."

When Alex heard this, he moved over to my bed and placed his head on my thigh. When he saw that I was receptive, he moved around on the bed so that his prick was just an inch away from my mouth. I watched in amazement as Alex moved his own head and in one quick movement caught the head of my cock in his lips and sucked with just a slight amount of wetness covering my prick. After a minute, Alex's saliva covered that entire length of my cock. As Alex worked on my cock, I pushed my tongue out and took a drop of pre-come from the head of his prick. It was not salty or bitter, just sticky. Then I moved my own head and let the head of his prick slide into my mouth. The warmth of his prick was a surprise to me, and the soft skin felt very good in my mouth.

I sucked on Alex's hard prick for a while, then let it slip from my lips and took one of his balls into my mouth. After sucking on his balls, I slipped my tongue to the base of his prick.

"Please take my cock back into your mouth," Alex implored me.

As I let his prick reenter my mouth, Alex let mine slip from his mouth and yelled that he was going to shoot a load, begging me not to stop. I felt Alex's prick grow in size, and then I felt it start to pulsate between my lips. All at once, Alex grabbed the back of my head and rammed his prick all the way to the back of my throat. Alex moaned a loud moan as shot after shot of his warm come splashed down my throat. I felt like I was in Paris or Budapest or some other place I've never been, but I was happy to be there. Feeling that gusher go off in your own mouth and knowing that it is due to your own ministrations, is the most amazing experience in the world.

After Alex was finished coming and I had licked his prick clean, Alex asked me to stand up next to the bed. When I was standing, Alex got on the floor and knelt between my legs, reaching a hand around my ass and pulling my cock deep into his mouth. Alex then started to push and pull on my ass, which caused me to fuck his mouth. I knew that at this pace I was going to come in no time at all. As Alex kept sucking and licking the head of my prick, my legs started to shake and Alex had to hold me up.

First gradually and then quickly, I felt my load of come start at my toes and move through my body. When I warned Alex that my come was on the way, he pulled me closer to him. Faster and faster his head moved. Then my come came rushing up from my balls, through my cock and onto Alex's tongue. Load after load shot out of me and into Alex's mouth. After he finished swallowing every last drop, we fell together on the bed and rested.

After that, the rest of the trip was spent in our room finding out all we could about each other. — *F.W., Chicago, Illinois* ○┼▬

LITTLE GUY FEELS STRONG WHEN HE FEELS BIG GUY'S COCK BEHIND HIM

My story starts about two days after my wife left me for, in her words, a "real man." To put it plainly, this guy is six-foot-two, weighs one hundred ninety pounds and, to hear my wife tell it, is hung like a horse.

I am a rather small man—five-foot-eight, a hundred and thirty—and I have a very small cock. But when we married we were both virgins, and for a couple of years my wife was satisfied—probably because she didn't know what she was missing. Then she met Arnold at work, and they had an affair. Soon she told me to hit the road because she had found a real man that could fuck like a wild man.

Two nights later I was sitting at a bar trying to drink my problems away. This club is next door to a large motel and truck stop. I picked this spot because it has lots of truckers who come in to drink, and I thought that I might feel more manly being around these guys.

After a while, a trucker sat down beside me at the bar. He was a large man with a beard and a rather large beer belly. His voice was very deep and his eyes had a rather vacuous look in them. He was dressed in tight pants and a T-shirt. His arms were very muscular and hairy. He also had a bulge in his pants that no one could help noticing. But at that time, I had no interest in other men's cocks, only the lack of mine.

We started talking and doing some serious drinking. After some drinks I was getting pretty drunk and started telling him my troubles. He was a good listener and told me that he felt bad for me.

Well, around two in the morning, the bar gave last call, and I was drunk as hell. My new friend, Gene, asked me where I lived. I told him across town. He said he had a room at the motel and that, since I was too drunk to drive, I should stay there the night.

We left my car in the bar parking lot and walked the short distance to the motel.

His room was small but clean. Also, it only had one bed, but he told me not to worry, we would be fine.

Well, I hardly remember getting undressed and into bed.

I don't know how long I slept, but something woke me up. I was still a little drunk and had a hard time remembering where I was, but knew someone was in bed with me, because there was a large hand rubbing my ass and a great mass of hair against the back of my neck. The face behind the hair was licking and biting my neck.

I could feel the hand going inside of my underwear and then a large finger sliding up and down the crack of my ass.

Suddenly I remembered where I was and whose hand it was. What a crazy night, I thought.

Finally, I asked Gene just exactly what he thought he was doing.

"You feel just like a girl," was all he said.

At first I thought I was with a crazy man, but then I thought about it and it made perfect sense. Except for the fact I don't have tits and a pussy, I am like a girl. I barely have any hair on my body, and my skin is soft and smooth like a girl's. Gene said that my ass was so round and firm that he couldn't help himself. It felt faintly intriguing to be attractive to someone, even though the someone in question was kind of like that big hulk of a man in *Moby Dick.* I thought I might as well relax and enjoy the attention.

Then Gene started removing my underwear, rubbing his hands and then his legs all over my fine little behind. All the while he was still nibbling my neck. It tickled, especially with that beard.

Needless to say, I was apprehensive, but my life had taken such a strange turn that anything new is welcome.

Gene then lifted my top leg and started sliding a very large dick between the cheeks of my ass. Then, still nibbling my neck, he reached a hand around and started tweaking my nipples.

I don't know what happened, but suddenly I was very turned on. Like I said, it was nice to feel attractive to another person after feeling inadequate for so long. I had heard how much pain is felt the first time someone gets fucked up the ass, but I needed the human contact. I then relaxed and started moving my ass against that great cock. Gene asked me if this meant that I wanted to fuck. In a very small, feminine voice that surprised me, I said yes.

With that, Gene got up and went into the bathroom. When he came back he left the bathroom light on and the door about half open. As he walked back to the bed, I could see him clearly, completely nude, for the first time. That is when I realized I was in for a wild night. Gene was every inch of six feet four inches tall with very wide shoulders and a massive chest. His legs looked like two oak trees, very thick and muscular. His whole body, including his shoulders and back, was covered with thick, black hair. And between his legs was the biggest, thickest dick I have ever seen, and that's not counting the two huge balls that hung beneath his ass.

He was standing next to the bed, and suddenly I had a very strong urge to touch him. I slid across the bed and very softly caressed his balls. Then I ran my hand up and down that beautiful cock. It wasn't all the way hard yet, but it was already eight inches long and as big around as my fist.

Gene then put his hand behind my head and pulled my face to his nuts. At first I only let them rub against my face. Gene asked me to lick and suck them. I slowly ran my tongue over and around each nut. I found that they tasted great, all sweaty and salty, so I took one in my mouth. It filled my entire mouth, and I tried hard not to bite him. The smell of him intoxicated me (even more than I already was) and I felt like I was on LSD.

After I licked and sucked both nuts, Gene moved me over on the bed and lay down beside me. In a gruff voice that I found made me weak and very ready to love him, he implored me to suck his dick. I had never done this before, but being a man I knew what would feel good. I slowly ran my tongue around the head of his dick, letting my saliva run down the shaft and onto his legs and balls. I then took the shaft into my mouth and started slowly swallowing that monster an inch at a time until I had about half of it in my mouth.

When I couldn't take anymore, I started sliding my mouth up and down very slowly, being careful not to let my teeth hurt him. Then I started going faster and, to my surprise, taking more and more dick down my throat. I wasn't even gagging. Gene started moaning and bucking his hips. I knew he was going to come, so I increased the speed and just kept swallowing dick. At last Gene grabbed me behind the head and pulled my head down real hard. I could feel the head of his dick at the back of my throat, his balls slapping me in the face and gobs and gobs of come squirting down my throat. I lay very still and swallowed all of his love jism that I could.

He shot off for a minute or so, and I felt like his cock was filling up my entire skull. After he was all done, I savored his dick as it went soft in my mouth.

We both fell asleep that way, with my face between his legs.

Later I was woken up by Gene pulling me up in the bed. He started kissing me on the mouth and I responded by kissing him back. He gave me a real hard French kiss, and then he spread my legs. He then started nibbling and sucking my neck, working his way down my front, covering my tits, belly, thighs and ass-cheeks with warm, wet kisses. This got me really turned on. He then put two pillows under my ass and spread my legs wide apart. He then produced a jar of K-Y jelly and started rubbing it on his big cock and putting some on my asshole. I knew then that it was going to happen, that in a few moments that big dick would be up my ass and I would be in for the biggest new experience of my life since I was born. I was excited. I had made up my mind that this would be my life from now on.

Gene started rubbing the head of his dick around the edges of my anus. Then I felt the head enter me. The head of his dick was so big and my ass was so tight that it was a difficult thing to pull off. But there was no turning back. As Gene stared passionately into my eyes and I stared back, I thought of all the women who would have killed to be in my position.

Gene then started slowly putting more and more dick up me until I didn't think I could take any more. In the woman's voice I had developed, I suggested that maybe that was enough. But Gene said that I was going to be his woman completely. With one huge thrust of his large body, he drove that whole ten and a half inches all the way up my ass. I was screaming with ecstasy, and Gene answered my cries of passion by saying, over and over again, "Oh, yeah. Oh, yeah. Oh, yeah."

Gene lay still until his cock settled in my ass, and then he started slowly fucking me.

Then the magic started. This ass-fucking I was taking started to feel better than anything I had ever done before. So good, in fact, that I started moving under Gene as he would pull his cock out until the head was barely in and then slam it back in, up to the nuts. This went on for a very long time. Then Gene started moving faster and faster, moaning loudly, those huge nuts slapping me in the ass. Then with a mighty thrust, he filled my ass with sweet come.

The next morning, he woke me up by putting that big thing back up my ass again. This time was even better because I had experienced it before.

When I went into the bathroom to shower, I looked in a full-length mirror on the bathroom wall. I looked like hell. I had hickeys all over me and large, dark circles under my eyes. But I felt great. Gene and I parted company promising to see each other often, which we have.

That night I realized I loved this kind of sex, so I decided to do all I could to become a woman—short of surgery. Since then I have started taking female hormones, had all the hair removed from my face and body and let my hair grow down to my butt. I wear clothes that show off my long legs and round, feminine hips. I now have more boyfriends than I can count. I still pick up men at bars and, when possible, I ride up and down the interstate with the top down on my car, trying to attract truckers. I also stop at rest stops and truck stops and fuck these great guys. Most of them already know I have a very small dick between my great legs, but some of them have had their dicks sucked by me and not known that I am a man.

None of them would have been pissed off, mind you, because I give the best head on the East Coast.—*Name and address withheld*   O+▪

JACK-OFF BUDDY HELPS OUT A FRIEND IN NEED

The following events happened over twenty years ago. This is the first time I've told anyone. While you're reading, please remember that truth is sometimes stranger than fiction.

During our senior year in high school, when we were both eighteen, Allen and I were neighbors and best friends. I spent a lot of time at his house after school because both of his parents worked. He had his own room and he had an older sister with fabulously large breasts who was in the habit of going braless. In time, we became jerk-off buddies, using Allen's large collection of magazines.

We'd sit side by side on the edge of Allen's bed with the door locked as we stroked our erect cocks while reading his latest magazines. Allen often reminded me that he admired my cock because it was so large. I had a very thick, six-inch circumcised cock with a large head. Allen had a thin cock barely five inches long with a small head partially covered by his foreskin. What he lacked in cock size, Allen made up for with a pair of enormous, low-hanging balls. He also shot off huge loads of come—about two tablespoons compared with my one teaspoon. I enjoyed watching Allen fill up his cupped left hand with huge loads of hot jism. One time, when I had trouble shooting off, Allen rubbed a handful of his hot come on my cockhead until I shot one of my best loads ever. I really enjoyed the feel of his hot sperm and slippery hand on my cock. Allen realized how much his hot jism turned me on because I practically passed out afterwards.

The next week, Allen came up with yet another way to jerk off. We both sat on his bed facing each other with our legs spread wide. Allen put his thighs over mine and we moved closer until we were cockhead to cockhead, sitting on top of an old towel. We'd shoot our hot sperm all over each other's organ. Allen always came first, shooting gobs of gooey sperm all over my cock, pubic hair and balls. As his hot spunk covered my organ and dripped down to the towel, I'd shoot my load—aiming at the huge balls hanging low between Allen's legs. Because I had a longer cock, I was practically touching Allen's balls when I shot off. I always hit my target.

Allen was a jerk-off expert. He taught me to wait for at least three days so I'd shoot a bigger load, to take a hot bath so my nuts would hang down like his, to fondle my balls before I shot off and to use a greasy finger to play with my asshole. In early summer I managed to get poison ivy on both of my hands and one of my arms. I had to wear cotton gloves on my hands to keep it from spreading. After about a week, I was extremely horny, but I wouldn't touch my cock with my hands and I couldn't jerk off with my gloves on. When I told Allen about my problem, he told me to come over on Saturday night and he'd help.

On Saturday night, Allen locked the door to his room and told me I had to smoke hash with him and get high. He dimmed the lights, told me to strip and complimented me on my large penis, as he usually did. I was so horny that my cock had juices dripping out of it. Allen told me to kneel on the floor and put my head and shoulders down on a pillow. I got into position with my ass up in the air as Allen lubricated his hands and began fondling my cock and dangling balls. My cock snapped to attention as he began greasing my asshole. This was the highlight of my life: I was extremely high and my best friend was handling my swollen, throbbing genitals. Allen stretched my asshole with one finger and then with two until I was fully relaxed. Then he put his thin cockhead against my asshole and very slowly penetrated my ass. When his rod was fully inserted, I could feel his warm thighs against my hips, and then he began stroking my greased cock. In this position, gravity caused my balls to hang toward the head of my cock so that he could stroke my cock and fondle my nuts at the same time.

Allen moved slowly in my ass—in deep, then back out. I never would have believed a real cock would feel so good in my ass-hole. His hips rocked back and forth and his heavy nuts bounced against me. He began to moan, and then he shot a huge load of come inside me. As he blew thick wads of jism in my asshole, I felt a pressure build up in my balls. They drew closer to my body and I knew I was going to shoot an extra big load of come. When I exploded, the first spurt rocketed out and splashed against the bottom of my chin. Allen slowly milked my cock and balls, giv-ing me sufficient time to shoot six hot wads of jiz on the floor. It was the best come of my life, and the largest load I'd ever shot.

For the next three weeks Allen serviced me every two or three days. When the poison-ivy rash completely healed, I paid Allen back by helping him jerk off at least once a week for the entire summer. I enjoyed cupping his long, heavy balls in my left hand as I reamed his asshole with my left thumb. With Allen facing away from me, I'd reach around his hips with my right hand to slide his foreskin back and forth over his glans until he shot his usual huge load of come. Allen would tell me when he was going to come so I could quickly get my left hand in position to catch his hot load. I'd rub his hot jism on my cock until I shot off, too. By the end of the summer I'd become a jerk-off expert. I could get Allen so hot that he'd shoot his first wad of come almost three feet—we had a contest and I measured it.

Today, just thinking about that summer makes my "trouser snake," now very thick and seven inches long, crawl down my leg and protrude out of my shorts. Honey is oozing out of the slit and my cockhead is throbbing near the bursting point as the poison-ivy summer adventure replays itself in my mental VCR. What a summer that was.—*Name and address withheld* ⚷▬

IT ALL HAS TO START SOMEWHERE, AND IT MIGHT AS WELL BE UP THE BUTT

Let me come right out and say it: Being bisexual is the best of both worlds. I have been married for almost twenty years. The two finest sexual things that I can think of are putting my cock in my wife's sweet, juicy pussy and wrapping my lips around a hard, thick, well-shaped penis.

My wife loves for me to tell her about the experiences of my late teens that helped me discover my bisexuality and my love for cocksucking.

One of my close friends was a stocky, hard-muscled boy who loved to have his cock sucked but would never suck anyone else. The strange part about Chip was, he felt that if you put a dick in his mouth it would make him queer, but he had no problem receiving a blowjob. Gradually he loosened up and began taking it up the ass. This is the story of how I took his virgin ass.

A week after we graduated from high school, we were fooling around in Chip's bedroom when I asked him if I could suck him off.

"Gladly," he said. "A hole's a hole, and I'm horny as hell."

"Great," I said, "thanks a bunch."

I lightly licked the head of Chip's cock and it twitched. I had sucked cock before, and I moaned in anticipation of that thing growing ever bigger. First it was a little small in my mouth, but soon it grew to where it perfectly filled my lips.

Wrapping my thumb and forefinger around the base, I sucked on the top third of his cock while stroking the rest with my fingers. Chip put his hands on the back of my neck and started fucking my face. Soon I could feel his dick going down my throat as if my mouth was one big pussy.

"I'm coming," Chip screamed, and I was in heaven. When that warm juice started pulsing down my throat, I nearly came in my pants.

When Chip was done, I looked up at him and said, "My turn, right?"

"If you think I'm gonna suck your cock, my man, you've got another thing coming."

"Okay, let me cornhole you, then."

"You want to stick your dick up my ass?" he asked.

"Indeed I do," I assured him.

"Okeydoke."

First thing I did was stick my tongue up Chip's ass, getting it all nice and lubed. Then I spit in my hand and rubbed it all over my cock. He was very receptive and I shot right inside. My cock was rock-hard, and his ass was so nice and tight that I dropped my load after only a few strokes. —*Name and address withheld* ⚬┼ ■

IF YOU CAN'T BE WITH THE ONE YOU LOVE,
LOVE THE ONE YOU'RE WITH

Sex with a man had never crossed my mind. When I was single and chasing women, I had been given a few blowjobs by a couple of my male married friends. I could never really understand why they would want to give head to a man when they were happily married, but I didn't argue. And now that I'm married, I have no need for sex with a man.

One night last week, however, while my wife was away, I went out drinking with an old friend of mine. When we returned to my home, I took him to my guest house. Since we were both drunk, we fell asleep in the guest-house bed.

In the middle of the night, still half asleep, I was stroking my dick to hardness. Something didn't feel right, however, and when I opened my eyes and looked down, I realized that it was not my own dick I was stroking but my friend's. He opened his eyes and we stared at each other in bewilderment. Then we laughed out loud. The warmth and texture of my friend's growing cock in my hand had my cock as hard as a rock.

Figuring he ought to return the favor, he grabbed my cock and started stroking it like I was stroking his. It had been a long time since another man had touched my cock, and I must say that it was refreshing, because he knew what he was doing.

Without hesitation, I leaned over to start an adventure I will never forget. I viewed the object in hand as my own. I lowered my lips around his shaft as far as my mouth would allow, closing my lips around him just tight enough to have the proper pressure.

Then I slowly slid my lips up and down the shaft, feeling the texture of the skin as it slid over the inner hardness. The swelling veins really turned me on. I moved ever so gently over the outer skin with my lips, up and down, up and down.

I stopped occasionally to run my tongue along the shaft to the head of his cock and around the bottom side of his helmet. Then I returned to my up-and-down movements on his stiffening rod. As I went up and down his cock, I could feel his thighs and butt tighten, and then his nectar erupted and shot down my throat. It was great—warm and sweet. His globs were so big that I felt like I was eating raw oysters.

As I cleaned off the subsiding shaft, I realized that my friend was still stroking me off. My rod had never been so hard. With a few more strokes of his hand I exploded like I never had before.

I have come to the conclusion that this form of masturbation can only be accomplished by another man. I still prefer women and so does my friend. We only did it that one time, and then he moved away. But I'd like him to come visit me.—*M.D., Big Sur, California* ○━━■

THE BASKETBALL ON TV CAN'T MATCH THE MAJOR LEAGUE BALLING IN THE BEDROOM

It was a long week. When I got home on Friday, I just wanted to take a shower and relax. My wife was waiting for me at the door. After a long kiss, she told me that my friend Grant had called to remind me that he was coming over to watch the basketball game like we had planned a week before. Fuck, I thought to myself. I forgot all about that.

Just after she told me this, I jumped into the shower so I could be out before Grant got there. I wasn't in the shower fifteen minutes when, out the corner of my eye, I caught a glimpse of Grant using the toilet. My wife must be in the front bathroom, I thought to myself. I was trying to figure out why he'd come all the way to the back of the house just to take a leak.

I thought nothing more of it and continued to wash myself. When Grant finished, I looked out the curtain to see if he was leaving, and to my surprise he was watching me with his cock in his hand.

"What the hell are you doing, you crazy loon?"

He didn't say a word. He just winked at me and started taking off all his clothes. In ten seconds flat he was completely nude. I shut the shower door and kept showering. Grant opened the door and joined me. At first I didn't know what to think as he began to soap up my body, working his way down to my cock. He looked up at me to see if I would stop him. Not sure why, I let him continue. He took my dick in his hand, stroking it with expertise. It was a nice surprise, I have to admit.

When he rinsed all the soap off my cock, he completely astonished me. He took my nine-inch member into his mouth all the way down to the base. He sucked like I have never been sucked before (or since, male or female). He hit all the right spots, and then he started licking my balls, sucking them each into his mouth. My eyes were closed, and when I opened them I saw that my wife was watching him suck me.

Not only was she watching, but she was buck naked, rubbing her pink clit. Pussy juice was running down her fingers. She licked the juices off. Grant, who had resumed sucking my shaft, let it pop out and suggested that we move to the bed. She ran out before he saw her and hid outside the bedroom door so she could hear and watch what was happening. Grant and I climbed on the bed and no more words were said. He grabbed his dick like he wanted me to give him a blowjob. His back was to the door behind which Angela hid. I looked at her through the crack in the door. She knew what he wanted and she gave me her look of approval.

She and I had, at one time, talked about a fantasy we both shared, and this was it! We share many fantasies, but we always felt that this one was going to come true for us. Staring at his seven inches of thick cock, I became so horny I didn't waste any time. I felt his hard cock hit the back of my throat and I was able to gently kiss his balls with my lips. I sucked so hard that pre-come oozed into my mouth. Licking every inch, I sucked up and down, licking his balls and sucking his head. He moaned with pleasure. I found myself actually enjoying the idea of sucking dick, like my wife does to me. A few minutes passed. I looked up at him and told him I wanted it in my ass.

"I want to feel what my wife feels during anal sex," I explained.

He said, "Rock and roll."

I rolled onto my stomach and he began spreading my cheeks apart. I felt his finger go inside me. The feeling was unreal! After only a few seconds, I was ready and relaxed. I gave him a tube of K-Y jelly from my wife's drawer and told him to be easy because this was a first-time thing for me and my virgin ass would need it slow. I could feel the head of his cock slowly enter my ass. He let it sit for a few seconds, then with long, steady, slow strokes, his cock was bottoming out in my ass. All the movement made his balls slap against mine. I was so turned on that I wanted it harder and faster.

About this time, my wife had apparently had enough, and she joined us on the bed.

"You guys just keep on going. I'm going to bring myself off just watching you."

My wife sprawled out next to us and started diddling her clit. She looked great as her cunt juice started dripping out of her sex. She could see how much I was enjoying getting fucked. It felt just like she had described it while I reamed her asshole.

Words, however, are not enough. Every thrust of his cock made my cock twitch. I could see him fucking me in the mirrored closet doors, my ass up in the air and his hard cock ramming inside me. I found myself yelling for him to come in my ass.

"I want your hot load deep in my asshole." With the next thrust I could feel his hot goo—five spurts deep in my ass.

My wife was so hot and wet, she had covered her rock-hard nipples with her own pussy juice. She screamed out, "I want both of you."

Grant pulled out of me and stuck his face in Angela's wet cunt. She teased him with orgasms and began lifting her legs around his head. I sucked her rock-hard nipples as she grabbed my rock-hard dick. She knew I wanted to come inside of her. She lay me on my back and straddled my waist, taking my rod deep in her wet cunt. Every thrust made juice run down my balls.

Grant, whose dick was ready to go again, moved toward Angela and eased his throbbing cock into her mouth. My wife looked so sexy, bouncing up and down on my pole as another pole completely filled her mouth. I started bucking wildly, and within seconds I was depositing my seed deep into my wife's abdomen.

She was yelling like a banshee, popping up and down on my cock so wildly that I feared she would hit her head on the ceiling.

When I was spent, she yelled, "Okay, Grant, add your two cents worth."

Getting behind my wife, he spread her cheeks apart and, with one smooth stroke, slid easily inside her.

"Oh, I thought you only did assholes," my wife said.

"Is that where you want it?" Grant asked her.

"You know it, baby."

So fast you couldn't even see it, Grant moved from one sweet hole to the other, and my wife let out an ecstatic "Ohhhh!"

The look on her face almost made me lose my load again.

"Have you got more, my darling?"

"I think so," I said.

With that, she leaned toward me and took me in her mouth.

"Yes," I whimpered, "oh, God, yes."

Right about this time, Grant's dick started throbbing, and I could tell by the look on his face that he was coming.

Then I could tell by my wife's muffled moans that she was coming, and I figured I better get on the ball.

Pumping my dick into her mouth, I released a load to end all loads. There was come everywhere—up my honey's butt, in her mouth and dribbling down her legs.

I was paralyzed. Angela crawled up to me and we shared my come in a passionate kiss. Then we hugged.

After we were all rested, Grant said he had to go.

"What about the game?" I asked.

"That's the only game I was interested in."

I looked at my wife. "Did you guys plan this?" I asked her.

"Who, us?" she asked innocently, and then the two of them burst out laughing.

After Grant left, the two of us lay together in bliss.

That was the night that our main fantasy came true. I felt what it would be like to be a woman.—*W.P., Reno, Nevada* ○┼▪

SURPRISE VISIT LEADS TO SURPRISE ENCOUNTER WITH SURPRISE GUEST

It was late Friday afternoon and I was driving to my condo. The music on the radio was interrupted by a warning of severe winds and thunderstorms. My girlfriend was away visiting her parents, so I wasn't looking forward to an exciting weekend. I stopped by a liquor store on the way home.

As I was putting my things away the telephone rang. It was a friend of mine, but one that I don't really know very well and who shall remain nameless. We met at the Y and we've played tennis several times and had drinks afterward. He's about my age, twenty-eight, tall, slim and a very competitive athlete. He called to arrange a tennis match for Sunday, then he asked about my plans for the evening. I told him that, because of the approaching storm, I expected to stay at home. Boldly, he asked if he could come over for a drink.

With nothing better to do, I said, "Sure, come on."

I pulled off my coat and tie, drank a beer and relaxed watching the news. At about seven o'clock I decided to take a shower. While I was undressing, the doorbell rang. I put on a robe and let the guy in. I told him I was about to shower, showed him the bar and asked him to make us drinks. I would only be a few minutes. When I stepped dripping from the shower, he was standing in the doorway. He handed me my drink. I took a big swallow and dried off. He followed me into the bedroom and examined some books as I put on running shorts. "I see you have a collection of classic porn novels, " he said.

"Yeah," I replied. "And some tapes also. Want to take a look at some?" "Sure," he said.

The storm was getting much worse as we went into the living room. Our glasses were empty so I mixed another round. I started the tape and sprawled on the couch. He sat at the other end.

The opening scene was of a male stripper at a girl's party. He danced around and peeled off his clothes to the encouragement of the women. He was soon down to just a pouch and that was soon removed, leaving the guy naked, displaying the beginning of a huge erection. It must have been eleven inches. "Where do they find these guys?" I said aloud. "Mine is only about eight inches."

"I'm sure yours is fine," my guest said.

The girls undressed and attacked the young man. They pulled him to the floor and were all over him. One sucked on his monster as another sat on his face. Then another rode him like a bucking bronco as the others cheered. The guy plugged another girl from the rear. Then two girls were licking his tool. The action was hot, and I was getting hot. My dick was twitching. I glanced over at Rick (oops!) and saw that he had his hands covering his crotch.

On the screen more guys had arrived at the party and the orgy really got going. The storm was getting much worse. I suggested to Rick that he stay and eat with me because of the weather. Also, we were getting too drunk for either of us to drive. He accepted. I asked him to fix drinks while I took a casserole from the fridge. My erection was very obvious when I stood up and so was his, but we'd both had enough to drink to eliminate our embarrassment.

I put the food in the oven, took my drink, and we sat back down to continue watching the movie. The couples paired off and

were screwing in every conceivable position. The girls were cli-
maxing and the boys were shooting off big loads of come. My
dick was throbbing. Rick was squirming and rubbing his cock
through his pants. Our glasses were soon empty again.

I got up, checked on the food and poured fresh drinks. I was
obviously getting pretty drunk. Rick wasn't too sober either. I
managed to serve supper on trays, and we ate while watching the
last part of the tape.

Suddenly there was a very bright lightning bolt, followed by a
loud clap of thunder. The lights flickered and went out. I found
and lit a candle. Rick turned to me and said, "Since we can't
watch the movie, tell me about your first sexual experience."

"Masturbation or the real thing?" I asked.

"Both," he replied.

"Well, one night, when I was eighteen, I was camping out with
a buddy. He began to beat his meat and so I tried it too. I'd never
done it before. When he saw my inexperience he offered to jerk
me off and I let him."

"You were eighteen when you first jerked off."

"Yep,"

"Wow."

"My first time with a girl," I continued, "was only a couple
months earlier. It was my eighteenth birthday and her parents
were out. She wouldn't let me put it in, that came later, but she
sucked me off. What about you?"

"I found a sex book in my dad's closet," replied Rick, and he
went on to tell how he showed it to a friend and they jerked each
other off.

Rick took my glass and fixed drinks. I was getting drowsy and
stretched out on the couch. Rick returned and sat down, placing
my feet in his lap. He rubbed my ankles as he told me how he
first fucked a girl while at a beach-house party. He moved my
feet against his stiff dick and ran his hands slightly up my legs.
"Have you ever had a guy suck you off?" he asked. His hand
moved farther up my leg.

I nodded.

"Did you enjoy it?"

"Sure," I murmured.

He placed his hand on my crotch and nervously asked, "Will
you let me blow you?" He grasped my cock. I was horny as hell.
I did not say no. He removed my shorts and exposed my raging
hard-on. Then he stood up and quickly undressed.

"God, what a dick," he said, as he leaned over me and began to rub my chest and stomach. He pinched and rubbed my nipples and then moved me around so that he could get between my legs. His breath was warm as he blew on my balls and gently massaged them with his hand. His other hand guided my prick to his lips and he licked around the head. Damn, it felt good. I was panting. He teased the full length with his tongue before sucking on the crown. I pushed his head down, hoping he'd get the message and take more into his mouth.

My hips were moving up and down, furiously fucking his face. Finally, he managed to take it all, his face buried in my pubic hair.

"I'm coming," I moaned. "Take it, eat it, drink it all, suck it all out."

My balls tightened and I shot my load deep down his throat. Rick kept on sucking until I became limp, then pulled away. I was about to pass out. Rick stood and pumped his cock, shooting big globs of come on my belly. I awoke late the next morning, naked, with a hard-on. Rick was sitting on the edge of the couch wearing only his briefs, gazing at me. "You feel like talking about what happened last night, or do you just want to forget it?" he asked. "I'm bisexual, as you now know, and I've wanted this to happen ever since I first saw you at the gym. You're probably confused right now."

"No, no, Rick. I'm fine."

Rick dressed, leaned over and patted my dick. "Hope to see you later, big boy. Don't forget our tennis match tomorrow," he said as he left.

I turned over and went back to sleep, trying to get over my hangover.—*A.S., Jekyll Island, Georgia* ◑▬

LOVING BOYS SPOIL THEMSELVES WITH SPARE ROD

I met Tony two months ago. He is nineteen, blond and cute. I get a hard-on just looking at his face, but with his loose-fitting clothes it was hard to tell what his body was like. We got to know each other after a couple of weeks, and I started to believe that he liked me. On Friday he asked me to come over after work to drink some beer in the hot sun. I put on my worn-out jean shorts, the ones with a few holes in the ass. I didn't wear a shirt.

When I got there he was washing his car. When he walked around the car to greet me, I was shocked to see his nearly naked body for the first time. He was awesome, standing there in his skimpy swim trunks. He got me a beer and started washing his car some more. Watching his tall, lean, muscular body scrub his car was giving me a hard-on. I started to help him dry the car off—he did the sides and I did the roof. He was squatting next to me by the door when he grabbed my ass and pushed me over, telling me to move. He kept drying, moving over towards me as I worked on the trunk.

When he stood up, he brushed his ass against my leg. Then I felt his finger through the holes in my shorts, feeling my ass. I grabbed his hard-on and looked him in the eyes. He smiled and so did I. He said we should go in the house and cool off. We sat on the couch and he turned to me and started rubbing my muscular chest and shoulders. I started feeling his awesome chest and smooth nipples. Suddenly we started kissing like crazy. Then Tony said, "Let's get naked."

We went into his bedroom, stripped and jumped into his bed. I felt his smooth ass-cheeks and almost came. He started feeling my ass and said he wanted a closer look. He crawled around so we were in a 69 position and took my thick seven-inch cock in his mouth.

I got between his legs and started sucking his long, eight-inch cock. It tasted great. His blond pubic hair and tight balls drove me over the edge. I started shooting my wad into his mouth. Almost instantly he blew his load into my mouth, and we sucked each other's pulsing cocks dry.

Then we went downstairs to drink some more beer. After a couple of beers, Tony wanted to take a shower with me. We hugged and kissed while getting wet. He said I was going to force the air out of him, I was hugging and squeezing him so hard. So I loosened up my embrace. We decided to wash each other. While he washed his hair, I did the rest.

It was great washing his chest and nipples, but when I washed his firm smooth buns I almost came. Then he turned around and I washed his blond pubic hairs and long hard cock and balls. Then I did my hair and Tony washed every place on my body, not missing anything. We got out and dried each other off, then back to his bed we went. It wasn't long before he had my cock down his throat and I had his down mine. I asked him if he'd ever fucked anybody up the ass before. He said no, and asked me the same. I told him he was my first taste of male meat.

"I wonder if it feels good," he mused. "Taking it up the ass, I mean."

I told him to get some lubricant, and when he came back he lay on his stomach, his muscular back and cute little buns making my cock rock-hard. I got down and started to lick between his ass-cheeks. He moaned as I licked his asshole. Then I got the lube and started rubbing it into his asshole and onto my cock. I rubbed my cock up and down his crack, then found his opening and started pushing.

After the head slid into his ass, I paused. He moaned as I worked my cock into his incredibly tight ass. I lay down on top of him, hooked my arms under his, grabbed his shoulders and started fucking him hard up the ass. He said it felt great and told me to go deeper. I tried to pick up the pace, but I blew my load up his ass after only five minutes of pumping.

He turned over and his come was all over the bed, his cock and his stomach. I licked him clean. Then we started kissing. It was great rubbing our sweaty chests together, trying to line my nipples up with his, while at the same time rubbing our cocks together. It wasn't long before we were rock-hard again.

We rolled over so that Tony was on top. He started licking his way down my chest and stomach to my belly button. He then took my cock and started to deep-throat it. I almost came again, but he pulled his mouth away just in time. He licked my balls, then grabbed my firm ass-cheeks. I spread and lifted my legs and he buried his face between my buns, licking my asshole. Then he grabbed the lube off the headboard and started greasing my asshole and his cock. He pushed my legs back and put a pillow under my ass. I took his cock and guided it in. He pushed the head of his cock in, then buried it in one push.

He started fucking my ass nice and slow at first, but soon he was pounding away. The sensation of having Tony's hot, smooth cock up my ass was so intense I started shooting my wad all over my chest and stomach. My asshole must have been contracting with each squirt, because Tony moaned louder and pounded my ass faster. Then I felt his cock coming deep up my ass. It was great.

Both of our assholes were sore the next day, so we resorted to blowing each other for the rest of the weekend. — *Name and address withheld.* O⊢▪

HAPPY WITH HIS GIRL BUT ALWAYS READY
FOR THE RIGHT GUY

I am a twenty-eight-year-old single male who used to consider himself strictly heterosexual. I realize now that during adolescence I was attracted to certain boys because of their looks, personalities and physical abilities.

I was involved in mutual masturbation sessions with a couple of neighborhood friends in high school, but that was when girls were the sole object of my desires and wet dreams.

In college I had a steady girlfriend; we fucked like rabbits for a year and I was devastated when she transferred to a school on the west coast. All through high school and college I seemed to attract the attention of gays, primarily because of my interest in dance and theater, but I ignored them and sought the company of the females in the drama department and elsewhere.

There was only one guy who really stuck out in my mind as someone for whom I felt more than the usual feelings I had about guys who were my friends. His name was Mark.

Mark and I met when we were seniors. He had transferred from another school. He was tall, dark and handsome — built like an Olympic swimmer.

We had summer jobs at a beach resort and shared a room in a cottage nearby. We would work until well after eleven in the evening, and we usually came home exhausted. I often had a date on my nights off and when I returned to the cottage Mark would be lying on the bed reading, usually just wearing his underpants. He would greet me with a hearty, "Well, did you get laid?"

My answer was "No" more often than it was "Yes." One night I staggered in so drunk that I tripped over the breakfast table and fell on the floor. Mark laughed and said, "We'd better put you to bed before you break the furniture."

Even drunk I realized that he was feeling me up as he removed my shirt, shoes and pants. It felt good. I didn't resist when he pulled off my briefs. He put me into my bed and turned off the lights. During the night I woke up to find that Mark had crawled in bed with me. His body was pressed against my back; his arm was draped over my waist and I could feel his hard cock against my buttocks.

I pretended to be asleep as he stroked my cock to its full size. I could feel his hot breath on the back of my neck. "Paul, Paul," he whispered in my ear. "Let me suck you off." I couldn't speak, but moaned and turned onto my back as an invitation for him to grant me some sexual release.

Mark caressed my torso from neck to crotch; he nibbled my nipples and tongued my navel, then sucked on my cockhead. It seemed like only a minute before I shot my load into his mouth. Drained, I drifted into sleep.

As we got out of bed in the morning Mark asked, "Are you upset about what happened last night? Want to talk about it?"

"I wanted it to happen," I said. "You must know that I'm attracted to you. What took you so long to make a move?"

"I was afraid of making you mad," he answered.

I was sitting naked on the side of the bed. "Come here a minute," I said.

He stood in front of me wearing only boxer shorts. Without hesitation I pulled his briefs down and fondled his dick and balls, making him hard as a bat. Then I pumped his cock until he spurted wads of come onto the floor.

We had sex fairly often after that. I finally gave him a blowjob as the summer ended and we parted ways.

I didn't have another gay experience until I met John years later.

We worked in different departments of the same large company and even though I had a steady girlfriend at the time, I was sexually attracted to him almost immediately. When I first saw him in the cafeteria, I couldn't take my eyes off him.

He was six feet tall, slim, black-haired, a very outdoors-type and masculine-looking guy. I finally met him when we were selected to attend a brief training course together in Toronto.

John picked me up the following Sunday morning. The drive was long and would have been boring except for the conversation. We talked of our education, work and interests and found we had much in common.

We checked into the hotel and as we unpacked, John suggested that we go swimming before supper. We grabbed our swimsuits and found we had the pool and dressing room to ourselves. John stripped and put on a tiny bikini. It was hard to keep from staring at his handsome body.

He had long swimmer's muscles without an ounce of fat. I swam fifteen laps but John swam about thirty without even tiring.

As we sat resting on the edge of the pool, the shape of his cock was clearly defined by the stretched fabric of his bikini, and I had an almost irresistible urge to reach out and touch it.

We swam a while longer and then went to the showers. Watching him soap his big cock made my dick swell. He noticed my staring and the effect it was having.

"Getting a hard-on, huh?" he said, amiably. "We'll have to take care of that later." I'm sure I blushed but I couldn't think of a word to say.

After a couple of drinks and a light supper in the grill, I suggested that we take in a movie. John said that he'd rather relax in the room and watch TV. We stripped to our underwear and stretched out on the beds. There was nothing of interest on the regular channels so we turned on an adult movie on pay-per-view.

It was one of those fun-in-the-sun films showing two sexy couples playing on the beach. The action got hotter when they moved into the nearby house.

They were soon naked and engaged in serious foreplay. John said that there was a glare on the screen from where he was lying and asked if he could move over with me.

"Sure," I replied. "And I'll turn off this lamp." John lay back on the pillow beside me. By this time the couples on the screen were engaged in some serious raw sex. One guy was getting a blowjob and the other was giving his girl a tongue lashing. Overwhelmed by the action on the screen and presence of the handsome, nearly naked man lying next to me, I began to get a throbbing, amazingly hard log in the crotch of my underpants.

I glanced over at John and saw that his shorts were poking up also. Shivers ran through my body when John's leg brushed against mine. "What's wrong?" he asked, "Are you cold? Let me warm you up."

His hand moved between my splayed legs and felt my firm cock. "Don't be embarrassed, I've got a hard-on, too. Here, do you want to feel it?"

He put my hand on his erection. "Don't try to tell me you've never had sex with a guy," he said. "You're too pretty and spry.

With all those guys wanting to fuck you, I know you must have given it a try. Did you like it?"

His fingers ran under my T-shirt and explored my chest. I trembled at his touch, but I didn't try to stop him. He became bolder and put his hand under the waistband of my shorts and gripped my dick.

God, it felt good. I moaned, "Yes, yes," and that was all the encouragement he needed. He pulled down my shorts and exposed my pulsating prick. John got up and removed his T-shirt and shorts.

His body was beautiful in the dim light. He leaned over and kissed the tip of my cock. "Get out of your clothes," he whispered pleadingly. I threw them aside and lay naked awaiting his next move. John spread my legs and sitting over me he pumped my rod with one hand and his own hard cock with the other. Leaning over, he rubbed our dicks together and scraped my chest and stomach with his fingernails.

My every nerve was on fire. "Now I'm going to suck you. You've been wanting me to, haven't you?" he whispered again, this time with more confidence in his voice.

It was a blowjob I'll never forget. He licked and nibbled on my shaft until it ached for release. He teased the knob with his tongue until I thought I'd go crazy, then stopped and began to lick and suck again. Finally he deep-throated me, burying his nose in my pubic hair as the big wad of my staff bulged his cheeks.

When I yelled that I was about to come, he wormed a long finger into my pliable asshole. My hot juice shot deep into his throat.

I was drained, of course, but he was raring to go. He crawled on top of me and straddled my chest. He held his dick and wiped the pre-come over my face. I refused to take it in my mouth. "Okay, then will you give me a handjob?" he asked.

I teased, tickled and stroked his cock until he tensed and squirted big globs of come, which he proceeded to smear all over my chest.

Sometime during the night he went back to his bed. I awoke when John turned on the shower. He walked out of the bathroom as I crawled naked out of bed. He stood there drying off, staring at me and grinning like he knew something I didn't. There was silence before he asked, "You didn't know I was gay, did you?"

"No," I replied. I honestly had no idea.

"Surprised?"

"Not really."

"Are you upset because we had sex?"

"No. I wanted it too, but I was afraid to let you know. I spotted you in the cafeteria several weeks before we met. Once in a while a guy attracts me the way you do."

I moved toward the bathroom but John stopped and embraced me. Our cocks rubbed together and he nuzzled my neck.

"We'll be together the rest of the week. I won't force you, but I can teach you a lot about gay sex if you'll allow me to," he said.

I was a willing student. Every night we eagerly stripped as soon as we were alone. We couldn't keep our hands off each other. The education was exciting. Our bodies joined in every possible way and position. John especially like being fucked in the ass, and I learned how to give an expert blowjob. I think we each came at least twice each night and were ready for more the next day.

The week was over too quickly. John and I see each other occasionally at work, where we continue to be flirtatious and sexy around each other in a very unassuming and subtle way.

For example, if I was bending over at the water fountain drinking water, and if no one was around, John would ease up to my backside and rub his tailored trousers against me, nudging me with a bulge I could feel between his legs.

One Friday afternoon, in a playful mood, I sent him an E-mail message on the computer system at work, asking him to meet me in the men's room, back stall, corner wall, for the treat of his life.

I sat on the toilet with my feet resting on the paper dispensers as John eased into the stall. Without a word being said, he whipped out his cock and let me suck him dry right there in the stale, dry atmosphere of the corporate world. I often wonder what would have happened if the CEO had been in the next stall, but luckily everyone had pretty much left for the day when we rendezvoused.

It was a risky deal, nevertheless, and we haven't done a thing since the restroom episode. Not that it might not happen again in the future, but I am very happy right now with my lady friend.

I realize now that I've always been bisexual and wouldn't change back to being purely straight even if I thought I could.
—*C.B., Chicago, Illinois* ○┼▄

STRAIGHT MAN LOSES IT AT THE MOVIES

Here's an experience that you might find worthy of inclusion in your "Boys-Boys" section.

I'm a straight, thirty-five-year-old, average-looking business-man. I'm married to a beautiful gal who is equally straight, and we enjoy a super sex life.

Gay sex has always been in the category of "fine for them, but not us." In other words, live and let live.

That changed about six weeks ago when I found myself out of town on a business trip and had the entire afternoon and evening to myself. About two blocks away from the headquarters of my client, there was a porno-movie house.

I haven't seen much porn so I paid my five bucks and went inside. It was an old classic movie palace, big, dank and dark. Downstairs were the hetero-sex films on a very large screen, while upstairs, on a walled-off portion of the old balcony, was a smaller theater for gay films.

I watched the straight films for a while until I was quite turned on. Since the theater was nearly empty, I rubbed my erect cock through my pants, and although I was dripping, I didn't come. I took my hands quickly out of my lap when a guy sat down right next to me.

In an almost empty theater, he picked the seat next to mine, which I assumed was some kind of strategy on his part. I figured I would sit there a couple of minutes, and then move to another more private seat where I could continue my self-indulgence. I didn't want to appear too obvious about it, however.

Before I got up to leave, this guy suddenly reached over and touched my softening penis. Startled by this violation, I pushed his hand away, and moved to get up. I don't remember saying anything to him, except for maybe an angry grunt. Instead, without saying a word, this guy got up and moved some distance from me.

I went back to watching the picture and, as a well-endowed guy filled a gal's mouth with come, I let my hand busy itself with my prick.

Now, I had never in my entire life ever had any sexual contact with another man, but watching the picture I got horny enough to think that maybe I should have let the guy play with me. It was fantasy watching the movie anyway; I could always pretend it was the woman on the screen doing me instead of this rank stranger.

I looked over and I could just barely see that he was still sitting where he had moved. I said to myself, What the hell, and I went over and sat down next to him.

As I sat down, he whispered, "Change your mind?" I nodded. As I looked around to be sure there was no one watching, he unzipped my fly.

I was surprised how soft his hands were on my cock. It was a few nervous minutes, though, before it began to feel good. I looked at him. He was good-looking, probably early twenties, with short hair, a clean shave and nice preppy-looking attire.

Like me, the stranger watched the movie, jacking me off slowly while his eyes feasted on the lusty action on the big screen. He stopped long enough to pull out his own cock, and while he stroked me, he also masturbated with slow, deliberate strokes.

Once, when I was about to come, I grabbed his hand, as I was sure I was about to ejaculate all over myself, but my signal was understood. He squeezed the tip of my prick between two fingers, cutting off the imminent flow of spermy glue. It certainly kept me from coming completely, but I did drip a little onto his fingers.

When he released his grip, a small amount of semen squirted out and I notice him lick the stuff off with his tongue. He looked over at me and smiled.

Without really being conscious of my action, I reached over and began to play with his cock, keeping my eyes peeled on the screen.

His boner was larger than mine, and I was surprised at how hot and moist it was. I realized it was pulsing with his blood and lathered with his saliva.

I stroked him slowly and cautiously, and by now I was enjoying playing with him and being played with. The action on the screen drove my passion.

I don't remember exactly how it came about, but suddenly he was on his knees, on the floor between the seats, with my cock in his mouth.

My wife sucks on my cock beautifully, but this guy was just as good, and at the same time, there was something even a little better about it.

He was holding the base of my cock with one hand, and had

reached into my fly and was playing with my balls with the other. His mouth was up and down on my entire shaft. I started to come a couple of times, but he sensed it and I was able to hold off.

After the second time, he said, "Go ahead and come." But I had another idea.

He got back into his seat, and I told him that if I came, I might not be too horny, and before that happened, I wanted to suck him.

Now remember, I had never even had fantasies about sucking another guy, but here I was, really wanting to put my lips around that hard, hot, wet thing he'd been fondling while sucking me off.

I kneeled between his legs and sucked his cock. I was really enjoying it too. Like I said, he was hung, and I couldn't suck as deeply on him as he had been able to on me.

A couple of times I felt him tense up, like he was going to come, and I backed off. Pretty soon, I wanted him to come in my mouth, and I speeded up the action, allowing him to gyrate in his seat, fucking my mouth.

He came, and I was again surprised because I didn't find the taste or the texture unpleasant one bit. My only surprise was the hotness of his come—like motor oil on a summer afternoon.

I swallowed as much as I could, but he ejaculated so much that some of his jism came back out of my mouth and down his cock. I licked it up, and almost frantically we swapped places and I found myself draining into his mouth the biggest load of come I'd had for a long time.

Now with my wife, when I come, I'm usually finished—no longer that interested in sex, but with this guy, I had just finished a huge orgasm and I was still ready for more.

My prick started to get soft in his mouth, but he kept sucking and, in what seemed like a short time, I was hard again.

He zipped up his pants, I did the same, and he took me to the men's room. In the light, he was not a bad-looking guy. As we both took a leak he asked me if I wanted to continue. I told him yes, and that I was surprised to find that I was eager to suck him again.

We went upstairs to the gay theater. There were five guys sitting in a group and we joined them. This guy I was with told them I had just lost my virginity, and wanted to get it on with anyone willing. One of the guys volunteered to "watch the door," and in the back corner of this small theater, me, Mr. Straight—

with wife, kiddies, job, etc.—sat comfortably in a theater seat and sucked and swallowed five guys.

One guy, the youngest, sucked me through two more climaxes, while I watched these two beautiful boys butt-fucking on the big screen.

I told my wife in pretty graphic detail of my "initiation," and it turned her on so much that she had an orgasm the second I penetrated her pussy.

She confessed for the first time that during high school she had bisexual activities with another girl, and that about three years ago, she had met the same girl for lunch. They went to a motel and made love to each other.

I hope to meet some other guys in the future. My wife wants to watch and, if they wish, take them on in a wild gangbang. —*C.M., Charlotte, North Carolina* ○━▪

FISHING BUDDIES ENJOY LIFE IN THE GREAT OUTDOORS

I'd like to share the experiences I've been having with two buddies of mine, Roger and Jim. We spend a lot of time fishing, often camping out on weekends.

Roger, Jim and I have become very close, not only from our fishing adventures, but because of our sexual recreation. Roger started it all three years ago when we were younger and a lot more experimental.

We had been fishing about two hours when he suggested that we stash our fishing rods and take a nude swim in deepest portion of the river.

We played around a bit in the currents, then Roger swam to the shore and emerged, sporting a truly beautiful hard-on. Jim and I swam up and emerged beside him. We all laughed and then Roger began stroking his dick and moving his hips in a rotating fashion.

This immediately caused Jim and me to get throbbing hard-ons. We all stood together in a small circle pumping our glistening cocks in a mutual jack-off session.

All of a sudden Roger put his arm around my shoulder and

grabbed my cock. I decided to do the same with Jim, who then took over Roger's prick. We had a glorious time stroking one another's shafts in an almost musical rhythm.

All three of us were moaning and thumping our asses to increase the pleasure of this wildly incredible experience. Believe me, we really had three raging erections all going at once toward one goal.

Jim gasped and said he was about to come. I immediately let go of his cock, dropped down on my knees and took his shaft deep into my mouth. I will never forget the feeling I got the first time I swallowed dick—buzzed!

Jim sighed with delight and began moving my head back and forth. It was a fantastic experience when he unloaded three huge wads of warm come into my mouth.

I lay down on the grass with my spent cock still unbelievably pointed to the sky. Roger quickly mounted me in a 69 position. It was great fun using Jim's come in my mouth as a lubricant on Roger's huge dong.

Then Jim said he wanted to join the party. He took over my prick and Roger began sucking Jim's penis, a homo orgy of glorious proportions.

After about five minutes of mutual sucking, Roger gasped and moaned that he was ready to come. He moved his prick faster and faster and deeper and deeper in my mouth. When he unloaded his silky wad, I greedily swallowed it in three gulps. I couldn't hold on any longer. I delivered my load in Jim's mouth and, at just about the same moment, Jim dumped his wad in Roger's mouth.

We stood up, laughed and kissed one another, letting the come drip all over our lips and chins.

Then we all jumped into the river pool and had fun diving down and playing with our cocks.

I still fish as often as possible with Roger and Jim, and we always look forward to our private jack-off party. We have made it a ritual.

Sometimes we even catch a few fish to take home.—*K.B., Roanoke, Virginia*   ⚬╾▪

Pursuit & Capture

EMPLOYEE BLOWS OFF COMPANY PICNIC TO PARTY WITH HIS BOSS'S WIFE

I want to tell you about a recent experience that I can't believe actually happened to me. A few months ago, the company I work for held its annual picnic for employees and their families. My boss, who was responsible for the picnic, spent the day of the outing making sure that everything went smoothly. I found myself talking to my boss's wife Kathy, who was left to herself as her husband took care of the details.

When my boss finally returned to his wife, it was obvious that he had been drinking. Kathy was upset over being deserted by her husband and then finally having him return drunk. She asked me if I would take her home. I said it wouldn't be a problem.

When we arrived at her house, I walked Kathy to the front door. I had turned to leave when she asked if I wanted a drink. Never one to refuse a drink, especially from such an attractive woman, I accepted the invitation. Kathy is in her late twenties, five feet, eight inches tall, with auburn hair and emerald eyes. Her perpetually erect nipples sit atop small but perfectly formed 34B breasts. She has the longest pair of legs I have ever seen. I'm thirty-five and good-looking, partly due to my love of biking and hiking and partly due to favorable genes.

With the drinks came conversation, and we soon discovered that she and I had more in common than her husband. Our conversation eventually turned to sex. I began to get an erection, and soon Kathy noticed the bulge in my shorts. Looking directly at my crotch, she asked if I was comfortable. I replied that I was as comfortable as I was going to get with my boss's wife. Smiling, she said, "We'll see about that." She softly began to run her red fingernails along the outline that my erection made under my shorts. In response, I cupped her breasts in my hands and rubbed her nipples with my thumbs through her blouse.

161

Kathy pulled off her top and reached behind her back to unclasp her bra. She sat there looking at me, her breasts unencumbered, waiting for me to make the next move.

Her erect, pink nipples begged for attention. I positioned her on my lap so that I had easier access to her beasts. I softly pulled and twisted her left nipple and sucked on her right nipple. Kathy's nipples stood out at least half an inch. She whimpered, "Don't stop, don't stop. Please don't stop!" I continued to play with her nipples until she pulled my head back and kissed me hard on the mouth. She jabbed her tongue into my mouth, plunging it as deep as it would go. My cock seemed to grow another inch as a result of her efforts. In a breathless voice, she said, "I want you now." I told her to stand up and take the rest of her clothes off. I wanted to see all of her body.

She took off her shorts and stood in front of me in a pair of skimpy panties. Then she began to rub herself through her panties while looking directly at me, with nothing but lust in those emerald eyes. Slowly, she pushed her panties past her hips and I saw the thin swatch of red pubic hair covering her pussy, which was oozing with her sex juices.

Her hands moved down to her cunt. She rubbed her clit with one hand, and with the other she spread her labia open so I could see the deep coral color of her hole. She stood in front of me with her legs bent and head thrown back in the throes of pleasure as she masturbated. Kathy leaned forward and I took her right nipple in my mouth and twiddled her left. With a moan, she crouched down on her knees between my legs and yanked off my shorts. My cock stuck out above the waistband of my underwear. She painstakingly licked up and down the outline of my cock under my underwear, never touching my cockhead. Soon I was leaking drops of come.

Kathy looked up at me, her face a mask of lust, and she moaned, "Give me your cock. I want to suck that big cock now!" I stood up, and Kathy nearly ripped off my underwear. My cock sprang out and a drop of come dripped on her breasts. Kathy rubbed it into her erect nipples, making them shine. Then she lowered her head and licked the precious fluid off her nipples.

She moved closer to my cock, wetting her lips in anticipation. She was totally unrecognizable as the woman I had met at the picnic. She licked along the underside of my cock until she got to the head, then slowly took it in her mouth, running her tongue around the head. I grabbed my cock and rubbed it over her face, smearing the mixture of her saliva and my semen from her fore-head to her chin. Looking down at Kathy, I told her she was the most beautiful woman I had ever known. She asked me, looking directly into my eyes, if I wanted her to play with my balls while she continued to suck on my cock. I could only groan in response. She smiled and resumed rubbing and sucking.

She rubbed my nipples when she was through with my balls. All I could do was moan and come in her mouth. My second blast of come went down her throat, the third splashed across her face and the fourth splattered her nose and dripped off her chin. I fell to my knees, drained and holding onto her for support. She licked some of my spattered come off her nipples.

After resting for a few minutes, I regained my erection. I laid Kathy on the floor and rubbed my cock up and down the slit of her cunt. Kathy arched her back and tried to impale herself on my cock, but I pulled away. I wiped up some of the come on her face with my fingers and offered my dripping fingers to her. She raised her head and sucked my fingers into her mouth. When she had cleaned my fingers, she moaned, "Fuck me."

I inserted my cockhead into her slit and then withdrew, running it up and over her clit. I probed her slit from the bottom to the top for several minutes before I inserted my cockhead into her cunt.

The sight of my thick cock penetrating her pussy beneath the small tuft of red pubic hair almost made me blast another load, but I continued to gently fuck her with just the head of my cock. Kathy's breathing became heavy and rapid. Her erect nipples darkened to a deep color and her stomach muscles undulated to a rhythm I had to struggle to match. She pulled her nipples and tickled them, trying to bring on the orgasm she so desperately needed. As I withdrew my cock and continued to tease her slit, she reared up, grabbed my shoulders and screamed, "Do it! Fuck me! Bury your cock inside me until it comes out of my mouth!"

I pulled her legs up until her knees pressed against her breasts and drove my cock all the way into her pussy with one stroke. Her back arched and she opened her mouth wide as if she were screaming, but no sound emerged. The muscles of her body quivered. Her eyes became glassy and she was covered in a sheen of sweat. Then Kathy went rigid, letting out a scream of release. Her juices ran out of her cunt and dribbled down the crack of her ass, soaking the rug under us.

When she started to recover, I rubbed her slit with two fingers and offered them to her. She sucked her juices from my fingers and tried to catch her breath.

Knowing that her husband would be coming home, I got dressed. Kathy walked me to the door and kissed me hard on the mouth while rubbing my crotch. We promised each other that we would get together again. —*S.G., Des Moines, Iowa*

HE BUMPS AND GRINDS FOR HIS BIG, BOUNCY BABE

I have an older client, a generously proportioned lady, who is young in spirit, if not in years. Sarah wears lacy push-up bras under low-cut blouses that she leaves half-buttoned. At first I was sure she wasn't interested in me at all. We had a couple of meetings in my office and she had been businesslike and formal.

One day I went to her apartment to review her financial file. I no longer entertained romantic expectations, but I still enjoyed her company and was only too glad to go out of my way for her. During a break in our work Sarah leaned over the table to hand me some iced tea. I resisted the urge to look at her cleavage (which was significant). Instead I noticed her eyes dropping to my crotch. I was certain she could tell I wasn't wearing undershorts, and that she could see my pecker through my thin, white slacks. But when we finished our meeting she didn't ask me to stay, and she didn't ask when we would need to meet again. I pretty much gave up hope of ever getting more intimate with her.

The next day, to my surprise, Sarah came to my office after lunch, dressed in a long skirt and designer sweater. She asked me if she had offended me in some way, and wanted to know why I had left her home so abruptly. I explained that I had thought she had been uncomfortable with my presence. Laughing, Sarah said that she had actually been trying to entice me to stay, and that she had long been intrigued by the possibility of spending some time with me.

I apologized profusely for misreading her signals and asked how I could make up for my mistake. As I waited for her answer, I reached for her hand and squeezed it gently. She stood up and drew me to her for a warm hug that blessed me with the feel of soft breasts unencumbered by a bra. She said she would let me know how I could make up for my error later. Before letting me go, she ground her hips against me and allowed me to lift her face and kiss her lightly on the lips.

I kissed her again, but this time more deeply, letting my tongue run over her lips until I felt the tip of her tongue searching for mine. I felt her left hand on my butt as her right hand held the back of my neck and fingered my hair. When we broke for air, I whispered in her ear that we should continue our conference at her apartment. We arranged to meet at three the next afternoon. After another lingering kiss she departed.

The next day I arrived at her place at the appointed time. She met me at the door, and we kissed lightly before she ushered me into her sitting room and told me she was not in the mood to work. She wore a white blouse and a short, black, pleated skirt. Sarah seated me on a large lounge chair and I watched her jiggle and bounce as she made her way to the kitchen to get wine.

When she returned I couldn't keep my eyes off her large, soft, jiggling breasts. She sat beside me on the settee, and leaned toward me in such a way as to reveal even more of her voluptuous figure. We sipped her fine French wine and made small talk till the bottle was empty. Then she offered to give me a tour of her spacious apartment. I put my arm around her waist as we walked from room to room. Once again, her hand found its way to my buns. I slowly moved my hand up her side until I could feel her boob through the thin material of her blouse. When we arrived at her bedroom she told me that once I entered I would be expected to stay there until she decided it was time for me to leave.

I could tell that all this was in good humor, and that she had no harm in mind, so I readily agreed, asking what she had planned.

"I want you to do a striptease for me," she said, "and you have to keep doing it until you get it right." I failed to notice the fancy stereo by the bed until she turned on some loud music with a distinct bump and grind beat.

I started to tap a foot in time to the music, at the same time slowly unbuttoning my shirt. Sarah sat in the middle of the bed with her knees lifted, showing that she wasn't wearing panties. When my shirt was off I turned my back, undid my belt and turned gracefully back around while I unzipped. My trousers fell to the floor and my pecker stood straight out at attention. All in all, I thought I'd performed rather well.

The lady, however, hardly smiled. She said my technique was very poor and that I needed to do more twisting and hip movement. Also, she said, she wanted more ass action and that if I couldn't do better next time she would have no choice but to show me herself.

I put my clothes back on and started over—this time trying to move more slowly and sensuously. She seemed to like it better, because I could see her cupping her breasts in her hands and licking her lips. As I stepped out of my pants I turned my back to her and leaned over. While leaning over, I reached between my legs, pulled my ass-cheeks apart and showed off my bunghole. This takes great balance, and I could only hold the pose for a few seconds. When I turned around, she was smiling approvingly. I went to the bed, reached for her face and kissed her deeply. My hand grazed her bosom and detected a hard nipple beneath her thin blouse. But she stopped me and asked me to dance one more time.

This time, however, she said she wanted my dangling penis closer to her face. She kissed it lightly, then turned me around and asked me to lean over. She got some lotion and rubbed it all over my buttocks, subtly bringing her fingers closer and closer to my asshole until one pressed against it and popped inside. She pulled out her finger, put a large amount of lotion on me and reinserted it, rubbing the insides of my ass and softly telling me to relax.

I could feel her finger well up inside me. I sensed that she was doing something that she hoped I would later do to her. I began to think about how it would feel to have my tongue inside each of her holes. She interrupted these thoughts by getting up and starting her own striptease.

She danced to the music, exciting me immensely, until eventually she was naked, showing me her asshole as she leaned over to touch her toes. Then she rubbed her boobs against my face as she turned around. After that we tumbled onto the bed. I licked and sucked her erect nipples and smooth breasts. Then I rolled onto my back and she pressed herself against me. Soon she was crouching over me and carefully placing my rigid pecker into her love-hole. Her strong muscles pulled me up farther and farther into her slick hole. We fucked gently, with her jiggling jugs bouncing up and down above me. After a good, long fuck we exploded in powerful, nearly simultaneous orgasms.

After a brief kiss, I asked her if she was as nice from the rear as she was from the front. She assured me that she was, and eagerly suggested that I judge for myself. I got the cream and greased up my pole, while she got onto her hands and knees with a pillow under her chin. I slowly pressed my middle finger against her dimple until it slowly slid in. When it was in as far as it could go, I pulled it out and put my member against her. It, too, slowly disappeared inside her. Soon it was all the way in, and I fucked her big behind till she screamed with pleasure.

I was about to blast off when she said she wanted to drink my come. I pulled out and fed my penis into her mouth. She finished me off gloriously, swallowing everything I could give. As I rested beside her, feeling her heaving breasts against my chest, I realized I had just had one of my greatest sexual experiences—at least so far. We have plans to meet again very soon and I may have to write in again. I can't wait.—*E.B.W., Fall River, Massachusetts* O━▄

HE MISSED A CHANCE TO GET IN HER PANTS, BUT THE DREAM LIVES ON

While in college, I once had a chance to have sex with my good friend, Allison. I didn't go through with it. However, I still think about how it could have been.

Allison and I have been friends since our first year at college. We lived in the same dormitories all through college. I was attracted to her from the beginning. She has luxurious brown hair, big, beautiful brown eyes, firm, grapefruit-sized breasts and an ass you want to grab with both hands and squeeze. Since she came to college with a fiancé from her high-school days, I didn't think we'd ever be more than friends. We did, in fact, become very close friends.

Eventually Allison and her fiancé broke up. By this time, her ex-fiancé was also a good friend of mine, and I wasn't ready to pick and choose between friends. Dating Allison would have been a quick (but certainly not easy) way to throw away a good friendship. That loss might have been doubled if Allison and I didn't work out romantically. Besides, Allison had never shown any sexual interest in me, so it wasn't as if I was turning down a real likely option.

Time marched on. Allison dated a few losers. I felt lousy when she started dating another friend of mine, a guy called Randy whom she had previously found very annoying. As luck would have it, they made a wonderful couple and I had to feel happy for them.

One weekend, Allison and I made plans to take a trip together. I was going to visit a girlfriend and Allison was going to visit her brother. We discussed the details Friday at lunch and decided to leave early Saturday morning. Allison then asked me what I had planned for that evening. Apparently, she was feeling sore and thought that a good friend like me would make the time to give her a back rub. I agreed demurely, but my mind was swimming with lewd thoughts.

Later that night, I went to her room prepared to work my hands off. Allison was working at her desk when I came in, and her desk lamp provided the only light in the room. She was wearing spandex leggings and a sweatshirt. She looked great! We sat around and talked for a while. Then she got up, pulled a bottle of baby oil out of her dresser drawer and asked me if I was ready. While my mind started working out the implications of the baby oil, Allison turned her back to me, pulled off her sweatshirt and lay down on the blanket on the floor. Her back was totally bare.

After my heart started beating again, I kneeled on the floor above Allison, straddling her ass. I had a raging hard-on. I rubbed, squeezed and pulled at Allison's lovely skin for over a half hour. As the time passed, I bravely made my way closer and closer to her ass, as well as around her sides toward her breasts. I was just getting ready to push my luck when there was a knock at the door.

Shit! A friend of Randy's walked into the room. He immediately flashed a suspicious look at us. I continued rubbing Allison's back in a very reserved way. We tried to act like it was just an innocent back rub. Nevertheless, our friend stuck around for a chat and didn't appear to be willing to leave before me. I told Allison that I hoped I had done some good for her aching muscles and that I'd see her in the morning. Then our friend and I got up and left.

After I left, I couldn't take my mind off Allison and what could have happened. I had to masturbate to two orgasms before I could get to sleep. It was a shame that we were staying at different places for the weekend. There was almost no chance of picking up where we had left off.

The next morning I knocked on Allison's door bright and

early. She was already up and waiting for me. I helped carry her bags to the car and we took off. Allison spent the weekend with her brother and I spent the weekend with my friend Diane. Allison and I didn't get to see each other much but (fortunately for my sanity) I spent a wonderful night having sex with Diane.

On Sunday I picked up Allison at her brother's house a little after noon. In the car, Allison and I made small talk for about three minutes before she asked about my Saturday night. She wanted the unexpurgated version, so I gave her all the details. I had a lot of fun describing it all to her. Then came the part I'll never forget.

"I'm jealous," Allison said.

"Huh? What do you mean?" I asked. "Jealous of what?"

"Jealous of Diane," she replied. I couldn't believe my ears. Allison was staring at me, and I couldn't think of what to say next. This was the pivotal point in a day that I believe could have turned out differently. Maybe it was because I had had such a sexually satisfying weekend. Or maybe I have a gallant streak I never knew about. I don't know. All I know is that I told Allison that if we acted on our feelings we would probably mess up a lifetime of choices for an afternoon of pleasure. I sometimes wish I had listened to my instincts rather than my reason.

When I think back to that day, I usually imagine it happening like this:

"I'm jealous," Allison said.

"Huh? What do you mean?" I asked. "Jealous of what?"

"Jealous of Diane," she replied.

Long pause. "Would you like to stay at a motel with me tonight?" I asked. Allison nodded.

I took the next ramp with a hotel sign, and soon we were pulling up to our room. After dropping our bags in the room, Allison said she wanted to take a shower. I headed out for champagne and rubbers.

When I got back, Allison was blowdrying her hair in front of the mirror, wearing a nightshirt that came halfway up her thighs. I grabbed the ice bucket and told her I'd be right back. After filling the bucket I went back and iced the champagne. I walked up to Allison and hugged her from behind.

"Mmmmm, you smell good," I said. "I think I'd better take a shower myself."

"I'll help," she said.

"I'm not sure I'm quite ready for that."

"It'll be all right," she said, taking my hand and leading me toward the bathroom. "It will be easier, and a lot more fun, if I give you a bath."

Allison walked around me and started the bath water. Then she told me to sit on the stool. She took off my shoes and socks. "Stand," she said. Turning me so I faced away from her, she hugged me from behind, burying her face in my back. Then she ran her hands up my chest and rubbed my pecs for just a moment before starting her hands back down my body. By that time my dick was throbbing and straining against my pants. She avoided it as she ran her hands down the inside of my thighs to my knees. She started back up my thighs and ran her fingers over the bulge in my pants on her way to my belt buckle. Next, she undid my buckle and unbuttoned my pants.

"Be right back," she whispered, and for a moment those wonderful fingers were gone. Apparently she was checking the temperature and turning off the water. "I missed you," she said as she picked up where she left off. She unzipped my pants and pulled them down to the floor. Next she started on my shirt, unbuttoning it slowly, starting at the top and then sliding it off my back.

Allison gave me a little kiss on the back, wrapped her arms around me and started rubbing my chest. Then she ran her hands down my sides, hooking her fingers in my shorts as she went, and pulling my underwear down and off.

As she straightened up, she gave me a little slap on the ass and said, "All right. Get in the tub."

So I did. As I climbed into the tub, Allison slipped out the door. She reappeared almost immediately with the champagne in one hand and plastic cups in the other. She popped the cork and poured a cup for each of us. We both sipped from our cups, and then put them aside. I watched as Allison pinned her hair up. "I don't want to get my hair wet," she said. "And I don't want to get this wet, either," she added, taking off her nightshirt.

Her body was even better looking than I imagined. Her neck looked long and lovely, especially with her hair up. Her breasts were larger than I thought they would be. Her nipples were bright pink and they poked out about a quarter of an inch. My eyes wandered farther down, focusing on her curvaceous waist and hips. Her bush was trimmed close and I could clearly see her pussy lips. Her legs were fabulous and they were moving closer.

Allison put a towel on the edge of the bathtub and sat down with her feet in the water. She then soaped up a wash towel and started scrubbing my back. Over the course of the next half hour, we sipped our champagne as Allison methodically washed every inch of my body. I was loving every minute of it, but I finally got to the point where I couldn't help myself any longer. I cupped a handful of water in my hand and poured it down her stomach onto her pussy "I'm sorry," I said. "I think I got you wet down there. Let me get that for you."

With that, I dove for the promised land.

Allison gasped as my mouth started working on her cunt. "Not yet," she said.

"I'm sorry, but I have to have you," I said, getting back to it. Allison grabbed my head and held it for a moment. Then she started running her hands through my hair. I really love that.

I was also really loving her cunt. My tongue teased her lips, up and down, left and right. Occasionally, I pushed my tongue as far up her pussy as I could. After a while she let go of my head and leaned back, with her hands on the bathroom tiles, so that I could get even deeper into her cunt. I put a finger up her pussy as my mouth started working on her clit. Allison started rolling her hips and gyrating her pussy; I could barely keep my mouth on her.

"Now!" she grunted as she shoved her cunt hard against my face. I used both arms to hold her legs and ass for extra support and to keep her cunt in reach. Then I stuck my tongue out and shook my head from side to side. Allison started shaking all over. I just left my mouth on her cunt and rode out her orgasm.

After she settled down, I took her hand and helped her sit up. She immediately leaned over and kissed me full on the mouth. Our tongues danced for a few moments; then she pulled away a little and gave me some quick pecks around my lips.

"Interesting," she said.

"What's that?" I asked.

"I think that's the first time I ever tasted myself. No wonder you really got into it," she commented.

She paused to regain her breath. "Thanks," she added. "That was really nice. Now let's get you out of that tub. You're probably shriveling up like a raisin."

"You might be surprised," I said. When I stood up my dick was stiffer than ever. After quickly drying off, I headed to the bed with Allison right on my tail.

Once in bed, Allison climbed on top of me. She wanted to take it slowly, and I wasn't about to argue.

First she kissed my chest. Next she kissed my stomach. Then

she kissed my waist. Then—big gasp—she kissed my cock right on the head. She trailed her tongue down the underside of the shaft, teasing the skin with her breath. Allison and I had had frank discussions about her oral abilities before, and now I was getting first hand proof that she hadn't exaggerated. She sucked my balls while her hand massaged my dick. Then she licked her way back up the shaft until she got to the head, which she sucked into her mouth. She lingered there for just a moment before plunging the length of my cock down her throat.

I was just lying back and enjoying the sensations when Allison stopped cold. "Aren't you watching?" Allison asked.

"I wasn't," I said, "but I will, now that you mention it."

She made quite a show of it, always trying to give me a good view of what she was up to. Watching Allison lick and suck my cock and balls, it didn't take very long for me to get that feeling.

"I'm getting close," I warned, but this only increased her fervor. She pumped her head up and down on my dick like a piston. While watching her lips sliding over me, I came hard and heavy. Allison swallowed every drop.

"Oh God, that was great," I whispered. "Thank you."

"Turnabout is fair play," Allison replied. "Now let's get a rubber on you."

"Sounds great," I said. Allison did the honors, which actually made the act of putting on a condom kind of fun. Then she climbed on top of me and lowered herself onto my dick. I really love this position. I hadn't tasted her tits yet, so I sat up and started kissing her breasts. Breasts always amaze me—mounds of soft flesh tipped with rock-hard nipples. I grabbed Allison's ass with both hands and hoisted her higher to get a better angle on her tits. Then, on a whim, I stood up. Still holding Allison on my cock, with my hands on her ass, I walked over to the wall and propped Allison against it. Making slow, deliberate movements, I pumped my dick into her all the way to the hilt.

After a few minutes of this, my arms started to get tired. I moved her over to the sink and set her down. I turned her away from me and bent her over the counter. Allison spread her legs and I shoved my dick into her from behind. Looking in the mirror behind the sink, I watched Allison's tits bounce while I held her hips and pounded my dick home. After a little while of this, Allison started moaning and thrusting her hips back while I thrust forward. I reached around her and rubbed her clit while I continued banging her pussy. She started moaning even louder, and then she came again. Her sticky juices squirted out and ran down my legs. I stood her up, hugged her and kissed her neck.

I led her back to the bed where I laid her down and mounted her missionary style. I kissed her and fondled her breasts while I achieved my second orgasm of the evening. Then she wrapped her arms around me and hugged me tight.

We spent the rest of the night getting very little sleep. We talked for a while. We snacked a little. We had sex on the floor and in the bathtub. We even gave each other massages before the sun rose again. After showering together, we checked out of the room and headed back to campus so we wouldn't miss our Monday classes.

Randy and Allison have been happily married for nearly three years now, and are considering having kids soon. I didn't get Allison, but I do have my memories of one of the best nights of my life. —*T.R., Ann Arbor, Michigan* ⊙╍▮

SHE'S SHIFTING INTO HIGH GEAR WHEN SHE SHOULD BE PARKING

I was living in Northern California and attending college when I met Debra. I had gotten a late start on my academic life at thirty-five years old. Debra was ten years my junior, and was everything I dreamed of in a woman. She was tall, athletic and adventurous. She also had a curvaceous body, slim-waisted with proudly jutting tits, and had a truly delightful pussy, with the fleshiest lips I had ever seen.

We were in a couple of classes together, and soon discovered that we lived near each other. When she asked me if she could catch rides with me to class, I thought it was a great idea. It wasn't long before our mutual interests led us to share an occasional glass of wine or a joint, and we finally hustled each other into my bed one rainy night, when my girlfriend was away in San Francisco.

Debra loved to fuck and to suck cock, and considered it a worthy challenge to take a big dick all the way down her throat.

She was extremely enthusiastic about sex, sometimes begging me to come on her face or do her in the ass. Although she lived with roommates, and I with my girlfriend, we arranged plenty of opportunities to get it on under the pretense of studying. At times we interrupted study sessions in the college library to sneak off to an empty classroom for a quick fuck, or into the stacks for a blowjob. On the way home from school we occasionally stopped at the beach, or in a deserted area, for a moonlight tumble of outrageous sex.

The backseat of my Ford Mustang had never seen this type of action. Once in a while Debra and I would whisper our fantasies to each other over the phone while we both masturbated. It was a great affair, with lots of memorable moments, but one truly amazing event occurred on a Saturday morning study date.

It was a rainy, foggy day. We drove to the campus parking lot in my car. On the way to campus I played with Debra's nipples while she unzipped my pants and lightly sucked on my hardening dick. By the time we got to school we were pretty horny, and we thought that, with help from the thick fog, we might be able to help ourselves to a piece of tail right there in the parking lot.

I drove to a deserted corner of the lot, and we started going at it—kissing open-mouthed and fondling each other's genitals. After a few minutes the car window steamed up and increased our cover. Before long, Debra had slipped her pants off and straddled my lap, facing me, with her feet on the back of my seat. It was easy to slide my cock into her tight, wet cunt. I grabbed her ass to keep it from blowing the car's horn, and Debra slowly rode up and down on my stiff pole.

We fucked for a few minutes, reveling in the glorious sensations. My balls were drawn up tight, and her rising and falling literally had me on the edge of my seat. I thought I'd blow my load at any moment. I was deliriously happy, but Debra, being inventive and curious, was restless. She mumbled something about "putting things into high gear," while carefully assaying the cramped front seats of my Mustang.

Debra slowly lifted herself off my cock, then moved sideways, so she wound up with a foot on each of the two front bucket seats. She was still facing the back of the car and squatting down, but what she did next totally amazed me. She reached down between her two legs where her purse was wedged against the seat, and pulled out a short, gold-colored vibrator. When she flicked it on its battery-powered buzz seemed to fill the whole car. She'd often talked about the "secret friend" who cared for her when we couldn't get together, but I'd never seen it, and was surprised at how loud it seemed to be.

"Hey, what if all that noise draws a crowd?" I whispered.

"The more the merrier," she responded, and touched the vibrating tip to her clit, which was protruding, round and ripe, from between her fleshy cunt lips. The sound of the motor was immediately drowned out by her responsive moans.

I didn't know what to say. At first I felt a little left out, but as I watched her masturbate I became incredibly excited. My expression seemed to encourage Debra more, because before I knew it she was burying the whole golden shaft of the dildo between those gorgeous pussy lips of hers until her juices ran down over her fist.

Her face contorted with pleasure and excitement as her juices ran down the knob at the base of the vibrator. The sight of her squirming was awesome. My motor was revving, to say the least. Debra pumped her hips a few times, then pulled the vibrator out again and ran it around her juicy pussy lips, as if it was a cock and she hadn't had any in months. She plunged it inside her pussy again, pumped away furiously, then suddenly stopped and sighed.

Her juices covered her fingers so that she could barely hold the humming shaft. I was amazed. By the slight tremble of her body and the way Debra's eyes were closed, I knew she had climaxed. I know this sounds weird, but I had never seen a girl getting herself off before. Everyone I'd gone out with always got embarrassed and said that was a really private thing.

Debra settled back down on the passenger seat with a very satisfied smile. She turned to me with a languid smile, then slid sinuously down to the floor. After asking me if she could go down on me, she proceeded to suck my cock. Could she, I thought to myself. I would have surely felt left out if she hadn't.

It didn't take long before I came, and just before I did she teasingly took my cock out of her mouth and rubbed it all over her face. One jet of come hit her square in the corner of her closed mouth, so she tilted her head sideways to let my come run across her full lips. She then sucked my come into her mouth and swallowed it. Then we got dressed and went into the library to study.

After that parking experience, I found myself fondly daydreaming about Debra's lovely wet pussy impaled on her golden wand. My only regret is that we never got the opportunity to shift into overdrive before the fog lifted! —*M.V., Redwood, CA*

SOMETIMES THE BEST LAID PLANS JUST LEAD TO THE BEST LAYS

I'm a twenty-four-year-old woman married to a thirty-three-year-old man who really knows how to fuck. I mean, he's incredible in bed and, being older and more experienced, he has taught me many pleasurable things.

He's six-feet-one-inch tall and weighs about a hundred and forty pounds, trim and muscular with an eight-inch cock. I'm five-foot-five, about one-thirty with 34C tits and shapely legs and ass. I'm going to tell you about the night I blew his mind.

Having been at home all day, I had plenty of time for horny fantasies, and they gradually evolved into a little scheme. Knowing that he loves black lingerie and having his cock sucked, I planned accordingly.

I dressed in a tight, black, crotchless lace outfit, stockings and heels. I finished the look with a tank top and a miniskirt that showed off my curves but hid the surprise. My cunt was hot and wet with excitement by the time I finished dressing up. It got a lot wetter driving to pick him up from work.

When Sidney got into the car and saw my outfit, his eyes widened with surprise and I saw his cock spring to attention. When he was settled I pulled up my skirt and flashed him a peek at my crotchless outfit and hot, pink pussy. He kept glancing over, and before long he had started fingering my cunt. Pretty soon he jokingly suggested we stop somewhere and fuck. He assumed I wouldn't, knowing that I'm shy and reserved, and have always resisted his suggestions about fucking in the open. He certainly didn't expect me to pull off on a side road and pull out his hard cock for a quick suck, but he made no move to stop me when I did.

One thing that invariably gets him going is if I stick my tongue out as far as it will go and swirl it around and around his penis. Every time it passes the underside of his dickhead he jumps, and he usually doesn't jump more than a couple of times before he starts spraying. That's what I did to him on this occasion, and when he started moaning like he was going to come I stopped and told him to save it until we got home. He was surprised at the sudden turn of events, but decided to be patient.

After we got back on the road, I kept reaching over every once in a while to make sure he was still good and hard. I was never disappointed, either by Sid's stiffness or the response I got. He sighed and humped his hips every time I touched the outline of his dick. Instead of rubbing him more, I'd just pat his thigh and say, "Just checking."

At home, Sidney went straight to our room, while I stripped off my outer clothes, leaving my sexy outfit and heels on. Sidney was lying on the bed, all six feet plus of him, naked, with his full hard eight-inch rod waving in the air. This man is a real treat to look at. He could have been a model if he'd been a little more vain.

My mother had told us of a little game her boyfriend plays with her called *Around the World*. It's an anything goes kind of game, except for one important rule: The recipient isn't allowed to touch the giver.

Straddling his body and kissing his neck, I informed him that he was not allowed to touch me. After being sucked so close to orgasm in the car, and watching me in my sexy outfit, he let out a groan and said, "I don't know whether I can do that."

"Try. For me," I requested with a coo. He didn't reply, but I saw his cock leap in anticipation, and that was enough of an answer for me.

Starting with his hard little nipples, I kissed, licked and nibbled my way down his love trail, purposely avoiding his thrusting, purple-headed cock. Knowing his stomach, inner thighs and balls are extremely sensitive, I centered my careful and lingering attention there. I licked slowly from his knee to his tight sac and nibbled on his balls, tongued his tight ass and kissed the smooth skin under his nuts.

Sidney was moaning and gripping the headboard, constantly directing his swollen cock toward my mouth and begging me to suck him. His hot rod was oozing onto his stomach, and I carefully and thoroughly licked up every stray drop. Then, sensing that he was as hot as he was ever going to get, I suddenly deepthroated as much of his huge prick as I could. He groaned loudly and came straight up off the bed, rolling me onto my back. Without any help from me, as I was giggling at the look of intense excitement on his face, he began jamming his pulsing rod at my midsection. I spread my legs and he found my soaked opening and began slamming into me for all he was worth.

Sidney stopped and asked me to get on my knees. With my rounded ass sticking up in the air, he shoved his cock into my slippery hole to the hilt. He was banging away so hard that his balls slapped against my clit with every thrust.

Getting close to coming, and wanting to do something spectacular to finish off this special event, I stopped him and asked him if he wanted to fuck my asshole. He immediately said that he did. I grabbed the K-Y off the nightstand and rubbed some on his cock and my virgin hole. I reached under and behind me and ran his cockhead up and down my crack, finally centering his head right at my tight opening. Slowly he shoved his cock into my tight asshole. He reached around to finger my cunt and clit as he sank his cock in my quivering hole.

When I started to moan and push against him he grasped my hips and started working in and out of me. I fingered my clit while his balls slapped my swollen lips. As we climaxed, I watched him pounding into me in the mirror beside the bed. Still connected, we slumped to the mattress. His cock kept pumping come into my ass and twitching. I could feel the streams pouring out of him so much more clearly than I can in my pussy.

Afterward he admitted it was the best fuck of his life. Then he started patting my breast. Looking at him with a satisfied grin, I informed him that he had touched me, and "Now we have to start all over." — *R.B., Tucson, Arizona* ⚬╍

LIFE IN PRISON LOOKS A LOT BETTER WHEN YOUR COUNSELOR IS A SEXY BLONDE LADY

I am a convicted felon, currently incarcerated for one to seven years in a state penitentiary. Feeling miserable because I no longer had the freedom to enjoy my favorite hobbies (sex, sex and more sex), I began my imprisonment by keeping to myself and not allowing too many inmates or prison officials to get near me. The one question constantly on my mind was, What will I do now that I can't have pussy six or seven times a day? Each time I would think of Debbi, Sara, Lynn, Bette and Kim, the girls I used to entertain every day, I would feel my fat black eleven-inch dick begin to throb in my brown jailhouse uniform. Then I would go to my cell and hang up a curtain so that no one could see me as I feverishly masturbated myself to climax.

I was indulging in this substitute pleasure one day when, just as I was about to reach orgasm, I was disturbed by a soft tapping on my cell door. With cock in hand I went over and pulled aside the curtain enough to see Rhonda, my prison counselor, standing there with my file folder.

Rhonda was a very petite but extremely sexy blonde lady, about five feet two and one hundred ten pounds. Her tits were small, and even though she wore somewhat loose-fitting pants, it was evident that she had a very shapely ass, and hips that flared enough to please any man.

I knew Rhonda could see the lustful expression on my face as I looked her body up and down, pausing at her breasts before meeting her eyes. Still, she gave me a friendly smile as she asked if I could come to her office to go over my programming schedule.

I asked her if she needed me to come right away and she replied, still smiling, "Yes, if you're not too busy." I wondered if she knew what I'd been doing. Deciding to test her out, I took down the top part of the curtain, showing her my naked chest and torso. When my cute and sexy counselor said nothing, but just stood there and looked at me, I boldly turned and walked over to my bunk, knowing she could see my strong hairy ass over the lower half of the curtain. When Rhonda still said nothing, I spun around quickly to expose my solid, meaty, still half-erect shaft to her gaze. I smiled to myself as I saw her swallow and lick her lips. Then she collected herself and turned away, telling me she would wait for me in her office.

After getting dressed (not bothering with my boxers or T-shirt) I walked across the unit, passing inmates playing cards, chess and dominos. I knocked on the office door just as my counselor was putting up a removable blind over her window. She motioned for me to come in, and I took a seat in a soft office chair in front of her cluttered desk.

I noticed that Rhonda had taken down her blonde hair, letting it fall to her shoulders. When she began to speak, her voice sounded kind of nervous. She cleared her throat and started again.

"Is there anything in particular you'd like to do or accomplish while you're here?" she asked me.

Immediately I said, "Do you mean in this office, or in the prison?"

She smiled nervously. "I mean what would you like to do here in this jail during your term of incarceration?"

I knew what she wanted to hear, so I said I wanted to do anything and everything that was necessary in order to make parole when the time came—adding that that included doing whatever pleased my counselor. Rhonda said she was working on my program plan, which included deciding which job details I would be working on. She then informed me that one of my jobs would be to clean her office every day.

"When do you want me to start?" I said.

"Now!" Rhonda replied quickly.

I rose to leave, intending to find some cleaning supplies, but Rhonda stopped me at her door, then got up and walked over to where I stood. Standing close and looking me straight in the eye, she asked, "Did you just get out of the showers when I came to your cell?"

"No," I said.

She took a deep breath.

"You are a very . . . healthy man," she said softly. "I've never imagined a cock the size of yours. I hope I didn't embarrass you by looking at you that way, but I was in shock."

"You didn't embarrass me," I replied. "You just reminded me of my favorite hobby."

Rhonda looked confused. "What does your hobby have to do with your—with you being naked?"

I smiled, looking straight into her eyes as I said, "My hobby is fucking beautiful women. Fucking them and sucking them and bringing them to orgasm."

My gorgeous counselor stared for a moment, licking her soft lips. Then she took my hand and brought it to her mouth, placing my forefinger on her bottom lip. Her tongue reached out to caress it, and I slid it into her mouth. She took it eagerly, closing her lips around it as if it were a little cock.

I liked what she was doing. I liked it so much I felt a stirring in my loins, and I automatically reached out to caress her face. She closed her eyes, still sucking on my finger, and I thought I saw her nipples becoming hard and rigid under her blouse. Feeling confident now, I placed my hand between her breasts and found that she wasn't wearing a bra. I slid the hand onto her breast, caressing its softness and moving my palm in small circles around the hard nipple.

Rhonda was moaning around the finger still lodged in her

slurping mouth. My own desire was mounting rapidly. I unbuttoned her blouse to expose her firm, creamy-white mounds, with nipples that stood out like little pinkies. After caressing both of them, I bowed my head to her chest, where my wanton lips and mouth eagerly enveloped her soft tits and hard nipples.

Rhonda threw her head back, moaning softly as I sucked and licked at her tits. She then reached for my throbbing dick, unbuttoning my fly and freeing my swiftly stiffening cock. Rhonda's hand glided up and down over the thick shaft, both of us moaning now with pleasure. With my free hand I reached down to rub at her pussy through the thin material of her dark blue skirt, and as I did she started grinding her crotch against my fingers. I quickly reached beneath her skirt and pulled the fabric of her lacy panties to one side, exposing her swollen clit to my touch. My middle finger slid into my counselor's tight slit as with my forefinger I started stroking the little man in the boat, feeling it respond by swelling and stiffening even further. She was so wet that her juices covered my palm. Sliding another finger deep inside her clutching pussy, I continued stroking her clit, rubbing it harder, and not stopping even when I heard Rhonda cry out as she approached her climax. Then she started bucking and twisting, grabbing my dick with both hands as she gasped out her orgasm.

As her climax subsided I moved her to the chair I had been sitting in, placing her with her knees on the seat and her arms resting on the back. I moved behind her and kissed her firm ass-cheeks as her juices ran down her inner thighs. My lips and tongue explored her smooth buttocks, and then I moved my mouth to her slick and shaven pussy.

I heard Rhonda moan as she felt my hot breath caress her wetness, and as soon as my tongue licked at her opening she cried out, "Eat me! Eat me!" The erotic effect of her words made my large black dick stiffen even further. I licked Rhonda's pussy gently, wetting the creamy flesh between her thighs as I murmured, "Do you like this?"

"Ooooo, yesss!" Rhonda moaned. "Suck on my pussy, oh, God, suck it good!"

I sucked and licked that sweet love-hole until I felt I couldn't wait any longer to fuck her. I stood up, resting my hard throbbing cock on her ass. Rhonda caught her breath.

"I've never had a cock half the size of yours," she gasped out.

"So take it easy, please. We could both get busted if I make too much noise!"

"Don't worry," I said. But even as she was saying that I noticed how she raised her ass and moved it back, trying to urge the head of my dick into her cunt. I aimed my eager tool at that waiting pussy, and Rhonda reached down with both hands to spread her lips as wide as they would go. I placed my dickhead at her entrance and let her ease it inside herself by moving her ass back and down. I couldn't believe how tight she was as she took more of my pole inside. I felt her pussy muscles expand to accept more and more of my eleven inches of black meat.

I let her take it at her own speed at first, but when I realized that she wasn't going to stop, that she wanted it all, I began to thrust deeper into her. The smooth snug flesh of her pussy gripped me so tightly that sweat broke out on my body. I put my hands on her tits and braced myself by holding on to them, and soon I was hammering my rigid tool into my counselor's writhing, twisting cunt.

Rhonda was going crazy with pleasure as I put all I had into fucking her, and when she managed to take the whole of my eleven inches inside her soaking wet pussy, she screamed out, "Yes! Yes! I'm there! I'm coming! I feel it! I feel your big dick all the way deep inside me! Oh, yes! It's sooo right! Sooo damn good! I never want it to stop! Never!"

And then she was coming, exploding over and over in a series of orgasms that she told me later were the most intense she had ever had. My cock seemed to expand and then burst open as the first spasm of my eruption shook the complete length of my rod. The warm hot cream gushed out into her spasming channel, pumping so hard and deep it would probably never come out. Even before I was finishing coming Rhonda experienced yet another orgasm, which rocked her body from head to toe.

As we recovered our breath I was thinking that it was lucky no one had come along to find out why we'd been in Rhonda's office alone for the last half-hour. But a minute later there was a knock on the office door. I looked through the blinds and saw another inmate standing there with a folder in his hand. It was Rhonda's next appointment. She called out for him to wait a moment, and hastily put on her panties and straightened herself out. When I finally let him in, he looked around with a puzzled expression and said, "I smell something!"

Rhonda and I just looked at each other and tried to keep from laughing.

Now I have a regular appointment to see Rhonda every Tuesday and Friday, in addition to cleaning her office every day. On the days I clean her office, she cleans my cock, and I do the same for her pussy. On Tuesdays and Fridays we have more time, so we try out every position and variation we can think of. In the intervals between fucking and sucking each other, we are working very hard to make me eligible for parole when the time comes, so that I can enjoy my special hobby with her on the outside too.

Not to mention with Debbi, Sara, Lynn, Bette and Kim!
—*Name and address withheld* ⊶▪

SHE LIKES THE LOOK OF HIS TRUCK, AND SHE LIKES WHEN HE GIVES HER A FUCK

It all started one evening when my friend Brad stopped by and asked me to go shopping with him. My wife and I had just had a fight, so I was happy to get away for awhile.

After doing a little shopping Brad and I decided to have a drink to relieve the stress of the day. We stopped by a liquor store and picked up some beer, then went cruising through town.

As we passed a local singles hangout I noticed this beautiful brunette waving at us. Naturally we stopped. The girl's name was Norma, and she said she really loved my four-wheel drive truck, and wanted to know if she could have a ride in it sometime. I told her there was no time like the present, and invited her in.

She sat between Brad and me as we rode around town. Soon Brad was ready to go home, and asked if I could drop him off at his car. The problem was that his car was at my house, and I could only hope my wife wouldn't see me dropping him off with this girl in my truck. When Brad got out I took off again down the street. I noticed that Norma didn't move over into the passenger seat, but kept sitting close beside me.

She asked me if I had a girlfriend. I told her I was married, but it didn't seem to put her off. She told me she was eighteen and had a boyfriend. She still sat close to me, so at the next stop sign I decided to seize the opportunity, and I turned to her and started to kiss her. We French-kissed for about two minutes. She was very cooperative, but it must have scared her a little, because after that she said she wanted to go home.

Well, I figured I would never have to worry about her again, but I was wrong. One night while I was working around the yard I happened to see her drive by my house. She was driving slowly, as if looking to see if I was home, and when I waved to her she stopped.

She was driving a Nissan Pathfinder and was smiling as I walked up to her. We said hi, and she told me she didn't have much to do because her boyfriend was out of town for the night, and she wanted to know if I could get away for awhile. I jumped into her car and said, "Let's go."

She drove a little way out of town and parked in a secluded area under some trees. A little surprised, I asked her why she had to leave so quickly the night I kissed her. She told me that what happened had scared her a little, because she was afraid of what it might lead to. My next question was, why did she come back? Her reply was that she had been so turned on by our kissing that she figured she wanted to try again.

Well, that was definitely the sign I was looking for, so I moved closer to her and began to kiss her. Her tongue responded to mine, and soon her breathing was getting heavier and we were French-kissing with great enthusiasm.

I moved my mouth to her ear and then to her neck, kissing and licking, and was rewarded with soft moans of pleasure. We played around for some time before I placed my hand on her breast. Oh my God, she had the greatest tits I've ever had the pleasure of fondling! But after a minute she moved my hand away. I looked her straight in the eyes and immediately pulled her sweater and bra up over her tits, then began to kiss and suck on her wonderful nipples. Any initial inhibitions on her part were soon swept away by her desire, which she expressed with murmured comments of pure satisfaction.

I was so hot and hard I was ready to explode, and I couldn't control myself any longer. I began to place soft, wet kisses from her tits down her stomach to the waistband of the shorts she was wearing. But when I tried to open the shorts she grabbed my hand, saying that no one but her boyfriend was allowed to touch her there. So I simply placed my hand on her crotch and started to rub very gently. Norma was too worked up to resist, and she spread her legs to give me better access as she began to squirm with pleasure. She was so hot I could feel her pussy juices soaking through her shorts. I asked her to remove her shorts so I could lick her pussy, but at that point she drew the line and told me she had to go home.

I was very disappointed, and tried to get her to give me a blowjob, or at least a handjob, because I needed to get off so badly. But she wouldn't. So I sighed and told her that I really wanted to make love to her, and that if she ever wanted to go that far she should let me know.

A few weeks went by, and then, to my delight, Norma called me and asked if she could see me again that night. I suggested she stop by my office after work, and then I called my wife and made up some excuse for being out that evening.

Norma arrived at my office right on time. I met her at the front door and invited her to see our new showroom area. As we walked around the showroom looking at all the products, I asked her if she was sure about her decision. I mean this girl was a total knockout, and as excited as I was, I didn't want her to do anything she'd regret. Norma stared into my eyes and told me she hadn't been able to think about anything else since I made that offer a few weeks ago.

She looked absolutely radiant, and I couldn't wait any longer. I moved close to her and our lips touched. Her body pressed close to mine, and I knew without a shadow of a doubt that this was going to be a night to remember. I slowly kissed her neck and gently nibbled her earlobes, and the low soft moans that I remembered began to escape her mouth.

After a few moments I unbuttoned her blouse and opened her bra to unleash her 36D tits from their confines. I held these breasts in my hands and buried my face in them. Norma seemed to be in a trance of pleasure as I sucked and licked her nipples. I slowly kissed her stomach and inched my way down to her shorts. She made no resistance as I unbuttoned the shorts and slid them down around her ankles. I slipped off her shoes and pulled her shorts off over her feet. After another kiss or two on her stomach I slowly removed her panties. Then I just knelt there looking at her perfectly manicured bush. My heart was pounding so hard I could barely hear myself think.

Norma just stood there waiting for my next move. Still kneeling in front of her, I looked up into her eyes and asked her if she would like me to lick her pussy. She told me that her boyfriend

had never done that for her, and that she had always wanted to
know what it was like. So who was I to disappoint her?

Moving her legs apart, I placed my tongue on her wonderfully
wet pussy and began to lick up her juices. Norma's knees almost
buckled when my tongue touched her clit, and she moaned
loudly with approval. I licked and sucked her for quite a while,
until she told me gasping that she wanted to lie down. She positioned herself on the floor on her back, and I knelt down in front
of her. I spread her legs, bending them at the knee to allow me
perfect access to her dripping pussy. Leaning forward I began to
eat that sweet twat once again. I couldn't get enough of the way
she tasted.

Finally I had to satisfy the raging desire in my loins. I positioned myself above her and French-kissed her, allowing her a
taste of her own juices. At this point Norma was going wild. She
looked at me and told me how much she needed to be fucked.
"Please," she begged, "please take off your pants and fuck me
hard and fast." I couldn't get my pants off fast enough. I lay on
top of her and asked her again if she wanted to be fucked. She
said "I don't just *want* to be fucked. I *need* to be fucked!" And
she grabbed on to my hard dick and positioned it at the entrance
to her soaking wet pussy. "Please," she said. "I need to feel this
hard thing inside me."

I rubbed the head of my dick against her opening, teasing her
just a little more, until she was begging me to put it in. Slowly I
inched my way into her, feeling the warmth of her so tightly
wrapped around me. I pumped slowly at the beginning, enjoying
every second of pleasure, but Norma asked if I could go faster.
Immediately I began to speed up my rhythm and she shook her
head from side to side, moaning, "That's it, fuck me. Oh God,
fuck me. Oh yes, that's it, fuck me harder!"

At one point Norma asked me to suck her tits, but I was so into
fucking her hard and fast that I couldn't position myself to give
her breasts the attention they needed. So she began to massage
them herself. Soon her moans and gasps changed to short, deep
groans, and I knew she was about to have an orgasm. I continued
my rapid, steady pace, and within seconds she put her hands on
my shoulders and cried out that she was coming. Her fingers dug
deeply into my skin, her groaning loud and irregular. I knew she
was right at the edge, and I pushed extra hard to help heighten her

explosion. Suddenly I felt her pussy tighten, and she came with so much force that it was all I could do to stay inside her.

I looked into her eyes and she smiled at me as her orgasm subsided. I moved down to her come-soaked crotch to get a taste of her juices. I ran my tongue upward from her asshole to her pussy to lick up her come. It was wonderful. She tasted so good! I continued to lick her opening until she asked if I could please fuck her some more.

I got into position and buried my hard dick inside her again, and this time she raised her head and began to suck on my nipples. At that point I think my dick grew another inch. My sensations intensified still more, and I knew my own orgasm was approaching fast. Norma placed her hands on my chest and began to rub my nipples between her index finger and thumb. I couldn't take it anymore. When I told her I was going to come, she rubbed my nipples harder and said she wanted to feel my jism deep inside her. Oh what a feeling! My heart was pounding a mile a minute, and my dick was pumping in and out of her pussy, and still I was trying to hold back in order to savor the moment as long as possible.

"Wait," Norma said. "Don't come yet. I want to make you come in a very special way." So I stopped, exerting all my control, with my hard dick buried deep inside her. She then began to contract and relax her pussy muscles. I felt a pulling sensation, as though my dick was being sucked in and out of her tight hole. It was absolutely fantastic! Within seconds my orgasm had peaked and I exploded into her. It felt like I was coming harder than I ever had before. Finally I collapsed on top of her with a feeling of total satisfaction.

After awhile we sat up and caressed each other, expressing our appreciation of this tremendous mutual experience. Norma told me that it was the first time she had ever had an orgasm, and also the first time she had tasted her own come. She said her boyfriend never took the time to let her really enjoy sex. She wanted to know if we could see each other again real soon. I told her I couldn't wait to see her again. Then she lowered her head to my still hard and dripping dick and stuck it into her mouth. She licked me clean and then said, with a grin, "How about right now?"

I had to remind her that I was a married man, and needed to get home before my wife got suspicious. We finally got dressed and passionately kissed again before saying good night.

Norma and I have made love several times since that night,

even though she recently got married to her boyfriend. She says he has his good qualities and she loves him very much. It's true that he isn't as sensitive to her sexual needs as she'd like, but she says as long as she can go on having great sex with me, she doesn't really mind a bit. — *Y.B., Amarillo, Texas*   O┼▪

HE WAS NEW ON THE JOB BUT A REDHEADED CO-WORKER BROKE HIM IN REAL GOOD

My wife and I have been married for twenty years and have two children. My wife is a very attractive lady, but is pretty straight-forward when it comes to sex. She's not big on experimentation in the bedroom. But recently I did get the opportunity to expand my sexual horizons, though not with my wife.

It began when I took a position with a new company. One of the women working there was a petite redhead named Ronnie, who had a personality that overwhelmed me. Over the course of several months Ronnie began to spend more and more time in the department I was in charge of. Usually our conversations would start out with small talk, such as what we did over the weekend, but almost always they eventually veered toward sex. We were both married, but Ronnie seemed to be struggling with her marriage, and she confided in me enough to let me know that she no longer enjoyed having sex with her husband. In fact, she made it quite clear that her life was in need of some excitement, and a few times she came close to asking straight out if I would like to fuck her.

There was definitely an attraction between us, and since we were both unsatisfied with our current partners, it seemed obvious that what we both needed was some raw untamed sex to help soothe the frustrations we were experiencing.

One Thursday evening I stayed late at the office in order to try and get caught up on a few projects. I thought I would be the only one there, but around eight o'clock I heard the office door open and footsteps approaching the entrance to my department. I looked up, and to my surprise there was Ronnie. She held up a four-pack of wine coolers and asked if I was thirsty.

We sat and talked for awhile, and Ronnie told me she was supposed to be out on the town with her girlfriends, but had decided to cancel at the last minute. She asked me when I was expected home, and I told her not until later. Ronnie looked at me with her beautiful green eyes and asked me if I wanted to go for a drive and talk. It sounded like a great chance for us to be alone, so I agreed.

We took my car, and it wasn't long till we were driving along an old quiet road, just talking about everything. Suddenly Ronnie asked me to stop the car. I stopped in the middle of the road and looked over at her.

Ronnie took a breath and then asked me if I had ever cheated on my wife. I told her that I had given it some thought a few times, but up to that point I never had. Then she looked at me and asked me to kiss her. I was so excited I could hardly breathe. I leaned over and pressed my lips to hers, feeling a bolt of electricity shoot down my body and into my dick. I pulled away and looked at her. She asked me to do it again, and this time our tongues went wild and my heart was beating like a racehorse. The next thing I knew there were headlights coming up behind us, and I hastily put the car in gear and drove off.

Ronnie looked at me and told me that she'd had two orgasms while we were kissing. I couldn't believe what I was hearing. She went on to say that she was so incredibly horny that if I didn't pull over and fuck her, she was going to remove her pants and finger-fuck herself right there in the car. Before I could find a place to pull over, she had her pants and panties off, with her feet propped up on the dashboard and her legs spread wide apart. She placed her hand between her legs and inserted her index finger into her pussy. In a moment she was moaning and panting.

I couldn't stand any more of this. I pulled the car onto the shoulder of the road and shut off the engine. In a flash I was totally naked.

Ronnie pulled her soaking wet fingers from her pussy and boldly stuck them in my mouth. The taste and smell of her juices almost made me shoot my load on the car seat. Then she leaned down to my crotch and began licking and sucking on my throbbing cock. She paused to look up at me with a smile and tell me how much she loved to suck cock, and how horny it made her.

After about ten minutes of what had to be the best mouth job I've ever had, Ronnie repositioned herself in her seat and told me it was her turn to be satisfied. I moved over and began kissing her full moist lips, then slid my mouth slowly down her neck. She quickly unbuttoned her blouse and unhooked her bra to expose

two small but wonderful breasts. Her nipples were hard and
ready to be sucked, but to my delight she pushed my mouth away
from her tits and down toward her wet and waiting pussy. I
slowly spread her legs and touched my tongue to her opening.
"Oh my," she moaned. "Oh my, oh, that feels so good!" And after
a few more licks she was coming again.

As soon as she caught her breath, Ronnie said she needed my
hard cock in her pussy. I lay down on my back on the seat and
she straddled me, reaching between her legs to grab my cock and
shove it into her pussy. I could feel every inch of my prick being
consumed by that hungry hole as she began to ride up and down
on my shaft.

Then suddenly she pulled away and moved to lean over the
back of the seat, legs wide apart and ass sticking out. This was a
fucking dream come true. I assumed a position behind her and
began to fuck her doggie-style with everything I had in me. Several times I was on the verge of coming, but I stopped to put my
tongue in her dripping pussy before entering her love channel
again. I couldn't get enough of her.

Finally Ronnie placed her fingers on her clit and began bucking like crazy, coming with a force that I had never experienced.
She drove me right over the edge, and I came so hard that I
thought my balls were coming out through my penis. After I shot
my load deep inside her pussy she slid down to my crotch and
licked my cock clean.

Since that night we have helped each other with our sexual
frustrations many times. For example, one night when we were
in my car again, fucking doggie-style, I removed my dick from
her pussy and began licking her asshole. Ronnie went crazy,
telling me how good it felt, and how she had always wondered
why her husband wouldn't lick her there.

I put my cock back in her cunt and began a slow rhythmic in-
and-out motion, and then I surprised her again. I licked my finger to get it nice and wet and began probing her ass with it at the
same time that I was pumping her pussy full of dick. She gasped
and moaned, and was soon begging me to stick my cock into her
ass. I wondered if she had ever had anal sex before. I knew damn
well I hadn't, but I'd always wanted to try it out. Now was the
time.

I pulled my cock out of her cunt and bent down to lick her asshole again in order to get it all lubed up. Finally I placed my

throbbing dick at the entrance to her anal cavity and slowly began to slide it in. It was slow going, and it took almost twenty minutes to get all of my meat into her, but all the time she was begging me to put it in deeper. As soon as I got it all in she pleaded with me to fuck her hard and fast. After five minutes of slamming my meat into her ass we both came so hard that we collapsed on the car seat, holding onto each other until we had regained our composure.

Wouldn't you know that after I got home, took a shower and went to bed, my wife wanted to ride the pony. Actually it didn't take long for me to get hard again, as I was still thinking of the fabulous sex I had had with Ronnie only an hour earlier.

Ronnie and I no longer see each other, because we felt it wasn't worth the risk of our spouses finding us out and turning a great sexual experience into a nightmare. But I'll always be grateful to her for opening up my sexual horizons, and I believe she feels the same. —*G.F., Charleston, South Carolina*   ○┼■

Different Strokes

ONE MAN'S BOXER REBELLION IS PROOF THAT PANTIES ARE DANDY

There's nothing I like more than the feeling of female flesh surrounding my cock. A nice warm, tight pussy, a hot mouth or a pair of firm tits are my dick's idea of a dream vacation. But I have my special tastes too, my favorite of which is the wonderful world of women's panties. As a matter of fact, I'm writing this letter wearing a fabulous pair of snug, red lace bikini panties that cradle my cock like a second skin.

Since the life-changing evening two years ago when I first tried on a pair of my wife Betty's panties, they are all I've worn under my slacks, jeans and shorts. Whether at work, shopping or out partying with the boys, no matter what I'm wearing on the outside, beneath the surface my life has been one continuous panty party. The only time I don't wear them is when I'm body-building or jogging—and that's only because I don't want to get my silky, frilly undergarments all sweaty.

I thought my wife would be reluctant to fulfill my desire to slip into a pair of her panties, but I was wrong. She must've read my mind that night when I looked longingly inside her underwear drawer, wishing I could slip into some of her finery. I'd worn panties quite often in my earlier days, but gave it up when I met Betty. I hadn't realized how much I missed the delicious feeling until that night when I peered into her drawer. I'd never told her of my earlier affection for panties, so I was surprised when she asked if I wanted to model a pair of hers. I'll never forget them. They were simple pink satin ones with tiny embroidered roses, and putting them on was thrilling.

Once Betty saw the raging hard-on I popped when she helped me slip out of my boxers and into her panties, a smile came to her face. From her lingerie drawer she pulled out pair after pair of silk, cotton and lace panties and laid them out on the bed for me to try on.

I think she was planning to have me give her a private fashion show, but it didn't exactly work out that way. My cock was night-stick hard from the moment Betty slid that very first pair of satiny pinks up my leg and into place. Betty saw the advantages of this right away. She asked me to turn around so she could see my ass in the panties. When I completed the turn, she knelt down and began to fondle my behind without removing the panties. She happened to be wearing panties too, and there was no mistaking the wet spot in the crotch of the pair she had on. Betty nibbled at my cock through the satin, getting the fabric all wet with a combination of her saliva and my precome. She freed my cock and took it into her mouth, bathing me with her warm tongue. I creamed almost instantly, soaking her gums with a helping of batter so huge it took her several gulps to swallow it all.

My hard-on didn't go away after I came. If anything, my dick was even more rigid than before. I lay back on the bed and Betty sat astride me. We were still both wearing our panties, which we pulled aside just enough to allow my cock to sink into her sopping well. She rode me hard, grunting and playing with her clitoris. I could feel her cunt muscles clenching my prick, just as I could feel the satin panties clinging to the skin of my thighs and ass. I erupted into her like Old Faithful, and kept drilling upward until I'd brought her to an explosive orgasm as well.

And still my erection would not quit! We fucked all night, with me trying on a new pair of panties after each climax. By the time morning arrived we were exhausted, but more satisfied than we ever thought possible. Needless to say, I haven't worn boxers since.

It's amazing how much more intensely erotic our lives have become since that night. Before we got married, Betty had no idea that I once wore panties. But now they're a very big part of our fun. We both wear the same size, so we can shop together and pick out pairs we know we'll both enjoy wearing. I feel very comfortable going into a department store, with or without her, and taking my time to find just the right style and size. Often I'll even ask one of the pretty sales clerks for help. When she realizes the panties are for me, she smiles and helps me pick out just the sort of thing she knows I'll like.

Once a week Betty shaves the hair on my balls and trims the rest of my bristly pubes so that the panties fit just right. She says that nothing turns her on more than the sight of my stiff log outlined in the smooth panty fabric. Over the past few months I've also started to wear sheer-to-the-waist panty hose. At first I just bought a pair on a lark, but I suspect that soon they'll be as big a turn-on for us as the panties.—*B.R., San Diego, California*

SOME MARRIED FOLKS JUST CAN'T KEEP A GOOD THING TO THEMSELVES

My husband Ross is a very successful contractor. He is attractive, intelligent, and has a beautiful cock that measures nearly seven inches when hard, with a thickness that is just perfect for my shaved, well-traveled pussy. Ross definitely has a kinky side. For the first year of our marriage I tried to ignore it. I finally gave in, however, and I'm glad that I did. The reason? It seems that I can be rather kinky myself.

At first I was really freaked out when my husband started asking about my old lovers. He pressed me for all the intimate details about whom I had fucked, how big their cocks were, whether I'd ever fucked two men at once, how many times I'd taken a dick in the ass—he wanted to know it all. But I soon learned that whenever I told him something juicy about my past, I got one of the best pussy eatings or fuckings of my life, so I didn't hold anything back.

In time he started hinting that he wouldn't mind it if I got in touch with one of my old boyfriends and fucked him—as long as I was honest with him about it and, most importantly, told him all about it in explicit detail. At first I absolutely refused, and was hurt that he thought I'd rather fuck someone else than him. But then I started thinking about some of my past lovers, and came to the conclusion that if the right situation came up, I could not only fulfill my husband's fantasy, but also enjoy a wild night of fucking another man.

I started thinking about who I could fuck to make Ross happy. I wanted someone who was, above all, a great lay. My husband always enjoyed when I told him about a young guy named Barry. I'd met him one summer while working at a restaurant, and we'd proceeded to fuck relentlessly for over a year. I was twenty-five at the time, and he was barely eighteen and always primed to pump! So one day when Ross was off at work, I called Barry's mom and dad to see if he was still living there. I was hornier than hell, and knew that the moment I tracked Barry down, I'd find a way to get my hands on his taut young buns.

I hadn't talked to Barry for two years, and when I dialed the number my heart was beating like crazy. To my surprise, he answered the phone at his parents' house. We talked for about five minutes, updating each other on what we had been up to, although I didn't tell him I was married. When he asked why I was calling, I confessed that I'd been thinking about how he used to fuck the shit out of me. He agreed that it was some of the best sex he'd ever had. I told him that if he was game, I'd be up for reliving the past.

Forty-five minutes later, Barry was at my door. I felt like a schoolgirl again. My heart was just going crazy, and my cunt was so hungry for the thrusts of his cock it was dripping juice down my leg. I had on a pair of my silk jogging shorts and a flimsy crop top when I answered the door. I got us each a beer, and we sat around and talked for a while. It was obvious that we were dying to get naked, but I think we were both too nervous to make the first move.

I knew Ross would be coming home soon, so I got the ball rolling. "Remember the first time you fucked me in the backseat of my car?" I asked Barry. "Your dick was so hard, it really stretched my cunt wide open. I still think about it."

I could see that my words were having the desired effect. Barry's pants were poked up like a tent in front as his big cock strained for room to grow. He stood up and turned me around, then began kissing my neck and ears. I ran a bare foot up his pants leg as he played with my tits through my crop top.

"We don't need this," I said, pulling the top off.

"I remember the first time I fucked your tits," he said. "I loved the way they looked with my come all over them."

"They're still big and soft," I said. "See?" I took my breasts in my hands and massaged them. By now it was all I could do to keep from jumping him. But I had to admit, the anticipation was really turning me on. My pussy was on fire, and I moaned and rubbed myself against him, running my tongue all over his chest and nibbling his nipples. Finally he unzipped my shorts and let them fall to the floor. I stepped out of them and spread my legs.

Barry knelt down and I stood before him, my bald, wet pussy

awaiting the touch of his tongue. Barry had always loved to eat pussy, and he hadn't changed in that regard. He lapped at my moist fuck-lips and drank up the nectar flowing out of me. He stuck a finger into my gash and fingered me fast while sucking my clit. I was literally thrusting my crotch against his mouth, and after only two or three minutes of his tonguing my pussy, I had a terrific orgasm that left me weak in the knees.

Barry pulled me down to the floor with him, and I slipped my hand into his pants. His cock was hard as cement, and I played with it like it was a toy. I'd forgotten what a nice dick he had. I'm not going to tell you it was twelve inches long, or as big around as a can of beer, but Barry's seven circumcised inches were just what I was in the mood for. I wrapped one hand around it and pumped, while rubbing his balls through his pants. Knowing that in a minute I'd be blowing this gorgeous boy. I was in heaven.

You might find this hard to believe, but I'd never sucked Barry's dick. In fact, until I met my husband I'd never sucked anyone's dick. Now I popped the crown of Barry's rod in and out of my mouth, then worked on the underside of his dick with my tongue. I took a little over half of it into my mouth and soaked it with my warm, wet tongue. Then I went for the gusto and deep-throated him. I caught a glimpse of myself in a mirror, bobbing up and down on Barry's delicious shank. I wished Ross were there to see me giving someone else such good head. Oh, well. I knew how turned on he'd be that night when I told him all about it.

I used my right hand to jack Barry off while sucking his hard dick. This is something that makes my husband come very quickly, and Barry was no different. I stopped when I felt his nuts draw up tight, because I did not want to catch his load in my mouth. My desire was to have him flood my cunt with a huge load of sticky jism. Ross had promised me that if I let a man fuck me, he'd go down on my freshly-fucked, come-filled hole and suck me dry. We'd fantasized about him doing just that many times, and it always led to him dicking me silly. I couldn't believe that tonight, after Barry left and Ross came home, we would finally experience the real thing!

I took Barry by the hand and led him into our bedroom, sat him on our bed and crawled on top of him. He kept thrusting upward, trying to get his dick into my super-wet hole, but I teased him for a few moments.

"Are you sure you want to fuck me?" I asked.

He answered by wrapping my hand around his shaft, which was hard as a baseball bat. Enough playing, I decided, and guided his cock into my pussy. God it felt great to have Barry inside me again. He pumped his dick into me hard, slamming against my clit with each thrust. I knew it wouldn't take long for either one of us to climax at this rate. My cunt was burning up, and the juices were pouring out.

I climbed off his dick after fucking him for a few minutes. The shaft was shiny with my dew, and I sucked it a while. Tasting my own dew got me even more excited, and I turned around, got on all fours and begged Barry to stick it to me from behind. He was giving it to me hard and deep. I could feel every inch as it slid in, then slid out, then plunged all the way back in again.

Barry's hard body was all tensed up, and I could see he was trying hard to keep from coming. I was near orgasm now myself, and said, "Come on, fill me up!" Even before Barry shot his load, I went off like a rocket. His cock was rubbing my clit, and it made me climax again and again. I could feel Barry's thick seed washing into me, and rode him until his cock was totally empty.

He rolled off me and kissed his way down to my twat. I knew he was dying to eat me to another climax, but I didn't want him sucking the sperm out of my cunt. I was saving that treat for my husband. But that doesn't mean I was done with Barry just yet. I proceeded to give him what my husband calls an "Ultra-Blow." This is where I coat his dick with a small amount of olive oil, then suck his cock and jack him off at the same time. I coated my hands with the oil and greased up Barry's pole, then started stroking his big prick.

My husband always tells me, "If you're going to suck a dick, then suck it like you mean it." I played with Barry's balls, picking up the pace of my blowjob and getting more and more of his steel-hard shaft into my mouth. My reward came soon enough. Barry tensed up and shot another big load. This one I let blast down my throat, coating my insides with his thick, salty spunk.

With the taste of his milk still full on my lips and tongue, I got Barry dressed and out of there fast, as I knew my husband would be home any minute. I slipped into a pair of sheer panties in hopes that they would soon be stained with the unmistakable proof of my adultery. I then lay down on the bed and waited to give Ross what he'd always wanted—a ride in my cunt where another man's cock had just been.

A short while later I heard my husband come in through the

garage door. I told him I was in the bedroom. When he came in and saw me in bed he didn't think anything unusual was going on, as I'm often lying there waiting to fuck him when he comes home from work.

He gave me a kiss, but the look on his face showed me that he tasted something different on my lips. Then he sat down on the bed, started to get undressed and placed his hand on my pussy. When he snaked a finger inside me, he knew what I'd been up to. He lifted the semen-soaked digit to his nose, sniffed it and then stuck it into his mouth.

"Have you been a bad girl?" he asked.

"A very good bad girl," I grinned.

He pulled the sheet away to reveal my pubic patch all matted with Barry's come. He kissed me for the longest time, enjoying the taste of spunk in my mouth, and fingered my drenched pussy until his fingers were squishing around inside me like toes in a puddle of mud. Ross asked me who I had fucked that afternoon, and I told him the whole story. He ate my pussy like a madman, sucking the jism out of my hole and swallowing it all down.

My pussy had already received quite a workout from Barry's masterful fuck, and now it was my husband's turn to drive me wild. He slipped me his big shaft, sinking it all the way in with a single thrust. There was so much come already in my cunt, Ross's penis slid into me like a hot knife through butter. He slammed into me like an eighteen-year-old, his plunges so deep and fast that Barry's come was literally splashing out of my hole.

I related the details of my afternoon with Barry as Ross made love to me like a savage beast. Although his cock felt great inside me, what really made me come was when I told him that I was going to call Barry the next day and have him service me again. The thought of having that magnificent stud taking me in every position imaginable made me feel like the happiest, horniest woman in the world. Ross loved the idea too. He must've fucked me five times that night, listening to me talk about Barry's hard dick and how good it felt inside me.

Barry did indeed come over the next day, and many days after that. As long as my husband wants me to seek out fresh meat, I suppose I'd be a fool to disappoint him. Lately he's been bugging me to ball one of his friends, Tony, who he says is hung like a donkey. I'm sure you'll be hearing from me again soon.—*V.B.,*
Hollywood, Florida   ⚬╼▪

MRS. BUTTERWORTH TOO SYRUPY FOR YOU? MAYBE YOU'D PREFER MRS. SEX

When it comes to sex, my wife Gloria is the best. Not only is she gorgeous and sultry, but she knows how to keep things exciting in the bedroom. Or the bathroom, the dining room, the carport—anywhere the mood strikes her to get nasty with that hot body of hers. Our friends have commented many times on the look of contentment that's usually on our faces. In fact, they call us Mr. and Mrs. Sex, because they realize that Gloria and I are always getting it on. But I'm not writing this to tell you all about one of our many fantastic lovemaking sessions. Instead I'd like to pass along some advice to any of your readers interested in keeping their partner happy.

First of all, be fresh. One major reason so many men and women seek out other lovers is that the person they're with becomes predictable. Women, surprise your man with sexy outfits. Come to bed one night with a jar of strawberry preserves and ask him to treat you like a piece of toast. Ram a vibrator up his butt the next time you give him a blowjob. As for you men, experience has told me that women love to fantasize while having sex. One of our favorites is when Gloria pretends she's a tourist visiting Alcatraz prison, and I'm one of the tour guides. She expresses interest in seeing one of the solitary confinement cells, and I show it to her—only in our version, there's nothing solitary about what happens to her next. With a little effort, I'm sure you can come up with some great ideas of your own.

Be bold. A woman who is brazen enough to plant her come-filled pussy on her man's face and beg him to suck it clean is a woman who knows something about lust. Soft and gentle sex is all right from time to time, but as Gloria once told me, "Deep inside, people like it dirty." Try French-kissing your lover right after giving him head. You'd be surprised how many men really get turned on when they can taste their come in their lady's mouth. And remember, sex is not limited to nighttime in the bedroom. Preparing a meal, bundling the newspapers or even cleaning the bathroom can be a lot more exciting when they're done in the nude—or with frequent interruptions for some spontaneous doggie-style screwing. Personally, I like to take Gloria when she's vacuuming the living-room rug. I don't have to tell you that a vacuum cleaner, when handled with care and imagination, makes one hell of a vibrator.

Don't be shy. If you want your man to eat your pussy while you're driving down the interstate, pull down your panties and see if he takes the hint. Men, if you've always wanted to see your wife's mouth full with a load of your sperm, tell her. I'm always amazed at how willing people are to try out their deepest fantasies with strangers, while they remain timid and unfulfilled with the person they supposedly love and trust most of all.

Remember, the biggest failure is being unwilling to try new things. Have you been dying to have your husband bone you in the ass, but just haven't been able to figure out a way to ask him? Would you like your girlfriend to suck your toes like ten little dicks, but are afraid she'll think you're out of your mind? So what! It's perfectly natural to be timid at first, but why should that stop you? Don't forget, there was a time in all of our lives when the thought of even kissing someone made us blush. Be willing to sacrifice a few minutes of embarrassment or feeling silly for a lifetime of sexual freedom and satisfaction. —*D.N., Columbus, Ohio* ○━▬

JOIN US FOR A TIGHT BROWN MIDNIGHT SNACK— BATTERIES NOT INCLUDED

I've just moved in with my new man. His name is Eddie, and he is a hunk. Every muscle on his body is well-defined. Just looking at him makes me want to mount him and ride him to orgasm. When Eddie kisses me, my nipples get hard and my cunt flows like a waterfall.

Last night I was alone with my vibrator, just starting to masturbate, when I heard his footsteps outside my bedroom door. The door swung open, and the look on Eddie's face was one of total surprise. His eyes were instantly drawn to my nakedness—and to the buzzing little toy between my legs. My legs were parted, and it was obvious from where he stood just how wet my pussy was. I could see his cock grow hard, and continued using my vibrator. My inviting smile told him he was welcome to join me.

Eddie quickly removed his clothes and came to bed. I gasped

at the sight of his gigantic hard-on, and my mouth watered in anticipation of what was to come. He leaned down and began tonguing my breasts, making my nipples instantly erect. I arched my back, pressing my firm breasts into his mouth. I could feel his tongue, lips and teeth on my tits, gently nibbling the turgid flesh. The sensation drove me insane!

We shifted positions so that I was sitting at the head of the bed, and Eddie was in front of me on all fours. The vibrator was still pressed against my clit, sending ripples of pleasure through my whole body. I reached around and took Eddie's cock in my hand. I slowly began to stroke it. His sinewy ass was poised in front of my face as I leaned closer to him.

I began to lick his balls, pressing the flat of my tongue up against his hard body while I continued to jerk him off. My tongue was hot and wet, and I traced my way toward his buns. I licked the crack of his ass, then used my free hand to spread apart the cheeks. I teased them with my tongue and began to trace circles around his asshole. My tongue never stopped. It constantly probed his ass, as my hand increased its speed on his cock.

Eddie trembled. He loves it when I use my tongue on his asshole, but I wonder if he realizes just how much I love doing it? I plunged my tongue into his ass and wiggled it around. He groaned with unbearable pleasure as I plumbed his secret depths. I got his anus all hot and steamy, and he wiggled and groaned with pleasure.

"I love eating your ass, baby," I whispered, then began to fuck the clenched bud with my tongue. The plunges of my tongue kept up with the rhythm of my hand on his cock. I must've been quite a sight, squirming against my vibrator while jerking Eddie off and making a meal of his butt, sliding my tongue in and out in a most wet and wonderful manner.

We were in a frenzy by this time, both of us about to come. I beat him to it, screaming out, "Oh . . . Jesus, I'm . . . coming!" As I thrashed against the vibrator, he turned around quickly and rammed his rock-hard cock into my open mouth. I felt the knob of his dick plunge all the way down my throat as his come spurted out. My throat muscles tightened around his reed as I swallowed a bellyful of his creamy brew.

Take it from me, girls. If you're in the mood for a late-night snack, you can't do better than feasting on some puckered anus and washing it down with a great big helping of thick, white sperm. —*M.C., Sioux Falls, South Dakota*   O⊢▪

PHOTOGRAPHER GETS A LITTLE BEHIND, AND FIANCÉE WINS IN PHOTO FINISH

Since we opened our relationship to include other sexual partners, my fiancée Caroline and I have found that our sex life is more fulfilling than we could ever have imagined. Our open relationship has freed us from the strictures of jealousy and deception, not to mention hypocrisy. Couples, even after they're married, often find themselves looking at other men and women in a sexual way, perhaps feeling that familiar spark of carnal excitement when the possibility of making it with a new partner arises. Caroline and I not only accept those urges, we allow ourselves the freedom to follow through on them.

Caroline greatly relishes every opportunity to express her sexuality in whatever way pleases or intrigues her. Usually this means pleasuring herself with another man, although occasionally she enjoys eating a bit of strange pussy. Although I've had a few memorable dalliances since I've been with her, I've found that it's not as interesting to fuck other women as it is to be part of Caroline's sexual adventures with other men.

Caroline is a shapely thirty-year-old brunette with bountiful tits, a firm, inviting ass and legs that have driven stronger men than I into a frenzy of masturbatory fantasies. She and I have been together for six years, and in that time I've watched her blossom sexually. When I first met her she was a virgin, but by the end of our senior year in high school she would alternate between blowing guys her own age and fucking the older men she picked up in bars. Since I'm not the jealous type, I've always been able to take great pleasure in the many ways she's put her insatiable body to use. After our prom, while most of our friends were off drinking themselves sick, Caroline and I were off having a hot threesome with the superbly hung stud who'd driven our limo.

Things quieted down for us during graduate school, but a call from an old college friend of hers got the ball rolling again. Roger and Caroline had never officially been a romantic item in school. They were just two good friends who'd occasionally get together in the posh home of Roger's parents to get high and fuck.

Roger had called her, these many years later, because he had just bought an expensive new camera and was interested in taking some sexy photographs of her both in lingerie and entirely nude. He even offered to pay her for her modeling services. When I told her it was all right by me, she immediately dressed in her sluttiest outfit, packed her assortment of sex toys and left for Roger's apartment.

When she came home six hours later (during which time I masturbated twice while thinking about what they might be up to), Caroline smelled of cigarettes, wine and reefer. In her hand was a thirty-six-exposure roll of film.

"I told Roger that I'd pose only if he let me take the film to be developed," she said. "We get to keep the negatives and a set of prints." Then she flashed a quintet of twenty-dollar bills arranged like a fan. "I could definitely get into doing this modeling stuff on a regular basis," she said with a smile. She tossed the money on our bed, and we fucked on it all night long until the sweat-soaked bills were sticking to her luscious ass.

When I saw the photos, I had to admit that Caroline had a natural ease in front of a camera. I riffled excitedly through shot after shot of my girlfriend tramping it up. There was a brazen quality about her that made me want to get my hands on the sizzling slut in those photos, especially when I saw the one of her spreading her labia with her glistening fingers. That photo was followed by a view of two of those fingers buried knuckle-deep in her cunt.

Each photograph went further than the one before it. In the last of the shots, she had about eight inches of her huge, double-headed dildo rammed up her canal, while her pink, penis-shaped vibrator was pressed against her clit. The look on her face was one of total abandon.

"I came twice while he was setting up that shot," Caroline said. We were on the bed looking at the photographs, and I was rubbing the head of my own big prick up and down her slippery slice.

"What happened after Roger ran out of film?" I whispered expectantly. "Did he fuck you?"

"No," she replied.

"Are you sure, you little whore?" I teased, growling as I rammed my prong into the furthest reaches of her twat.

"Quite sure," Caroline managed to gasp as I thrust into her. "I think I'm old enough to know when I've been fucked. But he did take his pants down and jack off in front of me."

That's what I wanted to hear. "Really?" I said. "What did he do when he came?"

Caroline stuck her forefinger in my asshole and admitted that she'd let Roger squirt his jism on her lush tits. Hearing this, the come burst forth from my own cock.

Over the next few months, Caroline did more than a few modeling jobs for Roger, usually ending the session by stroking his dick till he came, or letting him jack off onto her ivory skin. She told me that she especially liked the way his come felt when it splashed against the smooth cheeks of her ass.

But then, very late one Saturday night, Caroline showed up unexpectedly at my apartment. I could tell from the look on her face that she'd been up to something and that she was dying to tell me about it.

"I've been posing at Roger's," she said.

"Where's the film?" I asked.

"We didn't take pictures this time," she said. "I put on a sex show for him with my vibrators."

I was already steering Caroline toward the bedroom and removing items of her clothing. Her panties felt exceptionally damp, and my dick was stiffening fast. When I lay her on the bed and removed her panties, I saw that her pussy was exceedingly wet. Looking me right in the eye, she said, "I let him fuck me, honey."

I started to tremble. Not with jealousy, of course, but with uncontrollable lust. "In the pussy?" I asked.

"In the ass," she said. "I have a butt-plug in now. His come is still inside me."

My head swam. My sweet, hot Caroline was giving me the present of a lifetime! I couldn't decide what to do first: kiss her, or bury my tongue in her spermy anus and guzzle up Roger's pungent seed. Needless to say, I managed to do both.

As I munched her chute, she told me everything that had happened between her and Roger that night. She was masturbating for him while he beat his meat, the way she usually did. But this time, after she'd orgasmed a few times, Roger stripped off all his clothes and led her into the kitchen. He hoisted her onto the table and spread her legs wide. Then he worked two fingers into her— one in her cunt, and the other up her ass.

"Oh, yeah!" Caroline had squealed. "Fuck me with your fingers!"

"I'll go you one better," he'd replied, and pressed his throbbing prick against her tiny anus.

"Oooh, yeah," Caroline pleaded. "Do me like that. Make me your bitch."

Roger inched his thick rod into her. Caroline's eyes flew open as he took her through the back door. He fucked her fast and furious, making her completely lose control. His thrusts were so ferocious, he pushed the kitchen table all the way across the room until it was banging against the wall each time he entered her. Caroline said it was such an intense fuck, if her legs hadn't been locked behind his head she would've been thrown clear.

"What a fuck!" she said to me, reaching climax as I sucked her clitoris. "My ass is going to be numb for a month!"

I'd managed to hold off coming while she told her tale of lust, but now that she was finished I shoved my cock into her gaping anus and squirted out a sea of come. I'd never felt so satisfied or so much in love with her as I did at that moment. My cock swam in her sloshy chute for several minutes until it finally softened and slid out, all shiny and golden brown.

Caroline and Roger now fuck every chance they get, with my blessing.—*K.J., Memphis, Tennessee*

TEN LITTLE INDIANS AND TEN LITTLE TOES TICKLE HIS FUCKING FANCY

Cecilia's always been the sexiest woman I've ever met, and as she gets older she just seems to get better. Thank God I married her when I had the chance.

We've always worked hard at keeping our sex life interesting, but over the years I've discovered that some of the most exciting innovations come into our lives by pure chance. Just such a piece of luck happened to us a few weeks ago.

From time to time, like most women, Cecilia polishes her nails. She doesn't actually do it that often, or maybe this would have happened sooner. Anyway, we were getting ready to go to a party. Ceil had already had her shower and washed her hair. I'd come up behind her while she was drying herself off, because I love to smell her while she's all fresh and clean, and play with her breasts while they're warm and humid from the spray. She let me tease her nipples up to stiff, suckable points, but then she chased me away so she could finish drying off.

A few minutes later I came into the bedroom, and there she sat, her hair still turbaned in a towel, but otherwise naked, polishing her nails. She had just finished applying the bright red lacquer to the last nail, and I watched her slip the little brush back in the bottle and twist it shut. Then she tossed the bottle aside and sat very straight-backed, her fingers spread wide, waving her hands gently to help the paint dry.

Her nipples were still poking out, inviting me to fondle and fiddle them, and I hated to see them disappointed. I knelt by the bed and leaned over to suck one of those little cuties into my mouth.

Ceil made a face and whined, "Honey, not now. You're going to smear my nail polish."

Letting go my hold on her nipple I said, "No, it's okay. I'll be really careful."

"But if you get me all excited I'll start wiggling around, and then who knows what will happen," she argued, still pouting.

Ordinarily I'll do whatever my baby wants, but I realized that she wasn't going to do anything physical to chase me away because her nails were wet. Just to see what she'd do, I went back to work on her turgid nipple. In an effort to escape my efforts, she rolled backward. Bad move. Now she was lying flat on the bed, waving her fingers in a desperate attempt to make them dry so she could tickle me or chase me away. But she was completely vulnerable to my approaches.

I started to creep up the bed toward her, humming the approach music from *Jaws:* dum-dum, dum-dum, dum-dum, dum-dum.

Cecilia was giggling helplessly and shrieking when my lips descended on her breast. That was when I caught a strong whiff of her nail polish. I have a good sense of smell, and often form strong associations with smells. I don't know what the nail polish reminded me of, but my dick sprang up instantaneously like a flagpole.

Ceil noticed it, and spoke straight to my dick, as if I wasn't there. "Oh, so that's the way it is, is it?" she purred. "You poor fellow. Doesn't anyone ever pay any attention to you?"

"Wrap your hand around it," I requested.

"I don't know if it's dry yet, honey."

"Please. Just be careful." When she wrapped her flame-tipped fingers around my erection I swear to God it doubled in size. There was something staggeringly sexy about the look and smell of her long nails pumping away on my pink porker. Ordinarily I can fuck for hours. I pride myself on my control, but this time it wasn't going to be that way. She gave me about ten good jerks, and then I spouted. The intensity of my spasms doubled when I saw the sperm running down and coating her fingers, especially when a few drops went on her nails.

Ceil, as I said before, is the sexiest woman alive, and she proved it with her next gesture. Seeing how turned on her nails had made me, she asked, "Did that turn on my lover? Did you like those shiny nails jerking you off?" I looked into her eyes. That's when she raised her fingers to her mouth and slowly, deliberately, licked every drop of come off them. Watching those bright red fingertips disappearing one at a time between her lips turned me on so much that my pecker started throbbing with a fresh erection. Good thing, because my darling was worked up herself, and ready for a good dicking.

I gave it to her, and then I convinced her to polish her toes and I fucked her again. I couldn't tell you why this turned me on so much, and frankly I couldn't care less. I'm just grateful that we discovered it. Now it's a regular part of our routine. —*D.F., Flagstaff, Arizona* ○┼▮

A SHORT BUT POWERFUL NEW FOUNTAIN IS OPEN FOR EXHIBIT IN THE CITY PARK

Every guy should date a girl like Becky at some time in their lives. Not only was Becky gorgeous, but she had a gregarious personality to go with it. Her most distinguishing features were her thick, long black hair and her ever-present smile. The killer for me, though, was the sparkle in her eyes. It didn't take me long to realize that sparkle meant "I've got something sweet in store for you."

Becky was the girl who initiated me into the world of exciting, unadulterated, raw sex, as opposed to romantic, gentle lovemaking. Her imagination was unlimited, her spontaneity unnerving, her horniness unparalleled. Those qualities made our dates unbelievable. I quickly realized that one thing that dependably made her drip was to fool around where we might be seen, and that no place was off-limits.

Becky called me at work one day. "Do you like to look at naked girls?"

"Well, uh, of course."

"Does it make you want to jack off?"

"Well, uh, yeah, it does."

"I'll pick you up at seven." She hung up. My cock was hard with anticipation. I couldn't wait for what she had in mind. I was hoping it had to do with some of her college friends.

She showed up at my apartment dressed to kill. She was only wearing one piece of clothing, and it was pretty provocative. She grabbed my hand and said, "Let's go! I've been horny all day!" She hopped in the passenger seat of my car, and immediately had her dress up so I could see she wasn't wearing anything underneath. Becky also wanted to play with herself as she directed me to our destination. She loved to tease me, knowing that while I was driving I could not reach over and touch her. To make it even more tantalizing, she gave my hard cock a squeeze every couple of minutes.

We were driving down a main drag when she directed me into the parking lot of one of the local strip bars. I had been to my share of strip bars, but certainly not on a date. We strutted in. Becky was waving her butt provocatively, and I was rather proud to be seen with her. We took a seat, ordered drinks and started to take in the show. Becky was hanging all over me, while her clothes were barely hanging onto her. She wanted to know which girls I liked and she wanted me to be specific: blondes, brunettes or redheads; tall or short; petite or large; well-built or flat-chested; brown or pink nipples; bushy or bare pussies. All this talk, coupled with the naked dancers, made me as hard as I'd ever been.

And all the while, Becky was soaking it all up. "I love this place, you know. All these guys have hard-ons. What a great place!" And then came my explanation of her intentions. "And to think that you're the only guy here who brought his own personal masturbator!"

"What?" I asked, as she began to undo my pants.

"All these other guys are going to jack off in their cars or at home, but every one of them would rather jack off right here!"

"You've got to be kidding." She was pulling my cock out!

"Come on, feel how hard you are. Plus, don't you think these girls want to see some cock sometimes?"

"Well . . ." Becky was already starting to really stroke my cock.

"Oh, that's better. Now look at that girl: perfect little trim body, perky little erect breasts, neatly trimmed pussy. Come on, wouldn't you like to jack off for her?" She was beating my meat furiously, and it was all too much. The girl on stage could definitely tell what Becky was doing, and a few of the other guys were watching too. I exploded under the table.

"There, didn't that feel good?" She was licking her fingers, still watching their performance. "Come on, lover, I'm ready for mine now. You've got to lick my pussy. We can either go out to the car or I'll lie right down on this table!" I wasn't going to challenge her to lie on the table, because I was afraid she would, so I grabbed her hand and we headed for the door.

We got out to the car, and she hopped up on the hood and spread her legs. My face beat her own hands in a race for her pussy. She was sopping wet, and began screaming her excitement almost immediately. To my surprise, my dick was hard again. I had never had two orgasms within ten minutes before, but it seemed I was up to the task. It didn't matter that we were standing in a public place. We could have been in Macy's window at that point and I would have behaved exactly the same. I pulled Becky to the edge of the car and pushed my pants down. She was so wet that her pussy swallowed my cock in one thrust. She was beating her clit with one hand and diddling her nipple with the other while I pumped into her. We both came in a matter of seconds. I'm surprised the police didn't come, we were making so much noise.

Less than a week later, Becky surprised me on my birthday. I was fast asleep when I heard the doorbell. It was six in the morning, so I couldn't imagine who it was. Since I sleep naked, I pulled some gym shorts on and answered the door. To my surprise it was Becky, smiling and holding a bottle of champagne. "Happy Birthday," she grinned. "Come on, let's celebrate."

"Well, let me get dressed."

"Nope. Just go brush your teeth and I'll get you something to put on." She grabbed me a baseball cap and a T-shirt. No shoes or underwear.

When we got to the car, I noticed a picnic basket and blanket.

Becky glanced at her watch. "Come on, we have to hurry." How urgent could a picnic possibly be?

We arrived at a large local park, grabbed our gear and headed away from the parking lot and roads. We found what I thought was a pretty secluded spot, threw down the blanket and popped open the champagne. We were casually chatting and sipping when suddenly Becky jumped me. She rolled me over, kissing me, and started rubbing my cock. I naturally responded by beginning to touch her.

"Oh, no," she cautioned. "It's your birthday. I'll do everything." She laid me on my back and straddled me, sitting on my chest, knees on either side of my head. I was basically immobile, looking up at her smiling face. She kept her knees where they were, but lifted her rear end off my chest and positioned her pussy directly over my face. Like me, she wasn't wearing any underwear. "Smelling my pussy makes you hard, doesn't it?" she queried.

"It drives me crazy!"

She reached into her shorts. "You love to watch me play with my pussy, don't you?" By now my cock had grown out of my gym shorts, and was standing straight up in the air. "You love to have a hard-on out here in public, don't you? Doesn't that fresh air feel good on your cock?" Right then she rolled off me and lay down beside me. While she was straddling me, the only direction I could see in was up—up her shorts to her pussy or up to her smiling face. Needless to say, I was unaware of anything that was going on around us. So there I was, my erection standing out from my shorts, while Becky reached into the basket for some Vaseline. She quickly slicked up my cock.

About that time I noticed—with horror, I might add—that the girls' track team from a local college was headed our way. Becky had planned our picnic so that we'd be positioned about twenty feet from their path as they were out on their daily run. So here's Becky, lying on her side next to me, stroking my cock. As the girls approached, she crooned, "I thought we'd give the girls a little scenery during their run." I couldn't believe it, but knowing Becky it shouldn't have surprised me.

By the time the girls were running by us, she was beating my pecker furiously. I couldn't believe how large my cock looked. I don't think it had ever been so engorged. "These girls need to see this, they need to know how to jack a guy off, don't you think?" I was speechless. "Look at them, they're all staring. They love to see your enormous cock. I imagine their young pussies are drenched! You know what they'll be thinking about when they're rubbing their clits in bed tonight. Don't you wish a couple of them had enough guts to come over and help? Can't you just imagine three or four hands jerking your cock off?"

That was it. The entire situation was too much: the looks in the girls' eyes, Becky's verbal teasing and her skilled hand jacking me off. My orgasm exploded just as three girls were slowing down to get a better view. Becky rubbed my come all over my cock and balls. The girls just couldn't quit staring. I was surprised that Becky didn't invite them over.

As they were all running off to finish their daily run, hopefully with sopping wet pussies, Becky commented, "You'll have to wait until tonight to see what else I got you." I could hardly wait.—*M.R., Minneapolis, Minnesota* ⊶▪

THE MAN IN THE DRESS
FULFILLS FANTASIES FOR TWO

I'm a curious woman. I just can't let go when something strikes me as odd.

It started innocently enough in the laundry room of my apartment building. You meet just about everyone there, so I have a nodding acquaintance with the other people in the building. Doing laundry in public can be a bit embarrassing. After all, who wants the world to know what kind of underwear you prefer, or if there are holes in your socks. You have to get used to hanging your bra over a coat hanger to dry and then parading through the halls with it. Oh, by the way, any macho guys reading this need to know why you don't put a bra in the dryer: it wrecks the elastic, and your tits flop around when you wear it.

So anyway, one Friday a few months back I was doing my laundry very late at night. I was happily hanging my bras out to dry when Hiro came down to empty his dryer. He's a cute guy, lean and quiet and attractive. We had met a few times in the laundry room, and he had aroused my curiosity.

As far as I knew he didn't have a wife or girlfriend, yet I had occasionally seen him pulling a worn bra from the dryer and folding it up. On one occasion, I'd seen him washing an old housedress. So, since I spend all night sometimes reading *Penthouse Letters,* obviously the first thing I thought of was crossdressing. I mean, some of those crossdressing letters are really hot. When I'm reading them and getting myself off I wonder what it would be like to be fucked by a man in women's clothing.

I guess he hadn't expected to meet anyone down in the basement late at night, because I could see the outline of a bra beneath his shirt as he bent over the dryer. Suspicions confirmed!

I was overwhelmed with a desire to find out how a crossdresser screws, so by the trite expedient of pretending to trip, I knocked over his basket while dropping mine. As we sorted things out I noticed the loving way he folded my underwear. As I handed him back his bra I told him why he should air-dry it and, taking a big plunge, pointed out that the one he was wearing was rather too loose and puckered from too much heat.

I swear he looked like an eight-year-old caught with his hand in the cookie jar. Before he could recover, I offered to find a new bra that fit him properly. The eight-year-old regressed to a three-year-old with great shining eyes who had discovered something new and amazing. He stuttered and stammered, but soon agreed. I knew right then I was going to get laid by a man in a dress. The dripping in my panties told me I was going to have more laundry to wash.

I took him back to my place and got out the tape measure, which gave me a perfect excuse to run my hands over his body as I figured his sizes. I ran my hands over his chest, feeling the empty cups of his bra under his shirt, and decided a C cup would be about right. His hips were very slim, not feminine at all, but I took my time with the tape and blatantly grabbed his ass-cheeks.

What the hell. I went for broke, reaching around to loosen his belt. His pants fell to the floor and he was wearing red lace panties, which I slid aside. Since I was kneeling behind him I couldn't see his cock, but I began to stroke it while kissing his ass along the elastic of the panties. I began to play with his soft cock, caressing his balls and running my fingers along it as it began to grow. I love the feeling of a cock growing in my hands. It gives me a sense of power and seductiveness beyond belief.

He soon reached full length, and I happily pumped his prick with my hands, while nibbling on his ass. I loved the feel of the soft skin of his hard cock. As I kept stroking, my fingers told me he was endowed with a nice thick prick. I reached between his legs and fondled his balls through the nylon of his panties. It was sweet to play with his sac, sliding my fingers over the smooth fabric, then running them back to play with his asshole.

It didn't take long before he became unsteady on his feet. I laid him down on the floor, and got my first sight of his prick. I truly wished there was a rubber handy, but since there wasn't I bent over and began to suck his fat fuck-pole. I guess my aggressive behavior was too much for him, because he erupted in my mouth after only a couple of slurps.

When he stopped pumping, I stood and dropped my own pants and lowered myself over his mouth. He certainly knew how to eat a woman. His soft, strong hands on my hips supported me just enough to slide his tongue into my dripping hole. He burrowed into my slit, his face pressed against my crotch, so hard I didn't know how he could breathe.

He sensed that I was horny as hell and didn't want to play around, so he headed right for my clit and began to suck and lick with expertise. I leaned forward on my arms to give him a better angle, and went wild with pleasure. His hands left my hips and cupped my ass-cheeks, forcing me onto his dancing tongue. Far too soon I was writhing and grunting as waves of orgasm wracked my body. I couldn't support myself, and rolled to the living room floor beside him, where we shared a kiss and spent a long, luxurious time just holding each other.

No matter how great the lovemaking, the floor soon starts to get too hard to keep lying there, so I took him into my bed and we spent the night together.

In the morning we started out on our shopping expedition. On the way I asked Hiro about his crossdressing. He told me he'd been doing it since he was a teenager, but had never told anyone about it until I discovered his secret. He had a few things he wore, but not much more than what I had seen. He had been too shy to shop for himself, and had ordered his clothes through the mail.

I decided to head for a dress shop I really like, because it specialized in closeouts. Their selection was extensive, so I figured we'd be able to find something to fit him. I was struck by his childlike joy in picking out his new clothes. I was very naughty, wrapping a bra around him when we were hidden behind a display, and asking him if he'd found any panties that he wanted me to take off him.

I gave in to another impulse, dragging him into the dressing room with me to try on the clothes. It was a tight fit, but once inside I pulled off his shirt, slipped a red underwire bra over his arms and snapped it in place. A perfect fit. Too bad we didn't have anything to stuff it with. I soon divested him of his pants, and he tried on matching panties, which were a bit too small.

The sight of that lovely prick just hanging there before my eyes was irresistible. I took it into my mouth. Once again his velvet rod began to grow for me, and I savored his stick while he tried to be quiet so no one would notice. I couldn't believe how wanton I had become over this relative stranger just because he liked to wear a dress. Yet there I was, behaving like a giddy college girl and blowing him in a dressing room.

I began to massage his pecker with my fingers while I sucked. I ran my finger along the underside of his cock, lifting it up slightly until I reached the end. I watched enthralled as his pecker bounced up and down, then I caressed it again. I milked it, squeezing the head between my fingers as I pulled his pud. I ran my lips up and down his pole, flipping my tongue at the tip each time I pulled back. He lasted much longer this time. I was thoroughly enjoying myself when there was a knock on the door—the saleslady inquiring ever so politely if I needed any help.

The mood was broken. His cock deflated so fast I thought I could hear the air escaping. We quickly tried the rest of the clothes on him and gathered our purchases. He had a terrible time keeping a straight face when I bought a bra and panty set to match his, but the saleslady was professionally oblivious to our byplay.

On the way home I stopped at the drugstore for some rubbers, hoping to use the whole damn box if I played my cards right. I let Hiro get through the door before I attacked him, dropping his pants and pulling off his shirt. I relented long enough to get into his bedroom before helping him put on his new underwear. He opened a drawer and took out two breast forms that jiggled in his hands, then deftly slipped them into his bra. I hadn't even thought of pantyhose, but he took a garter belt and stockings from his stash, telling me they were much easier on his balls. He even had a voluminous half skirt that made him look like he had hips once his dress was on. For someone with such ratty bras, he certainly had an interesting collection of specialized underwear.

In a few hours, the man of my lustful dreams was an average-looking woman. I was still in my bra and panties, flaunting myself unmercifully. I couldn't tell if his prick was reacting under all the padding, but once he was completely dressed I took off my panties and sat down on the couch, spreading my legs in invitation.

To my surprise, he left the room, but was soon back with a little vibrating egg in one hand and something concealed behind his back in the other. He knelt before me and began to play with my pussy. Hiro was a tease, lightly stroking my bush with his fingers, drawing little rivulets of heat down my thighs. I felt him tugging my pussy lips apart, and felt his warm breath on my vagina, but he pulled back without tasting. There are some definite problems when getting it on with a man in makeup.

Not to worry. His fingers were soon buried in me and sending little shocks radiating from my crotch. He started to work on my asshole with something slippery from a tube. Even though I had teased his ass the night before, I had never actually done anything Greek before. He was gentle, but it really didn't do much for me. That is until he started to work the little egg up my ass. As soon as he pressed the buzzing beauty to my hole I practically levitated. When I was finally still again, he began to play the vibrator over my clit and slit, then moved down to my ass again. He worked the egg up my back door, and the vibrations were simply unreal. In a flash the thing was sucked into my rectum, and my whole body shook with its buzzing.

He reached down and revealed a great, hulking dildo, which he proceeded to thrust up my well-lubricated slit. I wondered in passing why a man had a dildo, but was simply too busy getting screwed to care. He was an artist, twisting and pushing the rubber prick into my hot box. I could feel it hit bottom, and cried out as he spun the thing around in my slash. He made lazy circles around my vagina with the tip, then suddenly drove the dildo deep into me, fucking me furiously.

I could barely form the words when I demanded he get one of the rubbers and fuck me with his living cock. He lifted his skirt and I had no doubt of his arousal. He rolled the rubber onto his shaft and plunged into me. My fantasies became true. I was in bliss as he drove his shaft into me, fucking me like never before. As he pistoned his hips I moaned in ecstasy. I lay back on the couch and watched as he plowed me, his thick rod spreading me open wide, then leaving a lonely hole until he came driving back into me.

Somewhere about then I started coming, the first of many orgasms I had while he filled my cavern with his warm flesh. I was floating in a wonderful erotic haze when I realized he was coming. He stopped plowing into me and thrust forward one more time, burying himself deep in my cunt. His body jerked and his boobs shimmered as he let go, filling the rubber with his juice. He pressed close to me, keeping his lovely cock in me as he told me how much he enjoyed screwing while he was dressed.

Eventually, we got up, and I found a black elastic strap at my feet, next to the abandoned dildo. So that's why he had a dildo. I wondered who used it on him, and decided that if I could get fucked by a man in a dress then I was going to fuck him back. I slid the rubber dong into the harness and tightened it around my body. The batteries for the vibrator were still dangling by their wire from my bunghole, so I slipped them into the harness. It was a really strange feeling to have a prick dangling before me, but I kind of liked it. Soon he was lying on the covers with his ass in the air.

It was my turn to use the stuff in the tube, and I lathered his hole thoroughly. Leaning forward, I placed the dildo to his exposed hole and thrust my hips at him. It was one of the most sexually exciting things I had ever seen, watching my rubber prick slide into his asshole.

After a nice, slow start I soon got the hang of fucking like a man. Hiro was moaning and begging for more as I reamed his ass. His prick was growing again as I slammed the shaft deep into his anus, and his boobs were swinging like pendulums.

It may be fun to fuck if you're a man, but I wasn't going to get any satisfaction out of the rubber rod. I pressed the thing home in his ass and undid the straps. I started the vibrator in my own ass, rolled a rubber onto his flagpole and seated myself on it. God, he felt good. I was doing squat thrusts on his manhood and could feel the bed bounce beneath us, driving his erect member deep into my waiting pussy.

What I hadn't anticipated was how good it would feel to have him stroke my body with his stocking-covered legs. I came in an instant, but he was still going strong. He thrust his hips upward, probing my pussy with his meat. Each time he thrust, his boobs rippled and shimmered. The makeup was a total loss, his mascara weeping darkly down his cheeks. Surprisingly, the wig was still in place and I really got off on being fucked by a woman—a woman with a real, live prick.

Things got a little fuzzy after that, but I must have come several times as he drilled me. When he came it was like riding a bucking bronco. He whinnied like a horse, too, while pouring his essence into the rubber.

As I came down I became aware of the buzzing in my ass, so I turned the vibrator off and collapsed beside him. My hand rested comfortably on his boob, and his hand covered my snatch.

Hiro turned out to be very helpful when I explained I wanted to use the entire package of condoms before the weekend ended. We still had one left at nine p.m. on Sunday, so I took him out for a walk and we screwed in the bushes behind the apartment building. I've always wondered what anyone who saw us would have thought. From a distance they couldn't possibly tell that one of us was a man in a dress. Hey, look, in this crazy world, anything's possible. — *G.K., Tupelo, Mississippi*   ⚷

EARLY EXPERIENCE ON THE FARM SHOWS HER THE VALUE OF A STRING OF STUDS

After reading *Penthouse Letters* for some time, my husband began urging me to write to you about the many sexual adventures I used to have. Here goes.

I was a virgin when I graduated from high school. While I'd had many dates, I was determined to wait until I was married. I was the girl-next-door type, and the guys respected me for it. I've always been on the thin side, with a great set of legs and a nice rear.

After I graduated, I spent part of the summer working, then took a week to visit my parents' best friends on their farm. I'd spent many summers there while I was growing up. Their son Greg picked me up at the station, and I was amazed at how he had matured. We hugged and kissed, then drove to the farm.

Greg is four years older than I am, and had just graduated from college. He was much more attentive than he used to be during my summer stays, and I knew he approved of the changes in me in more than a friendly way.

His folks went shopping the next day, and Greg asked me if I wanted to watch the new stud and mare mate. I walked with him to the barn, and when he put the stud in with the mare the big horse immediately mounted the mare and began pumping his huge cock into her. I was getting hot. I was a virgin, but I'd been masturbating for a long time and was not immune to getting turned on.

As we watched, I felt Greg move up behind me. When he reached around and cupped my breasts I didn't resist. He was kissing my neck and telling me how great I looked and how he never thought his little playmate would grow up to be so beautiful. Steam was coming out of my jeans. When I felt him pulling them down, I said, "We shouldn't," but it didn't sound very convincing, even to me.

He leaned over me, feeling my cunt, and soon had me on my knees. Next I felt his cock trying to enter me. I was trying to tell him that I was a virgin when he thrust forward and I felt my hymen splitting. He kept thrusting until I began to feel great pleasure. Greg fucked me for some time, and I was beginning to move with him when he came.

The next day we went into town. Just before we went back to the farm, he left me and went to the drugstore. When we got close to home, Greg pulled off into a field. He took me in his arms and we kissed. His hands were foraging all over my body. We were both hot again, and when he told me he had bought rubbers so I wouldn't get pregnant, I got even hotter. I was quickly ready to do it, and he again turned me around and entered me doggie-style.

While he was driving his cock into me he reached around and played with my clit, and I came harder than I ever had before. Greg just kept fucking me harder and harder until he shot his load.

Over the next few days, before he left for his new job, we fucked at least five times, always doggie-style. For a young guy, he had great staying power, and always kept fucking me until I came at least once.

Soon after that I met my future husband, Drew. We dated for a couple of weeks before we started having sex. I fucked missionary-style for the first time with him. He knew I wasn't a virgin, but didn't bring it up until after we were engaged. After we had a particularly hot session, Drew said, "I know you weren't a virgin when we met. How many guys were there before me? I'd really get turned on hearing about it, because I get hot thinking of you with someone else." I told him that I'd had just one other partner.

Drew was not the jealous type. In fact, he used to point out to me which guys were making moves on me (which I never noticed). He seemed to love talking about how they'd like to get me on my back and slip me the wet willie. This evolved into him talking during sex, saying things like "How would you like Tommy's cock in you right now?" or "I'd like to see you fucking Jimmy's brains out right now."

After a while his fantasies were infectious, and his talk about other guys definitely enhanced our sex life. One night, at his urging, I finally told him about Greg. That really set him off. He fucked me hard and fast, and for the first time he rolled us over so I was on top, and told me to fuck him for all I was worth. The feeling of being in control of the pace and how deep his cock went into me was new and sexy. I came twice before his cock went off like a firecracker and we collapsed.

The following week Drew asked if I would fuck another guy while he was in the room, and could he join in after we were through. I told him I didn't think I could. After several weeks, though, the idea was still playing around in my brain, and I came around to saying maybe.

Since we live in a somewhat rural area, it took Drew about four months to come up with a realistic plan, and I had all but forgotten about his threesome proposal. Then one weekend he took me to another city, and we stayed in a luxury hotel suite. The first evening we went to the lounge for drinks and Drew introduced me to Vic, who I thought just happened to be someone Drew knew. But when Drew said Vic was prepared to join us if I wanted him to, I got all giggly. After a hot conference on the side, in which I asked him was he sure he could handle it, we gave Vic the okay.

We went to the room. Vic and I got into bed, with Drew watching. Once I adjusted to the initial weirdness of feeling a strange new body next to mine, I really got into it. Vic had great staying power. He fucked me in different positions, and I came about four times.

Drew was on me as soon as Vic rolled off, and he came almost at once. The three of us stayed together all night, with Drew and Vic taking turns exciting me.

I will give it to Vic anytime, but Drew seems obsessed with getting Greg to visit so he can see me fuck him. I have thought of Greg often, and would like to get my hands on his hard prick again.

In the meantime, Drew has lined up another guy for this weekend. I hope he's as good as Vic, both in looks and performance.—
L.F., Boise, Idaho   ⊶▪

THE SWEET TASTE OF DARK MEAT TURNS OUT
TO BE THEIR NEW FAVORITE FLAVOR

Several years ago, my wife and I lived in a very old Victorian
house near the university. It was our first house, and financially
it was a stretch. We decided to rent out a room on the first floor
to a student. Mannie was a quiet, polite and well-built young
black student on the wrestling team. He was an ideal tenant,
pretty much keeping to himself. He was studious, and worked
out with weights regularly. He would occasionally have a couple
of his teammates over for an evening workout, and sometimes
brought girlfriends.

His room was directly below our spare bedroom, which
Rhonda used as a sewing and crafts room. In the center of the
floor was a big old grate open to the floor below. We usually kept
it covered with a small area rug.

One evening Rhonda spent much longer than usual at her
crafts, and returned to our bedroom flushed, sweating and with
her eyes ablaze with lust. She pulled down my shorts and engulfed my cock with her mouth as she pressed the heel of one
hand between her legs. She suddenly arched her head back and
exploded in a violent orgasm, her body twitching and writhing,
her mouth stretched open, her eyes tightly closed.

My cock was bone-hard at this wild display of lust. Rhonda
quickly shed her clothes and mounted my throbbing cock. She
was squeezing her breasts, riding me like a horse and pulling her
distended nipples. I asked what on earth had gotten into her. She
couldn't speak, only moan and grunt, as she exploded into another series of orgasms. Then my own eruption filled her with my
come.

As our breathing gradually came under control, she related details of how she had just spent the last two hours watching Mannie work out, then masturbate to four orgasms while lying on his
weight bench, just five or six feet below the ceiling vent. She

spoke of the smell of his come, the sight of him rubbing it all over his muscular chest, his swollen shaft that remained shining and hard the whole time, the soft moans of climax and the intense look of pleasure on his face.

When Rhonda realized that my own cock was still like granite, she rode it to yet another shuddering climax, and I filled her with another load of my come. Sitting on my cock, still hard after two climaxes in a row, she began to grin broadly as she looked down at my flushed face. "This is really turning you on too, isn't it?" she quizzed.

"I love seeing you this wild and turned on," I replied.

Our conversation gradually became more graphic. Our unspoken fantasies were slowly revealed, and finally I blurted out that it would be an unbelievable turn-on to watch her fuck Mannie. She admitted that her mind had been filled with images of his big, black, turgid cock blasting load after load of his come into her as she became delirious with orgasm.

Hearing that, I became crazy with lust, and pulled her body up my chest until she was sitting with her pussy just inches from my face. I was overcome by a need to suck the come oozing from her pussy lips. "Oh God, this can't be real," she kept saying, as she ground her hips into my face. "Suck me, suck me, suck me!" She kept moaning over and over until climax flooded her senses.

In the following weeks we screwed each other's brains out, talking about our fantasies. We watched Mannie beat his meat every night, and followed it with hours of the wildest sex, uttering words and thoughts we'd never imagined using with each other. We were intoxicated with the complex, gut-wrenching excitement, and knew we wanted to go further.

My wife began dressing very skimpy around Mannie. She stopped wearing a bra, so her nipples would be visible under her T-shirts and tank tops. She cut her cutoffs so short there was barely a strip of material between her legs. She engaged him in long conversations in the laundry room, bent over and found every way she could to show her flesh. Panties soaked with her juices were dropped from her laundry basket, and soon found their way onto Mannie's face as he masturbated. When she expressed interest in trying weight lifting, the stage was set.

She went downstairs for the workout wearing no underwear, just cutoffs with mere threads between the legs, and a loose tank top whose bottom edge barely covered her full breasts. I looked down from the room above as he showed her how to spot his bench presses. His eyes were right under her bare, moist pussy lips as she stood at the head of the bench. His view of the under-side of her breasts and hardened nipples was unobstructed as she reached for the bar. He soon had a raging hard-on that couldn't be contained by his bikini briefs. Seconds seemed like hours as they both realized how close they were.

Her legs trembled and became weak as she collapsed onto his face. I could smell the juice that was running down her legs. She reached forward and grasped his cock, and they both blasted off into instant orgasms. When Rhonda scooped his come off his chest and began sucking her fingers, I blew my wad.

I watched breathlessly as they fucked with animal passion in every conceivable position. This young black bull was relentless, pounding his cock into my wife. He deposited load after load into every hole of her beautiful body. Hours later, totally spent, Rhonda dragged herself up the stairs, her body covered with come.

When she entered our bedroom she crawled over me and kneeled over my stomach. Her pussy lips were red and spread wide. His come coated her thighs and dripped from her pussy and ass. She bent over and kissed me, our tongues entwined in battle as she pushed his come into my mouth. "Do you want it all?" she asked.

"Yes" was all I could moan as she moved up my body and sat on my face. She used what little strength she had left to milk his come into my mouth and flood my face. I could feel streams of come cascade over my face and down the back of my neck in a heavy dose of fantasy-turned-reality. Exhausted, we both col-lapsed into the deepest and most satisfying sleep we'd had in weeks.—*N.A., Cincinnati, Ohio*

FUCKING BEFORE THE EYES OF AN UNKNOWN STRANGER ADDS SPICE

I still remember thinking, How can I arrange for other men to see my wife nude? Here's how it happened.

We had gone out dancing and drinking. I asked Margaret to go into a dirty bookstore with me afterward. I'd been there a few times before, and knew there were small peepholes in the walls between the video booths.

We walked into a booth and put in our quarters. I immediately saw shadows appear near the holes, and knew someone was watching. I don't think Margaret knew about the holes, because it was dark, and I was keeping her busy.

I started kissing her and running my hands over her breasts. I couldn't wait to show off her tits, so I unbuttoned her shirt. I still remember how exciting it was for me, knowing that some stranger was going to see my wife's tits.

As I took her shirt off, I positioned both of us so the stranger could get a full frontal shot of my wife's titties when I took her bra off. I wanted him to see her tits fall free from the cups of the bra. I quickly unsnapped her bra and freed her C-cup tits. I massaged each one lightly, shaking them for visual effect. I could only imagine the stranger jerking off while watching the show.

Then I sat on the bench and had her stand in front of me. This put her ass directly in front of the stranger looking through the hole.

I slowly pulled her pants down and had her step out of them. I started kissing her stomach and thighs while caressing her asscheeks. Then I slowly started sliding her panties down her legs. I wanted to tease the stranger. I wish I could have seen his face when my wife's naked ass came into full view only inches from his face.

Then I parted her legs and started licking her pussy. I eased a finger inside her so she could enjoy it even more.

I slowly turned Margaret around to lick her ass-cheeks and ass, giving the stranger a full view of her trimmed pussy.

Next I had her lean against the television screen as I prepared to fuck her from behind. I dropped my pants and rubbed my cock between her ass-cheeks. Then I pulled her ass further back so she would be bent over a little more. Now he could also watch her tits shaking around as I fucked her.

I fucked her hard and fast. It didn't take long for me to come, knowing that another man was watching my naked wife take a hard dick.

Afterward, I sat her down on the bench to rest. I leaned over and kissed her while I slowly spread her legs with a hand. I wanted the stranger to see my come oozing out of my wife's pussy.

Then we got dressed and casually walked out of the store. I don't think she ever realized that a stranger had been watching us the whole time.—*O.P., New Bedford, Massachusetts*

True Romance

A HELPING HAND—IN KITCHEN AND BEDROOM

My wife was six months pregnant when she started pre-term labor contractions. This not only obliged her to stop working but made strict bed rest necessary for the final three months of her pregnancy. I adjusted my schedule so that I could handle the cooking, cleaning and grocery shopping. After a month or so, things improved. Julie's contractions stopped and it looked as if she would carry to full term, although she was still on strict bed rest.

One night, while we lay in bed discussing our day, we both talked about how horny all these precautions had made us. It had been five months since we had last had intercourse, and two months since any sort of sex at all. We got even more frustrated talking about how we would make up for lost time once we could fuck and suck without fear.

As the weeks passed, family members and Julie's friends all pitched in to come to her assistance. They sent over food or helped with the shopping whenever they could. Julie is fortunate enough to belong to a group of married girlfriends, all of whom have remained friends. A different one would stop by every day or two. I found myself fantasizing about those women in a wanton fashion, and eagerly awaiting the sound of the doorbell.

One Monday morning as I got ready for work Julie told me that her friend Vickie would be stopping over that evening. I told her "no problem," kissed her good-bye and left for work. Julie had been terrific throughout the whole ordeal, and I knew I couldn't love another woman the way I loved her. However, at different times during the day I found myself fantasizing about how Vickie would look that night. Vickie is a sexy woman with an outstanding personality. Her pouting lips and full breasts complement a firm backside and shapely, slim legs. After months

229

without sex, the thought of another woman—and such a magnificent woman—around the house made my crotch ache.

When I arrived home, Vickie was in the kitchen heating up
some soup for Julie. Her hair and makeup were perfect, as if she
were going out, but she wore a baggy gray sweatshirt and sweatpants. In my fantasies she had worn (for a time at least) a short
skirt and high heels, so I was a little disappointed. When we exchanged pleasantries and a kiss on the cheek, I inhaled Vickie's
perfume deeply. Vickie suggested I go on up to see Julie, and said
she would follow soon with the soup. On my way upstairs, I
turned and caught a glimpse of Vickie leaning over to taste the
soup. Her sweatshirt swung low enough to give me a quick
glimpse of her lovely breasts. The thought of her walking around
all evening with no bra under that loose top sent jolts of electricity into my sex-starved mind. In addition, it sent the blood racing
to my cock. My sexual euphoria quickly vanished when Julie
told me that Vickie was leaving soon to meet her husband for
dinner in town.

We shared a hug and a kiss and Vickie walked in with the
soup. Vickie asked me to clear out of the bedroom since she had
to get dressed for dinner. I told Julie I would attend to the mail
while Vickie dressed. As I left the room I pulled the door almost
shut behind me, and pretended to walk downstairs. But as a confirmed voyeur, I could not pass up this opportunity. Once on the
stairs, I slipped off my shoes and tiptoed back to the bedroom
door, still slightly ajar. I peeked in just as Vickie moved behind
the changing screen and started undressing. The screen stood between the bed and doorway, with a vanity to the left and a stool
to the right. This was perfect. I could see Vickie, but Julie could
not see me. Vickie and Julie carried on a conversation as Vickie
undressed. I thought my cock would burst out of my pants when
she dropped her sweatpants and pulled the sweatshirt over her
head. Vickie's body was impressive—long black hair flowed
over her shoulders and led the eye down to a slender waist and
an incredibly tight, rounded ass. I slipped off my shirt, pants and
boxer shorts, and laid them on the floor next to my shoes. I was
naked, standing outside my own bedroom, peering in at the
lovely naked woman whom I had fantasized about all day. The
adrenaline rush from the fear of being caught, coupled with the
sight of Vickie undressing—so close to me that I could again
smell her perfume—was intense. My prick stood out rock-hard
and pulsing. Vickie turned toward me as she reached down to

pick up her stockings and panties, on the vanity stool to her right. Her full breasts looked soft, yet firm. Her dark pink nipples pointed slightly upward. Her taut abdomen and her fine ebony pubic hair were all perfect. When she raised a knee and placed one foot on the stool, I realized she was going to put on a garter belt and stockings. Pre-come oozed from my engorged cock as I beheld one of my greatest voyeur fantasies come to life. I pushed the door a little bit further open to get an unobstructed view. Vickie now had her stockings on and was slipping on her black pumps. She paused to admire herself in the full-length mirror to her left. With her back slightly arched, she ran her hands over her hips and along her sides. Then she gently brushed her breasts with her upturned palms. Her nipples responded well, and a smile suffused her face. You could tell Vickie liked what she saw. I grabbed my schlong with my left hand and spread the pre-come over the head with my right. The pleasure was intense. My balls tightened and the muscles of my legs and ass contracted. Still gazing in the mirror, Vickie remarked to Julie, "I look pretty damned good for a woman who's had two kids." I turned my head to hear my wife's reply. "Don't let my husband see you like that," she said. "The poor guy hasn't gotten laid in five months."

When I turned my head to get Vickie's reaction, I saw her staring right at me. I froze, hands at my sides, stiff as a board. I had assumed she couldn't see me in the dark hallway. Now I saw that the hallway light was lit. In my haste to get back to the bedroom door, I had forgotten to turn it off!

I will never forget what Vickie did next. With the most incredibly sexy look on her face, she cocked her left leg up on the stool and slowly traced the outline of her now-exposed pussy lips with her right index finger. I was still in a panic, or so I thought, but my cock started pulsing wildly and spewed out one long stream of come after another. Vickie's eyes widened and she stared intently at my gushing prick. Without taking her eyes off my prong, she sweetly excused herself to Julie to go to the bathroom. At the doorway she grabbed my joint, and another thick rope of come splashed to the floor. She squeezed the joystick tight and whispered, "Save some for me."

She led my prick, and me behind it, down the hallway. Once in the bathroom Vickie leaned forward and whispered, "Thanks for a great show." I whispered back, "Likewise." She lifted her ass up on the sink, drew her knees up and spread her legs wide. "I'm not going to let you fuck me, I couldn't do that to Julie," she said. "But I'll take care of you." She still had a stranglehold on my cock, and she placed it right on her pussy as she pulled me close. When the head of my johnson brushed against her luscious pussy lips she tilted her head back, closed her eyes and released her hold on my prick. I watched one last wave of sperm splash onto her beautiful quim. Vickie sighed and took a new grip on my cock. Her hand was underneath and halfway up the shaft. She winked at me and rubbed the head of my prick, rapidly stiffening now, up and down the outer lips of her vagina. She rubbed slowly at first, and I could feel her wet, hot pussy lips grasp at the cockhead. The feeling was exquisite. She emitted a muffled groan and I actually felt her come on the head of my prick. It was an unbelievable pleasure, better than any fantasy, to see this beautiful woman shamelessly using the head of my cock to satisfy herself. As she started coming, she picked up the pace—rapidly, almost frantically rubbing the cockhead against her clitoris. She squealed with delight as my prick responded, unloaded again and absolutely covered that gorgeous pussy with come.

When we regained our composure, she told me she had known I was watching her undress. She had seen me in the mirror. I asked her why she had let me watch. She replied, "Julie told me earlier how depressed she was about not being able to take care of you. When I saw that nice cock of yours through the doorway I knew what she meant. Besides, it had always been a fantasy of mine to watch a guy masturbate. My husband would never do it in front of me, so when I saw you take your pants off it got my juices flowing."

I started to apologize, but she interrupted. "I was going to tease you, but knowing that you were in the hall watching me and jerking off turned me on so much I couldn't stand it. Then when you started coming without even touching yourself, that was it. I came too." Vickie then knelt down, eyed my cock for a minute and swallowed it right to the base. After sucking fiercely for a brief moment she took it out, smiled and said, "I had to know if it tasted as good as it looks." She then placed a delicate kiss on the head.

"Now, you be good till your momma gets better," she instructed my semi-erect prong. Then she washed and headed back to the bedroom. I marveled as I watched that superb woman saunter down the hall. I don't know that I have ever experienced two such intense orgasms or unloaded that much come in such a short time.

I crept back to the bedroom door, gathered up my clothes and headed downstairs. When Vickie had finished dressing, we met in the living room.

I told her, "Vickie, I owe you one." To which she replied, "If Julie doesn't start feeling better soon, I'll be back."—*J.B., Detroit, Michigan* ⊙━▪

LEARNING TO SHARE LATE-NIGHT ADVENTURES

I was awakened by the sound of the automatic garage door closing. Then I heard the back door closing. The red numeral 4:02 a.m. shone from the clock on the nightstand next to my bed.

My heart beat faster even as my brain cautioned me not to get my hopes up. My eight-inch cock stood rock-hard, pre-come dripping. I placed my hand around the thick shaft and pumped slowly as I recalled the events that had brought me to this moment.

Two days earlier, on Friday, my wife and I were in an exclusive department store. We wandered into the lingerie department, and soon acquired a valuable addition to Betsy's collection of sexy underwear—a black crushed velvet bra-and-thong set. Neither piece contained much material—just enough to tease.

Betsy then led the way to the clothing section. There I got my first hint of what her active imagination had in store for the weekend.

I found my soul mate in Betsy. We have been married for seven years, and these have been the most enjoyable years of my life. All our times together have been fantastic, and our relationship has never needed any work. In view of this, you might well wonder how I can fantasize about my wife fucking with other men. But I do, and she loves it.

Betsy and I share all our fantasies and act them out for each other. Some of mine are a bit wild for Betsy's tastes, and I respect that. But she throws herself full-heartedly into the ones with which she's comfortable.

Of all my fantasies, my favorite is seeing my wife's cunt filled with another man's come. That image gets my cock hard as a hammer—as it is while I write this.

The thought of cleaning her moist pussy folds makes me shiver in anticipation. And when my tongue has reached inside as far as it can, I look forward to easing my prick in her love-box to feel its warm contents—whatever I hadn't eaten out.

The combination of juices—hers, mine, and the new-comer's—brings me to some of my strongest orgasms. I say "brings me" because I have fulfilled that particular fantasy a number of times. I know I will always enjoy it, any time Betsy gives me the chance.

She gave me a great opportunity on Saturday night. Betsy had just finished her bath. I came in the bedroom and asked if she needed any help dressing. Actually I wanted to see her new bra-and-thong outfit, but she wasn't ready for that. She had thrown on a sundress for doing her hair. I turned to leave, but she grabbed my hand and guided it up her skirt. I was delighted to learn then that she had just shaved her pussy. My heart raced. I love the feel of her cunny when it is newly shaved. I knelt down and kissed her smooth mound and licked her clit until she pushed me away. She told me I must wait until she got home from the outing she had planned.

I left, and waited until she called me to come see her outfit. It looked fantastic and so did she, as she always does. Her get-up covered just enough for great results.

She must have spotted the enthusiasm in my jeans. She sat on the bed, pulled the zipper, hauled out Old Faithful and took it deep down her throat. Then she stopped cold. She loves to tease. She took the prick out of her mouth, and stood up all innocent, as if nothing had happened. Then she courteously asked me to leave the bedroom so she could finish dressing. I stuffed John Thomas back into my jeans as best I could and did just that.

Betsy stopped by to say good-bye on her way to her adventure. She kissed me and gave my dick a squeeze. She said she'd see me around four a.m. With that, my imagination went wild, and I told her my cock was begging for attention. But Betsy sternly warned me not to play with it. She wanted the joystick good and stiff when I came inside her.

I kept as busy as I could for the rest of the evening, but my prick kept stiffening. Finally, I went to bed and read myself to sleep. So I was far from alarmed when I heard those noises at four a.m. I heard Betsy make her way. She climbed into bed still in her bra and thong, as I had requested so that I could undress her in that outfit.

But that came later. She leaned over me and kissed me deeply. Now I smelled the faint scent of come. Betsy was cold to the touch, too. She explained that this is what happens when you spend most of the night without clothes. I pulled her close then. I knew that I was about to have my fantasy fulfilled once again. I rolled her over and kissed her neck and shoulders as she described her exploits. She and her girlfriends had gone out dancing as planned, and that is where she met *him*.

They had spent most of the evening together, dancing and talking, and at two o'clock, they headed back to his place. They made their way to his bedroom, Betsy continued. I removed her bra. She excused herself, went in the bathroom, and returned wearing only her panties and shirt. She said he really admired her outfit when he helped her out of her shirt. When he had removed her panties, she continued, he lowered his face to her bare pussy.

"He ate me slowly," Betsy said, "and told me that he had never tasted a shaved pussy before. He kept eating me until I came all over his tongue and face. Then he replaced his tongue with his cock. He fucked me, ever so slowly, until he couldn't hold back any longer. Then he flooded my cunt with his come."

I was enjoying this, as I'd known I would. Betsy told me to shove my cock inside her and feel his come. My stiff prick slipped easily into her, and we heard a sloshing sound from her contented pussy as I pumped it in and out. I nearly came after the first few strokes, but Betsy had an idea that delayed things.

"Why don't you taste me?" she asked.

I pulled out my prick and she pulled off her panties. I thrust my head between her open thighs and feasted on her juicy lunch-box. Both the scent and flavor were irresistible, and I savored some of his pubic hairs as I eagerly ate her out. Meanwhile, she continued her story.

"He came, long and hard. We lay there for a few minutes, our tongues intertwined. Then he began to kiss his way down my body. He said he wanted to eat his come out of my pussy. But I wouldn't let him do that. I told him I was saving it for you!" She went on to tell him about me and how much I loved to clean another man's come from her box. As she did this, Betsy told me, she sucked his cock, and it quickly grew hard again.

I shivered with delight and passion as she related the rest of the story.

"He lay me back down and entered me for a second time. His slow, rhythmic motions felt so good, and he filled my cunt again.

After a few more minutes of kissing and snuggling I told him I had better get home while my pussy was still full."

She pulled me close and asked me in a whisper to fuck her. I was hot, and needed no second invitation. My cock slipped into her love-nest once more, and she asked me to go slow. His juices lubricated and soothed my prick as I eased it in and out. When I couldn't restrain from orgasm any longer Betsy sensed it. She urged me to come, and fill her cunt for the third time that night. I shuddered with excitement and I did just that. My jism had to fight for space in her loaded pussy.

Then, "Eat me," she said. I dived into her pussy like a starved animal and sucked and licked the combined come from her swollen lips. While I feasted, she told me that he had a friend. He had suggested that another time, after he had had her by himself for a while, he and his friend might share her.

"That way," she said, "I can learn what it's like to have cocks in my mouth and pussy at the same time. And he said that you could watch!"

So this may be just the first of a series of letters that I can share with you and your readers.

I licked Betsy's pussy clean and we curled up in each other's arms, content. I can't begin to tell you how happy our marriage is now that I feel secure enough to relish her adventures with other men. You might think this is so I can be free to fuck other women. But that's not it. I am just one of those men who enjoy the idea of his wife's pussy full of another man's come, as well as the story of how it got there. I must admit, though, that I like the idea of watching some night—or even being the third or fourth person to share the adventure.

I look forward to years of fulfilled fantasies.—*M.M., Versailles, Kentucky* ⚬╂▪

FRENCH DRESSING—A PIQUANT TALE OF MARRIAGE

There was a time, only a few months ago, that the thought of having sex with a man wearing women's clothes would have been the ultimate turn-off for me. But times change. This is the story of how they changed for me.

My husband George and I had been married about three years, and I thought our lives ordinary. We both have jobs and we own two cars, a house and a couple of cats. We help one another with the housework, the yard work, and the mortgage payments. I thought we had a good, honest, loving, passionate relationship and that neither of us had any secrets. I know I didn't have any.

But one fall day I was cleaning out closets and drawers, collecting clothes for charity. In the bottom of a drawer, under a pile of sweaters, I found a collection of panties and bras. I knew they weren't mine. My first thought was that George had been having affairs, and had kept the undies as trophies. I was heartsick.

When George came home from work, I confronted him with the evidence.

"I didn't have an affair," he insisted. "These things are mine. I—ah—like to wear them."

I couldn't have been more shocked. "Are you gay?"

"No. I just like sexy things."

"You're sick!" I screamed. I left the house in tears, and spent the night in a motel. The next morning I returned, with an ultimatum. We were both going to be tested for H.I.V., and either he was going to get counseling or I was going to get a divorce. He agreed.

Both H.I.V. tests came back negative, and George kept his appointment with the psychologist recommended by our doctor. Two days after his first session, I got a call from the psychologist. Two things about the call surprised me. First, the therapist wanted me to attend the next session; second, the therapist was a woman.

"There is nothing wrong with me," I said. "Why do I need to take part in the sessions?"

"You need to understand the nature of his condition to help with the therapy," she assured me.

I thought about it, and it made sense. So I reluctantly agreed.

In several sessions, I learned a lot of things. The therapist explained the difference between homosexual, transsexual and transvestite behavior, and I learned what a fetish is. She assured me that everyone has male and female parts in their personalities, that men can be gentle and nurturing and women can be assertive without being bitchy.

"It's healthy," she said, "for each of us to get in touch with the man and woman in ourselves. For some people, clothing can open aspects of their nature that they need to be in touch with."

"But women's underwear?"

"When was the last time you put on one of your husband's shirts? Do you ever wear his T-shirts? Or sweats?" she asked.

"But that's different," I said.

She smiled. "Can you explain why it's different?"

I thought—really thought—for a long time. Finally I said, "It just is." But I was beginning to wonder.

As the weeks went by, George and I each explored our opposite-gender sides. George learned how to do my hair and we saved a fortune on beauty treatments. He cooks fantastic meals now, too. With the therapist's help, my self-confidence has grown. I've asked for more responsibilities at work, my suggestions have been carried out, and I've been given a raise and a promotion. I also joined a health club and took up bodybuilding. I've discovered that I can pump iron and enjoy being a girl— especially when the studs at the gym check me out in my tights and leotard.

I've learned that its okay to ask for what I want in the bed-room, too. As in: "I want to be on top," "do me from behind," and best of all, "eat my pussy!"

By November, things were getting back to normal. Normal means we were sleeping together again (and I'd really missed that part). It also means my spotting a few more pairs of panties in the laundry without wigging out.

One night when George crawled into bed and snuggled next to me I could tell that he was wearing nylon. We caressed for a while, and I have to admit the nylon felt sexy to me. George's cock stiffened in my hand as I rubbed it through the smooth, slippery fabric, and we both got even more aroused. He spread my legs and we rubbed our crotches together, panty to panty, both getting wetter and wetter. Then we made love—hot, hard, intense love!

Victoria's Secret got rich on us at Christmastime. We gave each other lingerie by the bunch! Our panties are the same size: six. But my bra is a lot smaller, 34B, while George wears 38C. (I suppose that if you don't have hooters you can have them any size you want.) I also bought George a pair of pumps and some nylon stockings that I knew he wanted.

George bought me something I had wanted but was too shy to ask for: a vibrator.

We kept going to therapy. I learned that it's all right to have fantasies. In fact, the therapist encouraged it as part of normal sex life.

Nowadays, when George and I are making love I sometimes close my eyes and I'm a motorcycle mama getting it on with her outlaw biker stud, or a cheerleader making it with the entire basketball squad in the locker room after the last game of a championship season.

My favorite is when I'm a cabaret star and after a particularly rousing performance I'm doing it with two horny soldiers at the same time in some grimy European alley. In that one I sit the handsome young recruit on a garbage can and suck his cock while he pulls down my peasant blouse and plays with my titties. (I'm not wearing a bra in this fantasy, and I'm a C-cup.) The well-hung sergeant gets behind me, lifts my skirt, and pulls down my panties to get his cock in me from behind. The recruit squirts sweet come in my mouth, I have a wild, shameless orgasm, and the sergeant pulls out and shoots hot sticky come all over my ass. Then the recruit does me again. We stand this time. I have my legs around his waist and my back against the wall. His hands grasp my ass and his dick pumps in and out of my cunt until we come in unison.

For Valentine's day, I decided to go all out in the fantasy and costume departments. When George got home from work he found a note on the front door. "Take a shower and shave," it read. "Legs too."

While he was in the shower I laid out his costume. I had bought a French maid uniform just his size, black with white trim, with a starched white petticoat. The costume included a black corset with garter straps (for the black nylons) and white panties. Black pumps and red lipstick completed the ensemble.

I had a costume for that evening, too. First I strapped on an eight-inch dildo. (Hey, if you don't have a dick, you can get any size you want.) Then I put on men's boxer shorts, baggy tan chino pants and a blue oxford shirt, high-top black socks and brown penny-loafers. No bra. The dildo made a lump in my pants so that it looked like I had a raging hard-on. I had to keep shifting the thing to be comfortable. It was easier to hide when I was seated. Now I understand why high school boys, with their perpetual boners, always seem so uncomfortable.

I mixed a pitcher of martinis. I was sipping my first one when the maid came into the kitchen. The costume was a knockout. The skirt came to the middle of George's thigh, and the petticoat fluffed around her bottom. The silicone breasts implanted in the corset, the lipstick and the subtle eye shadow made George particularly feminine. She wore earrings (mine) and a delicate gold chain that I hadn't seen before. To complete the illusion, George wore shoulder-length hair tied in a ponytail with a white ribbon. No wonder I had a hard-on.

"Hi, sweetie," I said. "Buy you a drink?"

"Thank you, I'd like one." She curtsied.

"What's for supper?" I asked.

"Would beef Wellington be all right?"

"That would be super. I'm hungry enough to eat a cow. Had a long day at work and good workout at the gym."

I patted her fanny, picked up my drink, and strolled out of the kitchen.

"Call me when dinner's ready. I'll be in the den watching the news or reading the sports page." I belched. I was getting off on being a male chauvinist asshole. It's fun. No wonder so many dipshits go for it.

Soon wonderful smells wafted from the kitchen. The TV was on, but I was too nervous to watch it. However, I did have time to finish my second martini.

"Dinner is almost ready," she announced from the doorway.

"Good. I'll open a Bordeaux and let it breathe."

The table was set with our best china and silverware. George had tossed a salad, and warmed some hard rolls to go with the beef, which was delicious. I read the sports pages through dinner, and polished off two glasses of wine. As you can imagine, I was getting a pretty good buzz on. The fact is, I wasn't totally comfortable with this gender-reversal stuff yet, and with what I had planned for the rest of the evening I was going to need a little emotional anesthetic.

George cleared the table and took the plates into the kitchen. When she bent over to stack them in the dishwasher her short skirt rose enough for me to get a shot of her panties and the smooth-shaved skin above the lace top of the dark nylons.

"Great meal," I said as I came up behind her.

"Thanks," she said.

I put my arms around her waist and softly kissed her ear.

"Don't," she said as my lips moved along her neck. "I have to clean up."

"It'll wait." I pushed my hips into her bottom, hard enough for her to feel my stiff prick. She pulled away for a second, then pressed her butt hard against my crotch. She closed her eyes and sighed.

"You don't know how much I've wanted this," she whispered. Without another word I turned her around and kissed her hard. She opened her mouth and my tongue danced with hers. I kissed her neck and worked my way down her chest. My fingers played with the hair at the base of her throat and I squeezed her breast through the corset. My hand slid down her back and under her short skirt to tease her through her panties. That audacity brought a short gasp and a moan.

"Let's go in the bedroom." I led her down the hallway.

In the bedroom I kissed her again as I unzipped her uniform and slid it off her. Her hand had found my swollen cock straining against the chinos.

"It's so big," she said, and I felt a rush of pride. I opened my fly and fumbled to get the dildo out of my pants and boxer shorts. She lowered herself to her knees in front of me. Once out, it hung in her face.

"I've never done this," she said as she took it in her hand and looked innocently up at me.

"Suck it," I said. "Take it in your mouth as far as you can."

She started licking the head, then took it into her mouth. She bobbed up and down on it, taking more and more until about half was down her throat. I undid my belt, let my pants drop, and stepped out of them. She never let go of my dick the whole time.

"Yeah, baby. That's great. Oh, yeah." My hips were rocking now, really getting into it. I was amazed. She was able to deepthroat the whole thing! Women are incredible.

"That's good." I slid it out of her mouth. "Now get on the bed. I'm gonna eat your pussy."

She kicked off the pumps and lay back on the spread. I got on top and lay between her legs. I kissed her gently on the mouth and slowly worked my way down her neck and chest. When I got to the corset I took one boob in my mouth and squeezed the other. Moving further down, I licked her navel and she squirmed under me. Finally, I was face-to-face with her white panties, soaking with pre-come.

"I'm gonna lick your cunt," I said.

Without taking the panties down, I took her cock in my mouth and sucked it through the nylon. I ran my tongue along the sensitive underside and nibbled the head. She nearly came several times, but I slowed and let her cool off before starting again.

While I was doing my mouth magic I slid a few fingers inside the boxer shorts and played with myself. There would be no holding back this time.

By this time, George's panties were soaked with saliva and she was straining and arching her back while I sucked. My fingers dripped pussy juice from the knuckles. She grabbed the back of my head and pushed my face against her crotch. I slid one of my long juice-drenched fingers right up her ass.

"Ah—ah—ah-h-h." Come gushed into the panties and soaked through the nylon into my mouth. I sucked up all I could, but didn't swallow. I wiped pussy juice on my cock, spit the jism into my hand and rubbed that on, too. Then I climbed on her chest and slid my big cock between her soft boobs.

"Now, sugar, you're going to suck a well-used dick," I said. I slid back and forth between the knockers, and she sucked me clean.

"We aren't done yet, honey," I said. I got a tube of K-Y jelly from the night stand. "I'm going to make a woman out of my girl tonight."

"What are you going to do?"

"Just what you've been asking for." I squeezed some K-Y jelly onto my fingers. "I'll be gentle. I know it's your first time." I was a virgin once, myself, I remembered as I started rubbing K-Y into her asshole.

"Please," she begged, "don't hurt me." Already her asshole was relaxing. "Want me to turn over?"

"No. I want it face-to-face the first time. Here, put this pillow under your butt."

"Do you want me to take my panties off?"

"Why do you think I got you crotchless ones, you little ninny?" I was rubbing my cock and feeling like a real macho stud. "Now, I'm going to give you a ride."

I put the head of my cock against her ass and moved it around, smearing the lubricant all over. Slowly I eased into her, taking it out when it hurt. Finally I was able to keep the head in. Then she took another inch and another. Finally she relaxed enough so that I could fuck her with long slow strokes.

"I love you so much," she said. "God, I love being a woman. Thank you, darling." She was moving with me now, moaning and meeting every stroke. "I think I'm going to come again!"

"Don't you dare! I haven't gotten off yet, and you aren't going to again until I do." I pulled out of her. "Now, you can take your panties off."

I got up and took off the dildo. "I'm tired of being a boy. If you still want to be a woman, you're going to have to be a lesbian."

I rummaged in my drawer and found the red satin panties I was looking for. I got the peasant blouse and ankle-length floral print skirt from the closet. Voilà! I was Carmen.

George had changed into men's clothes. I guess he didn't want to be a lesbian. Perhaps another time. . . .

"Let's get out of here," I said. "I feel like going to a bistro. You'd better drive, though. I'm still a little drunk."

We didn't go to just one cabaret, though. We went to—I lost track of how many. And by the end of the evening, I was more than a little drunk. We danced. We drank. I sang. As we were heading back to the car, I saw what I had been looking for all evening.

"Where are we going?" he asked, as I pulled him into the alley. "Are you trying to get mugged?" I took his hand and led him around a corner into the dark.

"Kiss me," I hissed. "Kiss me like you mean it! Hold me so tight that I couldn't get away even if I wanted to." He did.

I faced the front of the alley and leaned over a garbage can. I lifted my skirt and slid my panties down far enough for him to get it in me from behind. "Do me," I begged. "But don't come until I say you can."

He came at me from behind. I spread my legs for him. I felt the rough zipper and the wool of his pants against my naked rear. "Feel my tits," I said. He groped my braless boobs and they popped out from under the blouse. "Hard! Pinch me. Oh, yes."

His hot prick pushed against my ass, searching for my cunt. "Hard! All the way in." It found my sweet hole and slid in with one well-lubricated stroke. That was all it took to bring on my first orgasm. He pumped and pumped, and in less than a minute I felt my second orgasm building. It was the most intense orgasm I've ever had in my life, washing through my body like a tidal wave. I screamed. My knees buckled and I would have collapsed on the garbage can if George hadn't been holding me up.

We stood there in the cold alley, breathing hard, my naked ass pressed against his crotch. Suddenly I realized that his prick was still hard inside me. "You didn't come?" I asked.

"You said I couldn't until you told me to." That really touched me.

"There's one more thing I want to do," I said. "Then you can come all over me." I moved and the cock slipped out.

"Stick it up my ass."

"What?"

"Just like I did you, baby. Right where the sun doesn't shine."

"Are you sure?" But he was already probing.

"Just go slow. Let me relax. There. Easy. Yes." He slid it in, touching places that had never been touched before. It was a magical experience, like the first time I ever got laid, in the backseat of my teenage boyfriend's Mustang. And like that first time, I loved it. I was soon pushing back against his thrusts.

George squeezed my tits and pinched the nipples. I reached under my skirt, around the red satin panties, and rubbed my swollen clit.

He was breathing harder and I knew he was about to explode.

"I want you to come on my ass," I said. Three hard strokes and he pulled out, spilling gob after gob of milky semen on my butt, smearing it around with his dick. What a Valentine's day.

If there is a moral to this story, I guess it would be: Check your closets. Who knows what you might find?—*J.V., Topeka, Kansas* ⚬╾▪

COLLEGE DAYS—MEMORIZING THE ROSE TATTOO

I can't really explain my obsession. All I know is that I'm incredibly attracted to women with tattoos. There is something about a permanent picture on a woman's breast that arouses passion in me. When I find these secret surprises in the bikini area or beneath innocuous clothing, it excites me.

In college, I studied regularly with a Polish woman who had married an American only to get a green card. She had never loved her husband and was planning to get a divorce.

When we studied together, the sessions often drifted into flirtation. Olga is about five-foot-seven, and her golden brown hair falls to her shoulders. Her prominent Slavic cheekbones are classically beautiful, and her accent enhances her exotic appeal for me. But I never thought our flirting would lead to anything. For one thing, I had moral scruples against leading a woman to cheat on her husband.

Occasionally, though, our knees would touch under the table, and neither of us would hurry to break the contact. Fascinated, I would often gaze into her soft brown eyes and sometimes gently brush my fingers against her cheek.

In what I took to be a European fashion, Olga was quite open about her sex life and her fantasies. At times she shocked me with her boldness. Still, such conversations aroused me, and I took advantage of any opportunity to talk openly with her about sex. It was in one of these talks that Olga confided that she and her husband only fucked once every six months. I found that incredible, in view of the way she seemed to enjoy all aspects of sex. At such times, I would reach over and hold her hand to console her.

At one point, discussing sexual fantasies, I revealed my fetish with tattoos. Olga's eyes widened, and she huskily exclaimed, "Really! Do you know that I have a tattoo?" My heart raced. I hesitated, then asked what it was and, hopefully, where it was. She said she had a rose tattooed on her behind. I told her, quite sincerely, that I would like to see it one day. She winked. My time would come, she said.

Olga and I had made a friendly wager over the behavior of one classmate. I bet I could predict within two minutes when that girl would yawn, pull her shoulders back and stretch theatrically to show off her magnificent tits. Olga bet I could not call that shot. The loser had to drive on a public highway fully naked with the winner as passenger. In the next session of that class, I was delighted to win the bet. When the girl arched her back and stuck out her chest, I looked over to Olga and winked. She nodded cheerfully and winked right back. I could hardly contain my excitement. I was about to see her secret image.

That night, I went to her apartment. She greeted me at the door and wasted no time racing to the car. Once in the secluded driveway, she stripped. When she got into the car, she leaned over the seat to place her clothes on the backseat, presenting a glorious view. She was aware how much I longed to see her rose, and took the opportunity to show it off. She wiggled her ass and made it dance. I could not resist the temptation. I caressed her cheeks, and traced the figure of the rose with my finger. This was well worth waiting for. The rose was a fine piece of art, adorning an even finer image of beauty.

Olga plopped down in the driver's seat and laughed merrily. I took my place in the passenger's seat and we were off. On the road, we caused some commotion. One old man in a red Subaru did a double take at the sight of the bare Olga, and almost ran off the road. There may have been other reactions, but I didn't see them. I was concentrating on the main attraction. I placed my hand on Olga's thigh and slowly inched my way up toward her hip, but I went no further.

Eventually, Olga drove back to her apartment. She grabbed both her clothes and my hand and briskly led the way inside. I felt I should leave, even though her husband was not at home, and told her so. Before I left, she kissed me gently. I was afraid to push matters any further, so I left.

But eventually Olga got her divorce. I prepared a fine dinner for a celebration, and poured the wine generously for her. I explained I was taking medication and I drank ginger ale. Our conversation turned to sex, as it usually did. She inquired about my tattoo fetish, and whether I really enjoyed seeing her rose. I told her that for a divorce present, I would pay for another tattoo. But I specified the tattoo must either be on her breast or all the way around her ankle. Also, she must let me watch as she was tattooed. She was intrigued with my suggestion and agreed. We rushed out the door, and I drove to a downtown tattoo parlor.

At the tattoo emporium, she decided on a ring of flowers around her ankle. The tattoo artist was reluctant to let me watch, but a little bribery soothed away his objections. I stared away as he prepared her ankle for the tattoo.

As the artist shaved Olga's ankle and bathed it with alcohol, I felt my pants straining. Then he picked up his tattoo needle and got to work on one of the most graceful ankles in the Western Hemisphere. As I watched him adding new colors to her healthy pink, my John Thomas swelled even more. I realized now that this tattoo from me would be a permanent memento of her new-found freedom.

Soon the work was done. She had a beautiful ring of flowers around her ankle. She had to be careful to avoid infection, but the sight of her artwork made my blood race.

We returned to my apartment. As she walked in ahead of me, I gently stroked her pants-clad ass. She turned and smiled an invitation over her shoulder. I ushered her to my bedroom and asked for another look at that rose. She walked over to the stereo, put on a Clapton CD, and began swaying to the rhythm. She did a seductive dance, a striptease. She removed a little bit of clothing at a time. At one point, she draped her bra over my head. Her perky breasts had my undivided attention until she turned around and slowly lowered her pants. She wiggled her ass in my face, and teased me with the panties. Slowly, she peeled them off and revealed her little rosebud. That was all I could take.

I leaped to my feet and held her in a long embrace. Our lips met and our tongues explored one another's mouths. I ran my fingers through her hair and caressed her throat. She put a finger to my lips and slowly went to her knees. When her head reached the level of my fly, she zipped it open and pulled out my prick.

She licked the head of my cock while tracing the shaft with her finger. Then she engulfed the entire phallus in her mouth, and gave me the most mind-blowing headjob I had ever had. Within minutes I exploded in her mouth.

I collapsed on the bed. She leapt on top of me. After an intense embrace, she undressed me in leisurely fashion. When I was completely naked, she licked me all the way from my feet up to my face. We kissed again passionately. Then she straddled me and guided my penis into her sopping pussy. She rocked in a circular motion while she played with the hair on my chest. Soon she bit her lip and gripped my shoulders hard. She hung on tight as she squirmed on my joystick. She shuddered, and let out a scream of ecstasy as she came. She kept on rocking, and soon I erupted in my own climax. She collapsed in my arms then, and we both fell asleep.

Olga is a frequent visitor to my apartment now, even though we no longer have class together. I often take the time to admire the fine workmanship prominently displayed on this walking, moving work of art.—*M.C., College Park, Maryland* ○—▪

THAT'S WHAT WE'D CALL ONE FOR THE ROAD

My girlfriend Sarah and I live in a small town where you have to drive two hours to do any real shopping. We had long wanted to shop in Victoria's Secret or Frederick's of Hollywood for clothing to spice up our sex life. We finally made the trip one Saturday when we both had the day off.

Once we were on the way, with me at the wheel, I saw that Sarah's erect nipples were straining against her white T-shirt. That gave me a raging hard-on that strained my cock against my black jeans. She looked awfully hot, wearing the outfit I love to see her in, a white shirt over loose pink shorts that hug her ass. I love those shorts. When she sits a certain way you can see up her shorts to where her plain white cotton underwear barely covers the fold of her luscious lips. Every once in a while I reached over and rubbed those erect mounds of flesh. Each time she would tell me to stop—but not very forcefully.

We arrived at the mall we had in mind, but couldn't find either shop. So we decided to make do with Nordstroms. Sarah asked me to go to another department to look while she found something sexy. It seemed like hours before I saw her again, and to my disappointment, she had no bag in her hand. She said they had nothing that would turn me on. My former hard-on shrank to flab in a matter of seconds. Sulking a bit, I walked around with her as she did the rest of her shopping. On the way home, though, Sarah deliberately posed so that I could see up her shorts. I was intrigued to see that she had on a different pair of panties from those she wore on the way to the mall. These were made of white and lacy silk. My prick at once turned rock-hard. I looked up and saw a wicked little smile on her face. This got my schlong even stiffer.

She pulled the crotch of her shorts to one side and pulled the G-string tight. It disappeared between her glistening cunt lips. I had a hard time keeping my eyes on the road, especially when Sarah pulled down her shorts and started playing with herself. First she pinched her cunt lips together and pulled on the G-string so that it rode up her dripping slit. I helped her by pulling it down. After about two trips up and down between those luscious cunt lips, the fabric slid easily. It was lubricated with her cunt cream. The luxurious way she enjoyed the experience—mouth agape, eyes tightly closed, telling me how good it felt—nearly made me shoot my load then and there.

When I thought she'd had enough of that game, I pried the fabric from its hiding place and replaced it with my fingers. I stuck three of them deep in Sarah's juicy cunt. She bucked her hips to meet them. I finger-fucked her for about ten minutes. Then she said it was my turn for some excitement. She unzipped my fly, inhaled my swollen John Thomas, and sucked with all her might. Sarah's excellent technique combined with my high state of excitement. Quite soon I exploded come into her mouth. She swallowed every drop. Then she looked at me with sad puppy-dog eyes and asked, "Is that *it*?"

She then sat back and diddled her tiny clit. That instantly got me rock-hard again. Sarah saw that there was a lot of room on the driver's side. She crawled onto my lap, blocking my view of the road so that she had to do the steering. She grasped the steering wheel and told me to drive something else. I wasn't about to argue. Her pussy felt like it was at a thousand degrees, and it gripped my dick like a vise. As I fucked her I felt her warm cream sliding down my balls and onto the seat. I grasped her tits and played with the nipples—ever so sensitive now—until she yelled at me to fuck harder. Now I used my grip on her breasts to gain momentum and really pound into her. She cried out in pleasure. I could feel the load working up my cock. She ordered me to shoot all I had into her thirsty cunt. As I loosed my load, I stamped on the gas pedal. We spun out of control, onto the gravel shoulder.

I told Sarah to get off, and I got out to look for damage with my pants unzipped and my dick hanging out. While I was thus engaged, a helpful driver pulled up behind me. He got a weird smile on his face, and remarked that I must have been on a wild ride. He sure got that right. Apart from risking both our lives it was the best fuck yet, and probably the best I'll ever have. If not, it will do until the real thing comes along.—*E.M., Ames, Iowa* ⚷

ROCK CONCERT SERENADES TWO SLY LOVERS

My best friend and I had a great relationship. We had so much in common—we were both sleeping with her husband.

She didn't know it, and neither did my husband, who just so happened to be her husband's best friend. Now I know what the Moral Majority think, but this isn't an uncommon thing in today's world. More and more couples, I think, are staying together. Although technically we were not being monogamous, at least this way we thought we'd be safe as long as no one found out and got hurt.

For the past nine months, we'd collected quite a number of

great memories for ourselves, but we could only share them with each other, which we fondly did. There is one fond memory we would like to share with your readers, which pretty much brought this thing to a head and changed our lives altogether.

As usual, Jay and I spoke in quick conversations each day, planning when we could sneak away and be together. This particular Tuesday we planned to meet, but Jay called to tell me he had forgotten his buddy had tickets to a concert.

Now, normally I wouldn't have been disappointed because I knew we'd get together in the next day or two, but I had been rather horny that day. I was looking forward to our getting together and fantasizing about the things Jay would do to me, and the things I wanted to do to him.

As it turned out, my sister called me no more than ten minutes later. She asked me if I wanted to go to the same concert. She said there was a private party in one of the boxes that surround the entire coliseum.

"Well," I said, "sure, I'd love to," and the wheels started spinning.

By now Jay and I are very good at spontaneity. He couldn't believe it when I told him I was going too. I wasn't going to let him get away without giving me an orgasm that night.

He came up with the idea of me calling his beeper number, and we would meet in the main lobby and look around for a place to fuck, or at least grope. He told me to dress for an express. Our hearts were racing because the anticipation has always been half the fun.

I tore through my closet and picked out a short denim dress that snapped up the front.

The first thrill was me looking out over the entire concert and trying to find Jay. I didn't see him, but when I dialed his beeper number I saw him pop up and head for the main lobby. I knew we were going for the gold.

I went down in the elevator and he came up and we scouted out restrooms, hallways and elevators, but every place was so crowded with people. I said, "Let's try some of the boxes up on top, maybe we can sneak into someone's bathroom."

It didn't look promising at that point. Then Jay took out his credit card and opened the locked doors to the closed restaurant overlooking center stage as well as the entire arena.

He totally blew me away with his gutsiness. I could feel my wetness about to spew. It was such an amazing feeling being somewhere we shouldn't be—being with someone I shouldn't be with—and about to do something we'd never forget.

Well, down came his pants, and before he could say "suck on this baby," my mouth was all over his penis. I love it when I can feel his big erection growing deep down inside my throat. He was so hard I could no longer stand not having him inside of me. But he insisted on tasting me through my silk panties.

They were off, and so was my dress—so much for dress for express—let's get butt-naked! A security guard would have a field day dragging a naked gal with lace top thigh-highs and cowboy boots off to jail.

We did all kinds of positions in that closed restaurant, which had a line of seats in front of a huge wall of windows. When I pressed against them and accepted Jay's penis from behind with so much pleasure, I climaxed while envisioning sailing to our orgasmic deaths onto center stage. Doesn't, after all, the French word for orgasm literally mean "little death"?

Oh well, when I turned around Eric Clapton was bolting out his blues, and I was blowing Jay off into a screaming orgasm.

Neither one of us will ever forget this experience.

It was the beginning of the end.

At least with our respective spouses. Jay's friendship with my husband was over and so was my friendship with his wife. In hindsight, it's all turned out for the best. These things happen these days. Jay is my husband now.—*W.C., New Orleans, Louisiana* ⚷

THEY READ IT HERE, AND NOW THEY BELIEVE

After reading the June issue of *Penthouse Letters*, I wanted to write. I noticed how many times "solid marriages with good sex lives" are mentioned in the same context of these people sharing wives and husbands with every Tom, Tina, Dick, Denise and Harry and Harriet around.

What bullshit! These people must not inhabit the planet I live on, which is Earth. Granted, I believe many marriages are solid and the couples do have great sex lives, which has always been the case with me and my wife, but this business about throwing in other guys and shit has to be pure fabrication.

Or so I thought.

I know that my wife Kay and I had ten years of marriage, during which we enjoyed some hot, intimate times. We spiced up our sex by whispering and sharing our feelings about someone else. It was a fantasy. We playfully talked about the person(s) being single, another married couple, black, white, male or female.

Through my work, we met Jack and Bernice. This was very fortunate since Kay and I liked the company of people a little older. Both Jack and Bernice were in their middle forties. It seemed to help our friendship along. We began having dinner together often, and the sexy talk and the little hints began to come out.

Both Jack and Bernice had an easygoing kind of personality. Both were tall. Jack was a big man, about six-three, balding and on the plump side. Bernice was tall and kind of willowy, an attractive brunette.

"How's my fair lady," Jack said to Kay that one evening. Bernice kind of countered with, "Jack, maybe she's my fair lady."

I knew this thrilled Kay. She had said Bernice was so lovely. Kay didn't have to say it, but I felt she was getting the hots for Bernice.

But then, things do not always follow what you have in mind. Surprises can come along and blow you into another realm, right?

The following day Jack and I went to lunch. We began to talk about a few sexy things. Jack told me that he and Bernice had some experience with another couple some ten years before.

"But it was kind of disappointing," he said, "they were not the kind of people that you and Kay are."

I replied, "I'm sure Kay really goes for Bernice."

Jack nodded as if to say he realized that, and I told him I did have a little experience with another guy when I was pretty young, and he said, "I can get a hell of a jolt when I get it in the backdoor."

Whoaaa, I was thinking to myself.

I knew what he meant. I nodded, and he said, "Let's take the afternoon off."

After we called in, we went to Jack's place. Bernice was not there. She was doing some special work at a local hospital. After we were there Jack put his arms around me. I had never experienced another man holding me close, and with Jack being a big man, I didn't mind. I knew I would not care to kiss another man. I had seen Kay and Bernice kiss on the lips when saying goodbye.

"Getting a hard-on?" Jack asked, and I nodded. I did feel it.

I really knew then what he meant when he said, "I've got some Vaseline up in our room."

We went up to strip. After we did, I was glad Jack wanted to be the one to do the taking. His build seemed to fit together, even with the kind of body he had—his balding head, his plump belly, heavy legs and hands with stubby fingers. Then there was his cock, over seven inches easily, I knew, and it was thick with a big knobby head. What a little pony, I thought.

"Good one, you've got one," he said, seeing my hard-on. He walked over to the bed.

"Come on," he said, parting his legs and showing me his plump cheeks and the brown spot where he wanted my cock. After I knelt between his legs, he spread some Vaseline over the head of my cock. A second later I was entering his body.

"Uh," he sighed, and as he did, I knew I was glad that his ponylike prick was not entering my body. I remembered my homosexual experience when I was young. It was all touch, and now here I was for the first time actually fucking a man.

"Uh," Jack moaned. He moved, pulling me close and making more sounds of delight. I had heard that some men could derive pleasure this way. Now I knew it was true. He rubbed my back and said, "Phil, fuck me, lover."

"I will, I will, Jack," I sighed.

"Feel good, Phil?" he whispered.

"Oh great," I replied, feeling my cock all the way inside him. I was also feeling his big hard cock pressing between my body and his, and then his hand was feeling my tits and gripping his cock.

Then, "Phil, I'm coming," he moaned.

I felt his come flowing between our bodies. I kept on until I too came in a few more moments. I moaned, "Ah, ah, I'm coming."

Slowly and quietly we cleaned up and talked a while. Not about what had happened, but mostly about work. Then I went on home. Kay was out.

I didn't mention to Kay what went on that day. For the next

few days, for that matter, I was afraid to say anything. Then I seemed to sense that Kay was a little different. I love my wife very much. That evening I asked, "Kay, what's wrong?"

"Nothing's wrong," she replied, "just something's been on my mind."

"You know you can tell me," I told her.

Then I realized why she seemed so inward and shy. It was like a spark of recognition went off in both of our eyes because we know each other so well.

"Phil, Bernice and I did it the other day."

"Did it?" I asked. But I knew. I knew just what she meant, and I said, "To each other?"

"Yes," she said, "To each other."

Knowing the amount of oral sex we've enjoyed, I could have said it in many different ways, but all I said was, "Orally?"

"Yes," she replied.

"How was it?" I asked.

"Oh, nice," she said, "She's so nice. It was great."

Kay knew I had always complimented her on the taste of her pussy. "How did Bernice—I mean, how did she taste?"

"Good," Kay replied, "Nice, very nice."

With this kind of frank talk about her lesbian affair, it was only right that I come clean too. I told Kay that for the first time in my life I'd fucked a man. And I had enjoyed it. So we knew about each other. We thought of the future, the many possibilities.

I was affectionate with Kay. She was excited by what had happened.

"You kind of like Bernice, don't you?"

"You know I do, that body of hers," she answered. "I'm anxious to have her."

That evening Jack and Bernice arrived, smiling as usual. Jack usually had one drink. Tonight he had two. Bernice didn't drink. Kay had fixed a kind of buffet supper, but no one seemed that hungry.

Jack, though, was in a very good mood, and when he got the chance he felt my cock and smiled. But I seemed to know it would mainly be a ladies' night. I helped that along.

"Bernice," I said, "My wife has been so anxious for you to be here and I wonder why?"

"Oh, I don't know?" she smiled.

Kay said, "Phil, would you mind your own business."

We laughed and knowing that it was still early, I pressed,

wanting to speed things along. "It's never too early for bedtime," I said.

"Good idea," Jack said. I knew he was anxious for anything, and Kay did assist then in getting things moving in the right direction. "Well, that's alright," Kay said.

"Is that okay, Bernice?" I asked.

"That's fine with me," she replied.

In our room the four of us undressed. Both Jack and I had a hard-on. It was the first time Kay ever saw Jack, and for a few moments her attention was taken from Bernice.

"Oh my," Kay said, and Bernice smiled.

"Yes, he's proud of that," Bernice said, her eyes twinkling like she knew only too well how a well-hung hubby was a feather in her cap.

It was the first time I'd seen Bernice nude. I knew I had the impulse to fuck her. I reasoned that Jack felt the same about Kay, who in fact was younger and had a firmer set of tits. But again, Bernice had that mature womanly elegance that I find so sexy, and for her age her body was sumptuous.

"You're so lovely in the nude," I told Bernice.

Kay said, "Yes, isn't she? I hope I can maintain myself the way you have dear."

"You will," Bernice said. "You're naturally lovely."

Knowing women are the affectionate, emotional ones, my compliment seemed to help Kay go over to Bernice and put her arms around her. I had thought that Bernice would be the more aggressive one. She had some experience along these lines.

"Bernice, oh Bernice," Kay sighed, as she kissed her lips and pressed her larger, perkier tits against Bernice's smaller, slightly sagging pair.

Jack looked at me and smiled. His big cock stood up. He looked at Kay, then leaned over to me and said, "She has more than a nice ass, my friend. It's absolutely divine."

"I agree," I said. I was proud of Kay's looks, and I felt the same about her heart, which I knew no matter what occurred in this dalliance of extramarital experimentation, would always be just for me.

By the way they were kissing it was obvious they were really into it, especially Kay.

There was a complimentary manner in the way in which Kay led Bernice over to the bed. Hovering over her, Kay kissed her lips before slowly moving down to suck one of her tits.

I could see then that Jack was taken with it all.

Kay's hand fondled Bernice between her legs. Slowly Bernice parted her long legs. Then, just as I would do, Kay knelt between Bernice's legs and let her tongue lick the surface of Bernice's pussy.

"Hmmm," Kay sighed. She held on to Bernice's thighs, and her tongue worked even more, dipping and darting into her open cave. Bernice's hand came down in a complimentary way to pat Kay's head affectionately.

"Hmmm," Kay hummed with satisfaction. Bernice parted her legs more, allowing Kay's tongue to enter her pussy even deeper, and I could see then that Jack's interest in Kay's actions was taking on more than a passive interest. I knew what he was thinking. He probably wanted to slide up behind my wife and drill her from behind.

"Uh," Bernice sighed, moving her body some, so I could see Kay's cheeks draw in with the suction that she made. When she paused briefly to take in a breath, I could see what was happening. Those little flexible strands of fluid that drip from a woman's body when she is highly aroused were very evident.

"Uh," Kay sighed. She licked her own lips to take in the savory strands, and then returned to Bernice's pussy again, where Bernice's dark pubic hair smothered Kay's face. I was entranced by what I was seeing. Without even thinking about it, my hand reached to my cock, which was dangling half-hard in front of me. I entered a carnal reverie, imagining the secret sexual universe that only women truly inhabit. I pondered the idea that that secretion emitted by an excited woman could be transferred in the act of sex. In this case, it was flowing from Bernice's body into Kay's, and sparks seemed to be flying all over the living room as they embraced.

Bernice kind of whined. I was surprised by Kay's way of doing these things, eating pussy the same way I ate hers. Both Jack and I knew we had a real pleasure to behold here, seeing one woman making love to another, and in this case, one was sucking pussy the way she knew the other enjoyed it most.

"Oh my, I'm coming," Bernice moaned. Her body movements and her breathing told us she was having a bursting climax. Kay kept up her attention until Bernice's body movements stopped.

Bernice remained motionless as Kay knelt there, looking down at the hairy private parts of Bernice, which had just received such thoroughly enjoyable treatment.

Then Jack moved behind Kay. She felt him there, but was not the least perturbed by his presence. I knew just what Jack had in mind; he was about to take Kay from the old dog squat.

"Jack," Kay kind of whispered in a receptive manner while Jack took hold of her hips, "Oh yes, baby. Do me, do me, do me doggie-style."

Bernice kind of sighed, and then pulled her legs up to make more room. From the rear I could see the head of Jack's cock make contact. Kay dropped her head and upper body while Jack's cock parted Kay's pussy lips.

"Ahhh," Kay sighed. Jack was really inside her. Bernice moved away and stood up.

"Oh," Bernice said almost apologetically, seeing me there by myself. She came to me and we embraced. It felt so good to have her nude body next to mine. I kissed her knowing how soft and tender she made her lips, and I realized even more what a lovely woman she was.

We heard Jack humping over Kay in doggie-fashion. His big ass gyrated, sending his cock into Kay in forward-slurping strokes. Bernice smiled at the little sounds we heard. Squish. Squish. Squish. Oof. Oof. Oof. We knew that Kay knew she was getting fucked in the best sense of the word.

As we kissed again, my hand traveled down to feel that hairy place between Bernice's legs. I wondered if it was as good as Kay made it out to be. I led Bernice to a chair. After sitting her down, I draped each leg over the arms of the chair. That displayed her most hairy private parts to me, and she smiled knowingly as I knelt down on the floor at her feet.

"Phil," she whispered. My tongue began to lick the moist surface of her pussy, sampling it and tasting; it was as good as Kay said it was. After a few moments her aroused secretion was more evident on my lips, tongue and mouth.

"Ooh, ah," Kay said.

"Are you okay?" Jack asked.

"Yes," Kay kind of moaned, "But it's just that I'm . . . I'm . . . uh, coming."

Bernice had to smile at the way Kay expressed herself at having a climax as my hand fondled that juicy patch between her legs.

"I like a lot of hair down there," I told her.

"Well I've got that," she replied.

"Something else, too," I told her. I mentioned how Kay's actions did kind of surprise me with the way she went after Bernice's passion fluid, and Bernice smiled when I added, "I think Kay likes that stuff and probably will want more of it in the future."

Bernice smiled, "I don't think I'll have any problem when it comes to supplying it."

I assisted Bernice from the chair, wanting to go into the other bedroom and have the freedom of that bed. As we stood, we looked at Jack and Kay, still in the doggie-position. Kay's head rested on a pillow as Jack hammered her over and over. They remained carnally entwined, and it seemed they were content just to stay locked together that way forever. I bent down to get a better view, and I could see that Jack's cock was all the way inside Kay. His balls rested on the cheeks of her ass.

After we entered the guest room, Bernice immediately began to kiss me, and I didn't mind at all her aggressive actions. I had to compare her placid nature to that of her passionate one. Along with it, I realized just how great and loving and wonderful the feelings were between the four of us. This was not just about sex; this was a four-way love affair. I returned her kisses running my tongue in her mouth as far as possible.

"Did Jack tell you that I fucked him in that way?" I asked.

"Yes," she whispered as our bodies slipped down on the bed. Her long legs lifted up and my hard cock found the hairy opening it so desperately wanted.

"Uhhh," I moaned, and Bernice sighed when I yelled, "I'm coming."

"I am too," was her reply. "Your wife made me come and now you did the same."

We laid there for a while just looking at each other with admiration, and then Bernice smiled and asked, "What would your wife think if she knew you were doing this to another woman?"

"I think she would like it a lot. I know she really likes it with you, too."

Bernice smiled and kissed me.

"Why don't you stay the night? You know Jack is in there with Kay, and you're in here with me?"

"I'd love that," she said.

After laying there for a while we got up and went to the other bedroom. Kay and Jack were there, lying next to each other. After all that action, Jack's big ponylike cock was still almost fully hard. He was on his back and the big dong was resting on his tummy.

"How about staying the night?" I asked, and before Jack could answer, Kay said she was all in favor of it.

Bernice and I left the two of them and went to the other room. I knew we just wanted to make love nice and slow, and let things develop as they would.

It was about midnight when Bernice fell asleep, but with all the excitement of the day I knew sleep would not come to me easy. I was content to lay there for a while and observe how nice Bernice looked in the nude. I knew the more I observed the more excited I would become.

I got up quietly and went into the hall. I could hear Jack and Kay. I went to the doorway and they noticed me. I was surprised that Jack still had a full hard-on.

"Bernice is sleeping," I told them.

"Oh that's too bad," Jack said kind of apologetically.

I felt that Jack was getting the better deal, as Kay was still awake.

"It's okay, it's okay," I said. They both knew I meant it, and Kay said that she and Jack had been having such a good time.

"It's no wonder," I said, putting my hand on Jack's cock.

Kay smiled, but I knew she was surprised with me holding his cock.

"How many times have you done it since I saw you guys last?" I asked.

Jack replied, "Just once, but it just won't quit tonight, it just won't go down," he said, pointing to his erection.

"Honey, I'll bet you're not complaining are you?" I asked Kay.

"No," she replied. "You know, Phil, we never did it doggie like that."

I knew how taken Kay had been with Bernice's pussy, and it was somewhat in the same realm that I was fascinated with Jack's cock.

We all remain friends and lovers, and the true romance that exists with Kay has blossomed to include Bernice and Jack. Now I do believe in those stories I read in your magazine about swinging and swapping, but I still feel this is much more than the exchange of bodily fluids. This is real love. This is enlightenment. At times we have had sort of a commemorative night to simulate the wild freedom of what we did that night. It's always one of the highlights of our existence. —*Name and address withheld* O⊢■

Cluster Fucks

"I LOST TRACK, BUT I THINK THEY ALL DID ME"

I threw a fortieth birthday bash for my wife Patti. The theme was an old-fashioned toga party and I had invited all of her friends, including her best friend, Rosemary, who we hadn't seen in years. The party was a major success, and as the evening grew very late, Patti and Rosemary truly made it an evening to remember.

Both of the girls looked stunning in their outfits. They had spent the day before making their mini-togas out of white satin with halter-type tops that exposed their backs and barely covered their breasts. Patti still has the figure of a young woman at five-foot-four, one hundred thirty pounds and a tight 35C-26-36. Rosemary is petite at five feet and about one hundred pounds, and she's been blessed with a 36D-24-34 body that, rumor has it, she has used to excess on many occasions. Unfortunately, I had never been present at any of those occasions, but the stories about Rosemary and Group Therapy, a local club, were the stuff of wet dreams.

There were only a few couples left by about two o'clock, but the girls were still going strong, fueled by a combination of tequila and pot. Patti had gone upstairs to say good night to our guests while Rosemary had remained in the playroom with me and a couple of guys from the softball team. She had been a dancer years before, and when I put on some Santana, she responded by showing us her lambada. Pete, one of my softball buddies, was dancing with her, and he slyly untied her top, exposing her big tits. In all the times we had been together, I had never seen her breasts and couldn't help but stare as she continued to move to the music. Her tits were firm and her nipples were large and dark and stood stiffly before us.

There was a collective yes from all of us as we encouraged Rosemary, and she responded by dancing even more sensuously and slowly, stripping off the rest of her toga until she was naked, save for a white G-string. Pete had moved behind her and was running his hands from her breasts to her plump mound in rhythm with the music, and as we watched he slowly pulled upward on her G-string until the thick outer lips of her pussy popped into view. She moaned loudly at the pressure as he continued to slide the fabric between her lips, and then she arched her head back to kiss him. The heady aroma of her pussy filled the room as he continued to play with her body, sliding his hand inside her G-string, which snapped under the pressure. He had a long finger inside her and her knees began to buckle as he inserted a second until she was virtually supported by his hand.

Dwight, one of the other ballplayers, came forward and dropped his toga to the floor, exposing his swollen cock. "I'm cutting in," he said, taking Rosemary in his arms. She gasped when she felt his cock between her legs and moaned even louder when he cupped her ass in his hands and lifted her until the head of his cock lodged between the folds of her pussy. Then he slowly entered her body. She wrapped her legs around his back and tried to hump him but was powerless to do anything more than hold on as he lifted and dropped her over and over again onto his thick shaft. Her juices were running down over his balls, and white creamy come coated his shaft as their lewd dance continued. She cried out every time his long cock disappeared inside her, and I was afraid that someone upstairs might hear her, so I told Dwight to bring her into the exercise room where we would have some privacy.

The weight room wasn't huge, but the mats and benches offered numerous possibilities and we wasted no time exploring them. Dwight sat back on the bench and Rosemary quickly climbed into his lap and settled herself on his cock. She rode him like a jockey, and Pete and I had a great view as his big dick stretched her tiny pussy. She was very noisy. She grunted and groaned and cried out as they fucked, and I suggested to Pete that he put something in her mouth to quiet her down. He didn't say a word but quickly moved over and took her head in his hands and guided her mouth down over his cock. As she sucked, her moans diminished and she began to grunt quickly as her orgasm approached. She started to tremble and convulsed around the two cocks. Dwight couldn't hold back and stiffened as he pumped his come inside her. I could see semen ooze from around his shaft as he continued to thrust into her body. As Pete moved behind her to take his turn, I left them to go and check upstairs.

It was strangely quiet, and I thought for a minute that everyone had left and that Patti had crashed until I noticed that there were still a couple of cars left. I checked the bedroom, but it was empty. I didn't notice anything until I was passing the office and heard voices inside. I listened for a minute and couldn't believe my ears as I heard the unmistakable moans and murmurs of sex. I slowly opened the door, looked into the dim room and saw a man lying on the floor and my Patti lying on him as she sucked his cock. Two other guys sat on the couch watching and passing a joint. They were Chuck and Andy from the team, and they were both naked and both ready to fuck from the looks of their cocks. Patti was sucking on Bernie like a pro, and as he flexed up at her, she pumped his shaft and then released the head from her mouth as he came like a fountain. She sucked him back into her mouth and licked him clean while the other two slowly pulled on their cocks in anticipation.

Patti's face was a mask of lust as she pulled away from Bernie and moved toward the couch. I kept still so they wouldn't see me and saw her lean forward and lick Chuck's long shaft from bottom to top as he groaned. She licked him four or five more times and then quickly engulfed the swollen head, which caused him to gasp in pleasure. She is a terrific cocksucker, but I had never seen her with another man before, and the sight and sound of her almost made me come on the spot.

Bernie had gotten himself a good view of her pussy from the floor and had his hand up her toga, pinching and teasing her lips. He flipped her skirt up over her hips with one hand and I saw that he had two fingers buried inside her and was slowly pumping and twisting away. I could tell from her moans around Chuck's cock that she was enjoying herself and was getting close to coming when Andy suddenly sat up from the couch and said, "I can't wait anymore, I'm going to fuck you now," and he moved behind her. Bernie told him to go for it and moved out of the way as Andy knelt behind her.

Andy had a huge cock, and I could see why Patti had gone to Chuck first: she doubted she could have gotten Andy into her mouth. She didn't seem to notice when he moved. She continued to suck and lick on Chuck until she felt his cock stroking the lips of her pussy. "No! I don't think I can take it," she cautioned, but Chuck put his hands on her head and guided her back to his cock.

"My husband will find out. I'll suck all of you, but don't fuck me." We all heard the words she was saying, but none of us believed her—not even she herself. The look on her face had changed to one of overwhelming lust, and soon her words followed. "Oh, God, give it all to me. Now!" she screamed.

Andy was more than ready, and he slowly began to thrust his cock inside her. Her protests were a distant memory as the huge shaft slid inside. By the time he had buried all ten inches, the only sound was her panting and the liquid slurp of her pussy as he slowly withdrew only to thrust forward again with increasing force. He pumped her hard and fast and I heard her start to moan and grunt with every thrust until she cried out as her orgasm hit and she convulsed over and over. "It's so good," she moaned as he continued to pound his huge cock into her until he too stiffened and shot a tremendous load inside her that oozed from her pussy like a white river when he pulled out of her.

Bernie immediately took Andy's place and slid inside her soaked pussy, which caused more of Andy's juice to slurp out around his shaft. The sight had me ready to come, and as he too began to pump her, I decided it was my turn and went back to the weight room to check on Rosemary.

I found her lying on her back on the bench press, her jutting breasts capped by long red nipples, her legs spread on either side with her swollen pussy open and oozing. Dwight was straddling her head and she was sucking on his softened shaft as Pete lay on the floor and watched. I stepped between her legs and slid my cock into her pussy.

She was very wet and I slid in easily until my balls were pressed against her butt and I could feel the hard nub of her clit pressing against my shaft. As I began to pump her, I felt her pussy tightening around me. She began to squeal around the swelling cock in her mouth. I knew I couldn't last long but also that there would be more than one opportunity that night, so I fucked her as hard and as fast as I could. She began to buck and cry as her orgasm hit her, and as I felt my load building up, I pulled out and slid up between her sweaty tits and shot my cream all over her neck and chin. Dwight lifted his cock from her mouth as he too shot a load over her nipples until her upper body was covered with come. She rubbed it into her skin and caressed her swollen pussy tenderly as she looked up at us and whispered, "You're not finished, are you?"

"Not at all, babe, we're just starting the postparty part. But if you guys want to see a show, you should check out the office," I said. "It's incredibly hot. The guys are doing Patti." They just looked at me, unsure of how to react. "Don't worry, I've always tried to get her to do this," I continued. "Let's go upstairs. She's so horny she'll fuck us all tonight."

We took Rosemary by the hand and led her up the stairs. She was partied out, and when we got to the office she just collapsed on the couch. Andy took one look at her and went over to enjoy the view and explore her gorgeous body.

Patti was lying flat on her belly with her legs spread wide apart as Chuck fucked her juicy pussy. She was moaning and groaning in delirious passion as he pounded her faster and faster until he came deep inside her, adding his load to the copious supply she had already received. When he pulled away, her lips gaped open and then slowly contracted as she lay there, still coming down from her orgasm.

Dwight went to her, turned her onto her back and straddled her belly, laying his big cock between her tits. She opened her eyes and gazed at him with the dazed expression of a just-fucked woman, and as he slid forward, she grabbed him by the hips and pulled his cock into her mouth. Her eyes closed in pleasure as he slid his big dick in and out, and I could see her tongue working on the underside of his shaft.

Pete came over and inserted his cock into her pussy, and I watched as semen oozed from around his shaft as he pumped her. The feel of another man brought Patti to life again, and I heard her begin to moan around Dwight's cock. She wrapped her legs around Pete in encouragement and I was amazed to see my quiet little wife fucking these men with no inhibitions as they skewered her deeply from both ends. Her groans were deep and guttural as she took over twelve inches of hard cock into her body and climbed toward another orgasm. She had always been able to come rather easily but had entered into another level of excitement as she convulsed and trembled continuously. Dwight's cock slipped from her mouth as she came, so he moved down to cut in on Pete.

He had to pull her legs away from Pete, and she cried out as Pete pulled his heavy cock out of her. But Dwight hardly missed a beat as he thrust inside her.

"Don't stop, you're going to make me come again," she panted as he buried himself to the hilt and pumped her with short, hard strokes. "Anything you say, babe," he said, punctuating his words with his thrusts until she began to buck and thrash again.

The sight of them had my cock hard again, and as soon as Dwight shot his load, I took his place.

She was so lost in the sex that I'm sure she didn't even realize it was me as I thrust into her body. Her pussy was wide open and very hot, and I slipped easily to the very bottom of her hole. She wrapped her arms around me tightly and pulled me down to her as she tried to get me even deeper inside, and I could feel her hard nipples against my chest. Her pussy twitched and tightened around me spasmodically as she continued to come. And as I fucked her I could hear her voice hissing in my ear: "Fuck my pussy, big man, come for me. I love your big cocks. Just keep fucking me . . ." Over and over, like a mantra, she moaned until I couldn't hold back and shot my load into her soupy pussy.

I was immediately replaced by Bernie as the cluster fuck continued. He impaled her on his fleshy spike and then rolled over until she was straddling him. She rubbed her nipples against his hairy chest as he pumped up into her, and every time she stiffened in orgasm, a fresh flow of come would ooze from her pussy around his shaft until his balls were covered.

A sound from the couch caused me to turn, and I saw that Andy had revived Rosemary and had her sitting in his lap. Her back was against his chest and her legs were straddling him as they watched the scene in front of them. He was pulling on her nipples and she was groaning loudly as he did so. Her pussy was swollen and the pink lips were open and caressing Andy's shaft in a lewd kiss. As I watched, his cock began to harden and soon jutted impressively from between her thighs as she slowly worked her pussy on him and coated his shaft with her juices. She grabbed his cock with both hands and pulled on him as I heard him groan in pleasure. The swollen head of his cock extended halfway up her belly, and I didn't see how she could possibly take him inside her. But I didn't have to wait long to find out as she squirmed in his lap until he was positioned at the entrance to her pussy.

She teased her pussy with his cock, running the big head up and down her slit, slapping her clit with the heavy shaft as the rest of us watched her arousal. Her eyes were closed and she was panting as she masturbated with his cock. It was better than any fantasy, and I closed my eyes for a second and just listened to the sounds around me as Patti's moans and cries mingled with the slaps and slurps of hard cocks and wet cunts and the grunts of men rutting in the bodies of beautiful women. I opened my eyes again as Rosemary gasped loudly and tried to take the big cock into her body.

It looked like an impossible fit as the swollen head virtually covered her pussy, but slowly her lips parted and stretched wider and wider until her clit stood fully exposed above the flared head. Then, almost imperceptibly, the head began to slip inside and her clinging lips were drawn with it until about two inches had disappeared. Her clit looked so appealing that I reached up and lightly flicked it with my finger, causing her to jump, which allowed another inch of cock to sneak inside her. Her juices oozed around his shaft. As I played with her clit she began to come, and her frantic movements only served to impale her more deeply on his cock until he was totally buried in her body. She began to scream through her orgasm, saying "Oh fuck, oh fuck, oh fuck," over and over. I was ready to come, and although I tried to hold back, the scene was too much for me and I emptied my balls into the air. I was exhausted and lay back on the floor as Andy continued to fuck her.

Rosemary was virtually spent from the intensity of her orgasm and was too weak to move around the big cock, so Andy pulled out and quickly positioned her on the floor next to Patti, who was oblivious to us as Chuck fucked her from behind. Andy slid his big dick back inside Rosemary, and I heard her moan in pleasure as he pumped her with long strokes.

I must have fallen asleep, because the next thing I knew it was four in the morning and the house was quiet. I don't know what woke me, but I was on the couch in the office and it took a few seconds for my fogged brain to awaken. Soon my mind was filled with images from the party. The girls were nowhere to be seen, so I stumbled to the bedrooms in search of them. The door to the guest room was open and Rosemary was asleep, a single sheet covering her body. I was tempted to stay, but a moan from my bedroom caused me to open the door, where I found my Patti safely in bed but with insatiable Andy between her thighs again.

She was virtually asleep, but her body was still responding to the cock lodged deep in her pussy as he slowly pumped her. "I'm sorry, man," said Andy. "I just had to have her one more time. I've never had such good pussy. You're really lucky." He punctuated each sentence with a strong thrust into my wife and seemed to be getting off on fucking her in front of me. "Do you know how many times we got her? About fifteen times, easy. I've never seen a woman take it like that—in her mouth, in her pussy, on her tits. Rosemary was good, but your wife loves cock." He was fucking her harder now and she was panting as he brought her toward yet another orgasm. Her eyes were open, but she was so totally consumed by lust that she didn't see anything as her body trembled on the edge of ecstasy. She opened her mouth wide and extended her tongue in invitation. I climbed on the bed next to them and offered her my cock. She pulled me deep into her mouth and sucked as his thrusts drove me down her throat.

"Come for me, Patti," I said. "Show me how much you like his big cock fucking you. Make him shoot in your pussy while I shoot in your mouth." As I spoke, Andy began to fuck her faster until she threw her head back and her body convulsed over and over in orgasm. I pulled her mouth back onto my cock as she came, and then I covered her tongue with my load. Andy grunted as he came and his thrusts slowed until we were all lying motionless on the bed. She gasped when he pulled out and I kissed her in unspoken thanks as she fell back asleep.

I let Andy out, and as I went up to bed I looked in Rosemary's room and saw that she had thrown the covers off and was lying naked on the bed. My cock was worn out, but the voyeur in me couldn't resist one last look. I approached the bed. She was lying on her side facing away from me with one leg drawn up and her arms under her head. Her plump pussy swelled wetly between her thighs and was coated with the sticky remnant of her sexual activities. The pink inner lips protruded and curled back in invitation as semen oozed from within and ran down the back of her thigh. The sight of her was so sexy that I had to touch her. I lightly stroked her lips with my finger. As I played with the sticky liquid and spread it up and down her slit, she moaned softly. I pulled on the soft hairs of her pussy and opened her outer lips until her swollen clit came into view and she groaned and rolled over onto her back.

She still seemed to be asleep, and as I continued to stroke her pussy, I sucked one long nipple into my mouth and was rewarded to feel it stiffen as I teased it with my tongue. I tasted her other nipple and alternated back and forth between them as her breathing deepened and she spread her thighs slightly. I pressed her legs even farther apart and moved down and licked her pussy slowly from bottom to top. She was delicious, and as my tongue approached her clit, she gasped and began to slowly hump her hips as she became more and more aroused until she started to tremble and then climaxed with a grunt and spasmed violently as I tried to keep my tongue on her clit. "Put your cock in me," she hissed, "I want to be fucked."

My cock was only half hard, but having been fucked by so many men that night, she was wide open, and as I climbed between her legs and pressed the head against her opening, she just seemed to swallow me up and I felt myself swelling to full size inside her. Her pussy tightened around me as I started to pump, and she came over and over and soaked my balls with her juices until I finally succumbed and shot what was left of my semen inside her.

I covered her with a quilt and returned to bed with Patti. We woke up around noon the next day and I asked her how she felt. She claimed not to remember much of anything past midnight other than admitting to having kissed some of the guys good night and how they had tried to feel her tits. I smiled and kissed her and squeezed her pussy, which was still oozing with semen.

"Did you let them?" I asked, transferring some of the juice to her nipple. "Did they play with your nipples?" I continued, milking the juice from her pussy and smearing the sticky substance on her breasts as she looked at me with wide eyes.

"Promise you won't be mad? I know I should have stopped them," she whispered slowly, "but it was so sexy with them all around me. I was just kissing them good night and they said they wanted to play a game and brought me into the office. They had their hands all over me and I was getting hot. Chuck kept pulling on my nipples."

"Like this?" I asked, stretching her nipple a good inch from her big breast.

"Oh, yeah," she breathed deeply and continued, "and then someone was touching my pussy and I told them to stop but they kept touching me and then Bernie took his clothes off and his cock looked so good. He pulled me down on the floor and . . ." her voice trailed off as her breathing deepened and I finished the sentence for her.

"You sucked his cock." I kissed her hard and waited for her to respond as I continued to play with her gooey pussy and felt her clit swell under my fingers.

"Yes," she sighed and pressed her head against my chest. Her fingers curled around my cock as she moaned, "You always said you wanted me to, and I saw how you all were looking at Rosemary, so I did it."

I had my finger inside her juicy pussy and she looked up at me, her face full of lust and uncertainty, but she sensed my excitement and pulled on my cock with both hands as she continued.

"He was so big and so hot in my mouth. I love the taste of him, but he kept trying to get on top of me. I didn't want him to fuck me, so I crawled on him and sucked on his cock until he came. There was so much come, and then I saw the other two sitting on the couch. Two more cocks for me. Two more big cocks to suck." She was pumping me hard as she gasped out her story, her pussy creaming all over my hand.

"I went over to Chuck and rubbed his big cock on my face. His balls were so big. He liked me to lick them over and over, and then he was in my mouth, pumping into my throat. I just wanted him to come, and then someone was touching my pussy, and then Andy fucked me. I was so wet and he just put his cock in me. It was so big . . . And then he started to move and I just lost it."

My cock was hard as a rock, and as she spoke, I rolled on top of her and drove into her pussy and began to fuck her with long, slow strokes.

"Did he fuck you like this? Did you come? Tell me everything." She tried to talk, but she was too hot, and she gasped, "Oh, just fuck me, please." As I pumped her body, I said, "All day long, but I love hearing you tell me about the guys."

She looked up at me and her pussy squeezed tightly around my cock as she continued. "He did me from behind. His cock felt huge and he made me come so quickly, but he didn't stop, and I was so hot that I let them do everything to me. He came in my pussy. It felt like he shot gallons. When he pulled out, someone else started to fuck me. I couldn't stop coming. They kept shooting in me—in my mouth, inside me—over and over. I just couldn't stop. I lost track, but I think they all did me." And at that she spasmed around my cock and came so hard I thought she was going to pass out.

"I was there, babe. I watched. I fucked you too." Her eyes opened wide. "You were fantastic."

Her eyes glazed over as I continued to pump her. "All of them?" she moaned.

"Fifteen times, babe, for hours, cock after cock. I never saw so much come." She moaned louder and came again, her pussy wetter than ever.

"What about Rosemary? Did they . . . ?" I nodded and then stiffened as I came and filled her pussy with my come.

She whispered, "I love you," and slid down my body and took my cock in her mouth and sucked on me. I lay back and enjoyed her mouth and her new attitude until I heard a voice say, "Toga!" and saw Rosemary standing naked in the doorway. "Best party I was ever at," she said and came over and sat down on the bed. Patti stopped sucking me and looked up at her friend and smiled. "Breakfast in bed?"

I just lay back and relaxed as two sets of lovely lips played with my cock.

I don't know when we'll have another party like that, but I do know that softball season will certainly be interesting this year.
—*D.F., Fort Lee, New Jersey* O—▪

COLLEGE LIFE IS THE SAME AS IT ALWAYS HAS BEEN

I'm writing to tell you and your readers what can happen when six horny females decide to take advantage of three unsuspecting guys.

I'm a new student at an old southern university, and I live in a two-bedroom apartment. My roommate went home for the weekend, so I decided to invite some friends from my hometown down for the weekend. Eight people showed up, and their names have been changed to protect the guilty.

They arrived Saturday afternoon and, after going out and getting a couple cases of beer, Alan, Charles and I started playing a game of quarters while the chicks wandered around the grounds of the university. After an hour of this, we decided to go out and get a bite to eat.

When we got back, the girls were watching television, so we grabbed some more beer and joined them. After three more beers, I was getting pretty wasted. I dropped a beer and it spilled all over me. I stumbled into my bedroom, took off my wet clothes and was getting out some dry ones when I heard the door slam behind me. I turned around and there was Mariah staring at me. She looked down toward my crotch and said, "I was always wondering what kind of pistol you were packing. From the looks of it, I bet it's a twelve-shooter." She walked over to me, knelt down in front of me and grabbed my cock, which immediately became rock-hard.

She slowly lowered her mouth onto my pulsing piece of manhood. I moaned as her hot lips engulfed the head and her tongue started to flick at its tiny opening. With one hand she gently stroked the shaft, and with the other she massaged my aching balls. She kept this up until she felt me starting to come. She pulled her mouth off of my cock and grabbed it with her hand, jacking me off as jets of hot come shot in high arcs across the floor.

After my orgasm, it was my turn. I spread her legs and slowly lowered my head down to her gleaming cunt. I began to slowly tongue the length of her slit. She started groaning louder and pushed her pussy harder onto my face. By now Alan and Abby had wandered into the room and were watching us as Mariah moaned loudly and started to come. Lovely pussy juice flowed down my chin onto my neck. Happily I lapped the sweet nectar that flowed from her.

Just as I raised my head, Mariah said to Alan and Abby, "You got to watch us, now it's our turn to watch you." Quicker than a wink, they were both out of their clothes and down on the bed right next to Mariah and me. Abby grabbed Alan's cock and immediately started licking the head of his flagpole. Then she lightly sucked from the base up the shaft to the foreskin and back again. From his expressions, you could tell that Alan was about to come, but Abby didn't want that. Her mouth left his dick and started working up to his chest until her mouth met his and they French-kissed each other.

Alan then grabbed his cock and had Abby sit right down on top of it. Abby started bucking up and down like a jackhammer. My dick started getting hard at the sight of this, so I proceeded to roll over onto Mariah and stick my dick into her hot and wet pussy. I started with long, deep strokes but increased my tempo when Mariah started moaning. We both came together in a mindblowing orgasm. As I shuddered with my last waves of pleasure, I glanced over to watch Abby bring Alan to an orgasm that made his whole body start to shake. Abby screamed as she fell on top of him and started twitching as total ecstasy overcame her body.

We lay there for about five minutes until we heard some strange noises coming from the other room. When we walked into the living room, we saw Charles lying stark naked on the floor. He was underneath Natalie, Sinead, Joan and Melissa. Joan was sitting on top of his face, bouncing up and down, trying to get the deepest penetration of Charles's tongue that was possible. Natalie, Sinead and Melissa were each taking their licks at Charles's huge prick. This went on for about five minutes until Charles let out a loud groan and deposited hot come all over the girls' faces. They then proceeded to lick his cock and balls clean. Joan then pulled herself off of Charles's face and crawled down to his limp cock, which proceeded to jump back to life. He then pulled her away from his cock, turned her over and slowly slid his cock into her moist cunt. She started to grind her hips upward to meet his strokes and they began a long and furious fuck.

Not wanting to miss out on the action, Natalie, Sinead and Melissa each positioned themselves around Charles to get the most out of his young and virile body. Melissa got behind him and started licking his ass and balls as she fingered herself to an orgasm. Natalie lay down next to Charles's head and pulled it over to her waiting pussy. He ate her out until she screamed in ecstasy. Sinead grabbed one of Charles's huge hands and jammed two of his fingers up her cunt and he proceeded to finger-fuck her to an orgasm. After he was finished with the other three girls, he turned his entire attention to Joan and proceeded to fuck her in one of the best fuck sessions I have ever witnessed. They started to fuck so fast and hard that it looked like they had become one and would have to be surgically removed. Charles finally told Joan that he was going to come. That set her off and she bucked and shuddered her way to a hard orgasm as Charles pumped his love juices into her quivering pussy.

After we all cleaned up, we decided that we would resume our friendly Hide-the-Weenie games the next day, which is another story. — *T.W., Charlottesville, Virginia* ⚷

CHAPTER ONE: MY WIFE GOES CRAZY ON WHITE WINE

Now that my wife Darlene and I have opened our sex lives to the point where we are making and swapping amateur videotapes of our sexual liaisons (both by ourselves and with others that we fuck together and separately), it seems that it's time to tell the story of our rather unusual sexual relationship and how it got started.

The entire story of our sex life, up to date at least, will take time to tell, and more space than I have here. I'll start at the beginning. Call this letter Chapter One. I'm writing the accounts and Darlene is proofreading them and confirming their accuracy.

The initial months of our marriage were uneventful, except I soon found that Darlene had a sex drive that was always active but became insatiable whenever she drank white wine. While she simply became drunk on beer, whiskey or mixed drinks, when she drank white wine she would become uncontrollably horny. For example, one night as we left a bar, after she had been drinking wine, she pulled out my cock and blew me as I opened the car door for her. She wanted me to fuck her in the car in the bar parking lot. When I told her to wait until we got home, she reclined the seat, pulled off her sundress and fingered her pussy all the way home.

Several passing truck drivers got the view of a lifetime, made better by the fact that I left the interior light on, giving them a perfect view of my wife, bare-ass naked, stretched out in the seat, with two fingers pumping in and out of her sexy, tight cunt and the other hand rubbing her 36C tits. Knowing that passing drivers were watching turned her on even more, as she would put her legs on the dash and arch her back, thrusting her body above the window whenever a truck passed us.

When we arrived home, we fucked until I couldn't get it up without a rest. I left the room, leaving her naked on the couch. I thought she was finally passed out, but when I returned a few minutes later, her legs were spread, feet on the floor, and she was moaning as she continued to finger her pussy. I let her continue while I got two of her vibrating dildos. When I returned, I fed one dildo into her pussy and the other up her ass. Once inside of her two love canals, I moved the two vibrators toward each other, which set her off once again. It was obvious that no one mortal man could satisfy her when she was drinking wine.

It was also apparent that when she was in this condition, she had absolutely no sexual restraint and I could do anything with her that I pleased, so long as I allowed her the orgasms that she needed so urgently.

In those early days, there was a couple that we were close friends with, Bradley and Eloise. We spent a lot of time together. Eloise was always telling Darlene and me how good a lover

Bradley was and how he had the biggest cock that she had ever seen. However, despite Bradley's sexual abilities, Eloise suddenly left him one day. She found another man and dropped out of our lives. Bradley continued to see us, and our friendships became stronger.

I soon noted a change in Darlene's attitude toward Bradley. She was obviously becoming somewhat more than just friendly. There was a definite sexual tension developing. To her credit, Darlene made no attempt to hide this behavior from me. She would hug and kiss Bradley in my presence. She frequently patted him on the ass, and she often made reference to the claims that Eloise had made. I began to get the feeling that my faithful young wife was anxious to find out about Bradley's cock for herself.

Not being the jealous type, I came out and asked her one night, as we were making love, if she would like to fuck our friend. She would only reply that she would never sneak around behind my back. Since this answer was not exactly a definite no, the next night I opened a bottle of white wine and after several glasses, I again asked her the same question. This time she replied that she would only fuck him if I was there with them and approved.

Strangely, this situation began to sound interesting, so I asked her, "Do you want me to watch you fuck Bradley?" She replied that she would if it turned me on and if I wouldn't get upset. While this conversation was taking place, I put my hand between the legs of her jeans and found that her pussy had become so wet that she had soaked the crotch. I continued to excite her by asking her if she would like to suck Bradley's big cock while I fucked her from the rear.

"Yes," she replied. "I also want you to make me into a sandwich, one of you fucking my cunt while the other sticks me in the ass, like you do with the vibrators."

At this, she ripped off our clothes and impaled herself on my hard cock. She was so turned on that her juices literally ran down my thighs when she came.

After that night, Darlene became more aggressive with Bradley. The next time he came over for dinner, Darlene came downstairs wearing a pair of jeans that were obviously cut off just for the occasion. They were so short that the cheeks of her ass showed in the back and a tuft of pussy hair could be seen from the front. Her top was one of my old cotton-mesh tank tops that she'd cut off just under her breasts. You could plainly see the creamy undersides of her pendulous globes, and her hard nipples could be plainly seen through the material. Whenever she sat down, Darlene would spread her legs slightly, allowing her cunt lips to just barely be in view.

Bradley gave me a funny look, but I just smiled and shrugged my shoulders. On several occasions, over the next few weeks, Darlene would tease Bradley suggestively, grabbing and wrestling with him, telling him that she was going to "de-pants" him and see what Eloise had bragged about. Bradley still didn't know how to take Darlene's behavior. He would always stop her and hold her back. But on one occasion, she grabbed him by the crotch and briefly rubbed his cock through his pants as they wrestled on the living room floor right in front of me. As he reached for her hands to stop her, she hooked her thumbs under her T-shirt, and, as Bradley tried to push her back, she raised her arms and pulled the T-shirt up, exposing her tits to both of us, but making it look like Bradley had done it. Poor Bradley! He was still afraid of making me angry and didn't realize that he was about to become our sex toy. I know that Darlene wanted to fuck right then, but I was waiting for just the right moment. She wouldn't initiate sex with Bradley unless she was sure that I was agreeable, so I teased them both for a little while.

A few days later, Darlene hosted a bachelorette party for a girl from her office. This girl had a reputation as a wild child, and her fiancé had already gone out of town, so Darlene hired a male stripper from an outfit with a reputation for being somewhat sleazy. There were nine women present when the stripper arrived, and Bradley and I were there as well. Barbra was seated on a stool in the middle of the living room with the other girls seated around her in chairs and on the couch. The stripper, a young bodybuilder with an obvious bulge in his jeans, stripped down to a G-string, as per usual. But then, as he danced around Barbra, he leaned over her from behind and told her that he was getting hard as he fantasized about her and asked her if she would like to feel his hard-on.

Barbra reached behind her and touched the young man's G-string. Then she impetuously snatched it off, leaving him completely naked, with Barbra's hand on his impressive cock. After she had rubbed it even bigger, he danced around the room, shaking his cock in front of all the women. Several, including my wife, gave it a few good strokes. One gal even bent over and took it in her mouth. She was so turned on that she would have sucked him off, despite her being married to my wife's boss. But he pulled away and began gyrating against Barbra. She helped him finish his show by stroking his hard-on and rubbing his balls as he danced until the inevitable happened: the young stud tensed, groaned loudly and spewed an incredible load of spunk all over Barbra's hands, pants, top, and even a spurt on her face, which she licked off. Barbra then bent down and sucked the man's cock dry. I couldn't believe that this guy actually got paid for his work!

After the stripper left, Darlene, who had consumed more than a full bottle of wine, announced to the girls that she had it from a good source that Bradley had a cock that was even bigger than the stripper's. She asked if anyone was willing to help her find out. Several of the girls jumped up and gamely helped Darlene grab Bradley, pulling him to the floor. They would have successfully stripped him if I hadn't come to his aid. I acted as though I was angry that the girls would do such a thing, telling them all to back off. Actually, I felt that Bradley and I could have ended up in a two-man, nine-woman orgy, but I knew that this was the night that I would get to see Bradley's cock slide up my wife's canal, and I wanted it to just be us three. By now I was eagerly anticipating the inevitable and, to be honest, I was curious as to the size and stamina of Bradley's tool.

Soon after my "rescue," the girls left, leaving the three of us alone. I had made Bradley several mixed drinks during the evening, so he was feeling no pain. Darlene came to me as I was opening another bottle of wine and asked why I had stopped her and the other girls. "I thought you wanted me to fuck our friend," she complained. "I was really going to show off for you!" I replied that I didn't want to waste him on her friends. Darlene's eyes lit up as she realized that I wasn't actually angry. Then I told her, "If you still want to strip Bradley down, go grab him now. I'll help you."

She ran to the living room, and in seconds I heard the sound of them tussling. Bradley had finally realized that Darlene's flirtations had my approval. In seconds, Darlene had Bradley's shirt unbuttoned, and then she went for his belt. She took his jeans down and off in one jerk, leaving him wearing only his socks and open shirt. In spite of his nervousness, Bradley was beginning to rise to the occasion. I admit to being impressed, even at this early stage. As Darlene was tugging at Bradley's clothing, I had whispered to him that as soon as she was done, it was her turn to get naked. Darlene had little time to admire Bradley's equipment before we both turned on her. Bradley pulled off Darlene's Levi's while I excitedly took off her blouse. As she was not wearing a bra or panties, she was now as naked as Bradley. Darlene acted coy and shy and tried to cover up. She stood up on her feet, her back to Bradley, who was totally lost in the moment. As she mockingly struggled and squirmed, her ass rubbed against Bradley's rapidly stiffening prick. Feeling his cock pressing against her ass, she arched her back and leaned away from him. Seeing this, I teasingly said, "You nasty little girl, you strip another man naked, then let him strip you naked right in front of your husband, and now you're leaning up so he can look over your shoulder and see everything you've got."

At this, she leaned backwards, so he couldn't see. Of course, this forced Bradley's pole right back up against the crack of her ass, which had been my intention. Bradley let out a soft moan. Darlene was more than a little excited by the events taking place. I stepped up to them and continued, "Oh, sure, you hot little wench, now you grind your little sexy ass up against him and get him all excited. I'll bet you've got him hard as a rock now."

At this, I reached behind Darlene's ass and took hold of Bradley's tool. I must admit, Eloise was right, it was truly an impressive member. Mine is bigger than the average and never fails to get Darlene off, but Bradley's was at least nine inches long, nearly as big around as my wrist and hard as a marble column. I knew that Darlene was in for a real hammering, and, apparently, so did she, as I reached between her legs to find her pussy so wet that the juice was running down her thighs.

As I was directing this show, and my straining cock begged me to get on with it, I said, "Yeah, you got it rock-hard, you nasty slut, now you'll just have to get him off. I can tell that's what you want. Your cunt's all wet and ready to take it."

I quickly grabbed Bradley's rigid tool again, and before he could begin to wonder if I was turning gay, I pushed it down and slid it between Darlene's thighs. It slid up her belly and almost made her look like she had a cock. Darlene now gave up any pretext of embarrassment. She just wanted to be fucked. She began to thrust her pussy forward and back, rubbing her cunt lips and clit across Bradley's massive prick, drenching it with her pussy juice, making it ready. Events were now beyond anyone's control. I was committed to having my wife fucked by another man, right before my eyes. Everyone involved, including me, was too hot to stop the sex, even if we had wanted to.

I reached for Darlene's tits, gently pinching and twisting the nipples the way she likes. I pulled her forward in my arms, which caused Bradley's cock to slide down Darlene's belly to her pussy. The massive round cockhead found its opening. There was a slight hesitation as Darlene's pussy lips had to open wider than they ever had before. She had never been invaded by a missile of this size, not even a rubber one. Her wetness and desire quickly overcame the tightness of her sweet and tight little hole. She hunched back as Bradley thrust forward, and his rigid member slid smoothly up her pussy until the only thing showing was his bag. Darlene came instantly, screaming and bucking like a bronco trying to throw the man riding her. But she surely wasn't trying to throw him off. She ground down on his giant prick like she would never let it out of her. It struck me that I was actually watching another man's cock, and a huge one at that, slide in and out of my little Darlene's snatch. And she was loving every thrust, every slap of his pelvis against her ass, every moan and groan that she was causing him to make.

I reached for my own prick. Pre-come was dripping out of the hole and running across the head. I'd have never believed that watching my wife fucking another man would make me so hot. I took her by the head and slowly pulled her down to her knees as I also went to my knees. Unwilling to pull his prick out of her pussy, even for a second, Bradley followed us down. Bradley continued to fuck my wife doggie-style as I pulled her head to my cock. She took it into her mouth and began to suck the head and shaft, as she does so damned well, but this time it was a totally different feeling as Darlene rocked back and forth in time with Bradley's thrusts. I was too far gone to hold back, and in seconds I felt hot come explode out of my prick and into Darlene's throat. She came again, as she often does, as she swallowed my load.

Darlene's pussy walls contract tightly when she has an orgasm, and this was too much for Bradley. He arched his back, and slammed his cock into Darlene up to the balls as he shot his rocks off. He must have pumped a quart of spunk into Darlene's tunnel. He thrust his cock into her seven or eight times as he came. With his last push, he shoved her onto me and collapsed onto her back, where we all lay for several minutes, trying to catch our breath.

Darlene looked at me timidly and asked, "You're not mad at me for fucking Bradley, are you?"

Teasingly, I replied, "I sure am. You're a nasty girl. But you can make it up to me."

"How?" she asked.

"By letting me watch you suck Bradley's cock," I replied. "I want to see you make it as big and hard as it was when it was buried in your hot, wet pussy."

Darlene smiled and licked her lips as I continued: "I want to see you make him come in your mouth, like he did in your pussy. And I want to see you swallow every drop of his come."

Darlene replied, "Oh, you want me to put on a show for you? You just want to show me off to Bradley, to show him what a good little cocksucker your wife is. You know I want to suck Bradley's big cock for you," Darlene continued, "but while I do, I want you to lick my pussy. I want you to taste another man's jism in my snatch."

Often, Darlene would like for me to eat her pussy right after I'd shot my load into her. For some reason, the thought that I was tasting my own spunk turned her on. Being sexually liberal, I feel that lovers should accommodate each other's fantasies and kinks so long as no one is harmed. So I go along with this odd request. She always has a powerful orgasm whenever I do this for her.

Bradley had rolled over onto his back, his cock was soft and "only" five or six inches long. He protested, "Hey guys, I just got the fucking of my life, my poor dick's tired. Don't I have a say in this?"

"Sure you do," Darlene said in a sexy voice. Then she rolled over onto him, put her head between his legs and ran her tongue from underneath his balls up the shaft of his prick until she was circling around the head.

"You can take a nap now, if you want," she said. Bradley just moaned softly and pulled her head down onto his rapidly stiffening member. Darlene sucked Bradley's cock into her mouth, rolling her tongue around the head. His prick stiffened and grew to its former size as Darlene made her best effort to take it all down her throat. She got about two-thirds of the way down and then began stroking it in and out of her mouth, sucking so hard that her cheeks were sucked in and Bradley's tool could be seen sliding in and out of her mouth.

After a few moments of watching, fascinated, as my little Darlene enthusiastically sucked on another man's cock, I got down to business. Sliding my face between Darlene's legs, I found her pussy still gaping from the reaming that she had received a few minutes earlier. Her pussy juice and Bradley's come were mixed together and oozing from her cunt. Bradley must have shot a huge load of spunk, as it was not only dripping from Darlene's snatch but was also in her pubic hair and running down her thighs and under to her asshole. Knowing that my lapping her pussy in its present condition was going to get Darlene off, I dove in tongue first. She began squirming and moaning, clamping her legs around my head as I licked first her pussy lips, then her clit, then her asshole and then back again to her pussy. She soon had a toe-curling orgasm, which caused Bradley to lose control of his cock and blow another load of come into Darlene's throat.

All of this action, and tasting another man's come in my wife's pussy, had brought my cock back to life. I rolled Darlene over onto her side and slammed into her from behind. As I pumped Darlene's pussy, she gave Bradley a kiss, giving him back some of his own jism that she had been holding in her mouth. She stroked Bradley's cock as I fucked her, so that he was semihard again when I shot my load into her pussy.

Semihard for Bradley's cock is bigger than most men at full flag, and it was plenty big enough for Darlene. As my cock softened and I pulled it out, she guided him into her from the front. I rubbed and pinched her nipples as she rocked back and forth against me to the rhythm of Bradley's thrusts. He took a long time to come this time. As I lay beside them, watching my lovely, sexy wife being stroked by my friend, my tired cock began to show signs of renewed life. I slipped into the bathroom and came back with a jar of lubricant. I stroked the stuff onto my hard prick and massaged some into Darlene's tight asshole, working my finger into the puckered hole.

Darlene gasped and whispered, "Are you going to fuck my ass?"

"Yes, baby," I said. "Bradley and I are going to fill up both your holes at the same time. We're going to make you the meat of our pussy sandwich!" At that, I began pressing my cockhead against her asshole. She pushed back against me, eager to feel both our cocks inside her at once. "Oh, yes, baby, fuck my ass!" she screamed, now in complete wanton abandon. "I want you both fucking me!"

I had butt-fucked Darlene before, and I'd always been careful not to hurt her. This night she gave herself over to the sensations of sex and was feeling no pain. I steadily increased the pressure until the head of my cock pushed past her sphincter and the shaft slid smoothly in up to the hilt. As I began to stroke Darlene's ass, I could feel Bradley's cock through the thin flesh that separated us, thrusting in and out of her pussy. Darlene had begun to orgasm continuously. She was moaning, screaming and hunching her pubes at both of us as we stroked her, sometimes together, sometime alternately. Bradley was the first to shoot his load. Darlene's squirming and hunching was too much for his cock to stand. As he made his last thrust, his prick slipped out of Darlene's pussy and he pumped hot come all over her pussy lips and asshole.

Inadvertently, his prick rubbed up against my balls and shaft. This was a strange feeling. I'd never had another cock touch me like that. My cock was about to blow from stroking Darlene's tight butthole, and this new sensation put me over that edge. I shot a hot wad of come deep into Darlene's ass. Sweet relief!

Darlene had come at least a dozen times, but she was still not satisfied. She turned herself around and ground her gaping, sopping wet snatch into Bradley's face. Bradley was exhausted, but he was pleasantly surprised by Darlene's sexual stamina and grateful for the incredible fucking and sucking he had just received. He returned the favor, lapping his tongue into Darlene's tunnel and sucking her engorged clit. Incredibly, Darlene began coming again. As Bradley sucked Darlene's clit, she went into a series of continuous orgasms that had her screaming, "Stop, I can't stand it! Yes, suck my pussy, don't stop! Oh, I'm coming again, bite my clit, lick me, lick my pussy hard!"

Finally, mercifully, she passed out in the middle of her orgasm. We all slept the morning away, naked on the living room floor.

This was our sexual awakening. The next day, after Bradley had left, Darlene and I talked about what we'd allowed to happen. We both admitted that it had been a fantastic turn-on to do what is considered forbidden. She had been as excited by fucking another man in front of me as I was watching her. We both agreed that we would remain faithful to each other in that we would always include each other whenever another person, male or female, was involved. Neither of us would have sex with another person unless the other partner was present or at least knew what was happening and had consented. That way, we could do whatever turned us on without being deceitful. Being sexually liberal, this left us a lot of latitude. Now that we had broken the ice, our adventures were only beginning. —*B.K., Bloomington, Indiana*   O┼ ▪

"LOVE IN AN ELEVATOR" MEETS
"DUDE LOOKS LIKE A LADY"

I am a well-endowed college student at a large eastern university. I get more than the usual share of clit, but after a while it all smells the same.

One autumn afternoon, my roommate Graham and I were returning from a ball-busting English midterm when, as we boarded the elevator to crash in our sixth-floor sex chamber, five of the most gorgeous young girls we'd ever seen yelled for us to hold the elevator door.

Graham said, "Fuck 'em," but I had a feeling we were in for a good ride. These young goddesses looked sex-starved and could tell we were ripe for the taking. The elevator (as well as our cocks) proceeded to rise, and just as we passed the third floor, we came to an abrupt halt. The girls were obviously frightened and I felt it my duty to console them. As I reached for the trembling hand of the girl next to me, I heard Graham once again say, "Fuck 'em."

Much to our surprise, two of the more outgoing girls said, "Fine with us." We wasted no time disrobing and releasing our throbbing rods from their bondage. The girl whose hand I was holding reached to pull me closer by tenderly grasping my dick. We began to explore each other's mouth in great anticipation when she departed from my mouth on a long trip to my groin. She blazed a hot, saliva-laden trail down my torso to my aching hard-on. By now my flagpole was at full mast and she, being a good, patriotic American, soon engulfed Old Glory in a blaze of fire.

Meanwhile, Graham was on the floor, occupied with two of the beauties—one on his face and the other on his ten-inch black shaft. I thought he was going to thrust her up four floors by the way she was screaming in an agonizing yet pleasurable pain. The other girl, facing her friend, rocked in a rhythmic fashion on Graham's face. Her love juices creamed down the side of his black cheeks and into his ears. The two girls began to kiss, their outstretched tongues lapping up each other's saliva.

I was still occupied with my newfound lover when the fourth beauty slowly made her way to the other side of the elevator. She dropped to her knees and began nibbling on my ass. I nearly creamed when she worked her snakelike tongue into my virgin crack.

I soon became even more aroused when the last girl started to work herself free of her clothing. She removed her skirt to reveal a garter belt and long, black fishnet stockings. It was then that I noticed a peculiar looking bulge protruding from her . . . his crotch! This wolf in sheep's clothing began to peel off his erotic panties, revealing his immensely long but slender prick.

By now Graham had finished with his dynamic duo and they began milking what was left of his inventory of come. The two girls then switched positions and returned to their triangle of lust.

The female impersonator slowly made his way behind me. In addition to the pleasure of the lapping tongue on my crack, I felt a less moist and much harder organ protrude my anal opening. At first I was a little surprised. I'd never thought I'd be doing it this way, but I was soon overwhelmed by his manliness as he rammed my anal core.

We then all noticed a tinge of movement as if the elevator might soon resume its journey. All seven of us soon burst into a mass explosion of come. I looked back to see my girl lover lick the transvestite's shaft of passion clean as he withdrew his tool from my swollen hole. Everyone scrambled for his or her (or his) belongings as we again began to ascend to the sixth floor. The elevator doors opened, ending our ride of love.—*N.B., Chestnut Hill, Massachusetts* ⚷

CONVENTIONEER INITIATES VIRGIN SPRING BREAKER, THEN DOES FRIENDS

It is now Saturday—they did come back on Friday! I was sitting in the bar and one by one Sunny, Renée and Celia finally arrived and we went out for a leisurely dinner. The conversation centered around Renée and her desire to finally get fucked. The other two girls were very supportive of Renée's decision to lose her virginity.

When it was time to head to my room, however, Celia and Sunny were uncertain about coming. But Renée insisted she wanted to share the experience with them. It was a little awkward for me now, knowing what the other two expected, but I was too turned on to worry too much about it.

When we got to the room, the girls all hugged and Celia and Sunny settled in on the second bed. Renée and I started to kiss, and her body just melted into mine. My cock was like a rock immediately.

Then I slowly unbuttoned Renée's blouse and she shrugged it to the floor, followed by her bra. As I leaned down to kiss and suck her breasts, my hands opened her jeans and she slid them down over her slightly plump hips. When they were all the way off, my hand gripped her ass, holding her close again.

Her panties slid down easily and she lay back on the bed. I parted her legs and kissed my way up to her pussy, letting my tongue open her up. I licked and sucked her cunt lips and buried my tongue inside her, teasing her for a long time before turning my attention to her clit.

She started to moan, then asked for more. "Faster!" she yelled as I let my tongue fly. Her ass started to thrust and she cried out, telling me not to stop. She came again and again before relaxing, turning to the other two and telling them she was "pissed off" because they hadn't told her how good it really was. They just giggled amongst themselves.

I stripped and knelt between Renée's thighs. Her hand guided me to her waiting cunt, and I slowly started to enter her—meeting resistance, exhibiting patience, gently pressing harder, each thrust bringing me ecstatic pleasure. Finally she cried out and I slid in to the hilt as she held me tight. Her cunt was so tight and her muscles were squeezing me so firmly that I couldn't hold back. I gushed in her pussy. I thought it would be my turn to be embarrassed, but I looked over and saw that Celia had her hand in her panties and I could see her fingers moving in and out. Sunny was nude, one hand pinching her nipples and the other fucking herself, and she came with a loud cry.

My cock responded to the excitement and I was hard again. We slowly started to fuck again. Renée was slow to respond, finally starting to move with me. Her moans and cries told me she was getting close, and she finally came. Celia and Sunny had been coming regularly, and I could tell they were watching as they gave a big cheer.

I started thrusting faster and shot another wad in Renée's pussy, collapsing on her chest. Soon we had a four-way hug as the other two came over to congratulate her. This was an opportunity I could not pass up. I asked the girls if they wanted some of what they had just seen Renée get. They looked at each other quizzically, and I suggested I fuck them Bobby Fischer-style.

"How do you do it like that?" Sunny asked.

"I think I know," Celia enthused. "We both grab onto the head-board and present our young little asses to you. Is that right?"

"That's right," I said, instantly getting hard again. Before I knew it I was going back and forth from one luscious pussy to another, fucking Sunny doggie-style, then sliding over to give Celia the same treatment. My dick grew bigger and bigger, and each time I pulled it out to go to the other girl, I marveled at its size. Just before I was about to come for a third time, I stayed with Sunny for a while, really reaming her, preparing myself for the spew of a lifetime. As my cockhead mushroomed, Sunny started screaming like a banshee.

After I sent a couple of molten spurts into her loins, I tightly gripped my cock at the base, slid it out and rammed it into Celia's incredibly tight hole. She let out the most intense, hoarse scream I have ever heard and immediately started bucking back against my pelvis. She really wanted it, and when I let go of my cock I let forth with the rest of my orgasm. I felt like Celia and I were one and the same being, and even after I was spent, I was hard as a rock and I reamed her for another ten minutes. She wouldn't let me out!

"I feel like I just lost my virginity," she said when we finally collapsed onto the bed. "I've never had it like that before."

Before long, we all fell asleep. I woke up with a hard-on in the middle of the night and started to caress Renée.

"You want some more?" she whispered. I nodded yes. She got on top and lowered herself onto my waiting cock. We were as quiet as possible, and Renée bit her hand as she came to keep from crying out. She rode my cock like a cowgirl, and when I started coming her head almost hit the ceiling.

In the morning they were in a rush, but they each found time to say good-bye to me. With Celia and Sunny it was a simple kiss, but Renée bent down and kissed my cock good-bye. She said she'd never forget it, and neither will I. I consider myself the luckiest man alive.—*Name and address withheld* ⊙┼▬

THE PLEASURE OF THEIR COMPANY

My name is Sheldon. I'm six-feet-two, two hundred pounds, and have an eleven-inch cock.

One day when my girl Ursula and I had just finished an after-fuck shower, I checked the mail and found a cute envelope with a seal in the shape of lips, addressed to us both. It was an invitation to a party—not just any party, but one at Sheila's house. Sheila is the horniest, most erotic-looking girl I have ever seen.

The invitation was for Friday night at eight. Ursula and I arrived shortly after eight. To our surprise, the only people there were Sheila and two other women, Jackie and Barbara, and one man, Gerard. We had a drink and talked, and in a few minutes Sheila and her other guests casually took off their clothing. Ursula and I are always interested in a new experience. We exchanged glances and shucked out of our clothes, too. I, for one, was turned on by the sight of Sheila's swaying ass as she led us all to her bedroom, to say nothing of Jackie and Barbara, who were knockouts and not a bit shy about showing their bodies off to best advantage. I thought Sheila had an expectant eye on my rising prick, though she suggested that all the women in the room try some lesbian sex. Ursula, after an inquiring glance at me, enthusiastically agreed, and dived into the quickly forming pile of pulchritude on the four-poster bed. I had never thought Ursula had any interest in other women. But I knew very well she liked sex, and this was definitely sex.

Sheila had brought out a collection of dildos, French ticklers and vibrators, and the women grabbed them with enthusiasm. They began, though, by stroking and kissing one another, murmuring endearments that soon turned to obscene compliments.

"What a gorgeous pussy," I heard Sheila tell Ursula just before plunging her face into her honey-pot. Barbara, meanwhile, praised Sheila's well-rounded ass between licks and love-bites, and Jackie sucked Ursula's toes. For the moment, this left Gerard and me with nothing to do but watch, so we watched. It was great. They got right to work fucking one another with their dildos, fingers, ticklers and tongues. Soon the room filled with the marvelous musky aroma of pussy and females.

After some fifteen minutes of this, I was out of my mind with horniness, and Gerard seemed to be the same. We could have pounded rivets with our hard-ons. Just in the nick of time, Sheila called to us to join in. We eased into the pile and licked every bit of juice we could find in those four luscious women. When I got my fill of tasting, I lay Sheila and Ursula (who announced she was going to require about a mile of cock tonight) next to each other with legs upraised to give ready access to their sweet pink pussies. I gave each of them three pumps with my throbbing rod and the room seemed to steam up. Just as I was getting ready to shoot a very large wad, Gerard intervened. He'd been humping Barbara and Jackie and said he was ready to come now. At his urgent request, all four girls sat on the floor in a straight line with their mouths wide open. That seemed like a good idea to me. I joined Gerard, who also had a large prong, and we sidestepped on each side of the line of avid eyes and wide-open mouths. The girls swiveled their heads as we offered our pricks, and we both delivered four helpings of good, hot love-milk to the customers.

We took part in many sensual combinations after that. I came four more times, and Ursula told me she had at least four orgasms. Now that Ursula has discovered the joys of coose, she is insatiable. She lives for eating pussy. And so do I. We still fuck frequently, and Sheila comes over often for a bit of muff-diving and a good fuck. If you haven't indulged yet in sex with the lesbian set, I highly recommend it. —G.T., Pueblo, Colorado O┼▪

Three-for-All

EATING YOUR WIFE AND ANOTHER MAN'S
COME IS AN ACQUIRED TASTE

My wife Mika and I went to Ocean City, Maryland one weekend. We left early Friday morning to avoid weekend traffic. We checked into a hotel and Mika decided to take a swim in the pool. I can't tolerate the sun so I told her I'd unwind and join her later.

As I glanced out of the window, debating whether or not I should join her, I saw a tanned, handsome young man in spandex swim trunks approach her. He stood there beside her as she reclined in a lounge chair—his bulging crotch no more than a few feet from her face. I couldn't help thinking erotic thoughts. The young guy looked like one of those models that pose for Calvin Klein underwear ads. He pulled a lounge chair close to hers and began a conversation with Mika, who sat upright in her chair. In a few minutes I noticed her hand come to rest on his thigh. They talked for a while and then he got up and walked away.

Mika had confessed to me before that one day she'd have an affair. I didn't mind, of course. In our marriage the levels of sanity and self-respect, consideration and camaraderie are reassuringly high. The judicious use of the extramarital affair has seen each of us through an extended siege of each other's craziness. I mean, let's face it, marriage is not easy. I don't know when I first admitted to myself that another man fucking my wife had a tremendous hold on me. I would often ask Mika if this or that man appealed to her, or I would point out a good-looking guy and ask her if she'd like to fuck him.

Just as I was about to join Mika by the pool, I saw this stud returning with drinks in his hands. My wife stood up, flung her arms around his neck and they kissed long and passionately right there in public. After sunning themselves together for another half hour my wife got up and came back to the room. I was reclining on the bed as though I'd been taking a nap. Mika came in and told me she had met the sexiest man, Paul, who was Italian-American and lived not far from our home in the Washington D.C. area.

"Oh my, when I first saw him he was rising out of the water like a Greek god," Mika said. "Honey, don't get upset, but I think I've found my lover."

Upset? My cock stirred when she said that, just as it had when I saw Mika kiss this hunk by the pool. She said we were all to meet before dinner for drinks at the bar. I wondered about how I would react when I met my wife's intended lover. Mika noticed my bulge, and joked about whether I was more excited about her getting screwed than she was.

We met Paul at the bar for cocktails. He was quite friendly, but I couldn't help thinking he was disappointed that I'd come along. Mika introduced me as her "liberal-minded husband." Paul shot me this inquisitive look, trying to figure out exactly what my wife was trying to say.

We decided to have dinner in a small restaurant in a nearby town. As I got in to drive, Mika crawled into the backseat with Paul. She didn't hesitate one moment to come on to him. I heard him murmuring, keeping everything he said between himself and Mika. Then I distinctly heard him say, "Take them off." Then he started a conversation with me, but there was some shifting around back there, and I soon realized Mika was being fucked with Paul's finger. I tried to get a look at her face in the rearview mirror, and sure enough, she had that sensual look of ecstasy in her eyes. I couldn't tell for sure, but I would have bet that her hand was busy inside Paul's fly. As we neared the restaurant I did, in fact, hear him zipping up.

We had a wonderful meal, and carried on as though we'd been good friends for years. Mika excused herself to go to the ladies room. When she returned she slipped something to Paul, who went to the men's room while I paid the check. As we were leaving I stopped off at the men's room and found Mika's panties and her bra stashed in the trash.

During the ride home the action became more intimate. Mika bowed her head in the backseat, mouthing this young stud's penis. I could easily hear their soft-spoken interchanges, all of which signified some serious erotic interplay. Soon I smelled the distinct aroma of fresh, warm semen accompanied by slurping sounds. Mika didn't make much effort concealing what she'd done. I knew she would tell me all about it when we were alone.

As we were walking into the hotel, Paul asked if we'd join him for a nightcap. Mika declined, saying she was sure I was too tired from the driving I'd done that day. I was, indeed, ready for the sack, but also eager to relieve my aching cock and fuck the hell out of Mika. I knew her pussy had to be hot and oozing with her juices by now. When we got to the elevator Mika said, "You go on up to bed, dear. I'll join Paul for a quick one and be up in a minute."

It sure wasn't a quick drink she was talking about. I waited almost two hours before she came back. There was no doubt she'd had one good fucking. Dreamily she stripped out of her dress. I told her I'd seen her panties and bra discarded in the trash can at the restaurant. She thanked me for being so understanding and cooperative, and crawled into bed. Mika straddled my head and planted her fuck-wet cunt over my mouth. As I slurped and sucked the mingled fuck juices out of her cunt, she urged me on nastily.

"Taste that hot stud's cock butter! Do you like Paul's gooey dick snot? He shot a huge spunky load in there just for you. Eat it, baby—enjoy that stuff!"

Mika grabbed my tool and rubbed it up and down on her slick cunt lips. She said if I wanted to fuck her I'd have to do it really well because she'd been so satisfied by Paul's cock. "He's really hung! He's got a fat horse cock between his legs and he knows how to use it. You'll see how much he stretched my cunt when your cock slips right in."

I was like a starving man begging for bread. "Please, please let me fuck you. Let me fuck that wet, juicy pussy all primed with Paul's donkey rig. Please let me see how much he's stretched your tight cunt with his horse meat," I said.

With that, she sank her cunt right down over my cock without the least bit of resistance. Damn, I thought, she wasn't joking. He must have had a tower between his legs. As we fucked she related the sensational banging Paul had just given her.

The next day the three of us enjoyed the day as normally as friends would, although Mika was far more attentive to Paul than she was to me. After dinner at the hotel, Paul suggested we go to a club for dancing, but because I'm no dancer I said I was going to turn in. I was certain they would have a wild sex session in Paul's room before Mika returned to our room. When Mika returned late that night, I was asleep, but I was quickly awakened by Mika's urgent sucking of my cock. It was her way of communicating that she wanted to be fucked. It thrilled me immensely, knowing her cunt was full of Paul's sperm swimming around and lubricating her hole for me. I came much sooner than I wanted. And again, I ate up the deposits, savoring the love juices of the three of us.

The next morning we packed and paid a brief visit to the beach. After checking out, we had lunch and then parted with Paul for our drive home. I was certain we had embarked on a new lifestyle.

The next week Mika announced that Paul was coming for dinner on Friday night. I greeted him as a close friend and fixed drinks while Mika prepared dinner. We got on well. I really liked the guy. Paul was intelligent, charming and handsome, and added spice to our unique marriage arrangement. That night, however, he appeared to be uneasy when my wife was present. Mika suggested I go out for some ice cream. As I departed she asked that I not disturb them if they were upstairs when I got back.

I got home long before they were finished fucking. I listened intently to every sound I could hear—moans, sighs, words of encouragement and delight. It kept me rock hard. Eventually, they both came downstairs. Paul was fully dressed and Mika wore her short, sexy dressing gown.

Paul's attitude had changed drastically. He was much more arrogant, as if to say, I just fucked your wife, and you know it and can't or won't do a thing about it. He boldly took Mika in his arms and kissed her amorously while gliding his hands over her ass. Looking at me defiantly, he said, "Until next time, baby doll." Then he said to me, "See you soon, John boy."

The pattern was set from then on. I would wait downstairs while Paul would fuck my wife in our bed. After he'd leave I would get to eat their love juices and sometimes have sloppy seconds. I'm not complaining. I loved it.

Recently—and this is the reason I'm writing—Mika suggested that I join them during their fuck sessions, which occur now about twice a week. Mika said she'd enjoy it if I were present, not only to watch them fuck but to clean up with my tongue afterwards. I can hardly wait to be in bed with them, licking up the creamy evidence of their passion. I know it's kinky, but I have actually developed a taste for pussy secretions and spent jism, so much so that I'm posting a message on the Internet for others interested in this spicy, protein-packed indulgence.—*J.P., Reston, Virginia* ⚷

SWINGER AD LEADS TO
RISQUÉ RESTAURANT RENDEZVOUS

My name is Iggy and I've been married to Alanis for seventeen years. I'm forty-three years old and in good shape, but my wife, who is thirty-nine, is in excellent shape, with a tight body, a great ass and a heavenly set of 34D tits with big, sensitive nipples. Alanis has the looks and sex drive of a twenty year old.

During our marriage, we have experienced some great sex, everything from oral to anal and even double penetration with one of her many toys. She has everything from vibrators to rubber cocks from seven to ten inches in length.

In the last few years, I mentioned to Alanis that I would like to share her with another man. She was circumspect, but admitted to being real turned on by talking about it, especially while fucking, or whenever she read a letter in *Penthouse Letters* about threesomes.

One night while we were naked in front of the fireplace, perusing ads in a swingers magazine, Alanis saw a picture of a guy from our area. He had a huge hard-on and his comments included a notation that said "long-lasting, love to orally satisfy women and capable of staying erect all night." Alanis said if this guy lived up to his ad, he would be a god.

"Do you want me to contact him?" I asked.

"You're all talk, lover. It's a great fantasy. Come on, let's fuck," she said. I noticed that her pussy was wetter than normal, and we had a wonderful night of intimacy and really great fucking in the firelight.

Two days later I wrote a short letter to this guy, and sent three nude photos of Alanis. I also gave him my pager number to contact me because we have kids. Two weeks later I got a return letter from this guy, whose name was Jeff. He said he had received Alanis's photos and that they'd given him some great masturbation material. He included four photos of himself, all of which were great quality. In one photo, he was looking at one of the shots of Alanis that I'd mailed. He was jacking off and there were large gobs of come running down his shaft.

When I showed them to Alanis she just about came out of her panties with excitement. "Let's contact him," she whispered, reclining on the bed. While studying the photos, Alanis dreamily grazed her fingers across her clit and nipples. A couple of nights later, well after midnight, Alanis picked up the phone and called Jeff. She was immediately turned on by his sexy voice. They proceeded to get into some explicit, hot phone sex while I crawled between Alanis's thighs and ate her out. We set up a meeting to just talk and get to know one another, since Alanis wasn't keen on jumping in the sack with a stranger.

As we got ready to go and meet Jeff, I noticed Alanis's sexy attire—a tight skirt, crotchless panties and a tight white tank-top with no bra. "Just in case," she said. "If the vibes are right, I want there to be easy access."

We met in a dark restaurant in a town about halfway between our place and where Jeff lived. I think we were all nervous, sitting down in a booth in the back. We each had two drinks, which took the edge off and helped ease the anxiety. Things started progressing well after that. Just as the waiter was serving us, Alanis winked at me and began unbuttoning her skirt under the table. After dinner, at which point we were on our fourth or fifth drink, I could see Jeff caressing my wife's right thigh. Pinching me to get my attention, Alanis opened her legs and reached for Jeff's hand, which she brought to her pussy. Alanis leaned over toward Jeff and let him finger fuck her, while she squeezed his hard cock through his pants. That was the extent of our first meeting, but it led to some great sex that night in bed with my wife.

Our second meeting was on a hot summer night. Alanis wore a light sundress with nothing under it. She made sure she was freshly shaven so the area below her clit was silky smooth. When we got to the restaurant, Jeff was in the same booth where we'd sat before. Before our first drink, Alanis had pulled out Jeff's uncircumcised cock and began stroking it under the table. When the waiter took our order, Alanis's dress was above her pussy, and Jeff's fingers were buried inside her deep, while she was tugging away at his tool. From where I sat I don't see how the waiter could have missed seeing the action. Dinner was good and the activity kept both Jeff and myself hard. Jeff offered to walk us to our car on the third level parking lot when we left.

As we walked up the stairs with Alanis in front, we both fingered her pussy and ass. As Jeff kissed Alanis goodbye, he said he wanted to lick her pussy. Jeff opened the back door, laid Alanis out on the back seat, and proceeded to dip his tongue inside her box while she threw her legs over the two seats giving him full access to her crotch. He tongued her little rose-bud asshole, too. Afterwards, he was grinning from ear to ear and his face was shining wet from Alanis's juices.

We offered to give Jeff a ride to his car. He jumped in the back seat of our minivan with Alanis, and before I'd put the van in gear, Alanis had his shorts down to his ankles and had her hand wrapped around his huge cock, jacking him off. As we pulled up to Jeff's car, I parked under a street light, shut off the engine, and turned to see what was happening. Jeff had Alanis's legs spread wide as he was fingering her wet slit, while Alanis stroked Jeff's pecker. The large mushroom head was slipping in and out of the loose foreskin and precome was coating Alanis's hand.

Alanis bent down and proceeded to swallow as much of his cock as she could while he was rubbing her tits. I reached back and started to finger her pussy. It was beautiful to see my wife's lips sliding up and down his cock while she obscenely spread herself wide to allow me to finger fuck her with two digits. Alanis pulled away from his cock as Jeff pumped a large gob of come on her face.

Jeff bent down and kissed Alanis's pussy. "Next time we'll see if you can handle my cock inside here," he said.

"You didn't think I'd do it, did you?" Alanis said as we pulled away. "I can't wait to fuck both of you at once." I kissed her and could smell come on her face, which was still sticky in places. She gave me head on the way home and that night we had the absolute best fuck of our marriage.—*I.L., Gary, Indiana* ⌾━▮

BALCONY VOYEUR TIRES OF WATCHING BOUNCING BOOBS

I've been without a steady girl for two years. During this time I have become especially close with Bob and Kathy, who I've known since high school and who've been living together about five years.

With nothing to do, I called them last Friday and they invited me over to drink beer. I enjoy going over because from their balcony you can see directly into the bedroom. While having a cigarette on the balcony one night, I'd noticed Kathy rummaging through drawers before she changed clothes. I'd gotten a hard-on just knowing that I could see her and she couldn't see me.

Bob and I hit the brews hard that Friday night, pounding down about ten bottles apiece of dark imported German beer, which we chased with shots of Irish whiskey before Bob surpassed his limit and passed out on the couch. Kathy said she was going to get ready for bed so I took the opportunity to open the sliding glass door leading to the balcony and step out for a smoke. I watched as Kathy undressed, removing all of her clothing except for her bra and panties. Then, strangely, she put her cowboy boots back on and sprawled out on the king-size bed, not bothering to turn off the light. When she suddenly got up I returned inside the apartment. Kathy came into the living room in a white bathrobe, which was open in front so I could see her bra and panties, and she still had on the cowboy boots.

"Nice outfit," I said.

"Well, thanks, but you really haven't seen anything yet," Kathy said. "Come on, Bob," Kathy pleaded, rousing her boyfriend. "It's time to go to bed, you shouldn't sleep on the couch."

As they went to the bedroom, I once again slipped out onto the balcony. I watched in amazement as Bob slid Kathy's panties off. I saw her brown bush for the first time, and I thought my dick was going to burst if I didn't do something. As I began unzipping, Bob looked out to the balcony and acknowledged my presence with a smile and a wave. Then he turned to Kathy, saying something to her that made her break out laughing. Then, unexpectedly, Bob waved me inside. I practically ran to the bedroom, not the least bit embarrassed by the sizable bulge I had in my jeans.

"We want you to get naked and sit over there," Kathy said, indicating a chair next to their bed. As I stripped down, she spread her tan, luscious legs wide, still wearing those cowboy boots. Bob dove in and started tonguing that mop of pussy hair between her legs.

"Jack off for me," Kathy said. "I want to watch you beat off while Bob tickles my clit."

As I stroked my hardness with a slow, deliberate touch, Bob got on his back and removed Kathy's bra, letting those gorgeous tits go free. I couldn't believe the size of her pink nipples. Bob reached up and kneaded her right tit.

"Would you like to lick this tit, or this one?" he said, indicating the left one.

"I'm not picky," I replied.

"Why don't you do both, then?" Kathy said.

I came over and began fondling Kathy's firm globes, careful not to hurt her sensitive pink nipples. Bob was once again dipping his tongue into her rapidly widening slit. She was really getting into it, squirming and grabbing his head, slamming her pussy against his tongue and pulling my head harder to her breasts.

In the throes of getting her pussy and tits mauled and manhandled, she moaned something I couldn't understand. I thought maybe I was being too tough on her nipples, and so I asked her to repeat what she said.

"Cock," she moaned. "Give me your cock. I want it in my mouth."

I rose to a kneeling position with my throbbing penis poised right at her thick cock-hungry lips. Kathy sucked me as if Satan had taken over her soul. She cupped my balls, stroked the shaft, and suckled the pink cap of my cock before she went full force into a feeding frenzy.

By this time Bob had slipped on a condom and slammed his dick into her cunt. Her tits were really bouncing around, but remarkably, Bob's thrusting did not diminish the intensity of the blowjob she was giving me. Rather than distracting her, it seemed that Bob's cock was only making her hotter in her attentiveness to mine. I got tired of watching those boobs bounce around, so I began playing with them, the whole time watching Bob pound her twat and Kathy slurp on my tool. Her tits were no longer sensitive. "Squeeze them! Pinch them!" she beckoned.

In the next dizzying minutes I'm not too sure what happened. I had had a lot of alcohol that night, but I do remember Bob pulling out at the last minute, sliding the rubber off and tossing his cream all over her left tit. At the sight of that, I pulled back and shot my load all over her right one. It was a great night, and I'm looking forward to seeing my friends again next weekend. — *K.P., Albany, New York*

VIDEOS, VIBRATORS, HORNY WIVES
AND HOLIDAYS OF LUST

My friends Kevin and Dottie offered my wife and me the use of their Manhattan apartment while they were off on one of their numerous vacations. Audrey and I live upstate, but we enjoy coming to the Big Apple any chance we get. While I was getting acquainted with Kevin's state-of-the-art stereo system and CD collection, Audrey was unpacking our suitcases when she found a stack of video cassettes on the top shelf of the closet. Each tape was dated and labeled according to the travel site of their vacation. Kevin was always bragging about his exotic travels, so I suggested watching a few to see where all they'd been.

Audrey put a cassette in the VCR, turned on the TV and then our jaws nearly hit the floor. In the video Dottie was on a bed fingering her naked twat, while four men, none of whom were Kevin, surrounded her, stroking their meats. One of the men handed Dottie a dildo, which she stuffed inside her vagina, which caused Audrey to gasp in embarrassment. Audrey said we should turn it off and put the tape back in the closet, but because I was really turned on by Dottie's little video slut act, I overruled her.

On the screen the action intensified as one of the men removed the dildo from Dottie's cunt and placed himself between her legs, while another guided his cock into her mouth. She had one cock in each hand, and it wasn't long before these two guys unloaded streams of white spunk on her belly. Then the two others, the ones she was both fucking and sucking, screamed their pleasure in unison as they, too, reached climax.

The tape was still running when I grabbed Audrey and nearly ripped her clothes off in a frenzy. We fucked right there on Kevin and Dottie's living room carpet, the whole time watching Dottie on the screen as she was being drilled in her ass. When Audrey and I were done, we continued to watch the tape, fast-forwarding through the boring stuff such as museums, beaches and tourist traps, until we came upon more sex scenes.

Kevin and Dottie are both thirty, and Audrey and I have known them since college. Dottie is quite beautiful, and she carries that great body of hers with tons of sex appeal. Dottie is politically conservative and even supported Pat Buchanan's bid for the White House. I would never have guessed her to be sexually insatiable. I don't want to use the term nymphomaniac, but after watching the vacation tapes, I'd say she sure does like a cock, or two, or three, or four or more.

I asked Audrey how many tapes there were in the closet. "A couple dozen," she replied, flabbergasted. We watched several more, one of which showed Dottie having sex with ten men. At the end of each video, she seemed to have her own little trademark signoff: she would blow Kevin with her smiling eyes glued to the camera.

Another tape we watched appeared to be in the Caribbean, and it began with Dottie sucking a well-endowed black man's cock. During this salacious oral sex scene, Dottie coyly asked the black man if his friend wanted to fuck her tight blonde pussy. Audrey and I were in a constant state of arousal while viewing the tapes, but because I was spent after fucking Audrey three times already, I searched the apartment for some toys. I figured Dottie must have that kind of stuff around to keep herself satisfied. Sure enough, I found a neon yellow vibrator, which I used to ream Audrey's cunt and rectum. Audrey, who implored me to plunge the twelve-inch toy organ all the way inside her, reached a state of stimulation so high that she discharged a clear, fluid ejaculation of female come a good three feet across the floor.

The day Kevin and Dottie returned home, they acted really happy to see us. After some catching up over a few drinks, the conversation turned to sex. Kevin said his wife was the horniest woman alive. Dottie blushed. I mentioned that New York City, with all its energy, must make people horny because Audrey and I had been fucking like crazy since we'd arrived. When I said that, there was a silence filled in by an incredible sexual tension that settled over the room. Kevin then abruptly asked us if we wanted to see a video from their latest vacation.

As the tape began we saw Dottie wearing just a bra in a hotel room. Dottie removed her bra and began rubbing her tits and smiling at the camera.

"Audrey, don't be offended by this question," Kevin said. "But I'd like to know if you have ever fantasized about being with more than one man?" I swallowed hard and felt my dick flurry in my pants. Audrey said she had often dreamed of being devoured sexually by a group of men. Dottie was sitting quietly in the corner as the four of us watched the video, but on the screen she was fingering herself as three men groped at her tits and pussy.

Dottie moved over to the couch where Audrey was sitting and began licking her neck. Audrey looked in desperate need of getting her rocks off, even though we'd spent the past three days fucking like wanton baboons. My wife removed her jeans, then eased her panties to the side to allow Dottie to probe her ripe, fur-lined fig with the tip of the vibrator.

While the two wives explored female foreplay together, Kevin told me it all started in Florida a year after they were married. Dottie was seduced by three lifeguards in the hotel exercise room. Kevin had seen the whole thing. He jerked off as the three guys fucked Dottie. It was the first time Dottie had had sex with anyone other than him. When Kevin confronted Dottie she cried and swore it would never happen again, but Kevin, strangely enough, had insisted she invite the boys back to their hotel room for another session. It was then that I admitted to Kevin that Audrey and I had seen the tapes.

"What's it like, Dottie?" Audrey asked, "to be fucked by so many men?"

"It's total abandonment of your senses, inhibitions and all the crazy, puritanical hangups people in this country have," Dottie said. "We go to Jamaica once a year just for the sex—and the smoke—of course. The island men are long-lasting and they love to lick my blonde pussy for hours." Audrey was on the verge of coming as Dottie explained what it was like to be stuffed with a cock in each orifice.

"You guys can have Dottie for the night," Kevin said. "She'll be more than happy to do anything you wish."

The three of us went to the bedroom, where Dottie handed my wife a strap-on dildo. After I slipped my pants off, Dottie kneeled to take my cock into her mouth while Audrey plowed her with the plastic dick from behind. Later I fucked Audrey doggie-style while Dottie lay beneath us, licking at my pistoning cock and Audrey's clapping labia.

When it was time for Audrey and me to leave, Dottie and Kevin asked us to join them on their next vacation. "How about Jamaica?" Kevin suggested.—*J.D., Lancaster, Pennsylvania*   ⚬�┼▪

FRINGE—AS IN KINKY—
BENEFITS FOR YOUNG WORKING COUPLE

My husband and I started reading your magazine when we were both cheerleaders at the state university. We've been out of college for some time now, and although there have been many sexual encounters worthy enough to share with your readers, none are more deserving of publication than an episode that happened to us recently.

Dan, my husband, went to work right out of school, and I was hired by the same company three years ago. We both work directly for the president of the company, which has about seven hundred employees.

Brad, the president of the firm, is a handsome, charismatic and powerful individual, who at forty-four keeps his large physique very trim by playing tennis and handball three or four times a week. It's common knowledge that most of the women in our company, whether they're married or not, would readily sleep with Brad, and not just for career advancement. There has always been talk among the girls about how good-looking the boss is, including much speculation about the size of his cock. Indeed, Brad often had a noticeable lump running down the leg of his beautifully tailored Italian suits.

I'm in the marketing department of the firm, and my husband works in the acquisitions group. Consequently, we both travel extensively but almost never to the same areas or to see the same clients. Little did I know that that little detail had been arranged by the powers that be.

Two years ago, when Dan had been on an extended trip, Brad and I were working on a special project that required many late hours and weekends to complete. Working closely with the president and founder of our company, I could see how he became such a success at such an early age. He is a human dynamo, aggressive, confident and highly intelligent. Power is very sexy, and he had plenty of that. I was flattered to be receiving so much attention, but then I overheard a few of my co-workers' comments, including one allusion that I was getting "the treatment"—meaning Brad was setting me up so he could come on to me.

I didn't believe it, of course. During two weeks of working very long hours we never strayed from the task at hand. Brad never mentioned anything of a personal nature, and there were certainly no sexual overtones to anything he said. He was very complimentary about my work on the project.

In the middle of the third week, with Dan out of town, it suddenly changed. Brad, in that unpredictable way that propels him in business, stopped what we were doing. He physically picked me up and placed me on a small footstool in the office.

"I want to talk to you, eye to eye, Melissa," Brad said, which was funny because he's six-two and I'm four-eleven. Normally, I would be about eye to belt with him. When he set me down, I was startled, but also amazed since I could feel his strength in the way he lifted me. My whole body tingled. I don't mean just a little sensation, I mean it was as if every nerve in my body was quaking with sexual energy. My nipples stood erect and my clit pulsed wetly in my panties, all from this single act.

You can imagine how I reacted when Brad said, "I want you. I want to make love with you. I want you completely. I want to find places on you that you didn't know existed. I want to make you feel so totally alive that you will give all of yourself to me. Do you want this?"

I was stunned. I couldn't say anything. After what seemed an eternity, Brad ran both his hands up under my blue crepe skirt. Wordlessly, he pulled my panty hose down to my ankles, then grabbed my black panties and jerked them down with a quick motion. What came next was another fast blur of movement—he ran his hands to my mound, parted the golden strands between my legs, and found my clit. I felt the animal power of Brad. It was the most incredible feeling I had ever experienced.

When he grabbed my legs and shoved them apart, I gave in to the wildness of the experience, letting him roll my clit between his finger with one hand while he pushed my bra up to seek my hard nipples and firm tits with the other hand.

All that I really was aware of at this moment was that I didn't want him to stop, and that's what I said, finally breaking the awkward silence between us when I moaned, "Oh yeah, Brad, oh yeah, don't stop, don't stop ever!"

The boss smiled, stepped back as if to admire my semi-nude state, and then gave me a directive I had no trouble at all following.

"Take everything off and be quick about it," Brad said. As he stepped out of his suit I could only think his body—despite his good physique—was not as good as I was used to with my young husband. Somehow, it didn't matter. There was something almost comforting about being with this older man, whose power seemed to emanate from him like rings around Saturn.

Fully undressed now, I got on my knees to help him remove his briefs. I almost fainted at the sight of his cock. My husband is not small in the meat department, but Brad's cock looked like a club—just over ten inches long and God knows how thick. What a spike he had, and I wanted it. Brad—being the perceptive individual that he is—placed his hand behind my head and brought that fat prick to my mouth.

Although I've given head to my husband and former boyfriends on occasion, it has never been one of my favorite sexual practices. But this was different. Brad put his hips into it, and fucked my mouth. He came in quarts. He kept shooting, spurt after spurt, and it was flowing out of my mouth and running down my breasts.

When he finally quit pulsing his cock and rocking his hips, I thought it was over, but Brad lifted me up off my knees and stooped over to French me, getting a taste of his own come. Uncharacteristically, his oversized cock was still bobbing hard, and in one quick motion he had the head of that thing nudging the lips of my vagina. I couldn't believe how wet I was, and I really didn't believe Brad's cock was going to be able to penetrate me.

Slowly, he eased the head in. Once the big cap of his prick was secure in my hole, he allowed me a second to get accustomed. Effortlessly, he hoisted my legs while simultaneously driving that hammer hard so that I was impaled by his cock.

Brad removed his hands so I was literally being supported by his dick and my arms, which were clinging to the back of his head. In this position, Brad fucked me really hard and hot. I was screaming like a banshee until I sobbed uncontrollably with a heaving intense orgasm.

Over the next four days and nights, Brad would call me into his office at various times of the day. Usually it was a blowjob, which I'd taken an immense liking to, but sometimes he wanted to eat me. My pussy was shaven to perfection, with just a tiny triangular patch of pubic hair above my clitoris. Sometimes I would bend over his oak desk and take his monumental cock up my ass.

We'd been carrying on at work for about six months when Brad sent Dan out of town on an important assignment for two weeks. Before leaving, my husband seemed really anxious about it, and although he never complained about travel for business, he seemed both overly excited and nervous about this trip. I attributed it to a possible upcoming promotion. Brad was obviously fond of Dan, pleased with the progress of his work, and maybe a little guilty about fucking me. The two of them spent a lot of time together looking for businesses to buy; they played tennis, handball, and swam and lifted weights at the company gym. Brad towered over Dan, who is about five-seven, almost as much as he did me.

Thirty minutes prior to Dan's flight to the East Coast, I received a call from Brad, who told me to put on something sexy and meet him at his house in an hour. The palatial home is on a five-acre lot, surrounded by a high brick wall and a forest of trees providing privacy.

I selected a white wrap-around skirt topped by a black silk blouse, which I brazenly wore without panties or a bra. The silk felt good against my bare titties, and I was almost leaking down my legs with anticipation as I drove to Brad's.

I expected to be met by one of Brad's servants, which was usual procedure when ringing his doorbell. But no one came. I rang again and again, and still no answer. As I was about to leave, Brad came to the door wearing a short robe, the bulbous head of his monster cock dangling out the front. Passionately he wormed his tongue into my mouth, while I stroked his pecker, which was hanging out so invitingly. "Not now," he said. "I have something I want you to see."

We went through the foyer to the back of the house and into a room that was totally black. Not dark, but black, as in the color. It was black walled, black carpeted; there was a black ceiling, a black oversized chair and a black couch. It was a small room. I felt closed in. Brad turned on the light from a switch outside of the room and then led me in.

"It's completely soundproof," Brad said. "No one outside of this room can hear you, but you're capable of hearing and seeing whatever is happening in the next room. I think you will find it interesting."

Having said that, the boss motioned me over to the couch to sit down. Then he turned and left the room. I went to check the door, but it didn't have a handle or doorknob on my side. Suddenly, the black room was pitched in total darkness. Brad had turned off the light.

I found my way back to a chair, and wondered what this was all about. It was the strangest behavior Brad had ever exhibited.

Shortly afterwards, a light from another room came on. It dawned on me that I was looking through a mirror into another room. The room had weight benches, free weights, progressive resistance machines, a stairmaster, stationary bicycle, and an open three-nozzle shower stall with no curtain. At the far end of the room was a huge waterbed. I heard voices coming from the speakers in the ceiling of my cubbyhole.

The next thing was a complete shock. There was Dan, my husband, who still had on the suit and tie that he had on when he left on his "trip" that morning. Brad, still in his short robe, was showing the room to Dan. I was damn angry and totally perplexed.

"I wanted you to tell everyone you were on a trip," Brad said, stroking the leather seat of the stationary bike and eyeing Dan with an inquisitive look. "We both knew you weren't going anywhere, didn't we? See, I've been watching you, Dan, and I know you're curious. You're curious about me, what it's like for a man in my position, what it would be like to be close to that power. I've seen the way you look at me in the gym, after our workouts. You're interested in what it's like to make it with a man."

Dan had never shown any interest in other men. He had several girlfriends before he married me, and I knew how good he was in bed. I was waiting for my husband, though considerably smaller than his boss, to deck Brad with one punch. Dan, who was a gymnast at the university, was incredibly strong for his size.

Brad opened his robe, letting it fall to the floor as he approached Dan. His eyes never wavered although Dan's eyes dropped to look at Brad's humongous semi-erect cock. Brad reached out, took Dan's hand and placed it on his penis.

"You like this. You want it, I know it," Brad said. Saying nothing, Dan began to stroke Brad's cock, now lifted to its full glory. "I thought so," said Brad as he removed Dan's tie to unbutton his shirt. Placing his hands on Dan's shoulders, he pulled my husband down to a kneeling position. I recognized this routine. With only a moment's hesitation, Dan obligingly descended to his knees, careful not to lose his firm grasp on Brad's pole.

"This is what you've been wanting, isn't it, Dan?" Brad asked with the confidence of someone who already knows the answer. "Now you're going to get it all. In every way imaginable."

Brad pulled free of Dan's grasp and steered his big cock to my husband's mouth. Dan opened up and engulfed the head to a point just beyond his lips. Ever so slowly, Brad eased more cock into Dan's mouth, gathering a little sway in his hips while gently moving into a motion suggestive of face fucking.

"Desire, my friend, it ranks highly among those other traits I admire in men, like honor, loyalty, respect. I like it that you desire me, Dan. That's, ahh, so nice." I was amazed that Dan appeared to be nodding his head affirmatively, and genuinely enjoying having his boss's prick in his mouth.

"I'm close, Mister, ooh, ahh, drink my come, Dan!" Brad said. As he increased his rhythm, Brad placed both of his hands on Dan's head and unloaded down Dan's throat. Spunk ran out of the sides of Dan's mouth and all over his bare chest. Brad kept pumping. Dan kept sucking. Even after it was clear Brad was drained.

Withdrawing his cock, Brad reached down with his fingers and wiped come from the sides of Dan's mouth and then fed it to him on his fingers. I was a wreck of conflicting emotions, but mostly I was excited.

Dan quickly removed his boxers, revealing his eight inches of solid cock.

Brad stroked it hard until it gained its rigid maximum and erupted into a flowing ejaculation into his boss's hand. With sperm dripping over the sides of his hand, Brad lifted the pool directly to his mouth, letting his tongue take a small drop of the pearly goo before he smeared most of it as lubricant on his hardening dong.

"You are well hung, my friend," Brad said, "but nothing quite like this mighty manly joint, uh? Let's see how it feels, okay?"

Brad continued waxing his pole with Dan's semen, leading my husband to a bed in the corner of the room. As if reading Brad's mind, Dan assumed a position with his head and arms on the bed and his ass in the air—facing in my direction. Brad guided his behemoth cock to Dan's tiny rectum, easing in slowly but not without a lot of groaning and moaning on Dan's part. Brad stayed motionless until Dan had time to adjust to the penetration.

Soon, however, Brad grabbed Dan's hips, pulled himself hard against the cheeks of his skinny ass, and really started fucking his butt. I wasn't sure he could get that thick pole inside. Brad had taken several sessions with me before he could get it all the way inside my anus. But the boss was determined. Setting a rhythm, he inched his come-smeared fleshy dong into—and beyond—Dan's virginally tender, stretched sphincter.

His belly was flush with Dan's ass as he pounded into Dan.

Brad screamed with a blasting shot of his spunk, and then disengaged with his shrinking member. Amazingly, Dan's cock had become aroused and hard while he was being plugged, and he, too, was shooting a load all over the bed.

While Brad went to the open shower to bathe himself, Dan lay exhausted on the bed, gaining his composure, before he joined Brad in the shower. Under the running shower spray, Dan leaned over and grabbed Brad's cock to suck him hard once again. "Tell me, tell me what you want, Dan," Brad asked his young subordinate. "How do you want me? What will you do for me?"

"I want you," my husband said. Brad looked stern, as if he disapproved of the answer. "Okay," Dan continued, "I want to suck your cock. I want you to fuck me again. I want to taste your come." Brad looked pleased as he gently traced a finger on Dan's cheek.

"You have a smooth body. Your legs look good, too. Like a woman's, so I think you should dress in drag for me. Will you, Dan?" Dan nodded. "Good," Brad said. "I have some things in the room you'll be sleeping in tonight. Go put them on, please."

Dan hesitated. This was too much, too weird, too bizarre and kinky, but Brad placed Dan's hands on his elongated manhood. As Dan stroked, Brad motioned him to his knees again. There was an implied understanding. As Dan moved to suck him back to life, Brad moved away. The implication was clear.

Dan left the room to dress in a woman's attire, while Brad came to unlock the door to my room. I was beyond anger. I should have felt humiliated. I know that Dan and I should have left that instant, but I couldn't help myself. This whole thing was so erotic.

Brad positioned me on the couch so that my pussy was open for the taking. When he slid into my cunt, I was never more ready. I told him how excited I'd become watching him with Dan. "Good. Because you and Dan can move in with me. It will make you rich in a few years, because I'll advance you at the company."

After a quickie across the couch, I followed Brad to his bedroom. We were both naked when Dan walked in and saw me. He was three shades of bright red with embarrassment. Then he got angry, demanding to know what I was doing there.

He did look good for a man, dressed in sexy lingerie. He looked sweet and virginal, yet sensual. When I started laughing and pointed to his image in the mirror, Dan turned and smiled. "Guess I'm a fine one to talk, aren't I?" he laughed.

"We'll get you some falsies and I'll show you how to wear makeup," I said. His smooth legs and hairless body were feminine, and his face was prettier than many women I know. With an expensive human hair wig, he would have no difficulty passing as a teen. We both spent the night and the next two weeks with Brad, enjoying almost as much sex as a threesome as I'd had in my promiscuous college days. I'd go to the office during the day, and Brad continued working with Dan on a new project they'd started. Dan would dress accordingly: Liz Claiborne suits, Donna Karan hosiery and high heels, which he was getting good at getting around in for a novice.

We have decided to sell our home and move in permanently with the boss. No one at the office suspects there's hanky-panky. They think the arrangement is strictly a business necessity. Dan and I love each other; I'd like to think we'll always be together. — *M.Y., Provo, Utah* ⊶▪

PATIENT LADY GETS THE GIRL, SHARES WITH HUSBAND

My best friend Rosemary and I were separated last year when I got married and moved south. We were very close, and always discussed everything having to do with anything. I had become sexually active with my boyfriend—now husband—on my eighteenth birthday. Rosemary asked me for advice on blowjobs and different sexual positions. Nothing was withheld during our girl talks—except the fact that I'm attracted to her. Here's how she recently found out.

Rosemary came on down to visit me and my husband Trent during her spring break from school. One afternoon we were sitting on the couch, waiting for Trent to get home from work, and talking about how our men please us. The conversation got kind of raunchy, and we were soon comparing moans and groans. Then we fell silent and watched some television. My eyes roamed to her full, pink lips and the way she ran her tongue over them. What would it be like to kiss another woman? To feel that tongue on my body? I lowered my sights to her round, full breasts. What did they taste like? Sweet? Salty? And her pussy—did she shave it bald, or leave some fuzz up top? What did it taste like?

I wasn't startled by these lesbian thoughts, as I'd had them for years, and I figure they're natural. I'd never acted on them, but this time was different. I leaned over and pushed Rosemary's long blonde hair back over her shoulder. She turned her head and peered at me with her curious blue eyes. I ran a finger over her cheek, tracing her lips with my fingernail. I felt my pussy getting moist and my clit throbbed like a bass drum.

"May I kiss you?" I whispered. She slowly nodded her head. We leaned into each other and brushed our lips together. I felt a jolt of electricity shoot through me. She must have felt it too, because she jumped like she had touched a hot iron. We stared into each other's eyes for what seemed like an eternity. We kissed again, more sure of what we were doing. I slipped my tongue between her full lips, and nearly came in my panties when she tongued me back. Our kiss grew deeper, until we were devouring each other.

I slipped my hand under her T-shirt and fondled her naked breast. No bra—what a turn-on. I knew from her moans that she was enjoying it. Our lips parted long enough for me to remove her shirt. I kissed her neck, then ran my tongue down to her hard nipple. I sucked one tit and massaged the other, then alternated. Her breaths were short and huffy.

I took her hand and put it on my hot crotch. She immediately got the hint and massaged me through my shorts. I leaned back and she kissed my neck. Like butterfly kisses, so unlike the roughness of a man. I unbuttoned her shorts to expose her neatly trimmed cunt. I reached my hand into them and played with her clit. She tugged off my shorts and began playing with me. We bucked against each other's hand, and moaned a chorus of pleasure.

I took my hand away and licked her pussy juice off it. It tasted like honey. I tugged her shorts off, exposing her beautiful cunt. I kissed her soft belly and fuzzy pubes. I lightly licked her clit with long, electric strokes. She dug her hands into my hair, pressing against my scalp. It all seemed right. I'd always heard that women know best how to please each other. But a hard cock up my snatch has always been pleasurable too, I thought.

What timing, because a hard cock was at the front door, closely followed by my husband. I looked up, saliva and come juices running down my chin. "Oh my . . ." he moaned. He couldn't get out of his clothes fast enough. He stuck his rigid penis in my face. I sucked it and fingered Rosemary simultaneously. I offered Rosemary his hard dick, and she eagerly took it in her mouth. I leaned forward and continued eating her sopping wet snatch. I heard Trent moan, and I knew he was close to shooting a load in Rosemary's mouth. I eagerly took his cock from her and blew him until he came in my hungry mouth. I jerked him gently through the long period of aftershock, while Rosemary licked his come off my lips.

Trent positioned me doggie-style, so he could screw my throbbing cunt while I ate Rosemary's pussy. He rammed his dick into my hole repeatedly, until I felt like exploding. Rosemary shimmied down the couch underneath us and started sucking my clit. I nearly passed out from pleasure. I banged back into Trent, and felt my insides turn to mush as we came together in a chorus of moans and groans. He withdrew, and dripped his last jism into Rosemary's open mouth. I rolled off the couch onto the floor and lay there trying to catch my breath. Trent collapsed on top of Rosemary, both of them breathing hard.

Trent and I had been each other's first. I knew he wondered what another woman's hot cunt would feel like wrapped around his cock. Now was the time for him to find out. I told him to sit up and straddle Rosemary's thighs. I got on top of Rosemary and stuck my pussy in her face. She immediately began licking and sucking. I took Trent's semi-hard dick into my mouth and began blowing him. I ran my tongue lightly down the length of the shaft and tickled the head. He quickly got hard again. I poked a finger into Rosemary's snatch and tickled her G-spot. She took it out on my clit with her pointy tongue, until we were both squirming and moaning.

Once his dick was hard, Trent positioned himself between Rosemary's legs and slowly slid it in. Watching him bang my best friend was such a turn-on that I came all over Rosemary's face. He pumped faster as she reared up to meet his thrusts. I ran a finger over her clit to push her further toward the edge.

Trent withdrew his pistoning rod and jerked his come all over her pubes. Then he put a finger in her snatch and fingered her to an orgasm.

When all our climaxes had subsided, we sat back and relaxed. Trent had always fantasized about having two women. Who says fantasies don't come true?—*M.C., Marietta, Georgia*

GIVING HER A BIG DICK GETS HIM A LITTLE HEAD

I have been getting your magazine for quite some time now. My wife enjoys reading it almost as much as I do. I'm writing to you about our honeymoon a couple of years ago, without her knowledge. I hope she'll read it here, and be surprised.

It had been my fantasy to watch Angie make it with another guy who had a very large cock, and then to participate in a threesome. I would bring the subject up during our lovemaking by talking dirty to her. I would ask her if she would like to have a huge cock up her pussy, and tell her I would love to watch her fuck and suck a big old ten-inch cock. Then, I would tell her, I want to fuck you while you suck him off and make him come all over. When I talked to her this way she went off like a rocket, often coming twice before I'd even gone off once. As soon as we were through fucking, though, she would always tell me that I was all she ever needed. Worse than that, in real life she wouldn't suck my cock, even though it so obviously got her off in her fantasies.

I could never figure out how to go about making it really happen. Then a friend of mine told me about a nude beach he had gone to. I looked through some magazines and found a place to go where a little extra activity went on and nobody said anything, as long as it was hidden in the sand dunes.

I told Angie we were going to an island for the honeymoon we'd never had. The night before we left I did some repacking of her clothes. I replaced her conservative swimsuits with thong bikinis, added all her dresses that were either low-cut, mini, or both, and some crotchless panties and panty hose I had bought for her.

We got to the hotel late in the morning, and decided to hit the beach. She was not too thrilled to find out that I had switched everything, but she had no choice but to put on what she had. We got to the beach, and there was a sign saying that nude sunbathing was allowed. I acted all surprised, and asked Angie if she still wanted to go. She said we might as well, because she was eager to get out in the sun.

Angie was being checked out by quite a few guys, even though she was wearing a suit. She was a little bit embarrassed, but she was doing a lot of checking herself. I was checking the women out, but also the guys, looking for that one lucky fellow. After a couple of hours I got her to take off her top, but that was as far as she would go. Men frequently walked past us to get a closer look. I could see her eyes following all that cock. She was becoming quite aroused, her nipples poking way out.

I saw some cocks that were probably in the seven-to-eight-inch range when hard, but that wasn't what I was looking for. We finally headed back to the room to get cleaned up and go out for dinner and dancing. She put on her low-cut red mini and a pair of crotchless pantyhose with no other underwear.

At dinner she had a few drinks. Angie gets horny when she drinks. She was tipsy. We headed for a wild dance club I'd read about. Angie had a few more drinks, and was getting real horny, feeling my cock under the table and telling me she wanted to go back to the room.

About that time a good-looking guy came up to us and asked Angie to dance. I told her to go ahead if she wanted to.

Out on the floor she was laughing a lot, clearly having a good time. A slow song came on, and they started dancing to it. She had her head on his shoulder. He was feeling her ass and pulling her against his cock. She didn't pull away.

He walked her back to our table and thanked her for the dance. Angie was all excited. His name was Charles, and he had asked her to come up to his room for a while, but she had declined. She said that she could feel his cock through his pants. I hadn't noticed too much of a swell to his basket, so I just let it drop. Nonetheless, it had been an exciting development, because she was letting guys grab her ass and pull her tight.

The last guy she danced with that night was a little bolder than the rest. It looked like he was sliding his hand up her skirt, and she was doing a little ass-grabbing herself. When the song ended they gave each other a pretty good kiss. She came up to me and said, "Let's go back to the room. I want to fuck you." That night we had the best sex ever.

We got up late the next day. Angie took a long shower, then we ate brunch and hit the beach. I went for ice so we could take some drinks with us. I wanted her to get good and horny while we were out there.

As we walked to the beach Angie was wearing her towel around her waist. We parked ourselves in a spot a couple of hundred yards from a bunch of sand dunes. She laid the blanket down and immediately took off her top. When she dropped the towel, she had no bottom on. She was completely nude and had trimmed her pussy hair until she was almost bald. I got a hard-on right away. Angie wanted me to take my suit off too, which I did, but I had to lie facedown for a while.

We started on the drinks right away, and it didn't take her long to feel good. Men were walking by, checking her out, and she was openly staring back and making comments, her nipples popping out like pencil erasers.

After a while she rolled over on her stomach and fell asleep. A guy came up the beach, and I noticed a lot of women looking at him. When he got closer I saw that his cock was huge. It must have hung down a good seven inches. This guy was built, maybe six-two, two-twenty and good-looking. I said to myself, this is the lucky guy. He walked past us a short distance and I decided to go for it before some other lady beat me to him.

I caught up to him and explained that Angie and I were on our honeymoon, and that I had been looking for a guy with a huge cock to seduce her. He just looked at me with a blank stare. I said, "No joke. I want you to fuck my wife. She's lying right over there. Check her out."

He did just that, then came back and said he was very much interested, since he'd come to the resort specifically looking for some swinging opportunities. He said his name was Bobby, and he was from Philadelphia. He was recently divorced and on vacation with some friends. I told him to come over in a couple of minutes and I would introduce him to Angie as a guy I'd met at the bar while she was dancing. I told him to put his towel around him so she couldn't see his cock until he sat down. "This may seem a strange question," I said, "but can you get a hard-on while you're sitting there talking to her?" He said he probably could.

I went back over and sat down. Angie was still asleep. A few minutes later, Bobby headed our way. I yelled out his name, and told him to come on over. Angie woke up and made a vain attempt to cover up. I introduced them, and passed out drinks all round.

Bobby took off his towel and laid it down on the sand so he could sit down. Angie's eyes got huge, and she let out a very audible gasp when she saw his cock. As we sat there talking, her eyes never left his cock. It was limp, just resting on his legs, a relaxed but dangerous seven-inch viper. His balls looked like beachballs, they were so big.

Oddly enough, the conversation veered toward sex. Angie was

so excited that her voice was quivering. Her nipples were sticking out farther than I had ever seen.

Bobby's cock began to twitch and inch farther down his leg. Angie stared as it grew until it reached its full length, which had to be eleven inches. It looked as thick as a beer bottle. It just hung bobbing in the air between us. Angie quietly said, "Oh my God."

Bobby apologized. "Hey, I'm sorry the monster popped up like that, but he's got no self-control, and you're just so pretty."

I offered them another drink. Angie closed her legs. Later she told me it was because she was so wet just from looking at his cock. It was getting a little crowded around us. I had hoped for a little more privacy, to see how much further this would go. I suggested we move on down the beach, between two of the dunes, and they both agreed.

As we walked, Angie kept looking at Bobby's cock, barely paying any attention to where she was going. We found a nice spot where someone walking by couldn't look in. I told them I was going for a swim, and Bobby said he'd stay and talk to Angie. As I was leaving I told Angie she should put on some more suntan oil. "I'm worried about you burning," I said.

"Yeah, me too," she murmured.

I gave them about twenty minutes, then worked my way back up to where they were. I came over the top of the dune behind them. Angie was on her stomach, Bobby kneeling over her, rubbing oil onto her legs. He worked his way up her legs to her ass and began massaging it with great care. She began to spread her legs open. His hand slid down her ass to the inside of her leg. I could tell that he was working on her pussy. He slipped a couple of fingers into her, and she was lifting her ass up to meet his thrusting fingers.

Then he leaned over and kissed her butt. She looked back at him and said something, but not loud enough for me to hear. She rolled onto her back, with her legs completely open to him. He started right off massaging her tits, then bent over and hungrily started eating her pussy.

Angie was squirming around and trying not to moan out loud. She reached for a towel to cover her mouth, all the while thrusting her hips up to meet his probing tongue. In about two minutes she had a massive orgasm. Bobby never let up, and she had another one a few seconds later.

Finally Bobby lifted his head, and they spoke to each other. Bobby lay on his stomach. Angie kneeled over him and applied suntan oil to his legs. She worked her way up his legs, then started to massage his ass. Bobby slowly spread his legs, and Angie worked her hands down in between them. I couldn't tell whether she was playing with his cock or his balls. She then bent over and kissed his ass.

Bobby rolled over onto his back. His cock wasn't fully hard. Angie massaged his legs and his chest, avoiding his cock. She bent over and started sucking his nipples, finally sliding her hand down to his cock. Giving his cock a good, slippery few strokes with her oiled hand, she soon had him fully up. She lifted her head and looked at it while continuing rubbing him.

Bobby put his hand behind her head and tried to urge her down to his cock, but I figured he was wasting his time. She shook her head at first, but when he took his hand away she slowly bent over until she was a tongue length away. She then stuck out her tongue and licked that huge head of his. It was a mouthful in itself. My cock sprang up like a jack-in-the-box. Angie was licking all around his head, really getting into it, giving it little kisses and licking the entire length up and down.

She moved back up to the head and stuck it in her mouth. It was only possible for her to handle a few inches. She was doing a great job. She'd obviously paid attention to all the X-rated movies we'd watched, no matter what she'd said about not wanting to blow me. She was moving her head up and down and jerking him like a pro.

After a few minutes, Bobby started to move around a little and thrust his hips up. Then he started coming. The first shot must have gone into her mouth, catching her off guard, because she jumped back in surprise. The second and third shots hit her square on the mouth, and she put her lips back over his cock to catch the rest. A lot was running out of her mouth, though she was doing her best to catch it all. When he was done coming she pulled her head back, with come all over her lips.

Angie said something to him, then proceeded to clean the rest of his cock off with her tongue. That's when I started down toward them. I heard her say, "You taste so delicious. I wish I'd known about sucking cock before." She was still kneeling over him, playing with his cock, when she saw me. She jumped up, a scared look in her eyes and come on her face.

I said to her, "Now that you've tasted him, how would you like to take him back to the room and fuck him?"

She looked at my hard-on and said, "In a minute." She kneeled in front of me, took my cock in her mouth, and in less than a minute she was swallowing my come.

The second we were all in the room, Angie ripped off his towel and proceeded to suck him hard. Bobby lifted her up and carried her to the bed. "We have to lube you up so you can handle my cock," he said. He slid a couple of fingers into her and ate her to two more orgasms. By then Angie was yelling out, "Fuck me. Fuck me with that big cock."

He slid up her body and put his cock at the entrance of her pussy, slicking it all around her lips, getting it good and gooey. Angie was whining and whimpering, "Fuck me! Fuck me!" Finally he slid his cock in a few inches, then eased it back out. He did that a few times, while Angie thrust her hips up, trying to get him to go all the way in. "Please put it in," she begged. "Please!" Bobby slowly fed her his entire length. When she was able to absorb nearly his whole cock, he started his pumping action, pulling all the way out then pistoning it back home. After a few strokes she cried out, "Oh God, yes. Oh fuck, I'm coming!"

She bucked so hard against him that she almost threw him off. "Keep fucking hard," she demanded. "I want to feel your cock." She was matching his thrusts. "Yes! I'm coming again!" She was pretty much having one orgasm after another. I'd never seen anything like it. "Keep fucking me. Don't you dare stop. You feel so good. I want you to come inside me. I want to feel your come hitting my insides." He was really humping her fast now. Angie was moaning and thrashing about. "Yes, give it to me. I love your cock!" Angie yelled out that she was coming again, and that brought Bobby off. Angie was going nuts. "Yes, fill me with your hot come. Yes, I can feel you coming. Fuck me, baby. Fuck me hard!"

Come was running out of her pussy, down over her ass. Bobby slid his cock out, already going limp. She said, "Fuck me some more. I need your cock." She got up on her knees and slid his hose into her mouth, sluttily sucking both their juices off in her fever to get him hard again.

Bobby turned her around, still on all fours, and rammed his cock home from behind. A loud moan escaped her lips. "That's it. Fuck me! I feel your balls slapping my ass."

I moved in front of her and presented my cock to her mouth. She moaned and slobbered all over it as Bobby slammed her to another orgasm.

As this one subsided, she looked up at me, took my cock out

for a moment and said to me, "I love you." A few seconds later she went into another orgasm, and this one triggered mine. Even though I had just come an hour before, it seemed like I pumped a gallon into her mouth and down her throat. Bobby seemed to get her off in one hard climax after another.

Angie licked my cock clean, then turned to Bobby and said, "I want to fuck you." He pulled out, fetching a whimper from Angie.

Bobby got onto his back and held his cock up for her. She climbed on top of him and shoved her pussy down on his shaft. She started to raise and lower herself, slowly at first, then picking up speed. Angie was riding him like a rodeo rider. "Oh God, yes. I love fucking your cock, don't stop." Then she climaxed again.

Angie leaned forward on him a little to rest, and Bobby started to slide out from under her. She told him, "Hey, don't move, Bucko. I'm not done with you yet. I'm going to fuck you some more. Next time when you get ready to come, let me know, because I want to swallow your cum."

She started riding him again, but not as fast as before. She reached her hand back and played with his balls as she rode up and down. She was moaning and almost crying about how good it felt. Bobby started moving his hips a little faster, and groaned that he was ready to come.

Angie jumped off his cock and shoved her mouth down over it. Bobby arched his back and poured it into her mouth. This time she didn't miss a drop. She swallowed everything he had, using her hand to milk the last drops.

They rested a few minutes before Bobby said he had to leave to meet up with his friends. He said he hoped we would want to get together later on. Angie looked at me. "That was the greatest thing. You've introduced me to a whole new world. Can we do it again?"

"Any time, as long as I'm there," I said.

"Deal!" she responded.

After Bobby left, she said she wanted to do something special for me. She went shopping, but wouldn't show me what she'd bought until we went dancing that night. After dinner we agreed to meet at a different club than the one we'd gone to before. I waited there while she went to change. I noticed a lot of guys looking toward the door. Angie entered, wearing a sheer white blouse with nothing on underneath, and a very short, black miniskirt, that barely covered her ass cheeks. She has such great legs, and by then was so tan that she didn't need any stockings.

She came right up to me and sucked my tongue right out of my mouth. I slid my hand up to her ass and felt that she wasn't wearing anything. Every guy there got an eyeful. She sat down and told me how much she loved me. She had a few drinks and danced with a lot of men, including myself. Men were groping her all night, and she had her hand inside a lot of guys' pants, playing with their cocks. A couple of guys actually got her off on the dance floor by finger-fucking her. She declined all invitations to go to their rooms, saying she wanted to spend the rest of her honeymoon with me, but that on Saturday we would party.

We fucked like crazy the rest of the week. She was insatiable. Bobby disappeared until Saturday, when he suddenly showed up on the beach. Angie was elated to see him and his tubular accessory. That Saturday we met two of Bobby's friends as well, and believe me, the rest of the story is even better than what you've heard so far. If you publish this letter, I promise to tell you the rest. —S.J., Pittsburgh, Pennsylvania

THOSE WHO TEMPORARILY CAN'T DO, TEACH

I'm a twenty-eight-year-old male, and I love fucking my wife. In fact, after three years of marriage we still average twice a day.

Recently I had some surgery done that disrupted our usual lovemaking routine. We worked on bringing each other off manually, and after a couple of weeks we were able to work into a position where I could shoot my load into her pussy after stroking myself to the brink of orgasm, but it just wasn't the same. It was frustrating for both of us.

One day Cindy went to work early, so I slept in. When I got up I saw that my friend Craig, who is eighteen, was sunning nude in our backyard. We're accustomed to swimming and sunning in the nude and, since he lives only a couple of miles away, Craig has a standing offer to use our house and pool.

As I casually observed him from the house, he started to get an erection, which he proceeded to play with.

I hadn't come since the night before, and I was horny, so I figured I might as well join him. He was surprised to see me, having assumed I was back at work, but he never missed a beat. He said he was so turned on from the night before that he'd beaten off three times since. While making out with his girlfriend the night before, she'd let him slip his hand down her pants and feel her cunt. It had been his first exposure to the delight of a juicy pussy. That was as far as they had gone, but it had been glorious for him.

Just thinking about my own days of innocent discovery had me hard, and I asked if he'd mind if I joined him in jerking off. He said no, so I lay down near him, grabbed my sprout and went to town.

With our age difference, I had never done anything like this with Craig before, but it was fun watching that big penis of his ejaculate. Craig watched me shoot off, then dove into the pool to cool off and wash away the semen. Since I couldn't go in the pool yet because of my surgery, I went in the house to clean off and get us something to drink. While I was there, I called Cindy, told her about Craig and suggested that she take an early lunch.

When I went back out, Craig was sunning himself again. We drank some juice and I suggested to Craig that he put a damp towel over his head, as I find it quite refreshing when I lie in the warm sun. I dipped a towel in the pool and wrung it out. He did likewise, and we soon lost track of time.

I felt a hand on my cock, and lifted my towel to find a nude Cindy winking at me. She quietly moved to the other side of Craig, then lifted his cock and licked it. Startled, Craig threw off his towel and saw Cindy kneeling beside him stroking his growing shaft.

She led him over to the lawn, where she lay down, allowing him a close inspection of her treasures. Then I grabbed his cock and rubbed it up and down Cindy's slit, lubricating it with his pre-come. Cindy grabbed his shaft and showed him how she loved to have her clit massaged by a slick penis. Then she lowered the head to her opening and started pulling him with her legs.

Craig moaned in delight at his first feeling of a pussy completely surrounding his hard penis. Cindy gasped as Craig bottomed in her, reaching depths that I could only dream of. He took a couple of strokes, but I could tell by the tightness of his balls that he wasn't going to last. With a final long stroke he moaned, "I'm coming," and Cindy's eyes widened as he filled her depths.

Craig pulled out and rolled over on his back on the lawn, saying he didn't believe how good it had felt. His penis was still erect, so Cindy, pleased at having his semen in her but certainly not satisfied, mounted it for her pleasure. I stood straddling him, so Cindy could orally attend to me while she rode Craig. The sight of Cindy rising and falling, her cunt sucking up Craig's young, strong cock, had my come bubbling and spraying in no time. As excited by his second piece of ass as he had been by his first, Craig quickly filled Cindy up again also. While he was still shooting, I bent over and rubbed Cindy's clit with my fingertip to make sure she got off too.

When we were all satisfied, and Craig and I were drained, Cindy had to return to work.

We've given Craig several more lessons since then, but now I'm back to full fucking health, and Cindy is getting plenty of satisfaction again. Cindy says she loves the way his big cock fills her, but that he'll have to learn some of my techniques before he can really satisfy her.

Yesterday, Craig told me that he finally opened his girlfriend's virgin cunt last week, and that they've fucked several times since then. He thanked me for our help, saying that he learned a lot from Cindy and from watching us make love. He said that although the sex he had with Cindy was fantastic, sex with the woman he loves is even better. I told him that he has already learned a lesson that some people never learn.

Next week, we invited Craig and his girlfriend over to a barbecue so we can meet her. Craig says that he hopes she can get comfortable with us quickly, because he hopes we can work into a four-way so that she can learn as much from us as he has. I hope his dreams come true. — *L.N., Pontiac, Michigan*   ⊶▪

LAP DANCE TURNS INTO TWO-WOMAN TANGO

I am married to a very attractive and sensuous blonde, with full lips, beautiful eyes and a nice body. One week she told me to brace myself for Saturday night, as she had plans for me.

When Saturday rolled around she spent the entire afternoon at the beauty salon. She told me to take our son to the sitter's house at six o'clock. When I arrived back home, there was Carol-Ann, dressed in a short, overall-type dress, with a tight, black, ribbed and zippered shirt underneath. The shirt was zipped halfway down, so that I could see she was also wearing a black push-up bra that formed some delicious cleavage. I tried to get something going right there in the front room, but she stopped my advances, telling me I'd get plenty later.

At Carol-Ann's insistence, we drove to a topless bar. She handed me a hundred dollars, and instructed me to spend it on table dances. We entered the bar, and found a nice dark corner where we could see the entire bar and the two stages clearly. When we sat down, Carol-Ann reached under the table and rubbed my cock, telling me to enjoy the evening.

I found out that table dances were five dollars. I scoped out a blonde (I love blondes!) and requested her to dance for me. Wow! She was hot. She got so close to me as she danced that her sweet, sweaty thighs rubbed firmly against my crotch. I thought I'd come in my pants, but I controlled it. The song ended and I placed a five dollar bill in her G-string.

As she walked away, Carol-Ann asked, "How was it?" All I could do was shake my head in wonder. Carol-Ann tossed her hair back and laughed, asking slyly, "Wouldn't you love to fuck her?" My wife looked so sexy, and she was being such a tease, that between her and the blonde dancer I was having a hard time controlling myself.

I excused myself to go to the men's room. Since my wife was being such a tease, I came up with a plan. I walked over to the blonde dancer and found out her name was Sabrina. I told her that my wife had never had a table dance, and asked her if she would do a dance for Carol-Ann.

Sabrina said, "Sounds like fun. I'll be over at the next song." I went and sat back down. Just before the next song, Sabrina came over and introduced herself.

Carol-Ann said, "Oh, so my husband wants you again."

Sabrina responded, "Yeah, but not for himself. I'm here for you!" Carol-Ann turned bright red as Sabrina moved between her legs and started dancing for her. Seeing her dance for my wife was a great turn-on. Sabrina caressed Carol-Ann's face, shoulders and legs. At one point, she even brushed her hands across my wife's tits. I haven't seen a look quite like that on

Carol-Ann's face since the first time we made love over sixteen years ago. She was bursting with lust.

When the song ended, Carol-Ann put a five dollar bill in Sabrina's G-string and watched her walk away. Carol-Ann looked at me and said, "Wow, I've never wanted to kiss a woman before, but I had a hard time keeping myself from touching and kissing her. What a turn-on!"

I knew I had her. I excused myself again to go to the bathroom. I found Sabrina and told her that she had my wife in a trance. Sabrina laughed and said that my wife should be a dancer, she was so pretty. I asked her to dance for Carol-Ann again, then went back and sat down. I gave Carol-Ann a handful of bills and told her to enjoy. Carol-Ann looked puzzled, until Sabrina came back.

Just before a new song started, I reached over and unhooked Carol-Ann's bib overalls, displaying her unzipped shirt and her cleavage. Sabrina leaned forward and squealed at Carol-Ann, "Oooh, you have such pretty tits, too!" The song started, and her dancing was even hotter than before. At one point, I thought Sabrina was kissing Carol-Ann as she kept her arms wrapped around Carol-Ann's neck and her mouth almost touching Carol-Ann's lips, and I swear she licked Carol-Ann's at one point. Sabrina grabbed Carol-Ann's head and pulled it toward her tits. Then Sabrina dropped down to Carol-Ann's crotch, spread her legs and rubbed her face against both of Carol-Ann's thighs. She squirmed back to her feet again and moaned into Carol-Ann's ear.

Carol-Ann was in a lustful trance. The song ended and Carol-Ann once again put a bill in the G-string. Sabrina said she'd be right back. Carol-Ann told me, after Sabrina left, that she wanted to take Sabrina home and make love to her.

Sabrina came back to our table, and noticed that Carol-Ann had buttoned up her overalls. Sabrina said, "Oh no, you've covered up. No more playing?" When Carol-Ann reached up and dropped the bib, Sabrina smiled and started dancing for her again.

At one point during the dance, Sabrina had her head nestled into Carol-Ann's neck. At that point, I found out later, Carol-Ann leaned into Sabrina and whispered, "God, I want you, Sabrina." The song ended shortly after that.

Sabrina danced for Carol-Ann about ten times. Each dance got hotter and hotter. Finally it was time for the bar to close. Sabrina told us to wait for her by the front door. We did, Carol-Ann trembling and near tears at the thought of what she was about to do.

Sabrina came out, looking like a goddess, and we walked her to our van. Sabrina grabbed Carol-Ann, put her arms around her waist and pulled her close. They engaged in the hottest, wettest tongue kiss I've ever seen. Carol-Ann responded by feeling Sabrina's body as they kissed. After about five minutes of them making out, we got into the van. Sabrina sat on Carol-Ann's lap and they continued to make out and feel each other's bodies. I drove to the nearest hotel.

When I returned to the van after getting a room, they were still locked in a passionate embrace. They stopped long enough for Carol-Ann to jump on me and drive her tongue down my throat. God, my wife was hot. We all got out of the van, and Sabrina backed me against the van to kiss me and rub my crotch.

We finally broke our embrace, and Carol-Ann and Sabrina walked arm in arm to the room. I sat in a chair, and Carol-Ann and Sabrina melted into each other's arms. They frantically tore their clothes off, and in seconds Sabrina was on top of Carol-Ann on the bed. Their passion was staggering. I stripped and started stroking my cock.

Carol-Ann and Sabrina locked into a 69 position—both of them screaming into orgasm almost immediately. I've always envied women their ability to have an orgasm and keep going. Sometimes they need to have a quick come just to relax enough to really make love.

I walked up behind Sabrina. Carol-Ann saw me, grabbed my cock and shoved it into Sabrina's cunt. Carol-Ann licked both Sabrina's pussy and my cock as it slid in and out. Sabrina screamed as I flooded her pussy with my come. Carol-Ann continued to lick her pussy until she brought her off again.

Then we all settled down a little. Carol-Ann and Sabrina lay there softly making out. I started to get a hard-on again watching these beautiful women French kiss each other, and I went back to my chair to watch and jerk.

After a while they giggled and crawled off the bed and in between my legs. Directly in front of me, they started making out again. They broke their kiss. Both women went down on my cock and made love to it. You haven't lived until you have had two gorgeous blondes kiss, suck and swallow your cock. I managed to last for a little while, but not long, watching those two beautiful mouths fight for the right to suck my cock. I warned them that I was about to come. Carol-Ann took control as Sabrina looked on, massaging my wife's neck and shoulders. I came from the bottom of my toes. Carol-Ann then turned to Sabrina and kissed her full on the lips, sharing my juices with our new lover.

Carol-Ann and I made slow, passionate love until we both fell asleep in each other's arms. When we awoke Sabrina was gone. Carol-Ann told me the next day that she'd had no idea the evening she'd planned would turn out the way it did. She told me she loved me and thanked me for bringing such passion into our love life. Sabrina, if you are out there, we'll never forget you.— *Q.G., San Antonio, Texas* O⊢▪

BLACK AND WHITE IN LIVING COLOR

I'll die if I don't tell someone. I had sex with two guys at the same time. I felt like such a slut, but it was the most thrilling thing I've ever done.

I went to my friend Sean's house, and his buddy Kirk was there. We were hanging and drinking beer when Sean pulled out his video camera and began taping us. That made me feel like showing off. My clothes started flying, and soon I was dancing naked around the room. It didn't take long for the guys to strip too.

I grabbed Kirk, sat him down on the couch and started licking his toes. I proceeded up his leg straight to his balls. He started squirming like a worm. I started licking up and down his cock like it was candy. While I was bent over sucking Kirk's cock, Sean shoved his cock up my ass. It was the greatest feeling. Kirk and Sean then came at the same time.

What a letdown. They came so fucking fast. I started sucking on both of their cocks, and they both played with my tits. I was so horny. After sucking them both till they were finally hard again, I lay on top of Sean. He stuck his cock up my pussy, and Kirk got on top and pushed his cock into my ass. This time they lasted. We fucked in that position for twenty minutes. Having two gorgeous black males sandwiching one white pussy is a beautiful thing.

Finally, we changed positions. Kirk sat on a chair. I sat on his cock facing him, and Sean came and stuck his hard cock in my ass. As I jumped and bounced on their hard cocks, they had me coming like an ice cream machine.

After that we were exhausted, so we turned off the camera and cuddled together on the floor. We slept all night like teddy bears, and when we watched the tape the next day we got so hot we started all over again. — *P.D., Newark, New Jersey* O┼▄

THEY HAD TO GET SNOWED IN BEFORE
HE CAUGHT THEIR DRIFT

We had always been friends, Patrice, Kara and me, from seventh grade on.

Once we grew up I often fantasized about making it with either one or both of them. But mainly we were all just great friends and, while we shared every embarrassing detail of our sex lives, the three of us were rather proud that we had preserved a strictly platonic relationship for more than a decade.

Then one night it changed.

It was an extremely cold Friday in November when it happened. The blizzard that swept into town was unexpectedly fierce, and by noon of that day, just about everything was shut down.

By sheer happenstance, I bumped into Kara and Patrice on my way home. They frequently commuted together, since both worked in the same building. So there they were, struggling to get Kara's Suburban out of a snowy ditch, when I cautiously drove by.

Being a gentleman, I offered to give the girls a ride home. We headed to Kara's place first, since it was the closest. Her street was packed with snow, and it was only with the greatest difficulty that I managed to steer my compact up to her doorway. The snow was coming down even harder, and Kara's invitation to come up for a drink sounded pretty good.

Once inside Kara's house we shook the snow off, sat down and opened some beer. The cold Miller tasted good, but the knowledge of what I would soon be driving through kept me from having a second. Kara and Patrice, however, had no such inhibitions, and they finished off a six-pack in record time. I convinced Patrice that we had to leave, but our attempt to get out the door made me realize just how stupid it would be to tempt fate on the roads. The snow had piled up in front of Kara's door almost to the knob.

My announcement that we were trapped was treated with glee by my friends. "Now we can do some serious partying," Kara said, dancing around the room. Mindful that I was not quite as inebriated as my friends, Patrice insisted I do two quick shots to catch up. Within half an hour we were all pretty blitzed, and it wasn't even dark out yet.

Patrice was munching on some potato chips when she bit into a rather large chip, which immediately crumbled, spilling all down the front of her sweater. Some of the crumbs slipped down the V-neck opening, and Patrice pulled the sweater away from her body to pick the crumbs off her breasts. Normally I try not to leer at my friends, but as drunk as I was, I stared down her sweater at her rounded breasts, clearly visible in her bra.

"Are you looking at my tits, Bobby boy?" Patrice asked, noticing my stare.

I stammered for a minute or so, then finally admitted that yes, I was staring at her tits. "They look so nice, Pat," I said with a grin, "What's a red-blooded American male to do?"

Patrice smiled back at me, but Kara seemed to be a bit miffed. Staggering a bit as she jumped to her feet, she ripped open her blouse, sticking her bra-encased tits practically in my face.

"What about mine, shit for brains? Ain't they good enough to stare at?" Kara demanded, her face flushed with anger.

Taken aback, since I hadn't intended to insult either one of my buddies, I tried to think of what to say while admiring Kara's boobs, particularly the pointy pink nipples that poked through the thin cloth of her bra.

"Look, Kara," I finally said, "we've always been really good friends, and I've always wanted to be, you know, respectful. Of course your tits are nice to look at. You're both really sexy. I've always figured that if I made a move on one of you, I'd lose both of you as friends. Believe me, I've thought about you guys a lot, but I've always wanted to keep you both as friends, so I kept my hands to myself."

Kara looked a bit sheepish for a second, standing there with her shirt open, while Patrice sat on the couch, staring at both of us. Then Patrice started to giggle.

"So, you've had fantasies about fucking us, huh, Robert?" Patrice asked, snorting like she always did when she was really amused by something.

Kara looked at me and grinned, then started laughing.

"Oh, you should see the look on your face, Robert. It's a killer!" Kara said, laughing even louder.

"Okay, okay," I said, feeling embarrassed by my inability to keep my eyes off Kara's pretty chest. "I always thought if either one of you were interested in me that way, you'd've said something. Since you didn't, I just kept my mouth shut. I'm allowed my thoughts, you know."

Kara closed her shirt, and they both grabbed me and pulled me back down on the couch.

"We didn't mean to embarrass you, Robert," Patrice said, looking over to Kara, who nodded in agreement.

"And just so you'll feel better and stop sulking, yeah, I've had fantasies about you too."

Kara nodded her head in agreement, then let out a laugh and punched me hard on the left arm.

"Men can be such babies when it comes to sex," Kara said. "Robert, we all have fantasies. So we've all had dirty thoughts about each other, okay?"

I pretended to mop my brow in relief, which brought another laugh from the ladies. I lit a joint, took a big pull and handed it to Patrice, who took a hit and handed it to Kara. Kara blew smoke in my face as she handed me the joint. I put on my best bad-boy face, clamped the doobie between my teeth, and looked into both their faces.

"So Pat," I said. "Ever have any fantasies about Kara here?" Patrice looked shocked for a second, and I thought I might have overstepped my bounds. After all, we were just friends, not intimate, and—

"Yep," Patrice said, giggling nervously as she eyed Kara. "Her too."

Kara stared at both of us for a second, then smiled back at Patrice. We all realized in that instant that we had just crossed an invisible line. We finished the joint in silence, smiling and looking at each other. I guess all of us wondered who would make the next move.

Kara took a hit, handed it to me and stretched her arms high over her head, her blouse falling open again. I admired the view for a long second, noticing her soft belly and well-defined torso.

"Since we're all being so honest and buddy-buddy, Robert, let me ask you something. No shit now, which one of us is the best kisser?" Kara asked, looking into my eyes.

I hesitated before answering, because I was distracted by Kara's eyes. They looked especially blue in the dim light coming through the windows, and I was thinking how I had never noticed what great eyes she had.

"How the fuck would I know, Kara? I've never had the pleasure," I said, staring back at her.

Patrice put her hand on my shoulder and turned me around, looking directly in my eyes.

"It's something I'd like to know too," she said. "Can we trust you with such an important task?"

I smiled, looking into Patrice's deep brown eyes, which nicely offset her gorgeous dark hair. My friends, I thought to myself, really are a couple of sexy women. Kara reached over, cradled my face in her delicate hands and pulled me close. She leaned over and kissed me, lightly at first, then harder, her eyes staying open, looking at me with both amusement and affection. Her tongue tapped my teeth and I opened my mouth, letting her explore the recesses of my mouth. She was a hell of a kisser, I thought to myself.

Finally Kara disengaged and pulled back a little, smiling shyly at me. I grinned at her and started to say something, but then Patrice grabbed me and turned me completely around.

There was nothing light about Patrice's kiss. She immediately shoved her tongue down my throat, pushing insistently as our tongues swirled around each other.

After about thirty seconds Patrice pulled back, smiled and asked who was better.

I signaled that I needed to catch my breath first, and both girls laughed, hugging my arms.

"You know," I said, "it's different with each of you and you're both pretty damn good—"

"You too, babe," Kara said.

"—but it's too close to tell," I finished. Patrice looked at me, then at Kara. She winked at her friend.

"Maybe you need a further demonstration to make up your mind," she said, leaning close to me.

For the next ten minutes I went from one mouth to the other, gasping for breath between deep kisses and trying to shift my rock-hard erection without being obvious. They got better and better as we went along, and my head was literally spinning as Kara pulled back for the final time.

"Well, which one is it?" Kara insisted, her breath coming rather fast, I thought.

"Still a tie, ladies. You're both the champs," I gasped, hoping I didn't look as flushed and hot as I felt.

"Maybe we can break this tie," Patrice said, pulling her sweater off. Tiny beads of sweat perched delicately on the tops of her breasts, and for a second I pondered what would happen if I gave in to the urge to dive down her bra and lick those tits clean. She reached back, unhooked her bra and pulled it off. She tickled her growing nipples briefly, cooing softly.

"Oh, that feels good. They've been getting kinda hot," Patrice said. Before I could respond, a piece of damp cloth came whipping over my head and wrapped around my mouth. When I uncovered my mouth, I saw that I was holding another bra.

"Surprise!" Kara said, shaking her smaller, but equally nice boobs.

"Ooooh, you're right, Patrice, that does feel good. Now Robert, let's get that sweater off you, and we'll see who has the nicest chest."

My friends were more than helpful in getting my chest naked, and within seconds I was sitting between two half-nude women, whose nipples were hard and pointed, their breath coming almost as fast as mine.

"Well, ladies," I said, getting into this thing, "the examination of a woman's breast is a complex matter. This could take a long time." Kara just sighed and lay back on the couch. I leaned over and kissed her again, allowing my hands to glide down her neck and chest to her breasts. They felt firm and warm, the nipples poking into my palms. My cock was still painfully confined, but was plainly visible nonetheless.

I started by kissing my way down her neck and across her chest before letting my lips slip onto the tips of her breasts. Her skin was slightly salty from the sweat, but she tasted heavenly. I continued on, wrapping my lips around her right nipple while my left hand squeezed and stroked her left tit. Kara moaned softly as I suckled her.

Not wanting to be left out, Patrice reached around my waist

and unbuttoned my pants. I could feel her big tits on my back as she leaned over and whispered in my ear that she could see I was uncomfortable. Her hands peeled down my pants, guiding my hips off the couch so she could pull them completely off. As I moved over to Kara's left nipple, Patrice knelt in front of me, stroked my cock briefly through the cloth of my shorts, then pulled them off me. My rock-hard six-incher was now standing tall and proud in the cool air.

Suddenly I felt a pair of hot, wet lips plant a lingering kiss on the inside of my right thigh. My cock jumped a couple of times, then twitched and shook briefly.

What I didn't expect was the sound of Patrice's laughter. I pulled away from Kara's taut left nipple and glared down at Patrice, who was staring at my cock and just convulsing.

"Oh Robert, what do you call it, Bobby's Bouncer?" Patrice laughed, her tits jiggling in a most erotic way.

"What do you mean, Pat, what do you mean?" Kara demanded excitedly, pushing me back on the couch so she could lean over and look.

"Watch this, Kara," Patrice giggled.

Reaching down with her right hand, she jiggled my balls. Once again, my cock involuntarily jerked and twitched. Kara roared with laughter. I could feel my face turning red. Seeing my embarrassment, Kara leaned over and kissed me lightly on the lips. "We're not laughing at you, Robert. It's just so . . . so cute!" she laughed again.

While Kara's breathless explanation didn't mollify me, her next action did. Leaning farther down, she took the head of my cock into her warm mouth, teasing the tip of it. My God, I thought to myself, that feels damn good!

Patrice got up on the couch next to me and shook her tits at me. Getting the message, I leaned over and began an oral examination of her big tits. Her nipples were much larger and darker than Kara's but tasted just as good, and were marvelously reactive to what I did to her. I caught a whiff of some musky odor, and realized it was her pussy getting wet. That wasn't hard to believe, considering how much Patrice was writhing around underneath me and urging me on.

Meanwhile, Kara got up and stood in front of us, just watching at first. Out of the corner of my eye I could see her unbutton her skirt, letting it slide to the floor. Next came the panty hose, and finally her panties. She had a dark, small patch of pubic hair that did nothing to conceal her vagina, which was wet to the point of dripping. As I moved over to Patrice's left nipple, Kara came over to us, resting one hand on my back as she leaned over to kiss Patrice full on the mouth. We stayed like that for a few minutes, the girls wrestling with their tongues while mine thrashed Patrice's tits.

Kara finally broke away from the kiss and immediately reached down to Patrice's waist. Unsnapping Patrice's snug jeans, she began to roll them down, stopping occasionally to caress Patrice's thighs. Finally, she pulled Patrice's jeans completely off and grabbed the waistband of Patrice's thin panties. With a quick jerk, Kara ripped the panties in two, pulling them away from Patrice's writhing body in one motion.

I immediately slid my left hand down Patrice's soft belly into her crotch. Her crotch was hot and wet, her lower lips spread slightly as I traced their outlines with my index finger. My finger, slippery with Patrice's juices, teased her clitoris, which was hard as a button. Patrice moaned softly, spreading her legs wide, as I continued to rub her clit while inserting another finger inside her twat.

My mouth left her tits and roamed down her chest. I stopped briefly to kiss her thick mat of pubic hair, which was redolent of her odors.

As Patrice panted above me, I dove lower, letting my tongue retrace the actions of my hand. Pretty soon I was softly tonguing her clit, moving down occasionally to thrust the length of my tongue up her hole.

Not wanting to be idle, Kara sat up on the couch next to her friend and began sucking on Patrice's nipples. Patrice was getting louder and her movements more pronounced as we worked on our longtime friend.

Her hips started to buck, and Patrice's hand came down on the back of my head, pushing me firmly into her twat. Patrice let out a long moan as she came, her thighs contracting spasmodically around my head.

As soon as she stopped coming, Patrice pushed us both away, smiling hugely at us. Without hesitation, I grabbed Kara's thighs and pushed them apart, setting my sights on her puffy pink lips, which dripped with excitement.

My hands gripping the insides of her thighs, I spread her wide and dove in, slurping on her sweet twat like it was honey. Patrice started out on Kara's tits, but soon was pushing me aside to lick

Kara's labia up and down as I kept concentrating on Kara's clit. I looked up briefly to see Kara caressing her own nipples, eyes closed, head tilted back.

Patrice got underneath me to lick Kara's tight asshole and that was about as much as Kara could take. With a high-pitched scream, she came, cunt juice flooding my beard, her pelvis rocking up and down against my lips.

As Kara lay back on the couch, Patrice started kissing her way down my chest and stomach. Grasping my hard cock in her hand, she stroked me up and down, rubbing the head with her thumb. I was about to beg her to take me into her mouth when she slipped the head of my cock past her lips, tonguing the tiny slit on the top. Patrice began pushing more of me into her mouth, and I thought she might actually deep-throat me, but I was too excited. Within seconds I was coming, thrusting my hips forward, shooting a huge load into Patrice's mouth. She held on tight to my cock, swallowing my sperm as fast as she could, crooning softly in her throat.

Exhausted, I pushed my way up onto the couch, sitting naked between my two nude friends. Kara produced a joint and a couple of cigarettes, which we all shared in contented silence, caressing each other all the while.

Finally, Patrice broke the silence to tell Kara and me how much fun she was having, even though she had never considered doing anything like this in her life. Kara and I agreed, and I told my lovely, erotic friends how lucky I felt to know them. That brought some smiles and some kisses, which turned into longer, more passionate kisses. I could feel the blood begin to course back into my flaccid tool.

"Anybody up for a second round?" I asked.

With a smile, Kara leaned over and buried my stiffening cock in her mouth. Although different in method, Kara was just as good at giving head as Patrice, and I grew to full hardness, helped along by Patrice, who dangled her big tits in my face.

Breaking free from Kara's mouth, I told the girls I had to bury my schlong in a twat. Kara pushed me onto my back and mounted me, slowly easing herself down on my hard cock. Meanwhile, Patrice straddled my face, holding her dripping twat open as she descended on my tongue. I was in seventh heaven, buried under two hundred pounds of sexy female flesh. I alternated between sticking my tongue as far up Patrice as I could and sucking on her clit, while Kara slid up and down my shaft. I could hear Kara's breathing coming faster and faster. Then she howled as she came, her twat contracting around my member. That was enough for me, and I thrust my hips upward as I shot a second load of come deep into her wet twat.

Distracted by my orgasm, I let my head fall back from Patrice's cunt. But after a second or two to clear my head, I dove back in. I felt Kara lean over, and saw her face wedged between Patrice's ass cheeks, her tongue stroking Patrice's stretched asshole. Patrice came almost silently, moaning faintly as she bucked up and down between our faces.

Finished, Patrice climbed off my face and looked over at Kara, who had rolled off of me and onto the floor, lying on her back. I watched as Patrice smiled down at her friend, then leaned over and kissed her full on the lips.

That pretty well did it for us, and we all staggered to Kara's bed, where we snuggled under the covers and drifted off to sleep. My last thought before I slipped off was:

What a beautiful friendship.—*R.S., San Jose, California*   O⊢▩

MUNDANE ROAD TRIPS WERE THE NORM UNTIL SEXY PALS GOT HIS MOTOR RUNNIN'

I have a very routine job—moving motor homes from a display lot to a wash bay, then back. On occasion I have to go out of town to pick up a motor home from another dealer's lot and drive it back. One of these trips proved to be anything but routine.

At first, my journey home was as uneventful as all the previous ones had been. After I'd covered half the distance, I pulled into a rest stop for lunch. Before settling down to eat, I took a walk to stretch my legs. When I came back, I noticed two girls, one with red hair and one with brown, sitting near the motor home. They were both good looking, and their traffic-stopping figures were displayed to perfection in their tight jeans and T-shirts. As I opened the door, one girl asked me if they could hitch a ride.

They were disappointed when I explained that company policy prohibited me from carrying passengers, but then they asked if they could at least come inside, to see what the motor home looked like and to cool off. I certainly had no problem with that.

After they looked around, the three of us sat in the kitchen and talked. The tall redhead was named Lucy, and the brunette introduced herself as Barbara. They explained that the guy with whom they'd been traveling had had car trouble, so rather than wait, they'd decided to hitchhike. As fate would have it, they were headed for the same place I was. After some more small talk (and more than a few flirtatious comments and glances), I decided to take a chance and give them a lift.

Cruising along, the three of us talked about everything under the sun. After a while, the conversation turned quite personal, and we began exchanging stories of our past sexual experiences. All the graphic descriptions were turning me on, which was obvious by the bulge that threatened to poke a hole in my pants. They were also turned on, and soon the air was filled with the unmistakable aroma of their excitement.

Just when I thought I couldn't take it anymore, Lucy asked if we could pull over at the next rest stop for a quickie. I was stunned into silence. Mistaking my lack of reply for hesitation, she removed her shirt and bra, exposing a beautiful pair of tits, and said, "Maybe this will help you make up your mind."

Barbara did her friend one better. After she exposed her own perfect pair, she knelt beside me, cupped her hand around my hard-on and rubbed her erect nipples against my arms. I had to struggle to keep from crashing the vehicle!

By the time I parked, both girls were lying on the bed naked. Barbara got up to remove my shirt and shoes while Lucy yanked down my pants and shorts. They took turns sucking my dick and fondling my nuts. I was so horny, it didn't take me long to explode. I placed my hands on Lucy's head, pumping my dick into her mouth with each spurt. She gripped my ass-cheeks, pulling me closer to her. I could feel her throat muscles squeezing my dick.

After she'd swallowed the last drop of my juice, Lucy pushed me onto the bed, straddled me and slid her cream-coated pussy lips across my cock. Taking it in her hands, she pressed the head against her clit before shoving it into her pussy.

She sat there for a moment, fingering her clit as I fondled her breasts. Barbara came over and sat on the bed beside us, frantically fingering her cherry-red clit and pleading with us to hurry so she could have her turn.

The feel of Lucy's velvety pussy milking me and the erotic sight of Barbara's hands working her button gave me an irresistible urge. I asked Barbara to sit on my face. With a squeal of delight, she lowered her creamy pussy to my lips. As I swept my tongue through her folds, the taste and smell of her nectar caused my cock to swell.

Soon I felt Lucy's cunt muscles spasm as her climax began. When she fell back, sated and exhausted, Barbara took her place, lowering her love tunnel against my swollen dick. Her love juices drenched my shaft. She slammed all the way down and screamed, her eyes wide with delight as she started rotating her hips. I reached up and grasping her boobs, rolled her nipples between my fingers. Her cunt tightened as she moaned, "Now, now, yes, now. Give it to me! Fill my cunt!"

Never one to deny a beautiful lady, I let loose. Our pleasured moans and groans echoed around the motor home. Barbara collapsed against me and we lay motionless until my cock shrank and popped out of her moist cunt.

After another hour of three-way fondling, we dressed and headed back on the road. When I stopped in front of Lucy's house to let them out, they asked if they could visit me. I agreed, and they kissed me good-bye.

The girls have been coming over about three times a week (usually more). After the summer they will be headed back to college, but they're lining up some of their friends to stand in for them while they're gone!—*N.C., Wichita, Kansas* ⊶▄

DART-PLAYING LOVERS FORM
AN EROTIC LEAGUE OF THEIR OWN

Every Tuesday night, my wife, Marnie, and I play darts in a local league. My best friend, Greg, is also on the team, and for years I've been itching to arrange some action between the three of us. Greg and Marnie always used to laugh off my suggestions, but in recent months I'd noticed them making eyes at each other and giggling when I joked about threesomes.

Last Tuesday was the night when everything fell into place. Everyone was in a really good mood, and we won most of our games. As I was accepting congratulations from the captain of the other team, I noticed Greg and Marnie. Their heads were close together as they whispered conspiratorially and peeked over at me. I was just starting to get my hopes up when Marnie came over and said, "It's all set."

I looked over at Greg, who had a sly smirk on his face. He gave me a thumbs-up and pointed to me and Marnie, then himself. My jaw dropped and my cock popped when I realized they were serious.

Marnie suggested that Greg and I let her go to our house first so she could "prepare." She left each of us with a passionate kiss that gave Greg a hard-on to rival mine.

By the time Greg and I reached the house, we were so turned on thinking about what pleasures were in store for us we could barely speak. Marnie greeted us at the door wearing a sexy black nightie, a garter belt and sheer black stockings with lace tops.

The three of us looked at one another and smiled nervously. To break the ice, I suggested we play strip poker. As Marnie went to find the playing cards, I put an X-rated movie into the VCR to help enhance the mood.

Marnie's never been much of a card player, and soon she was down to her panties: (Though she denies it now, I believe she lost a few hands on purpose, so eager was she to get down to business!) After a few more rounds, I, too, was down to my underwear. Greg still had on his pants when Marnie removed her panties. Completely naked, she sat with her legs closed tight, stricken with a sudden bout of shyness.

She looked so cute sitting there, I decided to change the rules a bit and declared, "In this game of strip poker, the one who is naked first is the winner, and the winner can pick her special prize. Marnie, what would you like me and Greg to give you?"

Smiling coyly, she asked us to eat her.

Since there's nothing I like more than the taste of my wife's sweet pussy, I spread her legs wide and began licking away. Marnie quickly overcame her shyness, moaning with pleasure as I sucked the juices from her cunt. Before she could come, however, I moved out of the way so Greg could enjoy a taste.

Greg groaned as he savored Marnie's cunt, barely believing how wet she was. She came explosively when he took her clit between his lips and sucked ever so gently. I couldn't believe how absolutely gorgeous she was at that moment.

For the next hour, Greg and I took turns bringing my beautiful

Marnie to orgasm, again and again and again. She couldn't get enough, and neither could we.

Finally, she stopped panting long enough to gasp, "I want cock. Please, boys, share your cocks with me."

I took off my underwear and fed her my swollen dick. Greg didn't waste any time freeing his own. His long, hard shaft sprang from his pants, and he slid it inch by inch into Marnie's swollen pussy. She looked at me in shock, as it had been many years since any dick but mine had been inside her. As she writhed in ecstasy from the feel of Greg fucking her, I whispered in her ear how much I loved her.

I thought I was going to cream just watching them, so I put my throbbing stick back in her mouth. With each forceful stroke Greg gave her, she sucked my dick even harder. I couldn't hold out any longer and shot my load down her throat. It was the first time Marnie ever let me come in her mouth.

She looked me right in the eyes as her body bucked in orgasm. Greg came right after.

After a very brief period of rest, I fucked my wife as she sucked Greg's dick. It wasn't long before we all went over the edge yet again.

The fun lasted through the night.

Then it was back to the bedroom, where we fucked in every way possible. I had never seen Marnie come so many times or enjoy sex as much as she did that night. We kept at it until the early morning, when we fell asleep with grins on our faces.

Marnie has made me promise to set up another threesome, this time with another woman. I can't wait.—*T.N., Orlando, Florida* ⚷▪